D1251413

Ghosts of Futures Past

SIMPSON

IMPRINT IN HUMANITIES

The humanities endowment
by Sharon Hanley Simpson and
Barclay Simpson honors
MURIEL CARTER HANLEY
whose intellect and sensitivity
have enriched the many lives
that she has touched.

Ghosts of Futures Past

SPIRITUALISM AND THE CULTURAL POLITICS
OF NINETEENTH-CENTURY AMERICA

Molly McGarry

UNIVERSITY OF CALIFORNIA PRESS

BERKELEY   LOS   ANGELES   LONDON

University of California Press, one of the most
distinguished university presses in the United States,
enriches lives around the world by advancing scholarship
in the humanities, social sciences, and natural sciences.
Its activities are supported by the UC Press Foundation
and by philanthropic contributions from individuals and
institutions. For more information, visit www.ucpress.edu.

University of California Press
Berkeley and Los Angeles, California
University of California Press, Ltd.
London, England

© 2008 by The Regents of the University of California

Library of Congress Cataloging-in-Publication Data
McGarry, Molly.
    Ghosts of futures past : spiritualism and the cultural
politics of nineteenth-century America / Molly McGarry.
        p.   cm.
    Includes bibliographical references and index.
    ISBN: 978-0-520-25260-8 (cloth : alk. paper)
    1. Spiritualism—United States—History—
19th century.   2. United States—Religion—19th
century.   3. Religion and culture—United States—
History—19th century.   I. Title.
    BF1242.U6M34   2008
    133.90973'09034—dc22   2007037340

Manufactured in the United States of America

17 16 15 14 13 12 11 10 09 08
10 9 8 7 6 5 4 3 2 1

This book is printed on New Leaf EcoBook 50, a 100%
recycled fiber of which 50% is de-inked post-consumer
waste, processed chlorine-free. EcoBook 50 is acid-free and
meets the minimum requirements of ANSI/ASTM D5634–01
(Permanence of Paper).

For H.

CONTENTS

ILLUSTRATIONS

ACKNOWLEDGMENTS

Because this book has existed so long in the future of the "forthcoming," it is a particular pleasure to acknowledge past debts. At New York University, Thomas Bender was an extraordinary advisor. A model public intellectual, Tom provided not only the critical eye of a consummate editor but also an institutional space to exchange work. I thank him for his ongoing support. Also at NYU, I thank dissertation group members Mark Elliott, Saverio Giovacchini, Kathleen Hulser, Valentin Bvanck, Stephen Mihm, Kevin Murphy, David Quigley, Amy Richter, Andrew Schroeder, and Tracy Tullis. Robin D. G. Kelley, Molly Nolan, Richard Sennett, and Daniel J. Walkowitz provided crucial feedback and encouragement. Many years later, I returned to NYU, where Lisa Duggan became a particularly important advocate. I thank her for her magical powers, fierce intellect and friendship.

This book would never have been completed without the financial support of several institutions and the encouragement of friends and colleagues there. In addition to NYU, the National Museum of American History/Smithsonian Institution provided predoctoral funding, and Joe Dumit, John Hartigan, Anna McCarthy, Katherine Ott, Barbara Clark Smith, and Marvette Perez offered fellowship. At Bryn Mawr College, I thank Madhavi Kale, Jane Kaplan, Lisa Saltzman, and Sharon Ullman for making my short stay there so pleasurable. I am enormously grateful to my colleagues at the University of California, Riverside, for providing me with such a supportive scholarly community and to the College of Humanities, Arts, and Social Sciences for generously granting and aiding my sabbatical leave. This project was partially supported by funding from the President's Research Fellowships in the Humanities, University of California. The book was completed while I was in residence at the Center for Religion and Media at New York University, through funding from the Pew Charitable Trusts. There I was gifted with an extraordinary group of interlocutors, including Elizabeth Bernstein, Gregg Bordowitz, Ann Burlein, Elizabeth Castelli, Nikki DeBlosi, Lisa Duggan, Janet R. Jakobsen, Esther Kaplan, Richard Kim, Ann Pellegrini, and Kathleen Skerrett. Special thanks go to Faye Ginsburg and Angela Zito, as well as to Laura Terruso, Adam Becker, and Omri Elisha for making the center such an extraordinary place to work.

To put it simply, without archivists, historians' work is impossible. I am grateful to the librarians and staff at the National Museum of American History/Smithsonian Institution, the Library of Congress/Harry Houdini Collection, the National Spiritualist Association of Churches, the New York Public Library, San Diego Historical Society, Yale University Manuscripts and Archives, and the UC Riverside/Rivera Library Interlibrary Loan services. Jacklyn Burns, assistant registrar at the J. Paul Getty Museum, provided swift assistance with rights and reproductions. Michael Hargraves, Department of Photographs at the Getty and curator of the "Little Pictures" exhibit, found the haunting tintype reproduced here as figure 1. Howard Pearlstein, Book Junkies, located the Mollie Fancher image; Ziaa Szymansky at the Cora L. V. Richmond Archives taught me more about Cora than I can begin to recount; and fellow Spiritualist researcher John Buescher discovered the Walt Whitman link and offered to find it for me (again) in the maze of the Library of Congress.

Many of this book's chapters have had past lives as talks, invited lectures, or articles. I owe a special debt of gratitude to those individuals who offered invitations, read drafts, or commented on the work in its earliest incarnations. The introduction was artfully workshopped by the "Sex, Secularisms, and Other Religious Matters" writing group and by fellow fellow Ann Burlein at the Center for Religion and Media. Chapter 2 benefited from an especially incisive reading by Michelle Raheja. Chapter 3 began as a paper and later was revised as an article, but I believe it was hatched when Elizabeth Freeman rolled over on a blanket at Jones Beach and said, "It has something to do with the mail." Other readers of that piece include Rebecca Alpert, Jeffrey Escoffier, Terence Kissack, Kevin Murphy, Amy Robinson, Deb Schwartz, and the anonymous readers for the *Journal of Women's History*. Chapter 5 started as a talk at the invitation of Jim Schultz at UCLA's Center for the Study of Women. I thank Sue Ellen Case, Ellen DuBois, and Alice Wexler, whose questions and provocations made me rethink the project in important ways. I was honored to be a fellow traveler at the ALA with Betsy Erkkila, Elizabeth Freeman, Dana Luciano, E. L. MacCallum, Kathryn Bond Stockton, and Donald Pease, all of whom offered comments and incredibly smart suggestions on what would become chapter 5. Ann Pellegrini and Janet R. Jakobsen were the best of *Secularisms* editors and the most attentive of readers. Regina G. Kunzel read countless early drafts of all the chapters, and for that I am grateful.

At the University of California Press, I thank Niels Hooper for his initial interest, enduring attention, and key edits. Jacqueline Volin expertly shepherded the manuscript through production; Erika Būky unmixed metaphors and smoothed my prose; and Rachel Lockman just made everything easy. I thank the book designer, Claudia Smelser, for the arresting cover, and the anonymous readers for their razor-sharp comments.

This book is about mourning, memory, and the haunting presence of the past. But it is also fundamentally about contact and connection and the affinities that make worlds possible. Adina Back's name is first alphabetically, but she would have received the first acknowledgment even if it weren't. For guidance, support, vision, and conversation, I thank Pennee Bender, Pat Blashill, Joshua Brown, Erik Davis, Jennifer Doyle, Hazel-Dawn Dumpert, Jennifer Dumpert, George Edmondson, Linda Gall, George E. Haggerty, Janet R. Jakobsen, Michelle Johnson, Surina Khan, Richard Kim, Ming-Yuen S. Ma, Eric Miles, Sarah P. Miller, Jose Muñoz, Kevin Murphy, Miller Oberman, Ann Pellegrini, Sonnet Retman, Sharon Salinger, Janet Sarbanes, Deb Schwartz, Aretha Sills, Bill Stavru, Deb Steinback, Jennifer Terry, Karen Tongson, Matthew Trachman, and Devra Weber.

Elizabeth Freeman bridges the gap from friends and colleagues to family, categories which she both meets and transcends. I first learned the lessons of affinity and community from my aunts, uncles, and Kowal Kousins. My aunt Irene taught me the power of words and the lure of the numinous. My brother and sister-in-law, Mike and Caryn McGarry, and nieces, Gretchen and Clare, gave me an East Coast home. My parents, Frank and Sylvia McGarry, inspired me with their stories of the past. It is thanks to their love of a tale, the well-placed joke, and ardent support that I was able to imagine and complete this project.

Heather N. Lukes was this book's best reader, and for that alone she deserves a dedication. That she also has the seemingly endless capacity to transform the everyday into something more interesting (and entertaining) than I ever thought imaginable is beyond words.

Introduction

Eighteen forty-eight was a talismanic year in which revolution swept the world, reform movements flourished throughout the United States, and New York State in particular seemed scorched by the spirit of radicalism and revival. John Humphrey Noyes moved his experimental community from Putney, Vermont, to Oneida, New York, the center of the "Burned-Over District" and a hotbed of utopianism and religious communitarianism. In July, in nearby Seneca Falls, the first convention for women's rights met, drafting a "Declaration of Sentiments" proclaiming the "self-evident" truth that "all men and women are created equal." As the revolutions of 1848 spanned the globe, from France to Brazil to Hungary, Karl Marx and Friedrich Engels published the *Communist Manifesto,* opening with the line, "A spectre is haunting Europe — the spectre of communism." And in Hydesville, New York, two young girls heard communications from a different sort of specter, giving rise to a quite different revolution.

In the context of such a year, the founding of the Spiritualist movement, a popular religious practice conducted through communication with the spirits of the dead, may seem to deserve approximately the same amount of attention as the retail marketing of chewing gum, a development which also occurred in 1848. Yet, as this book argues, the history of American Spiritualism is much more than a cultural footnote, even as it may be considered the ghost story of the long nineteenth century. It begins like this. Late one night,

Kate and Margaret Fox, while sleeping in their family farmhouse, heard mysterious noises, raps, knocks, and bumps in the night. They soon concluded that the knockings were unearthly communications from beyond, produced by the spectral presence of a murdered peddler who had died in the house years earlier. Questioning the spirit, one Mr. Splitfoot, who rapped in response, the Fox sisters realized that they could operate a sort of "spiritual telegraph," allowing them to receive cryptic messages from the afterlife.[1]

Accounts of the ghostly events in Hydesville soon appeared in the popular press. As the nation spoke of the Fox sisters, the spirits began to speak to the nation, bringing similarly strange occurrences of raps, knocks, and levitating furniture to sitting rooms across the country. Soon Americans in both urban and rural areas, from Cincinnati to Maine, St. Louis to Massachusetts, were forming their own spirit circles and reporting tales of ordinary citizens spontaneously voicing extraordinary communications in words not their own. In 1854, fifteen thousand people signed a petition introduced by Illinois senator James Shields to the United States Congress, urging an official investigation of the new spiritual sensation. Although the petition was tabled, it created even more publicity for the movement.[2] What first attracted attention as a children's ghost story, and later as an after-dinner entertainment, quickly became a popular national phenomenon and a powerful new religion.

There were always many varieties of Spiritualism. Some were entwined with worlds of wonder and popular spectacle, others with metaphysical traditions like mesmerism and animal magnetism, still others with liberal Protestant circles linking Shakers, Quakers, and Unitarians. Many Spiritualists took seriously the possibility of channeling the voices of the dead as a means of connecting with the past and imagining both worldly and otherworldly futures, ranging from political reforms to an idyllic afterlife. Tracing these spiritual and political affinities, among the living and through the dead, reveals a map connecting the antebellum United States to the global twentieth century.

Some Spiritualists went west after the Civil War, founding new experimental communities in California, such as the still-extant Summerland, named for the Spiritualist afterworld. Others stayed in the Northeast and Midwest in quiet home circles or as public activists, some organizing for the cause of the American Indian, fighting for the rights of workers, crafting a unique brand of Spiritualist feminism, and eventually working against imperialism and for peace through disarmament.[3] Transported to England, Spiritualism was refigured as Theosophy, which spread globally, eventually bouncing back from the Indian subcontinent through London to Southern

California.[4] To call up these historically marginalized religious identities and communities attunes us not only to an apparitional netherworld often invisible to secular moderns but also to a set of material practices that informed the politics and dominant ideology of the era.

Writing as a believer and participant-observer, the medium Emma Hardinge, in her 1869 *History of Modern American Spiritualism,* estimated the number of Spiritualists worldwide at one hundred million, with "eleven millions of persons on the American continent."[5] Frederic Marvin, a New York neurologist and Spiritualist debunker writing in the 1870s, countered with the more conservative figure of four million.[6] Although the actual number of Spiritualists, curious or convinced, was probably considerably smaller than either of these totals, one must keep in mind that the entire U.S. population numbered only twenty-eight million at midcentury.[7] Commenting on the influence of the movement at the height of its popularity, Theodore Parker, a prominent theologian, remarked that "in 1856, it seems more likely that spiritualism would become the religion of America than in 156 that Christianity would become the religion of the Roman Empire, or in 756 that Mohammedanism would be that of the Arabian population."[8] That Spiritualism did not become the religion of America says less about the power and appeal of the movement at the time than about what counts as "religion" and where historians tend to look for and find its traces in the past.

Denominations and established churches are the most recognizable forms of religion in America's past and present. Evangelicalism, which first emerged in highly emotional tent meetings and revivals and only (and not always) later in churches and megachurches, represents a second strain. The historian Catherine L. Albanese has recently charted a third strain, which she calls "metaphysical religion," a long and winding tradition that includes Spiritualism, "beliefs about correspondence, resemblance, and connection . . . about what may be called magic."[9] Spiritualism was a form of magical metaphysics. This was a religion that had no churches, no membership rolls, and no formal governing body until its waning years.[10] Though it boasted a lively lecture circuit, Spiritualism was practiced mainly in domestic settings, around tables in dimly lit rooms. The séance circle was the ritual structure of spiritual practice and always more a private than a public event.[11] Mediums, mostly women, who conducted séances and were at the physical center of spirit circles, often rented rooms for this purpose, and Spiritualists also made room for mediums in their own home circles.[12] Indeed, many mid-Victorian American families became Spiritualists when they discovered that they had a medium in their midst. As with the Fox sisters, where one medium was found in a family, another would often emerge. Like the ghosts that signaled the new movement, unearthly power sometimes came from within the house, even as the practice and the practitioners refused to respect the diaphanous divide between public and private or between this world and the next.

Through speaking tours and a flourishing regional and national press, Spiritualists created a public, and often political, community. Many Spiritualist freethinkers were united in their belief in the "family of reforms," which included abolition, temperance, and women's suffrage. The connection between Spiritualism and reform culture was apparent to many nineteenth-century commentators. The white abolitionist Gerrit Smith remarked in 1859 that the Spiritualists he met in "tours through the state last fall, were nearly all reformers. . . . I have no doubt that, in proportion to their numbers, Spiritualists cast tenfold as many votes for the Abolition and Temperance tickets as did others."[13] Spiritualists were not only abolitionists and suffragists but also in some cases advocates of dress reform, vegetarianism, and free love.[14] Indeed, in reading the Spiritualist press, as well as the writings and speeches of prominent Spiritualists, what emerges is a picture of a large group of Americans who found impetus in their spiritual life for their political beliefs and who were deeply involved in reforming the world.[15] Actively engaged in a politics of the body and the body politic, Spiritualism encompassed a set of utopian practices and imaginings that, when understood together, uniquely linked many of the disparate political movements of the day.

Spiritualists and anti-Spiritualists began to write their own histories only moments after the first raps and continued to do so into the early twentieth century.[16] Emma Hardinge chronicled mediums and manifestations, and such writers as Arthur Conan Doyle and the utopian socialist Robert Dale Owen attempted to explain themselves and their embattled beliefs to their respective circles.[17] More recently, there has been renewed historical interest in Spiritualism in the United States: a number of important studies have been published in the last thirty years.[18] Yet in the wider cultural field, this movement remains largely understood as an easily parodied parlor game or an apolitical and marginal mysticism.

The best work on the subject, Ann Braude's *Radical Spirits,* documents Spiritualism's relationship to antebellum reform efforts, especially women's rights. Braude has subsequently noted that one of the most controversial aspects of her book has been its linking of Spiritualism and suffragism, religion and politics, a fusion that was ubiquitous in the nineteenth century. She finds "a certain squeamishness," especially among post–second wave academic feminists, in imaging that religion might be a reasonable font for politics and that religious feminists might be rational, political actors rather than women suffering from false consciousness.[19]

This resistance has everything to do with the politics of secularism. If secularization is a progress narrative that culminates in the freedom from religion, religion can function only as an anachronistic invasion into public life that logically aligns with conservative and reactionary returns to moral values. Hence a liberal-humanist secularism has become the naturalized ground of opposition to right-wing religious dogma. Yet this assumption erases significant structures of belief that, at least at times, have sustained progressive politics. Excavating a narrative in which secularism does not simply or inevitably triumph over an antimodern, atavistic religion not only provides a more nuanced understanding of the past but also reveals a more complicated politics of the present.

That this broadly popular movement has been marginalized in standard histories of the nineteenth century tells us more about historiography and the history of secularism than it does about religious life in the nineteenth-century United States. Scholars have long contended that in the last half of the nineteenth century, Americans shifted their faith to science and placed their belief in an ordered public sphere. The generation between 1850 and 1880 was a pivotal one, with 1848 representing a revolutionary moment of possibility and 1877 a moment of radical retreat.[20] After this point Americans seem, at least to historians who have chronicled a dominant, white Protestant culture, "less religious, less optimistic, more concerned than ever to embody their cultural values in institutions."[21] These narratives accord with the historiography of the end of the Reconstruction period, which similarly positions this era as marked by failed radicalism and exhausted reform, an "age of incorporation," a society in "search for order."[22] As the historian Robert Wiebe writes, "An age in which the Supreme Court justified oppression of the Mormons because no right-thinking man could consider theirs a religion would not be remembered for its cosmopolitan tolerance."[23] Wiebe's implicit dichotomy between "tolerance" and "right-thinking" men interrogates the imagination of this era as one of liberal rationality and national unification; yet the fact that his point is forged precisely over the status of a new nineteenth-century religion also underscores the presumed secular acceptance of established religions over the grave of antebellum spiritual ferment.

In contrast to this narrative of religious decline and consolidation, I have found that Spiritualism not only thrived but also continued to engage with social questions through the 1870s and beyond. Into the 1880s, the Spiritualist press reported packed lecture halls, conventions, and camp meetings. Invoking and reworking the notion of Reconstruction, one speaker at a gathering in 1872 argued that Spiritualism could be "a grand revolutionary movement: a vast scheme for social, political, and religious reconstruction; a new dispensation of divine truth and power, for the liberation, civilization, and spiritualization of mankind."[24] Refusing both the discourse of failure, which was already attending Reconstruction by the early 1870s, and the term's original signification as a mandate to reconstitute the nation, this heralding of a "new dispensation" through the language of reconstruction at once acknowledges the current state of the nation and transcends it.

Spiritualists felt the burden of the present, and the call of both the future and the past, as a mandate that was always both religious and political. In narrating the cultural formations of modernity, scholars too often ignore such religious imaginaries, which offer historiographic techniques of remembrance and theories of affiliation that challenge basic assumptions about secular history. Whereas linear, secular history demands the transcendence of the past, Spiritualist practice collapsed time and refused to accept the past as over. Spiritualists, then, can only ever seem out of time. In looking backward, one might find a nineteenth century more seemingly premodern than modern, one in which the dead spoke to and through the living, the world revealed daily wonders, and the realm of the invisible shaped individual and social subjectivities.

Listening uncritically to an aging generation of reformers describe loss and decline in a new culture of skepticism, historians have ventriloquized Spiritualist detractors and debunkers. I would argue that the movement did not decline so much as become illegible. Subcultures of a dominant ordering culture are often seen as taking on an order-defying, antirational romanticism. Rejecting this binary reveals a more complicated history, one which elucidates the ways in which both insides and outsides, cultures and subcultures, depend on stable demarcations at the same time that they refuse this opposition, each showing itself as containing the defining characteristics of the other. Spiritualists did not see themselves as antimodern. Mystical Spiritualists drew their language from popular tracts on scientific empiricism, invoking a secular optimism and faith in human, material progress. They believed in science and the possibility of making "all things new." In this sense, Spiritualists were as profoundly American and mainstream as they were countercultural.

Although Spiritualism may appear at first glance to be a fringe religion that rose and fell in the United States during the nineteenth century, this history entwines with fundamental questions of mourning and memory in our own time. This project was initially conceived in a recent moment of United States history, during the height of the AIDS epidemic in the 1980s and 1990s, when the political questions of how to give collective voice to grief took on ethical urgency: What is the relationship between mourning and militancy?[25] How might a single death be transformed from an individual occurrence into an occasion for collective praxis? How can the dead speak through the living as something other than the haunting, seething presence of absence? *Ghosts of Futures Past* traces a spiritual movement born of a particular historical moment, yet the questions of love and loss that animate the project have been persistently revivified in the contemporary public sphere.

In the wake of death—whether death on a national or global scale, or the—often private and lonely grief attending the death of a loved one—mourners have developed historically specific performances and practices that refuse the encryption of loss, bringing the dead into an active engagement with the living. Recently, a growing number of scholars have insisted, perhaps counterintuitively, on the productive possibilities of loss in reconstituting both an ethical relationship to the dead and to history in our at once necrophilic and necrophobic culture.[26] Yet despite this renewed interest in the politics of mourning, dominant scholarship has largely followed a narrative, first charted by Philippe Ariès in a series of classic studies, in which mourning as shared, community practice declines and the dead are displaced from the public sphere to the private by the beginning of the twentieth century.[27] Commenting on the loss of rites of collective mourning, one writer notes that it is the absence of these practices, "rather than their presence[,] that has merited scrutiny."[28]

In these accounts, mourning has declined for a variety of reasons. In particular, technology, both in Ariès's formulation and in critiques of it, is ascribed the magical power to banish mourning and death, and seemingly community, from the world. The critic Alessia Ricciardi counters Ariès's thesis of privatization and decline and instead notes the "displacement" of mourning "from the sphere of ritual or sacred activity to the larger context of society in general, which now primarily consists in mass culture."[29] It seems that if the public sphere is haunted at all, it is now primarily through spectral reemergences in representation: the photograph keeps company with death by marking stopped time; the flickering film screens the phantasm of technology. Implicit in these arguments is a modern mystification of technology that takes place as a sublimation of that which refuses demystification from a past world of sacred ritual. The ghost has become not just the ghost in the machine but the ghost *of* the machine.

Here I would ask whether these discussions are themselves haunted by the unexamined assumption that our secular moment has, or should have, left the sacred and the supernatural in the past. As secular subjects, we are no longer literally haunted, but we seem haunted by the idea of haunting. Literary critics and social theorists have long turned to spectral metaphors to signify everything from ethereal materiality to amorphous subjectivity. Similarly, spectrality has become a means to explain the social status of marginalized subjects as well as a powerful politics of living with the past as both memory and harrowing presence.[30] While all of these uses of the spectral work differently, haunting is more than a dead metaphor.

Deploying the metaphor of the ghost to depict, among other things, alienated subjectivity and an alienated relationship to history tends to belie the ways in which certain historical subjects engaged spirits precisely in order to resist such alienation. This book examines such alternative possibilities realized in a historical moment in which communing with the dead offered the potential for affective connection across time, personal transformation, and utopian political change. The contemporary urge to make specters into metaphors reveals the excessive rigor of a secular belief system as much at odds with the supernatural as with the affective. In Avery Gordon's words, "Being haunted draws us affectively, sometimes against our will and always a bit magically, into the structure of feeling of a reality we come to experience, not as cold knowledge, but as transformative recognition." In taking the lived experience of being haunted seriously, one arrives at a historical appreciation for "a very particular way of knowing."[31]

In the nineteenth century, many Americans took literally the possibility of conjuring the dead. Gathering around séance tables in darkened rooms, Spiritualists enchanted technologies of modernity—from spiritual telegraphy to spectral photography—for purposes of spiritual contact and connection. Unlike other religions, in which faith was a necessary prerequisite for belief, Spiritualism asked only that one become an "investigator," attend a séance under "test" conditions, analyze "evidence," and weigh whether or not to believe. Spiritualists described theirs as a "religion of proof."[32] An alchemical combination of science and magic cloaked in the language of popular positivism, Spiritualism called into question the very categories of the material and immaterial, knowledge and belief, the living and the dead.

In 1867, an editorial writer for the *Nation* marveled that the numbers of Spiritualists seemed to be growing with each passing day. Wondering if the popularity of this faith was due to a kind of "sublimated mysticism," a "natural reaction from the intense materialism of the age," he concluded that, in the end, Spiritualism was newly popular because the Civil War decade was one of profound loss in the United States. The continuing power of Spiritualism, he argued, lay in the ubiquity of death: "Still, mothers are losing their children by death; fond fathers unwillingly give up the only son of their name to the grave; each day how many die, some of whom are long and some of whom are bitterly mourned by the survivors—mourned with 'blind longing and passionate pain.' And this being so, it is vain to look for a speedy ending to a belief that offers the living one more opportunity to speak with the beloved dead."[33]

Nineteenth-century Spiritualism was a movement of consolation that grew out of, and eventually away from, middle-class Victorian cultures of mourning. American Victorians' obsessive attention to death is rife in the literature, theology, and advice manuals of the period as well as in the antebellum material culture of memento mori.[34] Funerals strewn with black crepe, elaborate mourning costumes, and black-trimmed notecards became de rigeur for the grieving upper and middle classes; lockets enclosing cameo death portraits were treasured objects for the working poor. Mourning manuals dictated specific dress and corresponding obligations, guiding the choice of appropriate outer emblems to reflect the inner bereavement process. These intricate rituals of middle-class sentimental culture effectively shifted the social focus from the dead to the living, from those who were mourned to the mourners themselves.

With their refusal of death as the ultimate loss, Spiritualists' direct communication with the afterlife obviated the need for mourning at the same time that it performed a materialist critique of the aestheticized pageantry of sentimental culture. Spiritualists saw this commodified Anglo-American culture as a form of solipsism that arrested the social, political, and spiritual development of nineteenth-century America. Spiritualism gave believers a community of mourners who could take them beyond personal grief and the domesticated, sentimental rituals of middle-class mourning, offering instead new possibilities for life. Indeed, a faith in Spiritualism and the experience that the dead continued to connect with the living allowed some nineteenth-century Americans a new way of being in the world.

Spiritualist optimism, born of the faith that this world and the next were merely two stages in an unbroken process, produced a Spiritualist reform politics. That many Spiritualists would move from their own personal loss to a belief in the prospect of the reformation of personal and political life is less than intuitively obvious. Yet it is in this connection between a relationship to the dead and a transformative politics of the living that Spiritualism might be understood as something other than either magical melancholy or a form of "spurious consolation."[35]

Though belief in personal communication with spirits has historical antecedents dating back to the ancient world, nineteenth-century American Spiritualism was born of a particular set of historical and cultural confluences. Nourished in the religious and cultural climate that the historian Jon Butler has termed "the antebellum spiritual hothouse," Spiritualism blossomed alongside other pre–Civil War religious and utopian experiments.[36] Spiritualism found its place within the popular utopianism that Henry James dubbed the "Puritan carnival." This was an era of sectarianism and revivalism, one in which "farmers became theologians, offbeat village youths became bishops, odd girls became prophets."[37] The antebellum period saw a broad interest in supernatural phenomena and the rise of a religious syncretism that wedded popular supernaturalism to a Euro-American Protestantism. African religious practices, including conjuring and faith healing, shaped both black and white evangelical Christianity in the South.[38] The widespread popularity of movements like Swedenborgianism, Shakerism, and mesmerism laid the groundwork for the growth of nineteenth-century Spiritualism in the white, Protestant Northeast.

Nineteenth-century Spiritualists often wrote their own genealogies of belief, drawing parallels between their understandings of the spirit world and those of earlier generations of Americans. Allying themselves with the persecuted men and women of Salem, Spiritualists constructed an American counterhistory in which the suspects of the Salem witchcraft trial were like the "poor mediums of that day" who "were made to believe that they were 'witches.'"[39] A small percentage of Spiritualists understood witchcraft as a sister belief, a past manifestation of otherworldly power, born of an American culture more likely to persecute the messengers than to attend to sacred signs. During its heyday, Spiritualism was often attacked as a recrudescence of either the demonism that led to witchcraft or the superstitious credulity that led to the Salem witchcraft trials. Elaborating this connection, one Spiritualist countered that "the history of Salem Witchcraft is but an account of spiritual manifestations, and of man's incapacity to understand them."[40]

In some ways Spiritualism is a distillation of many of the seemingly paradoxical combinations of modernity and belief attending the Victorian crisis of faith. The Anglo-American, "secular" late nineteenth century was also a high point of moral uplift and religious missionary activity in inner cities and colonial outposts. It was a time when the numinous, traditionally imparted by established religion, did not so much disappear as rematerialize, newly domesticated, in daily life.

As Max Weber argued, religious asceticism culminated in worldly abstemiousness and sublimation in the Protestant ethic. In spite of Weber's further claim that the tide of capitalist secularism "disenchanted" the world, the American nineteenth century shows that magic itself was not so much eliminated from the world as it was rechanneled.[41] Nineteenth-century consumerism transmuted the mystical into the prosaic, as Americans purchased stereocards of cemeteries and photographs of dead loved ones in record numbers. The uncanny found its way into sitting rooms as consumers played with objects that were not what they seemed. Americans collected money boxes disguised as books, painted trompe l'oeil doorways onto walls, and purchased unusable "floating" chairs cast of papier-mâché.[42] Not only did furniture levitate during Spiritualist séances, but the materialism of the Victorian home was itself haunted. The cultural fascination with the supernatural extended to reading practices as well. More ghost stories were written during this period than at any time before or after.[43] American Protestants did not merely replace or reject the religious impulse; they sublimated and diffused it into the everyday.

This transformation was intimately connected with what historians have termed "the feminization of American religion."[44] During the middle of the nineteenth century, Protestant culture gradually rejected a harsh Calvinism for more liberal theologies like Unitarianism and Spiritualism, in which women were central as mediums, speakers, and investigators. The idea of infant damnation died a happy death during this period and would have done so earlier, as Theodore Parker rightly noted, if women had had a greater role in the creation of theology.[45] The feminization of religion did produce more humane, less rigid institutions and increased the prominence of women in religious organizations as leaders and laypersons. Many deplored this turn: Orestes Brownson abandoned what he saw as a weak and effeminate, middlebrow Protestantism for the proper hierarchy and severity of the Catholic Church. Whether commercialized or feminized, these alternative structures of belief show the Victorian crisis of faith to have been not so much a mass secularization as a widening of a search for answers in newly crafted theological terms.

The continuing attraction of Spiritualism for many nineteenth-century Americans points to the resiliency in American culture of the seemingly nonrational commitments to belief, devotion, magic, folklore, and faith healing. It raises the question of why historians, particularly American historians, have so resolutely chronicled what Max Weber termed "disenchantment" in the face of the continued refusals of the world to be disenchanted. The resilience of Spiritualism, then, brings into focus the historical specificities of the marginal and local forms by which dominant practices were resisted, deflected, or shown to be imperfectly constituted.

In a formulation that depends on what it purports to explain, European historians typically record the long secularizing tide brought on by the Enlightenment as the cultural force behind this religious transformation. According to one characteristic argument, from the latter half of the seventeenth century, rationalist and positivist currents in the European temperament grew increasingly skeptical of the existence of fairies, goblins, and ghosts; devils and wood demons; the powers of astrology, witchcraft and magic; the hermetic "world soul"; and perhaps even of Satan and Hell.[46]

Entities like the "European temperament," however, remain difficult to track and even harder to historicize. Keith Thomas, in a parallel formulation, substitutes "intelligent persons" for the European temper. He begins his magisterial history, *Religion and the Decline of Magic,* with what he presents as a universally held truism: that "astrology, witchcraft, magical healing, divination, ancient prophecies, ghosts and fairies, are now all rightly disdained by intelligent persons. But they were taken seriously by equally intelligent persons in the past, and it is the historian's business to explain why this was so."[47] Despite his problematic use of "intelligent persons" as a category of analysis, both Thomas's narrative of the decline of magic and the reception of his work on the subject provide a useful historical corollary when analyzing the mass acceptance, and later demonization, of the scientific occultism of nineteenth-century American Spiritualism. They also shed light on historians' understanding of this presumed transformation. Thomas argues that the radical paradigm shift from magic to science would not have been predicted at the beginning of the seventeenth century because magic and science had until that time advanced side by side. Mystical and magical astrology fed developments in scientific astronomy; heliocentrism birthed Copernican-Keplerian planetary models. Here Thomas follows Thomas Kuhn in arguing that sometime in the seventeenth century, the partnership between magic and science collapsed.

E. P. Thompson counters that the occult not only survived but flourished among the working classes in eighteenth-century rural English culture.[48] Newer studies have demonstrated its persistence, documenting a belief in the occult not only among the English working classes but also among the English and American middle and upper classes well into the twentieth century.[49] Given these counterhistories, the question remains: does magic decline or does it just seem that way to academics? And if the latter, why? The anthropologist Hildred Geertz has provocatively commented that Thomas "takes part in the very cultural process that he is studying" by accepting the categories of the actors and using them "as analytical categories to develop his own casual hypothesis of decline." She argues that "it is not the 'decline' of the practice of magic that cries out for explanation, but the emergence and rise of the label 'magic.'"[50]

The work of the word *magic* in the mouths of moderns has the ideological effect of relegating a series of affective and ritualistic practices to the temporal past, to a spatial periphery, or to a narrative of underdevelopment. Weber describes "the elimination of magic from the world" as "that great historic process in the development of religions," which "repudiated all magical means to salvation as superstition and sin" and culminated in the "worldly asceticism" of Reformed Calvinist Protestantism.[51] If Weber's model of developmental religion and increasing societal rationalization leaves magic as modernity's remainder, an atavistic trace preserved by culture's various others, *belief,* a less obviously charged term, can be similarly impervious to secularism's analytics. Belief is not equivalent to magic but, within developmental historical narratives, survives as the indivisible remainder of religion *minus* magic, a recalcitrant reminder of the past in our putatively rational present.

A generation of anthropologists and postcolonial theorists has bemoaned "the social sciences' view of the world as disenchanted" and pointed to what Dipesh Chakrabarty calls "a certain kind of intellectual bankruptcy, a paralysis of imagination, and a certain spell of reductionism" in scholarly attempts to understand religious practices and beliefs.[52] Talal Asad's *Genealogies of Religion* traces this contemporary problem by charting the shift from religion as a "site for producing disciplined knowledge and personal discipline" to that which resembles "the conception Marx had of religion as ideology—a mode of consciousness which is other than consciousness of reality, external to the relations of production, producing no knowledge, but expressing at once the anguish of the oppressed and a spurious consolation."[53] Beyond accounting for the way religion has come to appear "spurious" in the secular mind, Guari Viswanathan has argued that, although the various ideological and political investments that underwrite intellectual engagements with belief cannot be conflated, "the ultimate significance of such work lies in its being a vehicle for secular intellectuals to express the difficulties of communicating the idea of religious belief—as distinct from religious ideology—in and for a secular community."[54] Rather than imagine a dissolution of the divide between belief and ideology, these critics underscore what is lost in refusing to recognize belief as a continuing source of knowledge production.

Returning to Spiritualism in the context of these recent interventions, we must ask whether we can think of consolation as anything other than spurious. It has been suggested that the very rationalization of society and its "desiccating effect" on everyday life have encouraged older forms of belief, vestiges of ancient myths, and arcane lore in a backward search for new sources of power. In this formulation, religion remains counter to a larger culture and unthreatening to social systems.[55] Yet can religious belief be understood as a transformative and progressive project, as opposed to escapist consumerism and entertainment or always already a form of revivalism? Spiritualism in American history might be understood as the old New Age, not a restitution of old institutions or beliefs but a transcultural and transtemporal expansion, heralding a "new dispensation." Whether a flight from a dominant order or a continued belief in the ability to craft a new one, Spiritualism denied the warfare between science and religion, disavowed the divide between fact and fantasy, and, most important, refused the idea of the past as irretrievable and the future as the inevitable result of calcified sociopolitical structures. If a "ghost is precisely an intermediary 'apparition' between life and death, between being and non-being, between matter and spirit, whose separation it dissolves," Spiritualism haunted nineteenth-century American culture.[56] Rather than counter that emergent culture, Spiritualism, specterlike, refused to acknowledge its deepest divides.

Chapter 1, "Mourning, Media, and the Cultural Politics of Conjuring the Dead," explores the antebellum foundation of Spiritualism, in which many Americans found the possibility of uniting politics and faith in a transformative vision of society. Spiritualists' embrace of the modern revelations of science and technology was more than an analogy: communicating by telegraph may have seemed no less magical than speaking to the dead; spirit rapping was dubbed the "Spiritualist telegraph"; and Thomas Watson, assistant to Alexander Graham Bell, imagined the telephone as an aid to spiritual connection. The relationship between new media and an old spiritual belief in the permeability of the boundary between the living and the dead cast the movement as modern and scientific. Yet speaking to the dead provided more than a vernacular science; it offered solace to those looking to abandon an increasingly remote, impersonal Calvinism. This was a solace beyond the Victorian cult of mourning, opening believers to other forms of communication, other voices, and other bodies, and allowing them to imagine new social worlds and to forge diverse political affinities.

Chapter 2, "Indian Guides: Haunted Subjects and the Politics of Vanishing," examines the relationships between Spiritualists and the "Indian question." Mapping the colonial role of the Indian as guide for the white man onto the spirit world, Spiritualists positioned Native Americans as a vital link between this world and the next. On the one hand, Spiritualists saw Native Americans as powerful spiritual predecessors, evincing romantic attachments to an ideal or imagined Indian that sometimes amounted to unexamined cultural appropriation. On the other hand, Spiritualists called for the protection of native lands and sovereignty, laboring to right the wrongs of colonists while also salvaging the spiritual life of white Americans. The history of these ambivalent forms of affiliation raises questions about the importance of a specifically religious worldview to the construction of secular progressive politics.

Chapter 3, "Spectral Sexualities: Free Love, Moral Panic, and the Making of U.S. Obscenity Law," traces a post–Civil War battle over the specter of obscenity, a secular replacement for the idea of sin. The inception of U.S. censorship law was in part a response to the spread of Spiritualist affinities with movements that sought equality for the sexes, free love, and dress reform that subverted dominant gender codes. When Anthony Comstock successfully lobbied Congress for a new law stopping the spread of sexual representations in the public sphere, he was seeking to squelch these reform movements while also responding to larger cultural fears that the phantasm of obscenity was penetrating the American body politic through the U.S. mail. Recognizing the role of Spiritualism in the history of censorship illuminates how this nineteenth-century moral panic continues to inform the nation's anxious relationship to new technologies of circulation. From the mail and spectralized spiritual bodies in the 1870s to the Internet today, such new media have provoked fascination as well as the fear that the putatively private home can never be fully protected from the many dangers beyond.

Chapter 4, "Mediomania: The Spirit of Science in a Culture of Belief and Doubt," moves from the law to examine Spiritualism in relation to the emerging profession of medicine. Beginning in the 1870s, a growing number of doctors pathologized mediumship, naming it as a particularly female disease akin to hysteria. One New York neurologist coined the term *mediomania*, linking Spiritualism to insanity and siting pathology in the body of the female medium. In doing so, these doctors staked a professional claim to the expert knowledge necessary to distinguish between the normal and the abnormal, mysticism and madness. These border wars between medical men and mediums over definitions of religious experience and forms of revealed speech provide an entry into nineteenth-century debates over understandings of the soul, brain, and psyche.

Chapter 5, "Secular Spirits: A Queer Genealogy of Untimely Sexualities," brings the book from the nineteenth into the twentieth century to ask how contemporary theories of sexuality might understand Spiritualist subjects who, in séances and through trance speaking, reembodied themselves in the opposite gender. Some varieties of religious experience may have been markers for an incipient, not yet materialized sexuality, and perhaps a sexual dissidence located outside both the medico-juridical matrix and the expected spaces of subculture. Tracing a transatlantic genealogy from American Spiritualism to British Theosophy, I excavate sites for queer self-fashioning from the superstars of the Spiritualist lecture circuit and alternative press to such literary luminaries as Walt Whitman and Radclyffe Hall, contending that these subjects made sense of their own queer time through spiritual theories of embodiment that offered forms of meaning that secular science refused.

Spiritualism ghosted major battles of the nineteenth century, from religious utopianism to women's rights, from the professionalization of the scientific and medical establishments to the role of the state in controlling the circulation of information. In the following pages, I track the contests for authority in the antebellum and reconstructed United States, and also, more importantly and less obviously, the multiple forms of affiliation channeled through Spiritualism.

ONE

Mourning, Media, and the Cultural Politics of Conjuring the Dead

From his snug home in an atmosphere in which pianos float, "soft warm hands" bud forth from vacant space, and lead pencils write alone, the spiritualist has a right to feel a personal disdain for the "scientific man" who stands inertly aloof in his pretentious enlightenment.

WILLIAM JAMES
"Sargent's Planchette," 1869

In the last third of the nineteenth century, as William James and many of his contemporaries mourned the ability of religion and science to function as mutually productive explanatory systems, the movement calling itself Modern American Spiritualism promised "an experimental science," affording "the only sure foundation for a true philosophy and a pure religion."[1] At a time when science was meant to have pushed religion to the cultural margins, and when the forces of positivism, realism, and rationality should have washed magic from the world, this practice offered a popular religion buttressed by scientific "evidence" of human immortality.[2] A half century after the inception of Spiritualism, William James would find the divide between religion and science intolerable and irrational. As a response, he eventually founded the American Society for Psychical Research with some of the most prominent scientists of the day, to investigate the paranormal using scientific methods. For a much larger, diverse set of Americans, Spiritualism supplied the language and technology to test the unseen boundary between this world and the next.

Spiritualism called into question not only the categories of religion and

Figure 1. "Seated woman with spirit of a young man," ca. 1885. Unknown maker, American School, active 1880s. Catalog no. 84.XP.447.1. The J. Paul Getty Museum, Los Angeles. Spirit photographs, in which a spirit double appeared as a whispery image within a traditional portrait, were nineteenth-century memento mori, cherished objects in which the living and the dead were reunited through the magic and manipulations of photography. Most of these images, like those by the photographer William Mumler (figures 2, 5, 6, and 10 and discussed in chapter 3), were made as infinitely reproducible paper *cartes de visite*. This is a rare example of a tintype spirit photograph. Neither the photographer nor the subjects pictured are known.

science but also the divide between the living and the dead, giving nineteenth-century Americans unique access to the afterlife and the possibility of communing with departed loved ones. It thus posed a counterdiscourse to both an aging Calvinism and a growing materialism. Spiritualism extended the promise of a gentle, supermundane afterlife. The Other Side, or the Summerland, as it was often called, was imaginable, familiar, and attainable.[3] This vision held enormous appeal, and Spiritualism was, in the words of one historian, "ubiquitous on the American scene at mid-century."[4]

Spiritualism's appeal was as diverse as the many practitioners it attracted. As the historian Ann Braude has argued, women played particularly important roles in the movement as mediums and speakers, often crafting a specifically feminized, and sometimes overtly feminist, spiritual practice.[5] For many Spiritualists, small-group communalism took the place of institutionalized religion; alternative healing replaced male-dominated medicine; and the voices of priests and ministers were drowned out by those of the spirits themselves. Many Spiritualists denied basic categorical binaries: the distinctions between men and women, science and magic, life and afterlife, the past and the present. They repudiated the power of experts and the necessity of mediating hierarchies at a time in which these forces were taking on a renewed cultural importance.

Nineteenth-century Spiritualists were predominantly middle-class Anglo-Americans of a very specific historical moment.[6] Although they were never of a single political mind, their convictions grew from an optimistic perfectionism and the belief that the world could be radically remade. Indeed, all around them, on a daily basis, nineteenth-century America was being transformed. Concurrent with the birth of modern Spiritualism, as one believer explained, was "the demand for exact justice and equal rights for the sexes. The same impulse was moving the world in a determined moral protest against the institution of human slavery. Under the same divine impetus the theological authority which was the bulwark of despotism was analyzed and criticized in a manner and degree which no previous period would have tolerated."[7] Spiritualism was born of an era of enormous social change and fervent antiauthoritarian impulses.

Yet Spiritualism was more than an antiauthoritarian antinomianism; it was a unique practice centered on communication with the spirits of the dead. A specter of the once-living materialized into being, a ghost is a visitation from the past to the present. Given that tens of thousands of Americans took to the séance table to commune with spirits, it is worth asking why, in certain historical moments, people need to speak with the past. Why, in the middle and late nineteenth century, did Americans want to converse with their dead ancestors, to look backward as they strove forward? And, beyond their desire to do so, why did they imagine that they could?

In some ways, Spiritualism bears similarities to the most radical, anticlerical strains of Protestantism in the nineteenth century: it too sought to make religious hierarchy and expertise obsolete. Yet Spiritualism also took the concept of mediation literally, at once transforming ordinary Americans into spiritual mediums and transfiguring new forms of information and technological media into the means of the movement's proliferation. Moreover, it was popularized in an era when anything seemed possible, when speaking to the dead may have seemed no less strange than communicating across cables or capturing the living on film. Like freezing an image on a photographic plate, the Spiritualists' ghost catching was a collapsing of time: the past preserved in the present for the future. To view this nineteenth-century religion from a contemporary vantage, then, is to engage with emergent technologies and inexplicable occurrences, modern vision and phantasmic visions.[8]

The revelations of modern science provided new language for spiritual communication, but Spiritualists' embrace of technology was more than mere analogy. Samuel Morse's electrical telegraph was introduced in 1844, four years before the Fox sisters' invention.[9] Spirit rapping was almost immediately dubbed the "spiritual telegraph," as was one of the first Spiritualist newspapers, which extended the metaphor as it spread the news. In a literalization of what the critic Jeffrey Sconce has termed "haunted media," the Spiritualist press was driven by the information-gathering power of contributing mediums as well as worldly editors. During the Civil War, "spirit helpers" played an important role as Spiritualist newspapers competed with one another to disseminate information about battles and war dead faster and, arguably, more accurately than the mainstream press could promise.[10] Even Thomas Watson, the famed assistant to Alexander Graham Bell, experimented with the telephone as an aid to spiritual communication.[11] Nineteenth-century phenomena such as spiritual telegraphy, automatic writing, and spectral photography functioned as new media; at the same time, Spiritualists understood their own embodied religious practices and practitioners *as* media. Spiritualist media and performance were not merely attendant to the religion, a way to get out the word: mediation was Spiritualist practice itself. The medium's bodily transformation in the séance circle was an individual experience collectively mobilized.

Mediums extrapolated the new ability to communicate across land and water via wires and cables to a link across time itself. Spiritualist communication became more than either popular science or an amusing parlor game: it functioned as a powerful means of connection, offering grieving Americans an outlet for mourning. Collective consolation, as well as disparate personal longings for community, however, gave rise to another voice within Spiritualism, one that renewed the call for utopian reform and reimagined the obligations of citizenship in this world.

After situating Spiritualism within antebellum mourning cultures, this chapter illustrates the ways in which the sense of collectivity forged by consolation, in presence and in print, opened a path to interconnected political practices. While tracing Spiritualists' broad involvement in myriad personal, social, and political reform movements of the nineteenth century, I ground Spiritualist politics in Spiritualists' own unique relationships to dying and to the dead. Untangling the relationship between mourning and social change on the one hand and a rising consumer culture and middle-class sensibility on the other, this chapter charts the ways in which, in this moment, mourning became militancy.

CONSOLATION AND CONNECTION

In some ways, Spiritualist media predated Spiritualist mediums. More precisely, the popular religion that became known as American Spiritualism was rapidly disseminated by an existing group of skilled writers, editors, and lecturers who came of age during the mesmeric movement that laid the intellectual groundwork for its successor.[12] At the same time, Spiritualism grew out of American Victorian mourning cultures that were themselves made manifest through new markets in commercialized memento mori and flourishing print media. This particular confluence of markets and media contributed to the movement's explosive growth and widespread circulation. Within a few short years following the Fox sisters' "Rochester Rappings," the Spiritualist press became a community in print, linking disparate local spirit circles into a national network.[13]

The *Shekinah,* one of the first Spiritualist newspapers, included pages of letters from readers to the editor, Samuel B. Brittan, asking for comfort, consolation, and sometimes assistance in contacting dead loved ones. Likewise, beginning in the late 1850s, the Spiritualist newspaper *The Banner of Light* published a regular column, "The Messenger," which included communications to readers from the spirits of the dead through the mediumship of Mrs. J. H. (Fannie) Conant, whose services were engaged "exclusively for the *Banner of Light.*"[14] Some mourners directed their letters personally to well-known Spiritualists. Judge John Worth Edmonds of the Supreme Court of New York became a prominent spokesman for the spiritual cause when, mourning his wife's death, he approached the nation's first medium, Margaret Fox, to help him make contact with his deceased spouse. After attending séances led by the Fox sisters, Edmonds converted to Spiritualism; he resigned from his final post on the New York Court of Appeals in 1853 to devote himself fully to spreading the spiritual news.[15]

In 1853, the *Shekinah* published an exchange between Edmonds, described as "one of our most distinguished citizens," and a woman identified only as "an intelligent lady at the South." She wrote to Edmonds because she knew that "he too had lost a spirit mate." Edmonds answered one of her letters with the assurance that "the intelligent lady's" dead mate was still with her: "Believe me, if you have in the Spiritual World one dearer you than life, he is ever around and near you, watching over and guarding you, conscious of your every thought, rendered more happy by every evidence of your purity and affection, and striving to make his presence known to you." Edmonds further offered his condolences and the possibility that he might contact the departed on her behalf. "I feel that this letter will not afford you all the consolation you deserve," he wrote, "and if at any time you desire more, do not hesitate to write me. If I knew who your dear one was, perhaps I might be able to converse with him for you."[16]

Judging from literature and artifacts of the period, as well as exchanges in the Spiritualist press, the burden of mourning seemed to fall primarily on white, middle-class women, reflecting their position as keepers of domesticity and pillars of home and society.[17] Though their letters to Spiritualist newspapers mourned spouses as well as children, little girls seemed to hold a particularly treasured place in women's hearts. A typical letter ran: "She was but a little child, my little ——, scarce five years old; but as an only daughter, had become doubly dear to me."[18] Both women and little girls figure prominently in this discourse. Men were largely absent from these exchanges as mourners, though they did function as purveyors of advice and solace.

In many ways the epistolary "consolation literature" printed in the Spiritualist press, and Spiritualism itself, fit squarely within a larger mid-nineteenth-century, middle-class sentimental culture, one that had a particular fascination with death.[19] In attempting to understand the Victorian cult of the dead, a scholar's first impulse is to assume that the mortality rate rose during the period. Indeed, historians have shed new light on Americans' relationship to death in the antebellum period by charting demographic trends in life expectancy. As Nancy Isenberg and Andrew Burstein detail, the Revolutionary War generation saw a "gradual increase in life expectancy between 1750 and 1790, in spite of the Revolutionary War; yet, while survival statistics vary among geographic regions, we have also learned that the average American's life span *declined* after 1790, from approximately fifty-six to forty-eight years by the time of the Civil War."[20] Scourges of typhoid, yellow fever, and tuberculosis undid the expectation—at least among the more prosperous classes—that medical science could reduce mortality. An additional seven hundred thousand Americans died during the Civil War. The epidemics of the "cholera years," which spread with a new rapidity in increasingly populated cities and among the urban poor, combined with the devastation of the war years, cast the shadow of death over the promised progress of the nineteenth century.[21]

Evidence of the Victorians' obsessive interest in death is widely available in the literature and theology of the period, as it is in memento mori.[22] A remarkably high proportion of the lyric poetry of the era, especially by women writers, addresses the themes of death and dying, bereavement and mourning. The historian Ann Douglas has termed the memoirs of women and clergymen written in the 1850s as veritable "exercises in necrophilia."[23] Indeed, the deathbed scene was a ubiquitous literary convention in the mid-nineteenth century, not only in fiction but also in sermons, memoirs, and biographies. In this genre, a moving death was more important than a significant life: the deathbed was the focus and telos of every life, however short.[24]

Intricate rituals of sentimental culture effectively adjusted the social focus from the dead to the living. Antebellum mourning manuals functioned like etiquette books, prescribing elaborate funerals and bereavement rituals. Dress marked different stages of mourning, each with its own corresponding rituals and obligations. The first stage of mourning demanded black: " 'A dead solid color' of black that gave no hint of blue or rust."[25] This stage mandated lockets, brooches, earrings of black jet, and a veil, which could be lifted in the second stage of mourning. The so-called rural cemetery movement of the mid-nineteenth century, which saw rolling cemeteries on the edge of townships replace family and church graveyards in town centers, was another sign of change in community practices as well as in the physical place of the dead. Like the new mourning culture, resituating the dead from a central place in daily life to its spatial periphery marked a shift from communal grief to broader societal mourning.[26]

Historians have described Victorian mourning customs in both the United States and Britain as "extravagant displays" that imposed a heavy burden on bereaved families.[27] As the historian Karen Halttunen has argued, in a society increasingly stratified by class, pomp-filled funerals and imposing grave-stones became a means of asserting status and respectability, of differentiat-ing oneself from the lower orders. These rituals became visible signs of a mourner's "Christian piety, social benevolence, and sincere sensibility."[28] A baroque protocol was used at once to mark proper Christian bereavement and to unmask the insincere mourner or pretender to middle-class status.

Spiritualist and sentimental mourning practices, however, constitute dis-tinct practices born of a shared wellspring of culture. Comparing the heart-wrenching words published in Spiritualist newspapers, bespeaking a deeply personal anguish, with the sentimental rituals steeped in convention and designed to perform sincerity, one runs up against a fissure in middle-class cultures of mourning. Spiritualist bereavement stands in stark contrast to these prescribed displays and seems to express quite different needs. The critic Jeffrey Steele has suggested that it may be more useful to think not of "one culture of mourning, but multiple cultures that overlapped and inter-sected in a variety of ways."[29] Spiritualist mourning practices, then, may be understood as one culture of mourning that coexisted alongside a similar sentimental culture.

Although letters to publications like the *Shekinah* and the *Banner of Light* were intended for circulation, and were thus more public and performative than purely private acts of mourning, they did not function as spectacle. Correspondents almost always wrote anonymously or at least were published under pseudonyms. Editors replaced names and references to correspondents' family members with double dashes, circumventing both social and familial recognition. Neither were these exchanges overtly pedagogical. In contrast to Victorian advice manuals like Nehemiah Adams's *Agnes and the Little Key: Or, Bereaved Parents Instructed and Comforted* or the Reverend Theodore Cuyler's *The Empty Crib*, Spiritualist epistolary consolation literature did not dictate behavior or suggest that mourners strike a particular emotional note.[30]

Letters of grief written to the Spiritualist press, however did hew to the sentimental convention that "only those who had been mourners could sym-pathize with the bereaved."[31] Letter writers expressed their sorrow as some-thing that was intelligible only to those who had experienced it; they there-fore sought solace from like souls. To Judge Edmonds, another woman wrote: "To others my grief may appear excessive, but you, who have lost children, may conceive of the anguish of a mother's spirit, in seeing suddenly snatched from her arms, in the space of a few hours, the idol of her heart . . . and who in that Spirit-world can replace the mother in this?"[32] Writers almost always communicated that no one in the world understood their pain. What most characterizes this literature is a sense of social isolation among the correspondents, of being without collective comfort and alone with solitary grief. It is hard to say whether these bereaved individuals found themselves actually excluded from the materialistic cult of mourning and untouched by the era's mostly literary ethos of sentimentality or whether they were voicing grief as a longing for connection that these social forms repressed. In some ways, the very existence of these epistolary exchanges speaks to the shared sense among letter writers that their immediate social circles had failed them and that another imagined community, in this case a community in print, was required to assist in the mourning process.

Writers to the Spiritualist press did not always identify themselves as Spiritualists, though it is likely that many arrived at this belief system through their mourning processes and through the collective solace provided by Spiritualist communities in print and in person. Grieving "seekers" received assurances that they were not alone or, as Judge Edmonds put it, not "solitary instances."[33] While it did not guarantee seekers contact with dead loved ones, Spiritualism provided a community of the living for the living. This transformation of the grieving individual into a member of a collectivity was particularly important at a moment when individualism was taking on a new ideological power—especially for the middle classes and particularly for middle-class white women.

The shift from communalism to individualism was a slow and uneven process, one that was intimately related to the growth of industrial capitalism in the nineteenth-century United States. For the working classes and most immigrant groups, community concerns remained paramount well into the twentieth century. While ethnic and class affiliation continued to shape communities, changing ideas about time and work in a new age of capital stressed the role of the individual in shaping his or her own life. On a theological plane, the focus of most Americans shifted from preparing for death to enjoying life. Calvinist predestination became increasingly unacceptable to American Protestants whose daily lives underscored the necessity of creating their own earthly and eternal futures. The spirit of capitalism was the spirit of the age and, for many nineteenth-century bourgeois Americans, individualism was a pragmatic component of life and of death.

The nineteenth century marked the beginning of death as an individual or familial concern, rather than one involving an entire community. Although the theological conception of individuality in death emerged over centuries, as Philippe Ariès has argued, it was not until the twentieth century that most members of society were allotted a personal burial space.[34] On the one hand, affluent classes engaged in these increasingly private observances as a demonstration of individuality and economic autonomy. On the other hand, many families experienced this circumscription of death to the nuclear family as a loss of community and a mounting sense of social isolation. This process was hastened by urbanization, as many Americans were distanced from the communities into which they had been traditionally integrated. In these circumstances, death took on new meaning and power; the evisceration of community consolation made it intolerable.[35] In this context, Spiritualism emerged as an alternative to both an increasingly individuated society and the commodified rituals of sentimental culture.

Some Spiritualists publicly criticized "the showy and utterly hollow rituals" connected with sentimental rites of burial. Many chafed at the empty materialism of a culture that equated the quantity and quality of mourning's accoutrements with the depth of felt loss. "These [rituals] make themselves manifest in the imposing styles of funerals, and the pageantry with which these decent ceremonies that naturally pertain to death are overlaid. . . . The style of dress, the cut of the cap, the width of the ribbon, the breadth of the crepe, indicates the depth of grief and the nearness of the relative dead," explained a Spiritualist editorialist, opining that "all this parade and pomp will avail nothing."[36] Others saw the performative nature of grief in these rituals merely as a reification of the griever: "Much of mourning is rooted in selfishness. The more external, the more conspicuous the weeping."[37] One critic went so far as to directly challenge the sincerity and faith of the mourners, writing: "Weeping, mourning, and darkened drapery are not signs of intense sorrow, but rather of doubt."[38] Yet Spiritualists were not looking to purify sentimental rites of mourning with a more vigorous faith but rather to address doubt through an interrogation of death itself.

Spiritualism gave believers a community of fellow mourners who could take them beyond personal grief and the increasingly domesticated, sentimental rituals of middle-class mourning, offering instead new possibilities for life. In a formulation that, at once, recapitulated a focus on the living and denied the existence of death, one believer explained: "We shall only think of what lives and have no fruitless lamentations for what dies."[39] Indeed, a faith in Spiritualism, and in contact between the dead and the living, allowed some nineteenth-century Americans a new way of being in the world. However, Spiritualism did function in this way for many nineteenth-century Americans. Once-private grief could be assuaged by public solace and by the assurance that the dead did not die. In this sense, the significance of

Figure 2. "Unidentified man with three spirits," ca. 1861.
William H. Mumler (photographer, American, 1832–84,
active Boston, Massachusetts). Catalog no. 84.XD.760.1.24.
The J. Paul Getty Museum, Los Angeles.

Spiritualism may be in its attention to the specificity of the dead, the conjured voice, hand, or message. In an Anglo-American society obsessed with mourning only as a performative practice that tamed the power of loss and displaced the physical bodies of the dead to the spatial outskirts of culture, to attempt to draw the dead nearer was to move against that current.

WOMEN, CHILDREN, AND OTHER LIMINAL SUBJECTS

The anthropologist Victor Turner's concept of liminality as a space or transitional period between two established social roles is useful for understanding both cultural practices of mourning and the making of a Spiritualist medium. Mourners and the dead might be understood as passing through analogous liminal spaces: mourners journey from grief through mourning and back to the world of the living; the dead travel from the land of the living to the other side.[40] Mediums were thus doubly liminal figures, traversing two worlds, literally mediating a space between the living and the dead while obviating the necessity of mourning. Moreover, Spiritualism implicitly intervened in the liminal spaces of secular time, at once adhering to and challenging the Victorian invention of the child. A number of historians have charted the way the movement drew women from the margins of society to the center of this religious practice. However, combining a study of women as a marginalized identity with the liminality of the newly figured child offers a more complicated view of Spiritualism's unique negotiations with the era's notions of religion and gender.

Although women and—somewhat less often—effeminate, "gentle" men were called to spiritual service, it was young girls who held a privileged and foundational place in Spiritualist practice. The first mediums, the Fox sisters, like many who followed in their footsteps, were in the borderland between childhood and adulthood when they began their spiritual communications. The middle third of the nineteenth century, the founding years of Spiritualism, also marked a crucial point in the making of childhood, a concept deployed for both class regulation and the production of sentimental innocence. School reformers shaped a major revolution in classroom discipline, primarily in schools for the poor and working classes. Many middle-class parents who sent their children to school incorporated these disciplinary lessons into home life. The 1840s and 1850s saw the rise of child-rearing guides and advice books, instructing middle-class parents how to shear children from their playful, impulsive ways and direct them toward sober, industrious futures.[41] At a moment when their childhood dreamscapes of ghosts and night visitors should have been fading into the decidedly unfanciful realities of work and marriage, Spiritualism offered a different vision. As mediums, girls in particular occupied a privileged place as intermediaries between this world and the next at the very moment when their possibilities for power, speech, and imagination were fast diminishing.

Mediums were often from rural areas and of the working or lower middle classes. Yet they also embodied less material, more numinous qualities. Biographies and autobiographies of nineteenth-century Spiritualists sketch remarkably similar patterns in the making of a medium. The early life history of Emma Hardinge, who wrote her own autobiography as well as histories of other movement leaders, was typical: she described herself as serious, solitary, imaginative, and a daydreamer. In this regard, her childhood is similar to those of other nineteenth-century Spiritualist autobiographers; yet her account of her youth takes a decidedly morbid turn. She recalls never being "young, joyous or happy, like other children; my delight was to steal away alone and to seek the solitude of woods and fields, but above all to wander in churchyards, cathedral cloisters, and old monastic ruins." She adds that she also liked "to be laid on a bed of sickness" to "pass away in dreams . . . and go off to the unknown and fascinating fairyland."[42]

When she penned her 1869 history of modern American Spiritualism, Hardinge fittingly began with the children who inaugurated the movement. She wrote that "a score of years ago the name 'Spiritualist' was unknown on the American continent, whilst all the sum of Spiritualism was contained in the persons of three young girls, ignominiously designated the 'Rochester knockers.'"[43] These "three young girls" took their place in history when the two youngest, Kate and Margaret Fox, were eleven and fourteen years old; the third sister, Leah, was in fact quite a bit older and a married woman, though she is often included in this youthful triad.[44] The "miracle" of spirit communication was understood by nineteenth-century contemporaries as all the more miraculous because of the guileless innocence attributed to girl-hood—especially to the rural white girlhood of the Foxes. As one nineteenth-century Spiritualist historian asked, "What more fitting instrument could be found by the heavenly messengers to confound the wise and to reveal the things of the spirit than innocent children, little girls whose souls reflected the truths as the perfect mirror does its surrounding objects?"[45]

The story of the first rappings places children and ghosts at its center, alongside a playfulness hardly befitting the founding story of a new religion. But Spiritualism as a popular religion in fact played with and in the contemporary genres of entertainment and belief. Thus believers as well as debunkers tended to retell the creation story of Spiritualism as a sort of ghost story. Hardinge wrote the story of the Fox sisters with the cadences of a tale told at a campfire or a child's bedside: "Imagine the place to be an humble cottage bedroom in a remote obscure hamlet; the judges and jurors, simple unsophisticated rustics; and the witness an invisible, unknown being, a denizen of a world of whose very existence mankind has been ignorant . . . and breaking through what has been deemed the dark and eternal seal of death, which not even the fabled silence of the tomb could longer hide away."[46] Once the scary scene is set, the story emerges that, late one night, Mrs. Fox heard strange noises emanating from the floors and ceiling of her rural farmhouse. Blaming Kate and Margaret for the disturbances, Mrs. Fox insisted they stop. As the raps and knocks continued, the girls maintained that not only were they not making the noises, but that the communications were made by a spirit who rapped in response to their questions. Kate, the youngest of the Fox sisters, imitated the ghostly sounds by snapping her fingers. Naming her ghost "Mr. Splitfoot," she said, "Mr. Splitfoot, do as I do," clapping her hands, to which the specter responded with the same number of raps.[47]

The power and pull of the Fox sisters' story not only derived from a gothic literary tradition; it also evoked local folk traditions of extrareligious spiritual happenings. For this was not the first time unexplained events had been reported in Hydesville. Earlier residents had also heard strange scrapings and noises in the old farmhouse, and neighbors came forward to tell stories of hauntings there. The Fox family decided that the mysterious communications came from a peddler who had been murdered in the house.[48] Observers were called in to witness the disturbances, reporting noises from the attic and cellar and sights of moving furniture and slamming doors. In her book *The Missing Link,* Leah Fox [Fish] Underhill told of these nightly knocks and strange disturbances. "Articles of furniture were moved, doors opened and shut, the sound of persons walking about was distinctly heard, the beds upon which they were sleeping would be raised from the floor and dropped down again, until they were obliged to take the bedding and lay it on the floor."[49] Mrs. Fox swore in signed testimony that she was not "a believer in haunted houses or supernatural appearances" and apologized for the "excitement" over the rappings. "It has been a great deal of trouble for us," she continued. "It was our misfortune to live there at the time; but I am willing and anxious that the truth be known. I cannot account for these noises; all that I know is that they have been heard repeatedly."[50] In some ways, Mrs. Fox would become the model for the doubtful "investigator."

Hearing news of these spiritual visitations, locals came by to ask questions of the spirit. Quizzing this supernatural being about the most mundane aspects of their lives, Hydesville residents were thrilled to get correct responses, in the form of knocks, to their queries about the ages of their children and the births and deaths of relatives. A local lawyer dutifully recorded all statements.[51] When Kate Fox was taken to Rochester to visit her sister Leah, she found that the raps traveled with her. Spirits soon began to clamor in Rochester in private gatherings held for prominent guests. From their debut, the spirits seemed to have a wonderful knack for publicity. The first meeting, in what would come to be called a spirit circle or séance, was held at the residence of Isaac and Amy Post, prominent Quaker abolitionists whose home had been a stop on the Underground Railroad. Among the invited guests at this first séance were celebrated activists, writers, and editors. Frederick Douglass, then the editor of the *North Star*, was a frequent visitor to the Post residence.[52]

When strange noises began to circulate around the bodies of the Fox sisters, it was not assumed that the girls were deceiving either themselves or the public. Their credibility derived in part from the many witnesses to the supernatural events in Hydesville and Rochester, respected community members whose testimony was thought to be reliable. Within the belief system of Spiritualism as well as in a broader Victorian context, seeing was believing. Neighbors of the Fox family and Rochester séance-goers had all posed questions to the spirits, who had revealed knowledge of human events that was considered by the listeners as inaccessible by natural means. Questioners eventually concluded that the raps were coming from many spirits, including the spirits of their own dead relatives, rather than solely from the murdered peddler who had set off the first storm of effects in Hydesville. The raps occurred, for the most part, only when the Fox girls were present, but investigators did not grill the young mediums as to how they might have produced the noises: they did not verbally question the sisters. As one historian astutely puts it, "Americans wanted to talk to spirits, and they would have found a way to do it with or without Kate and Margaret Fox."[53] The mediums' youthful innocence, and most significantly their middle-class femaleness, lent them an unbroachable sincerity reinforced by believers' own desire for communication with the dead.

The Fox sisters' communications with the afterlife were eventually debunked, but the desire they had inspired in average Americans took on a life of its own.[54] Americans who wanted to speak to spirits had to do so through mediums, but not everyone could become a medium. Mediumship was something visited on a person, and, according to memoirs and accounts in the Spiritualist press, it came unannounced. These visitations produced a spectrum of emotions, ranging from excitement to terror. As chapter 4 details, young girls who found themselves conduits for strange voices or subject to hypnotic trance states would have been as likely to be placed under the care of a doctor or clergyman as embraced by a spirit circle. Many incipient mediums had spent much of their early lives in sickbeds prior to discovering Spiritualism.

The *Banner of Light* editor, Luther Colby, referred to mediums as "tender susceptible plants."[55] Indeed, little girls were seen as ripe for mediumship in part because of the cultural assumption that they were passive, guileless, and incapable of producing feats of skilled speech or writing through normal means. The language used to refer to the onset of mediumship was as passive as its subjects: one was "developed" as a medium. This process was linear and progressive, a spiritual journey that brought unschooled girls and women, theoretically without their own volition, to epiphanies of spiritual understanding.

Soon after the Fox sisters' 1848 revelations, young girls throughout upstate New York discovered hidden spiritual talents. For the most part, Spiritualist writers and the newspapers that published them described the onset of mediumship as a momentous event, celebrated by the community. In the family of a "Mr. Anson Attwood," of Troy, New York, "a gentlemen of prominent position and high character," one of his little daughters, a child of about ten years of age, became suddenly developed for "marvellous phases of the strongest physical character." The tiny medium extracted payment in the form of a "liberal supply of candy," and while she "munched away at her sweetmeats the spirits lifted her about and moved her from place to place." She conjured spirit raps and translated them; she performed feats of automatic writing and clairvoyance. And, as Emma Hardinge gushed, similar manifestations "continued to spring up like grass beneath the feet in every place and with a variety of developments."[56]

Among the many mediums of the 1850s, none was more renowned than Cora L. V. Scott.[57] She was a trance medium and spiritual speaker whom the press took great pleasure in describing as "a delicate-featured blond" with "flaxen ringlets falling over her shoulders." She was depicted as both sexualized and innocent, with accounts typically waxing eloquent over Scott's "ethereal beauty" and femininity while also expressing admiration for "her movements, deliberate and self-possessed, voice calm and deep, and eyes and fingers in no way nervous."[58] In a photograph that circulated widely in the 1850s, Scott is pictured with flowing, pre-Raphaelite hair and a look of angelic innocence befitting one who made her New York debut as "a young lady of scarce seventeen summers."[59] Unpacking and analyzing this combination of female virtues and masculine endowments not only sheds light on the making of mediums in the nineteenth century but also opens up broader questions about the meanings of female sexuality and subjectivity during the era.

Cora Scott's "development" as a medium began in 1851, when she was eleven years old, living with her family in Lake Mills, Wisconsin. Born in Allegheny County, New York, in the same region of the state that nurtured the Fox Sisters and many other prominent Spiritualists, Cora found her spiritual gifts soon after leaving the region. It was then, as her biographers tell it, that Cora went one day to an arbor of trees in her family garden to write a composition for school. She awoke, as she supposed, from a sleep, and found her slate "covered with writing not her own." Assuming that someone else had written on the slate while she was sleeping, Cora brought it inside for her mother to read. Her mother found the communications to be addressed to herself, from a sister who had "been in the spirit world some years." Cora had never been told of her mother's dead sister. The only other person in the garden while Cora slept was her four-year-old sister, who could neither read nor write.[60]

This "singular manifestation" was considered the first evidence of Cora Scott's mediumship. Immediately after, she was developed as an "unconscious trance-medium." Cora communicated to her family that she had been "directed by spirit guidance, through her own organism" to leave school. At age eleven, having ended her formal education, she prescribed cures for various diseases while entranced and under the control of "a celebrated German physician."[61] People came from miles around to be healed by the child medium. Mediumship offered the possibility of work for young women, which would have paid more than other forms of labor and certainly more than a typical eleven-year-old could earn. Nevertheless, the question of whether mediums should charge for their spiritual services and, if so, how much was hotly debated in the Spiritualist press.[62] Most did earn money for their work, often after male breadwinners had somehow failed the family.

Emma Hardinge, who began her career with a British theatrical troupe and ended it as one of the most prominent mediums of the nineteenth century, embarked on her public life soon after her father died. As she wrote in her autobiography (in the third person), "Being deprived of her good father's care at a very tender age, the young girl, like the rest of her family, was compelled to depend on her own talents for subsistence."[63] Another famous Spiritualist, Victoria Woodhull, found her calling in her father Buck's traveling medicine show, where she and her sister, Tennessee Claflin, sometimes

Figure 3. Portrait of Cora L. V. Scott
Hatch, ca. 1850s. Photographer unknown. Collection of the author.

known as the "Wonderful Child," performed feats of psychic healing and
clairvoyance for paying customers. The Hardinge, Woodhull, and Scott
families may have been crassly delighted with the financial rewards of their
daughters' spiritual callings. However, it is equally likely that they found
religious justifications for allowing these young girls to perform public work.
"There are certain good works to accomplish which it is permitted the young
girl to leave the domestic sanctuary, and if necessary, even to throw aside that
reserve which characterize her age," wrote a prominent Spiritualist. Advising
a girl with gifts that she may do more than "assist her mother in household
duties" or "lend her arm to support her aged father," he concluded: "Go, my
daughter, go without hesitation, and may God be with you."[64]

The Scott family, in particular, came out of exactly the antinomian Protestant reform tradition that gave rise to Spiritualism. Cora's father, David W.
Scott, described variously as an "independent" or "free thinker," had some
interest in Spiritualism and more than a little in utopian reform. Scott had
begun correspondence with Adin Ballou after reading about his utopian

colony near Milford, Massachusetts, in the pages of Horace Greeley's *New York Tribune*. Scott visited Ballou at Hopedale and was inspired by this cooperative colony dedicated to "Practical Christian Socialism."[65] Scott moved his family to Wisconsin in 1851 to gain access to land on which to begin his own colony, modeled after Hopedale. However, Scott's plans were disrupted, and later completely abandoned, when his daughter Cora was developed as a medium. In a match made in heaven, one of Cora's first spirit guides was Ballou's son Adin Augustus Ballou, the dead scion of Hopedale.[66]

Cora's mother, Lodensy Butterfield, later found her own spiritual talents, and it was soon discovered that there were several mediums in the family besides Cora. Her grandmother, her aunts Olive, Catherine, and Cordelia, and her Uncle Edwin were all developed as mediums, and much of the rest of the extended family converted to Spiritualism.[67] Cora Scott, at age eleven, had effectively altered the direction of her entire family's lives. David Scott gave up his dream of a Western Hopedale to guide Cora's career, and they soon took her talents on the road. At age fourteen Cora landed in Buffalo, New York, where she spent two years as a regular speaker at a western New York Spiritualist society.[68] There she developed "joint mediumship" with a Miss Sarah Brooks, with whom she "frequently held trance séances, at which one would be controlled to speak in foreign tongues, whilst the other interpreted the mystic utterances."[69]

Although Spiritualism offered a world in which young women could craft unique forms of autonomy, many depended on their spirits, who were often male and socially powerful. The spirit of the "celebrated German physician," who came to Cora at fourteen and brought her knowledge of pharmaceuticals and medical treatment, inaugurated Cora's relationships with eminent and not so eminent men. In 1853, her father died, and sometime between her fourteenth and seventeenth year Cora married the much older Benjamin F. Hatch, a dentist.[70] The marriage did not last long. In *Spiritual Iniquities Unmasked, and, the Hatch Divorce Case,* Dr. Hatch excoriated Cora for leaving him for another man. He also rebuked Spiritualists in general for encouraging "free love." His account of the marriage, written in the aftermath of a bitter separation, is nothing if not self-serving; but it nevertheless traces the outlines of a story that his ex-wife and other Spiritualists corroborated elsewhere. According to his account, Hatch discovered Cora and rescued her from the peripatetic life of an impoverished Spiritualist traveler. He described supporting both Cora and her mother and training the young medium in how to best use her unformed gifts. Hatch depicted himself as working with "untiring toil" to advance Cora's career.[71]

Cora's account, written many years later, not surprisingly presents a somewhat different story. She accused Hatch of taking advantage of her innocence, lying about his own social status in order to marry her under false pretenses. (Hatch stopped practicing as a dentist soon after marrying the young ingenue.) She accused him of keeping all of the profits from her work for himself and forcing her and her mother to beg for money.[72] Hatch admitted that he kept firm control over the profits, but by his own account he was extremely generous with his wife and her family: "My rule was to anticipate her wants as far as possible, and thus supply them before requested to do so."[73] While he was working to develop her career, Hatch claimed, Cora lazed about, doing nothing to prepare for her appearances. Still a teenager, Cora had arrived in New York a little over a year earlier, attended by great success on stage and in society parlors; her divorce was closely tracked by the press, especially the respected *New York Daily Tribune*.[74]

In New York City, Cora attended regular Sunday meetings with other prominent Spiritualists, where they discussed events of the day and performed spiritual anthems, hymns, and oratory for an audience. From 1853 through the 1870s, the New York Spiritualists met at the Stuyvesant Institute, the Hope Chapel, and later at Dodworth's Hall, where they attracted the attention of the popular press as well as building a loyal following in the Spiritualist press.

The connections between the popular and Spiritualist presses were more tangled than one might imagine. The *Tribune* editor, Horace Greeley, was an early Spiritualist investigator. Having lost four small children during the 1840s, Greeley asked Margaret Fox to perform a séance so that he and his wife could commune with the spirit of their son, "Pickie." Greeley's newspaper covered the travels of the Fox sisters and other spiritual events through the 1840s and early 1850s, and in 1859, Greeley allotted a column to the Spiritualist and retired judge John Worth Edmonds.[75]

Cora Scott, like the Fox Sisters before her, became a celebrity, often lecturing to packed crowds that flowed out into the streets. A contemporary account reported: "She has carried the New Yorkers by storm, and every one of her lectures in that city have been attended by wondering thousands."[76] Entering the hall and climbing the lectern in a noticeable trance state, she expounded on subjects as diverse as medicine and science and the history of Christianity.[77] A committee of Spiritualists gathered from the audience would propose a topic of scientific, religious or philosophic significance thought to be beyond the ken of an ordinary woman. At other times, the controlling spirit, voiced through the medium, would choose the topic.[78]

Cora Scott bears more than a passing resemblance to Henry James's Verena Tarrant, the trance-speaking heroine of *The Bostonians,* who is manipulated by a series of political, amorous, and spiritual figures. Like the fictional Verena, who was first mesmerized by her huckster father, Selah Tarrant, Cora Scott performed under "controls." Nineteenth-century Spiritualists understood trance mediums as being under the power of a spirit stronger than their own. Controls typically worked from the spirit realm: that is, Spiritualists recognized mediums as being ventriloquized by spirits of the dead. In a process suggestive of mesmerism, however, the controlling operator might also be a mere mortal, who entranced the medium and guided her to channel a spirit. In either case, controls were typically men.[79]

Yet to assume that Cora Scott was merely an instrument of either the spirits or the living men who orchestrated her career is to underestimate the subversive power of both the practice of mediumship and of this particular medium. Scott's sermons were regularly reprinted in the *Banner of Light,* often with accompanying commentary. Praise for her words was as common as the belief that they could not have been her own. Nathaniel Parker Willis, the editor of the *Home Journal,* reported on Scott's performances at Dodsworth's Hall and remarked on how "very curious it was, to see a long-haired young woman standing alone in the pulpit, her face turned upward, her delicate bare arms raised in a clergyman's attitude of devotion, and a church full of people listening attentively while she prayed."[80] Indeed, in histories of the nineteenth-century women's movement, the image that is typically cited to illustrate the movement's transformative power is the appearance of the woman speaker before a "mixed audience."

Willis had clearly never seen a young woman holding an audience rapt. But "how to explain it, with her age, habits, education," he concluded, "is the true point at issue."[81] As a nonbeliever, Willis was unwilling to attribute Cora Scott's feats to spiritual agency, but neither was he willing to attribute them to her own ability. Asking "how to explain it," Willis never even entertained the possibility that the alacrity of speech could have been the medium's own. He also failed to notice the genius of an even more extraordinary woman in his milieu: Harriet Jacobs toiled in Willis's Brooklyn home while writing *Incidents in the Life of a Slave Girl.*[82]

The Bostonians evokes and yet never really entertains the spiritual dimension of female mediumship, providing instead a critique of female impressionability and a damning exposé of the political as too personal in nineteenth-century U.S. reformist circles. By contrast, Scott's history offers a more generous and collaborative account of a medium's development.

Although Cora Scott's formal schooling had ended at age eleven, the constant company of adult Spiritualists thereafter may very well have provided a richer education. A teacher quoted in her official biography remembered Cora as a remarkable student with a photographic memory: "She did not seem to have to study her lessons at all."[83] And, regardless of whether she actually channeled spirits, Scott was unusually adept at channeling the religious spirit of the age. The texts of her lectures reveal her thorough knowledge of the generic Protestantism that was in the air among Spiritualists and many others in the 1850s.

In a speech titled "Christianity in America," Scott spoke of John Calvin and Martin Luther, "the great institutors of the present forms of Protestant religion" who "are as familiar to you as your own name." Like many religious figures of the day, she was pushing the logic of Protestantism beyond its institutional manifestations. Speaking in the first person plural to represent herself and the spirits, she asserted that "we still have to tell you that the form of Protestant religion is susceptible of almost any interpretation; and that the standard of present Christianity is not the Bible, but humanity; that the Bible was just what it is now in the days of the Romish church in their greed and prosperity; that the new Testament was just as it is now when the Pope reigned over all Christendom, and the thunders of the Vatican gave forth their tones, and the terrors of the Inquisition gave way."[84] Scott, as well as the audience she addressed, would have been well versed in critiques of institutionalized Calvinism and aware of a broader anticlericalism and exaltation of individual conscience. Scott at once evokes standard antipapal sentiment to reject biblical fundamentalism in favor of a religious humanism.

From a twenty-first-century vantage it is hard to imagine that these far-ranging speeches were thought beyond the capability of a woman speaker. However, without fail, the argument adduced to support the authenticity of her gifts was the fact that she could not have produced these speeches without spirit direction or delivered them unless in a trance. "She is evidently under the control of a higher order of spirits," wrote one admirer. "Her use of language is almost perfect, while it is obvious to everyone that she has not above ordinary intellect, and her years preclude the possibility of her being conversant with all the topics that come before her."[85]

Scott held private circles for interested, paying New Yorkers who sought spiritual guidance. In these "investigating" circles, "the most distinguished savans of the country" discussed the philosophy of Spiritualism with Scott. The circles typically concluded, as did her lectures, with an opportunity for an interested inquirer to ask questions "propounded on the spot."[86] That she could answer these questions was, again, proof that she was under spirit control. When speaking, she did so in a trance, the most passive of states, performing masculine prowess in a stereotypically feminine embodiment. On the one hand, she spoke, but her speech was understood as ventriloquized; she received no credit for her own intellectual, verbal, or performative skills. On the other hand, she carved out a space and commanded a public unique for a woman of her day.

Scott conducted her private life with some of the same combination of classically feminine passivity and scandalous, unwomanly acts that characterized her public life. When she freed herself from her first husband, B. F. Hatch, she found reason and defense in Spiritualism for doing so. While the New York *Tribune, Herald,* and *Post* all ran stories on Mrs. Hatch, "free love," and the rumored "forty mediums" who have "separated or are wanting to separate from their wedded partners," Spiritualist newspapers defended their belief system as one in which people live as "happily with their companions" as any others do, "many of them much more happily than before they became Spiritualists."[87] Benjamin Hatch fueled this media fire, penning bizarre articles with accusations that "all who have sought for divorce, have, to a greater or less extent, possessed mediumistic powers."[88] One editor of a Spiritualist paper countered with the notion that if a woman "fell from virtue" in marriage, then it was most typically evidence of "her husband's blameworthiness," as men "pretend to the right of roaming."[89]

Other writers pointed to the implied support of Spiritualism for "free love." One editorial writer admitted that inasmuch as Spiritualism "breaks down the barriers of wealth and caste, and places its disciples—or aims to do so—on a platform of common brotherhood," it also opens the door to a sometimes dangerous "freedom of action."[90] It was precisely this freedom of action that allowed Cora Scott Hatch to find sanction to leave Benjamin Hatch. Her Spiritualist achievements gave her a level of control over her life and career that was rare among her peers. Indeed, Scott's career lasted another half century after her divorce. Although she continued to attach herself to sometimes difficult men—marrying four times—Cora L. V. Scott Hatch Daniels Tappan Richmond wrote hundreds of books and articles and remained a favorite trance speaker at Spiritualist camp meetings and lectures well into the twentieth century.[91]

Many depictions of mediums adopted the genre of the conversion narrative to contain the tangle of contradictions that characterized Cora Scott's life. The story that circulated about the making of the medium Anna M. Henderson was told as the classic tale of submissive service to the spirits.

Henderson's story ran as part of the "history of mediums" series in the *Banner of Light*. Like all the others, it employed a narrative formula in which women were drawn to the calling by what Calvin called "irresistible grace." Young girls or women were called to service and then "developed" by the spirits. Anna Henderson's narrative began:

> At the age of twenty-one, seven years since, she attended the first circle for spiritual manifestations, when she received the following communication, by raps: "You are a medium. Be submissive to the will of God; a great work is before you to do." She felt a thrill of happiness, such as she never felt before; felt a deep and earnest interest in the subject that she could not describe, or resist. She felt drawn by an unseen power to devote her time, her thoughts and her soul, to this new and seemingly strange influence. Thus, for a few months, she continued constantly to think, talk, and attend meetings on the subject, until she became developed as a trance medium.[92]

Anna Henderson was unusual in that she wrote to the *Banner* to correct her story. Among other details, the article claimed that Henderson did not believe in taking money for her services. She wrote to say that this was not the case. In righting this one error, Henderson provided a rare glimpse into a medium's own sense of her calling as work. She wrote: "It is true, during the first years of my labors, when I was engaged in lecturing mostly in country villages, I made no demand—that is, I had no set price—and many times left my home with barely enough of the needful to bear me to my place of destination, leaving it altogether to the guardians and the good friends that I visited, to furnish means for my return home. My experience is that it costs a medium just as much to ride in a railroad car as it does any other person."[93]

Some openly criticized the commodification of mediumship (while freely availing themselves of mediums' services), but Henderson found this view a particularly galling act of hypocrisy. She explained that people expected her to do her work without pay, sometimes offering only food or lodging. As she tells it, these "customers" would announce that "we do not believe in paying mediums; this is a free gospel and we must not turn it into merchandise." She observed that this goodwill would not feed or clothe her and that "mediums, as well as others, are generally too tangible and material to live on faith. . . . [E]very reasonable person will justify me in demanding an equivalent." She signed this letter: "With a heart warm and willing to aid in this great work, in my humble way, for the good of humanity. I am very cordially yours, Anna M. Henderson."[94]

Mediums were indeed intervening at the nexus of a new theology and economy. Henderson made a case for paid labor while still casting her words in the language of humility and service. Similarly, Cora Hatch used her mediumship to craft a public career and a radically free personal life, buttressed by a belief system that supported her actions. The complicated contradictions of Spiritualism allowed these women to be at once in this world and of another and to find a place for their own versions of work, sexuality, speech, and spirituality.

WOMEN, RELIGION, AND REFORM

That women were central to Spiritualism is not surprising given the rise of female participation in religious movements, sentimental mourning cultures, and political reforms following the Second Great Awakening, the second major religious revival in U.S. history. The privileging of female mediums, however, radically challenged the binary notions of the private and public sphere, the personal and the political, the religious and the secular. This new religion's renegotiation of gender was so radical and pervasive that it is inseparable from the movement's other, multiple concerns. It is perhaps this expansiveness that threatened Spiritualists' nineteenth-century contemporaries and has rendered Spiritualism only partly legible in our own time.

In an essay written in 1973, which defined a new field of historical inquiry, Barbara Welter pointed to "the feminization of American religion." Welter argued that in the first half of the nineteenth century, American religion—specifically American Protestantism—saw an "increased prominence of women in religious organizations" and a "new catering to this membership."[95] This change in American religion, she contended, was more important for women than "anything which happened within women's organizations or in related reform groups."[96] The desire to "perfect" human institutions was the product of a specific moment in the history of reform Protestantism. The Second Great Awakening swept away Calvinist predestination and presented believers with the possibility of acting to save one's own soul and a deep-rooted faith and belief in the individual's ability to do so. This combination gave rise to a peculiarly American form of industrial capitalism, as well a sense among a segment of white Protestants that reform of self and society was a duty and a right. A mixed group of reform movements, addressing education, temperance, prison conditions, the rights of women, the evils of slavery, and the dangers of immigrants and their Catholicism all fell within the reformer's—and often the Spiritualist's—purview.[97] This reformist impulse took distinctive shape in different regions of antebellum America and was given different meaning by women and men of the working, middle, and upper classes. Emerson's oft-quoted notion of reform as "the conviction that there is infinite worthiness in man, which will appear at the call of worth, and that all particular reforms are the removing of some impediment" characterized the general religious humanism of the era.[98] Among many Spiritualists, however, the experience of a worldly incarnation of the afterlife informed more concrete and political versions of this ethos.

Spiritualist freethinkers were united in their belief in these reforms, including abolition, temperance, and women's suffrage. In 1857, a *Banner of Light* editor answered his own rhetorical question, "What does Spiritualism call for?" with the answer: "Reform," the "watchword of the day."[99] Yet many Spiritualists tended toward specific and unconventional theological formulations that both a generalized optimism and dominant reform movements would find hard to assimilate. As one reader wrote to the editor of the Spiritualist newspaper, the *Banner of Light*, "the *Banner* . . . is certainly doing a noble work, in directing men and women to the worship of the true and infinite God, who is perfect cause and perfect Providence; who is the Father and Mother of us all, and of all; who neither recognizes war, nor slavery, nor the degradation of women, nor any other wrong."[100] This reader was not unusual among nineteenth-century Americans who felt drawn by an impulse to perfect society. Yet his evocation of a Spiritualist notion of a dualistic, egalitarian Father and Mother God turns a broadly enthusiastic response to the ethos of reformism into a radical reconfiguration of theology.

In one sense, Spiritualism was a popular phenomenon that paralleled the rise of a print culture, which in turn gave voice to a noisy, eclectic reform culture. The *Banner of Light* newspaper, the longest-running and widest-ranging of the Spiritualist newspapers, circulated among religionists who were part of a broader, white reading public. Advertisements for Spiritualist newspapers targeted former Calvinists and aging Transcendentalists. These readers could fulfill their wants with weekly "verbatim phonographic reports" of the sermons of Henry Ward Beecher and Edwin H. Chapin; the "Philosopher and Metaphysician" could find the writings of Ralph Waldo Emerson; the "Lover of Romance" discovered serialized stories and sentimental novelettes; and the "Reformer" could follow "the lectures of Cora L. V. Hatch, Emma Hardinge and other distinguished speakers who visit Boston and New York."[101]

From these readers and writers emerged an activist community in which women were central and gender was a key organizing principle. Reports from Spiritualist conventions reveal the leading lights of the Spiritualist

Figure 4. "The Spirit of Temperance," tintype, ca. 1875.
Wm. B. Becker Collection/American Museum of Photography
© 1989 Wm. B. Becker. Spiritualists were active in myriad reform
movements, including temperance. Here the medium of spirit
photography conjures the double entendre of alcoholic spirits
and double vision.

movement uniting behind the abolition of slavery, the "Right of woman to decide how often and under what circumstances she shall assume the responsibilities of Mother," and a range of other "progressive" reforms. Undergirding these social resolutions was a religious individualism in which "the authority of each individual soul is absolute and final, in deciding questions as to what is true and false in principle, and right or wrong in practice" and a belief that "the individual, the Church, or the State, that attempts to control the opinions and practices of any man or woman, by an authority or power outside of his or her own soul, is guilty of a flagrant wrong."[102]

Spiritualism had a particular importance for those who sought alternatives to an outmoded Calvinism and an incipient secularism. Beginning in the 1830s, in the historian Sydney Ahlstrom's characterization, a national "cry went up against hierarchies, seminary professors, dry learning, 'hireling ministers,' unconverted congregations and cold formalism."[103] Many Americans, whether or not they considered themselves Spiritualists, would have agreed with one Spiritualist editorial writer's lament that "God has not been brought near enough; He has rather been kept away, and a class of men arrogating authority from Him have presumed to thrust themselves between."[104] As a religious practice, Spiritualism was a heterodox belief system that found adherents among disaffected white Protestants, especially Quakers, Unitarians, and Universalists, many of whom discovered in Spiritualism the immediacy and experiential solace absent from other liberal Christian theologies. Universalist clergymen like Uriah Clark abandoned their old associations for the new dispensation.[105] In a few cases, entire Universalist congregations deserted the denomination to embrace Spiritualism. The Spiritualist lecturer Warren Chase made the assertion that, judging from his 1859 visit to the state, "most of the Universalists in Vermont had become Spiritualists."[106]

Many of these converts were women. Spiritualists appropriated the characteristics that had been used to deem women unfit for public life—piety, passivity, and purity—and transformed them into ideals of spirituality. In so doing, they made women not only appropriate purveyors of religious knowledge, but also influential public figures. Around séance tables and in public performances, mediums spoke in public at a time when very few other women did.[107] Paul's admonition to the Corinthians (1 Corinthians 14:34–35) that women keep silent in the churches was interpreted in the nineteenth century (and before and since) as Biblical justification for circumscribing women's preaching. It was used to silence women on the podium as well as in the pulpit.[108]

Historically, women have been excluded from positions of power in traditional Judeo-Christian religions; at the same time, they have been central as believers.[109] Historians of Spiritualism and other forms of female mysticism have argued that the religious movements in which women have been prominent are those that embrace direct spiritual contact. Arthur Conan Doyle, in his two-volume history of Spiritualism, published in 1926, observed that "the early Spiritualists have been compared with the early Christians and there are indeed many points of resemblance." He continued, "In one respect, however, the Spiritualists had an advantage. . . . The women of the older dispensation did their part nobly, living as saints and dying as martyrs, but they did not figure as preachers and missionaries. Psychic power and psychic knowledge are, however, as great in one sex as in another, and therefore many of the great pioneers of the spiritual revelation were women."[110] Personal and even corporeal spiritual experiences obviate the need for a learned clergy to mediate that experience, rendering religious practice open to women in ways that a more structured, hierarchical religion might not be.[111]

In the nineteenth-century United States, women often found power in marginal religious movements that reinterpreted Biblical tradition or found other sources of prophecy or inspiration.[112] A striking number of new religious movements were founded by women. Examples of such leaders include Ann Lee, the "mother" of the Shakers; Ellen G. White of the Seventh-Day Adventists; Helena Blavatsky, the founder of the Theosophical movement; and Mary Baker Eddy, the originator of Christian Science.[113] (The few religious movements that were founded by men following the Second Great Awakening established unconventional relations between the sexes as central to religious practice.) New Thought and Pentacostalist churches continue to have a higher proportion of women preachers and members than other Christian denominations.[114]

Spiritualism appealed to nineteenth-century Americans who were already conversant with the language and belief systems of sects like the Shakers and Swedenborgians. These religions utilized a notion of an androgynous deity: the Shakers, for example, referred to the Holy Mother Wisdom and Father God. Universalists and Transcendentalists similarly embraced a concept of a universal spirit.[115] The writings of the Transcendentalist Margaret Fuller constructed a gendered cosmos, which on closer inspection showed itself to be structured by a permeable and unstable divide. In *Women in the Nineteenth Century,* Fuller wrote that "Male and Female represent two sides of a great radical dualism. But in fact they are perpetually passing into one another. Fluid hardens to solid, solid rushes to fluid, there is no wholly masculine man, no purely feminine woman."[116]

Spiritualist writers and speakers similarly called on, and disrupted, cosmo-logical and social dualisms. Many discussed the importance of a balanced universe and the reintegration of matter and spirit, male and female. Some noted women's particular suitability to this restoration and healing.[117] However the "balance" that many Spiritualists sought was also one which unsettled the immutable binaries that midcentury science and culture rooted in the body.

In an 1859 speech in Boston's Ordway Hall, the medium Amanda Spence spoke on "the Masculine, or Positive organization" and "the Feminine or Negative Organization." Beginning with nature, she made a rhetorical move designed to valorize the feminine as necessary and coequal with the mascu-line. She argued that everything "from the lowest form of vegetable life, to man, and even to the Deity himself, is dual," and "it is the equilibrium of these positive and negative forces, which creates balance, and harmony, and health. It is the preponderance of one of these in our physical being which causes physiological disease. . . . [I]t is the preponderance of one of these in our social system which gives rise to all our social evils." However, she added an impor-tant coda. While acknowledging that woman is typically the negative, and man the positive, she insisted that "each organization should be judged by its own laws, irrespective of its sex; that a man of feminine organization should . . . assume the duties to which his nature calls him, and that a woman of execu-tive temperament ought, without accusations of manliness and coarseness, to be permitted to take her due part in the executive business of the world."[118]

Spiritualism, then, developed in a context where speakers could find recep-tive audiences for radical ideas about the relationship of gender to spirituality and the proper place of women in religion. In 1859, one Spiritualist medium spoke of women as "the half of which must complete the angel; the dual principle which makes our God, our father and mother."[119] More than three decades later, a prominent male medium voiced a similar sentiment when he wrote that "people cannot entertain an exclusively masculine idea of Deity and at the same time believe that motherhood is as divine as fatherhood."[120]

The most visible manifestation of the link between female empowerment and Spiritualism is the historic connection between suffragism and Spiri-tualism elucidated by Ann Braude. Both movements can be dated from 1848, and their early development was intertwined. Many Spiritualists were suf-fragists, though of course not all suffragists were Spiritualists. Although his-torians of the American women's movement have, for the most part, ignored this pairing, the earliest historians of suffrage—and its first leaders—were well aware that "the only religious sect in the world . . . that has recognized the equality of woman, is the Spiritualists."[121] The *History of Woman Suffrage,* compiled by Elizabeth Cady Stanton and Susan B. Anthony in the 1880s, paid homage to the movement, writing that Spiritualists "have always assumed that woman may be a medium of communication from heaven to earth, that the spirits of the universe may breathe through her lips."[122] The *History* went on to recount the testimony of a person "familiar with Spiritualism since its beginnings in 1848," who "has known but very few Spiritualists who were not in favor of woman suffrage. All their representative men and women, and all their journals advocate it, and have always done so; that expressions in its favor at public meetings meet with hearty approval, and that men and women have spoke on their platforms, and held official places as co-workers in their societies." Most striking to this nineteenth-century observer was that all of "this has taken place with very little argument or discussion, but from an intuitive sense of the justice and consequent benefits of such a course."[123]

Chicago's Spiritualist newspaper, the *Religio-Philosophical Journal,* was not alone when it announced itself "a stalwart advocate of woman's rights."[124] Boston's *Banner of Light* regularly featured editorials and writings on "the rights of woman." It endorsed legislation like the 1859 bill before the New York State legislature that ensured married women better protection of their property and earnings, calling it "this salutary and most humane measure."[125] Unlike many champions of women's rights, Spiritualists called for more than guarantees of property protection, suffrage, or citizenship. Spiritualists constructed a unique politics of the body, claiming sexual rights—especially "voluntary motherhood"—and focusing on dress, diet, and health. During an 1865 Spiritualist convention in Chicago, Dr. Juliet Stillman declared that "the great demand of the day was health." According to the conference report, she "ridiculed the idea of women going to the polls in a fashionable dress" and argued that women needed to reform their own bodily habits to strengthen themselves for citizenship. Stillman felt dress reform should take precedence over suffrage itself.[126]

Spiritualists like Juliet Stillman distinguished themselves from both suffragists, who directed their energies toward securing women's public rights as citizens, and male health reformers, like Sylvester Graham or Orson Squire Fowler, who attended to the body without seeking to change society.[127] Many practiced abstinence or moderation in food and drink, and many mediums were vegetarians. Arguing that animal food was injurious to health, they crafted a vegetarianism that was advocated as both a "better influence on the nervous system" and an aid to spiritual development.[128]

The ghost of Sylvester Graham, the inventor of the graham cracker, was a frequent visitor to spirit circles. One medium, Mary E. Frost, regularly channeled his spirit.[129] However, Graham apparently held much more radical social views in death than he had in life. His regimen stressed a mainly vegetarian diet, built around the staples of fresh, cold water and graham crackers or bread; abstinence from all stimulants, including coffee, tea, and alcohol; and limited and controlled "amorous reveries."[130] Through Frost, Graham counseled the faithful to avoid fried foods, pork, liver, mushrooms or any other fungi. In one séance, however Graham quickly dispensed with advice about meat and mushrooms and turned instead to the rights of women and the unlikely topic of marital rape: "That which is a horrible crime, deserving a decade in State Prison when found without the cover of a marriage certificate, is no crime under such cover, but one of the rights secured by marriage; and if a poor victim appeals to the public, even to her sex . . . she is only treated with scorn, and told that it is good enough for her; the law would not protect her though her life were destroyed in a few months by the treatment which, if not covered by a marriage certificate, would send her murderer to prison or the gallows."[131]

Needless to say, this voice is hardly Graham's. But the occasion to speak on diet and the care of the self brought the medium, Mary Frost, to a subject quite beyond, though intimately related to, the theme on which her spirit might have held forth: the protection of the body, particularly the body of the married white woman. In this jeremiad, the dangers of excessive consumption were displaced by the dangers of excessive and uncontrolled (male) sexuality. Linking the private concerns of dress, diet, and health reform with public demands for citizenship and reform of the marriage laws recapitulated the Spiritualist ethos uniting spheres of belief and action. It also pointed to the failure of the abstracting logic of liberal suffragism to address the complex embodied desires and concerns of many nineteenth-century Spiritualist feminists. At the same time, orations like Frost's highlight the ways in which Spiritualist speech itself stretched the limits of rational discourse.

As mediums, women were able to take center stage as public speakers; once there, they did not always confine their speech to spiritual matters. Spiritualism offered women more than leadership positions or even a constrained cultural power. By 1860, it functioned, in the words of the medium Cora Wilburn, as a "release from the dominion of the senses, . . . liberty from the bondage of the passions of the body, . . . and the resurrection of the soul life of love."[132] Trance speaking and mediumship offered the possibility of disembodiment and a kind of purifying transfiguration and release from the earthly, sexualized body. At the same time, as a political practice, Spiritualism functioned as a material reform movement. In performing or speaking "out of body," as well as by championing reform causes such as alternative healing and dress reform, Spiritualists created a religious and social movement based on a reimagining of the corporeal. Indeed, the Spiritualist press became a site for a national conversation about female sexuality, particularly feminist critiques of bourgeois marriage, calls for voluntary motherhood, and discussions of free love. It is these conversations, as well as the radical antinomianism and individualism of the movement, that led to a split between many suffragists and their typically more radical Spiritualist sisters after the Civil War.

PEACE DURING WARTIME

If there was one way in which nineteenth-century Spiritualists distinguished themselves from most Americans, it was in their insistent, often strident pacifism. This attitude was intimately connected to Spiritualist religious practice and communion with the dead. Beginning before the Civil War, and for decades thereafter, Spiritualists pressed the cause of peace. In so doing, they stood almost alone in mid-nineteenth-century culture. In the 1898 "50th Anniversary Edition" of the *Banner of Light,* the president of the National Spiritualists' Association declared pacifism and anti-imperialism as the great Spiritualist projects of the new century.[133]

For many Spiritualists, peace had been one of the great causes of the "old" century. On the eve of the Civil War, in January 1861, the lead editorial in the *Banner of Light* conceded that "our mode of government, apparently, is in a state of dissolution." In recognition of the possibility of the final abolition of slavery, he went on to argue that the country could "now go forward with all the silence—comparatively speaking of course—of peace and harmony."[134] However, on April 13, 1861, the day after Confederate guns opened fire on Fort Sumter, the *Banner* sermonized in lead editorials that "in this day it would be a long standing disgrace to either side, that civilized political communities could not dissever former relations without proceeding to war."[135] Eventually the *Banner* ended its cries for peace, lamenting that "the Past is all closed up; we can only hope and labor every one of us, that it may stand for a still prouder and more noble future."[136] The *Herald of Progress* issued a different pronouncement on the war, declaring a unanimity among Spiritualists belied by the range of opinion in its own pages: "Unanimity, enthusiasm, and unswerving fidelity to the government, and an abandonment of all party divisions and animosities, characterize the manifestations of popular feeling everywhere," declared an April 1861 *Herald* editorial.[137]

Spiritualism had a newly important role to play during the war. The massive dislocation, loss, and grief accompanying the Civil War called for new forms of communication and consolation, both of which the Spiritualist movement provided. Those with loved ones at war, as one Spiritualist described it, "were thrown into an impressionable state, in which the longing desire predominated to hear from the beloved ones who had gone before. Spiritualism was at hand with its words of comfort and consolation. It cheered those who put their faith in its teachings, and took from death the rudest and most hideous of its features. . . . Death never was so generally thought of and talked of among the people; and by that very way was Spiritualism to gain a foothold in the public heart from which nothing would be able to shake it."[138]

Even accounting for the hyperbole of partisanship, Spiritualist and non-Spiritualist sources alike attest to the growth of the movement during the Civil War. Emma Hardinge wrote of Spiritualism's "triumphant flourishing amidst the disruptions of war and national agitations, that were calculated to sweep every institution not founded upon some constituent element in human nature out of existence."[139] She stressed Spiritualism's role not merely as a source of consolation to the bereaved, but also as a means of understanding the conflicts that drove the country to war. "And so people still seek Spiritualism," Hardinge argued, "not only to comfort them in the bereavement of the war by its phenomenal communion, but because its just and reasonable doctrines clearly point to the cause of the nation's failure, and its source of reconstructed health, namely, the supremacy of just laws on earth, as in heaven."[140]

The language of reconstruction infused Spiritualist writing, as well as the larger political culture, before Reconstruction itself. Many Spiritualists believed that the political slate-cleaning induced by the war had opened up new possibilities for making "all things new" again. One Spiritualist proposed that as "war's confusion" gave "place to new visions," it was now "a fitting time to commence in earnest some great and noble work—some work that shall challenge the attention of the world. The mind of man cannot remain inactive. When the excitement of the war is quelled, what shall next attract the public mind?"[141] The answer, for many, was a global, pacifist movement.

In February 1866, the *Banner of Light* called for all, "irrespective of sex, color, creed, nationality or residence" to assemble and "exchange fraternal expressions of sentiment, to consider what ought to be done in behalf of the Peace cause, and, if practicable, to organize a new uncompromising, vigorous and well ordered movement against the war system, on the force among mankind, between individuals, families, communities, states and nations."[142] Organizers imagined and described a "radical peace movement" that would connect multiple issues ranging from the "Woman Question" to the "Indian Question." The Universal Peace Society, as it came to be called, argued in its organizing document that "there is no peace, and can be none while the *conditions* of war remain."[143] Maintaining that "war is opposed to the inalienable rights, of life, liberty and pursuit of property," it also called for an International Court of Arbitration.[144]

As some Spiritualists stressed internationalism and a more general idea of the rights of man, others invoked Spiritualist cosmology as its own justification for peace. The séance circle, with its emphasis on balance between "negative" and "positive" forces, corresponded with many Spiritualists' support of equality between the sexes as well as their often expansive understanding of masculinity and femininity, which sometimes transcended the sexed body. Women of masculine mind and men of feminine character played a particularly powerful role in Spiritualist practice. Above all, the Spiritualist emphasis on balance often translated into calls for peace. "Balance is the need, not destruction and rooting out," argued one Spiritualist.[145] Spiritualists invoked the language of balance in their hopes for society as well as in descriptions of their own spirituality, and they called over and over again for a peaceful body politic. "The experiment of masculine rule has been tried long enough," wrote the Spiritualist Thomas Hazard in 1868. "Six thousand years of war, bloodshed, hypocrisy and crime have pronounced it a gross failure. It is high time that the feminine element was called to its aid."[146] The "feminine element," as Spiritualists typically formulated it, included both the empowerment of women and a societal ideal of a peaceful, cooperative, nurturance equated with femininity, which could also function as an essentialist recapitulation of "true" womanhood. Often both possibilities coexisted in any given formulation of the Spiritualist feminine element.

Spiritualists analogized from cosmology to politics, uniting the spiritual and material, the public and private. And if the private could be made public, the local could also be made national and international, as Spiritualists across the country wrote to and for one another, read each other's words, met at conferences and camp meetings, and joined together in a the remaking of the nation. Two years after the Civil War, the Spiritualist Payton Spence described his spiritual compatriots as those who "do nothing after the old fashion, and seem determined that old things shall pass away and all things become new."[147] This biblical call from Revelations to make "all things new" marked an enduring utopian impulse in American culture, one to which Spiritualists gave new voice in the 1860s and beyond.

Despite the restitution of peace, the decades that followed the Civil War were marked by vast accumulations of wealth, sharpening class differences, and enormous poverty. However, the "Gilded Age" also saw the persistence of utopian strivings, charismatic perfectionisms, and spiritual radicalisms.[148] As the historian Alan Trachtenberg has asked of the period: "Was the true America best represented by its most successful citizens, those for whom laws protected the private means of employment—private property and con-tract—and permitted accumulation of private wealth? Or did utopian 'America' demand for its realization a new social order, the abolition of pri-vate property, the emergence of the nation as a collective body of shared wealth as well as culture?"[149] In the space between successful America and utopian America, Spiritualists imagined a different nation.

Nineteenth-century American Spiritualists looked simultaneously for-ward and backward. Spiritualist speeches, writings, and philosophy from the 1860s through the 1880s display, with very few exceptions, an enormous faith in progress. Spiritualist cosmology was structured by a series of teleologically ordered spheres through which evolved souls could hope to advance. Even as they looked fervently forward, Spiritualists were drawn by their social imagi-nation and perfectionist leanings back to the remembered radicalisms of the antebellum years. "They were radical in every way, and hospitable to novelty of all kinds," William Dean Howells wrote in the late nineteenth century of the residents of the Ohio town of his youth. "I imagine that they tested more new religions and new patents than have ever been heard of in less inquiring communities. When we first came among them they had lately been swept by the fires of spiritualism. . . . They were ready for any sort of millennium, religious or industrial, that should arrive."[150] Howells remembered Spiri-tualism as "rife in every second house in the village, with manifestations by rappings, table-tippings, and oral and written messages from another world through psychics of either sex, but oftenest the young girls one met in the dances and sleigh-rides."[151]

Howells's recollections of this ferment accord well with historians' under-standing of that period.[152] What confounds traditional historical character-izations is the persistence of a vision of a new America in the Reconstruction years. The historian Robert Wiebe, in analyzing the contested nature of American society, argues that ostensibly competing political visions actually rarely competed; rather, they constituted parallel visions, which themselves characterized a generally "segmented society." Wiebe states: "A properly ordered society, therefore, would comprise countless isolated lanes where Americans either singly or in groups, dashed like rows of racers towards their goals. What happened along other tracks might be a matter of intense interest for competitors, for they were all sprinting there, but it was seldom a matter of emulation. Each lane, testing a unique virtue, would trace a unique experience."[153] A cultural "segment," then, could coexist alongside another segment, the two barely noticing one another's existence.

Only in the later historical chronicling would one of these segments emerge as "culture" and the other as "counterculture," one as the "public," the other as a "counterpublic." As Nancy Fraser has argued in an attempt to complicate and democratize Jürgen Habermas's notion of a public sphere, "The bourgeois public was never *the* public. On the contrary, virtually contemporaneous with the bourgeois public there arose of host of competing counterpublics, including nationalist publics, popular peasant publics, elite women's publics, and working-class publics."[154] Spiritualism after the Civil War, however, constituted neither Wiebe's model of a "unique" or "isolated" track toward an ideal American life nor any kind of "public" containable in Fraser's implicitly secular formation. For just as Spiritualists' lives, both private and public, were still centrally occupied by spirits from the afterworld, their political convictions and affiliations challenged the Gilded Age's ideas about an "ordered society."

Despite the intense desire on the part of a coterie of industrialists and politicians to create a coherent national culture, the country remained striated by the conflicts of the prewar years. In 1867, the year closely most associated with "Radical Reconstruction," Payton Spence could not describe his community as "revolutionary" without also acknowledging growing public opposition to the radicalism of Spiritualists. "Spiritualism," Spence wrote, "is profoundly radical and revolutionary in all of its movements. This is evident to the most casual observer; and it is this fact which, more than any other, has excited the most alarm, apprehension, and hostility in the public mind."[155] Postwar political retrenchment resulted in a climate increasingly hostile to spiritual freethinkers.

Although the Reconstruction years marked one of the most genuinely revolutionary periods in American history, culminating in the fulfillment of the decades-long struggle by African Americans for full citizenship, the 1870s ended in financial crisis and a large-scale political retrenchment that resulted in new forms of racism and legal discrimination. By 1867, Congress had crafted a series of laws, including the Fourteenth and Fifteenth amendments to the Constitution and the Reconstruction Act of 1867 enshrining African-American suffrage in federal law, which was passed in an override of President Andrew Johnson's veto. Together, these laws enfranchised the freedman and provided federal power to enforce the new legislation. Civil rights for African Americans marked a new stage in a political revolution, the outcome of which was far from inevitable before the War. Indeed, as a writer for the *Nation* declared in February 1867: "Six years ago, the North would have rejoiced to accept any mild restrictions upon the spread of slavery as final settlement. Four years ago, it would have accepted peace upon the basis of gradual emancipation. Two years ago, it would have been content with emancipation and equal rights for colored people without extension of the suffrage. One year ago, a slight extension of the suffrage would have satisfied it."[156] Implicit in this history are both amazement at the pace of progress and a silent suggestion that perhaps too much had changed too quickly.

African Americans gave their own meanings to freedom as they rebuilt families, founded new communities, and exercised their new rights.[157] In the fall of 1867, between 70 and 90 percent of eligible freedmen used their voting rights in every state in the South, and a total of 265 African Americans were elected as delegates to state constitutional conventions.[158] At the same time, a backlash developed in both the South and the North, reacting to the gains of African Americans and an inchoate sense that things had gone too far during the Reconstruction years.

The Spiritualist publications with the broadest circulation during the antebellum years were uniformly abolitionist. The proceedings from the Garrisonian American Anti-Slavery Society received regular column space in Andrew Jackson Davis's *Herald of Progress* during the 1860s. In 1862, the *Banner of Light* printed the Emancipation Proclamation in full on the front page (a space typically devoted to "spiritual news") under an unusually large and bold headline: "Freedom of the Slaves in Rebellious States on the First day of January next." It published a separate editorial backing full citizenship for African Americans.[159]

After the war, however, some Spiritualists sounded more like radical carpetbaggers than former Garrisonian abolitionists, seeing in a reconstructed, free-soil South new opportunities for "enlightened" capitalism. "Northern men do not yet see the great field for labor, and even for money-making on a most liberal scale, which is opened to them by the possession of the cotton-fields of the Southern States," declared a *Banner of Light* editorial in 1864. "Land [should be] leased out to men who are accustomed to work and know how to till the soil themselves. . . . These farmers, thus leasing the lands, would at once proceed to hire the blacks, not enslave them—pay them good wages, and finally buy the farms outright when the Government proceeds to put in force its Confiscation law."[160] It is, however, difficult to measure which Spiritualism was *the* Spiritualism, and whether it was the reformers or the consolidators who best characterized the movement as a whole. Clearly, multiple Spiritualisms coexisted, and individual Spiritualists represented a range of religious and political viewpoints.

Following the war, white Spiritualists were increasingly cast as "wild-eyed, long-haired reformers" out of step with their time.[161] In some ways this was nothing new. Since the birth of Spiritualism in 1848, the popular press had published numerous articles denouncing believers as fanatics and dupes. Many of these were reprinted or refuted in the Spiritualist press. The *Herald of Progress* reprinted a damning piece from *Hall's Journal of Health* in 1864, which linked Spiritualism to all other radical "isms," asking, "But how is it when we meet a vegetarian, he is almost sure to be a phrenologist, a free lover, a root doctor, a woman's rights *[sic]*, a mesmerist, a Spiritualist, a socialist, a cold waterist, a ranting abolitionist, an abnegator of the Bible, the Sabbath day, and the religion of his father?"[162] An editor of the *Herald,* probably the prominent male medium and theologian Andrew Jackson Davis, responded, arguing that "One-idea-ism is no finality, and every advocate of a single reform idea, is sure, ultimately, to become a true Cosmopolitan Reformer. . . . And as for the danger from extreme views, the Doctor forgets that not a page of his journal, but would at some day have been regarded as 'extreme.'"[163]

The fact that this *Herald* editor countered the skepticism of *Hall's Journal of Health* in a discourse of dialogic reason was hardly a rhetorical innovation for Spiritualists, as they had always understood science as part and parcel of their practice. What is unique about Spiritualism after the Civil War is the mode of its critics' assaults, ranging from such mockery of coalitional affinities to a new denunciation of Spiritualists' bodies and affects. The literary magazine *Round Table* likewise labeled Spiritualists "lank, long-haired and cadaverous," morbid zombies, "fattening on the ignorance of the public."[164] The paradox of how the inherently "lank" come to "fatten" may simply be an effect of mixed metaphor; or it may illustrate the desire of the writer to construct these cadaverous subjects as at once threatening and irrelevant. Whereas antebellum critiques of Spiritualism pointed to the frailty, effeminacy, and suggestibility of mediums and their followers, postwar critics took on the "long-haired" believers as insufficiently masculine to embrace a reconstructed America and as overly identified with the dead subjects they conjured.

Whether male or female, prewar mediums were typically portrayed as lively in their channeling; the Spiritualist of the 1860s and beyond increasingly came to stand for an unnatural morbidity. Spiritualists' seemingly aberrant interest in death allied them with the dark side of antebellum sentimentalism, while their radical social views thrust them further from the mainstream.

Attacks on Spiritualism were a reaction not only to general reform culture but also to the Spiritualist advocacy of specific and broad rights for women. A few Spiritualists recognized this issue right away. Lois Waisbrooker, an advocate of free love and a purveyor of frank sexual advice for women, was among the most radical of nineteenth-century Spiritualists. She wrote, edited, and published a weekly newspaper, *Common Sense,* out of Kansas from 1874 to 1875; a monthly journal, *Foundation Principles,* subtitled "The Rock upon Which Motherhood Should Rest," from 1885 to 1894; and numerous novels.[165] Her unblinking radicalism is best expressed in the frontispiece to one of her novels, which reads: "I demand unqualified freedom for woman as woman, and that all the institutions of society be adjusted to such freedom."[166] In her column in the *Banner of Light,* Waisbrooker argued that dismissals of Spiritualism were rebukes to female reformers, and vice versa. She wrote: "Another taunt against reformers comes in the following shape. Speaking of a lady lecturer in England, [a male commentator] says, 'Judging from the description of this female apostle of infidelity, she must resemble some of the talking women in our own country, who advocate Spiritualism, and other delusions, preferring the light which is darkness.'"[167]

In the eyes of its detractors, Spiritualism's alliance with movements like women's suffrage was proof of its danger. In 1855, a pseudonymous "Fred Folio" published a book-length tract attacking women's rights and Spiritualism. Its rambling title said it all: *A Book for the Times, Lucy Boston; Or, Woman's Rights and Spiritualism: Illustrating The Follies and Delusions of the Nineteenth Century.*[168] *Lucy Boston,* a tale in which the curmudgeonly bachelor narrator, Amaziah Badger, is awakened by a spirit who admonishes him to help "the disenfranchised woman," was a product of a small cottage industry of nineteenth-century Spiritualist satire.[169] However derogatory in its aims, *Lucy Boston* made the link between Spiritualist religious and political tendencies in an unusually direct way.

Not all Spiritualists were political: many attempted to disentangle religion from politics, Spiritualism from radical reform. "Fanatical" Spiritualists came under fire from within their own ranks as more and more Spiritualists during the 1860s constructed their own "reasonable" or "rational" belief system, in direct contrast to supposedly irrational, unnatural Spiritualism. Typically, this distancing involved associating a segment of Spiritualism with the political or religious excesses of the antebellum era and then contrasting the older Spiritualism with a new, more rational belief system. The *Banner of Light* editor Luther Colby announced the end of revivalism in 1866, decrying these gatherings as cultures of superstition and sites of fantasy and "unnatural ecstasy." In their place, he offered a calm, rational, spiritual knowledge: "The charm of revivals . . . is gone. There was that mixture of superstitious awe and unnatural ecstasy about them, which secured wide and profound attention to them, as a general rule; but mankind is generally outgrowing its superstitions, and for the matter of spiritual ecstasies it prefers to put in their place something that has the texture of a firm spiritual knowledge and belief."[170]

Similarly, Emma Hardinge wrote to the *Banner of Light* in 1865 to defend the "just and reasonable doctrines" of Spiritualism from the "tangle of 'isms'," the "hobbies falsely labeled 'Spiritualism'—From the vastly momentous movement of ladies riding astride, and resolving the weal and woe of all future generations to depend on their wearing pantaloons . . . to the doctrine of 'affinities,' so prominently preached and practiced in the notables of New York."[171] As hard as some Spiritualists tried to untangle their Spiritualism from the array of other movements for freedom, the perfectionist taint was a difficult legacy to shed, precisely because the "tangle of isms" and the so-called hobbies falsely labeled as Spiritualism remained firmly held beliefs for many.

As the reformer and medium W. J. Colville argued: "When, in 1848, the Rochester knockings called attention to the fact that communication between the two states of existence commonly called the two worlds was a fact, the majority of investigators were solely intent on proving this rudimentary fact of spirit communion . . . but a fact, nevertheless, like all facts, when standing alone is inadequate to transform existing conditions of social life."[172] Colville, like many Spiritualists, was committed to transforming the material world while communing with the spiritual. Free love, as I discuss in chapter 3, tore Spiritualism apart in the 1870s. Spiritualists held multiple and divergent viewpoints on the "woman question." Indeed, many individual Spiritualists held stances that were themselves rife with internal contradictions. Much of this tension turned on Spiritualist understandings of the body.

OTHER BODIES, OTHER WORLDS

The radical individualism that characterized Spiritualism as a religious practice also structured individual Spiritualists' notions of the "use" of the body. If the role of the feminine element was to guide the world to peace, it needed to be nurtured in living bodies. This view had a number of implications. Spiritualists' call for free, unfettered bodies translated into demands for everything from health and dress reform to spiritual marriage and free love. Spiritualists' understanding of the feminine element (and the body) was a messy combination of expansive and conservative notions of womanhood, marked by race and class as well as gender. In a notion shared by generations of nineteenth- and twentieth-century feminists, Spiritualists saw middle-class white women as crucial to building a healthy society. To do so, these women needed to be strong.

"If women are to civilize us," began the women's rights advocate Warren Chase in an argument for full equality between the sexes, "we must begin by a better system of education and physical culture to have bodies as well as souls for American women." "American" women, according to Chase and many others, could civilize society only if their bodies were strong enough to complete the task. "There is no use talking about religion with no flour in the house," Chase continued, "and we say there is little use talking about women's work and wages, with no physical strength to perform the work."[173] When Chase and other Spiritualists spoke of either the feminine element or "women," they invoked their own middle-class, white Protestant sisters, wives, and daughters. These were the women whose bodies might vanquish the warlike masculine element. Spiritualists, for the most part, did not include either African American or white immigrant women in their notions of embodied citizenship. These other women could not provide the "innate" spirituality that would presumably civilize society. In this sense, they bore a striking resemblance to other middle-class white reformers and suffragists.[174] However, Spiritualist practice offered other, less constricting notions of embodied womanhood.

Spiritualists had many interpretations of what bodily freedom for women and men might mean. As one reformer wrote in 1868 in a particularly strident call for free use of the body: "The uses of our physical bodies are to indulge in any enjoyment that affords us real comfort and happiness—any enjoyments that bring no stain hereafter. We have a right to do anything that is not repudiated by our own conscience. Are not the dictates of our own conscience sufficient to guide us in the right path of life?"[175] Others saw an escape from the binds of the gendered, material body through disembodiment. Bodily transcendence was an accepted belief among Spiritualists, but, in true democratic, Spiritualist fashion, believers often asked the most mundane questions about this mystical and arcane practice. The "experts" at Spiritualist newspapers who answered questions took them all equally

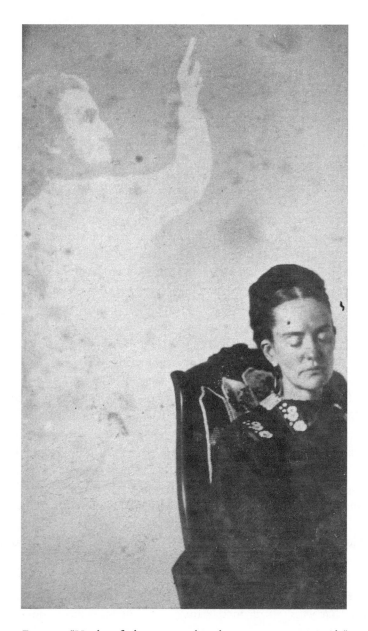

Figure 5. "Unidentified woman with male spirit pointing upwards,"
ca. 1861. William H. Mumler (photographer, American, 1832–84,
active Boston, Massachusetts). Catalog no. 84.XD.760.1.4. The
J. Paul Getty Museum, Los Angeles.

seriously. One Spiritualist wrote the *Banner of Light* to ask: "Is it possible for the spirit of the medium to commune with friends when apart from her own body?" An editor responded, "It is possible. Notwithstanding there is a sympathy kept up between spirit and body, yet the spirit itself is free to go wheresoever it wills; free, if it finds conditions adapted to its use, to employ them at any time or place, however distant."[176] One issue of the *Herald of Progress* provided answer to readers' questions about spirit bodies, which included: How much does a spirit weigh? Can spirits see? Do they wear clothing? And do they reproduce as we do?[177]

The somewhat childlike fascination and interest in the practicalities of the afterlife coexisted with another strain in Spiritualism. While believers kept newspaper editors busy with questions about the folkways of ghosts, Spiritualist mediums wrote of their own experiences "out of body": leaving their own bodies while in trance state. Cora L. V. Richmond (née Scott) chronicled her voyage in *My Experiences While out of My Body and My Return after Many Days*. "It was true then," she wrote, "I was suddenly and finally released from my body; 'this time,' I said, or thought: 'I will not have to return.' Many times, almost numberless, I had experienced the wonderful consciousness of being absent from my human form, of mingling with arisen friends in the higher state of existence, but, until this time I had always known that it was only for a brief season and that there was a tie—a vital and psychic tie— binding me to return to my earth form." Richmond contended that "although not usual, this class of experiences is not so unusual as many imagine or assert." The medium, having been from childhood accustomed to the "other state" of consciousness, could "distinctly trace her experiences in that inner realm as forming fully a third if not one-half her life experiences." The realm of spirit in which she so often found herself was not an unfamiliar one; in fact, if called upon to decide which state was the real one, "'the life,' she would unhesitatingly say: the inner state, the super-mundane realm." For Richmond and others, disembodiment produced another world "within and about us, revealing dormant powers within each person: Soul powers more active than perhaps any are aware! . . . It is of the Substance that dreams are made that we shall ultimately find our divinest realities, our very lives refashioned."[178]

While Spiritualists like Cora Richmond were refashioning their inner lives and constructing divine realities in new realms, others were constructing utopias in this world. Beginning in the 1850s and increasingly after the Civil War, Spiritualists traveled west to create new communities. For many groups of Spiritualists and utopians—the mystical disembodied mediums, the Spiritualist organizers and editors, and the health-conscious seekers—California provided new and fertile ground. As early as 1857, Spiritualism was openly advocated by some "advanced thinkers" in California. Most prominent among these was "Colonel" Lyman W. Ransom, publisher of the *Marysville Herald*, who was an avowed Spiritualist, and one of his sons, Elijah, who was a medium. When the *Banner of Light* first made its appearance in that year, Colonel Ransom "scattered the newspaper among the people in the city of Marysville." In San Francisco, séances were held in the 1850s at the house of Russell Ellis on Sansome Street, at the International Hotel, and also at the residence of J. P. Manrow on Russian Hill, where "the most remarkable manifestations" occurred.[179]

During the middle decades of the nineteenth century, the *Banner of Light* regularly published letters from California Spiritualists, urging New Englanders to come West. "The interest in Spiritualism in this place seems to be rather increasing than otherwise," wrote Margaret Booth to the *Banner* in 1862.[180] "Just say, Mr. Editor, to these New England lecturers," another Californian wrote in 1866, "that if they want to do a good thing and reap a rich harvest, materially and spiritually, the Pacific coast is the place for them."[181] Midwesterners made their own pitch. "Thinking that perhaps there are many good Spiritualists throughout the Eastern States who are desirous of emigrating to the far West, let me say we should like their company; and as Kansas is one of the most desirable localities of the West, having a congenial climate, with very rich and fertile soil, we invite them here."[182]

Women soon emerged as central to California spirit circles, taking on an even greater prominence than they had in the East. Julia Schlesinger, the longtime editor of the *Carrier Dove* and later the *Pacific Coast Spiritualist,* chronicled the West Coast movement beginning in the late 1850s. The New England Spiritualist press regularly published columns by Schlesinger and other California Spiritualists.[183] In November 1865, a "Friend of the Cause" wrote announcing that Mrs. Laura Cuppy, a suffragist, Spiritualist and longtime reformer for "progressive" causes, had arrived in San Francisco and was soon to take up permanent residency there. The writer noted: "Spiritualism is spreading rapidly in this coast, and I never saw anywhere such an eager desire to investigate the phenomenon and listen to its philosophy."[184]

Julia Schlesinger recorded the first lectures on Spiritualism in San Francisco, given by Mrs. Eliza W. Farnham in 1859. Farnham also lectured in Santa Cruz in the 1850s with her "intellectual and energetic friend," the former Brook Farm Transcendentalist Georgiana B. Kirby. In 1864 Emma Hardinge went west, where she lectured and organized meetings of the

Spiritualist "Friends of Progress." She was soon joined by "Mrs. C. M. Stowe and Mary Beach, mediums, who arrived overland," as well as the famed Cora L. V. [Scott Hatch Daniels] Tappan, and the feminist reformers Laura Cuppy, Laura De Force Gordon, and Laverna Matthews.[185] Circles were instituted in San Francisco, San Jose, Sacramento, and San Diego.

It is particularly significant that California Spiritualists were building their movement at a time when Eastern Spiritualists complained that a lack of organization was impeding the movement's growth nationwide. In 1867, the National Convention of Spiritualists met in Cleveland, Ohio, and prominent on their agenda was the problem of organization. "We have stood upon the platform of individuality for the past fifteen or sixteen years, and what have we done?" asked one Spiritualist. "Numbering as we do more than any sect upon the civilized earth, we have nowhere to lay our heads, whilst the most insignificant sect upon God's footstool enjoys the advantage of beautiful churches and buildings for their use, wherever they desire them. Our forces are disorganized, scattered and so individualized, that they can accomplish nothing. Let us marshal and equip them for the contest between sectarian bigotry and free thought. Disintegrated, we can do nothing. United, what can we not do?"[186]

For their part, Western Spiritualists organized, building institutions and a thriving Spiritualist press. Spiritualists who had been present in California since the 1850s reported a resurgence of interest after the Civil War. In 1867, they announced the birth of San Francisco's Spiritualist newspaper, the *Banner of Progress,* an "exponent of liberal religion while denouncing revivalism and all dogmas and creeds."[187] "The *Banner of Light* is read with interest here, and our *Banner of Progress* is also growing into importance," wrote a follower, who went on to say: "A very pretty idea is suggested in the names and location of these two papers: each a Banner of the Spiritual faith—one leading its army along the shores of the Atlantic, through the Eastern America, the other waving over the Pacific wing, and leading it gradually to the new faith, floating over the new America that sits so stately beside the sunset shore."[188] Despite the language of manifest destiny, however, the California Spiritualists struggled with each beachhead.

The San Francisco *Banner of Progress,* which survived for two years, was followed by *Common Sense* in 1874, published by W. N. and Amanda M. Slocum; it managed to survive a little longer than a year. *The Philomathean,* birthed in 1875, and the short-lived *Light for All* were followed by the *Carrier Dove* in 1883; it continued until the latter part of 1893, when its name was changed to *Pacific Coast Spiritualist.* Also inaugurated in the 1880s was the

Golden Gate, edited by J. J. Owen, the founder of the *San Jose Mercury News,* and his wife, Mattie P. Owen.[189] In 1865, Spiritualists established a Children's Progressive Lyceum in Sacramento, and in 1876 another in Oakland. The first Spiritualist society incorporated under the laws of the State of California as the "First Spiritual Union of San Francisco" in the same year. The "Golden Gate Religious and Philosophical Society" organized and incorporated in 1885, a year after the California "Spiritualists' State Campmeeting Association" was founded by the irrepressible Julia Schlesinger and fellow traveler Frances Logan.[190]

Back east, prominent Spiritualists preached conservatism, warning Californians to move more slowly. "The schemes set on foot by these reformers, are, in our estimation, entirely Utopian," wrote the increasingly conservative Luther Colby in 1865. "Communities cannot be changed in a day or a year or a series of years. Reforms that are effective are necessarily slow in their culmination."[191] Some Eastern transplants found California lacking in the community so evident in the East. After discussing her incredibly arduous journey west, Laura De Force Gordon summed up her new home: "I have heard the same statement from other lecturers here, and I know whereof I affirm when I say to those lecturers in the states contemplating a trip to California, 'You must expect to engage in the most thankless, soul-wearing work of your life, if you look to profesed Spiritualists for aid, encouragement, or appreciation with a few noble exceptions.'"[192] Despite these less than encouraging reports, Spiritualists flooded west in the years after the Civil War.

Spiritualists migrated to California for many of the same reasons as other nineteenth-century Americans, including greater economic opportunities and access to open land. However, they also came seeking a climate suited to bodily health and healing, as well as new spiritual frontiers.[193] Spiritualist colonies grew quickly in the West and, to this day, carry the mark of their origins. Summerland, a town near Santa Barbara, was named both for the Spiritualist term for the afterlife and for the local climate. Founded in 1888, Summerland advertised itself as perfect for those in "search of a quiet home where they can commune with mortals and immortals as freely as they may desire." Summerland offered more than spiritual freedom: it also provided a salutary climate for invalids, a large class of nineteenth-century immigrants to California. As one partisan described it, Summerland afforded "great inducements to eastern people in poor health, for its invigorating climate, beautiful scenery, and life-giving magnetic forces are well adapted to the physical needs of invalids."[194]

The pursuit of bodily health with water cures and vegetarianism, as well as the hope of abolitionism and perfectionist reform, waned for the most part in the East after the Civil War. However, Spiritualists, especially in California, found renewed optimism after the war, and some of that optimism was channeled into health reform. They merged a vision of social perfectionism in the outer world with the achievement of bodily health and wholeness within.[195] Moreover, Spiritualist individualism melded well with the anti-elitism of self-help medicine first elaborated in the United States through Thomsonianism in the 1830s and 1840s. This popular health movement rejected the calomel and bleeding of "regular" physicians in favor of herbs, and replaced a belief in medical orthodoxy with Samuel Thomson's slogan "Every man his own physician."[196] Spiritualists added psychic healing to the mix, and, because many Spiritualists were women, they sought to strengthen the weakened female body in order to further both individual spiritual development and societal health.

Some found new models for female empowerment in California. The Spiritualist Anne (Annie) Denton Cridge left her home in Washington, DC, in 1871 for a new life on a Southern California citrus farm. Cridge envisioned her orange grove both as a means to fund the publication of her four-volume manuscript on the "rights of children" and "to demonstrate that the self-salvation of women lies in the culture of the soil."[197] Julia Schlesinger used her Spiritualist newspaper, the *Carrier Dove,* to campaign for women's suffrage and economic self-sufficiency for women, arguing that "in order to be free women must be financially independent."[198] The soil of California provided new ground for a generation of Spiritualists, especially women, to build new communities and renew old political commitments. Yet the utopian vision of the Spiritualists, premised as it was on a forwarding-looking activism built on a radical, perfectionist past, placed them outside an emergent American ethos.

That Spiritualism's radically individualistic, syncretic religious practice flourished into the late nineteenth century and beyond, casting roots into movements like Christian Science, Theosophy, and the New Age movement of the late twentieth century, points to the enduring appeal of eclectic, spiritually minded politics and transformative religious impulses. Nonetheless, in the years following the Civil War, the cultural fit between mainstream America and Spiritualism became less comfortable. During the 1870s, Spiritualists were targeted by doctors as hysterics, by suffragists as "irrational" citizens, and by moral reformers as purveyors of obscenity and vice.

Spiritualism provided a foil of the irrational against which both a growing scientific establishment and a postwar women's rights movement defined themselves. Although the early history of the American suffrage movement is filled with names of women who were suffragists as well as Spiritualists, a divide gradually widened between the two. At mid-century, the rare woman who spoke on public rostrums was often an abolitionist, suffragist, trance speaker, or all three; by the end of the century, women's public speech had become more common. Many Americans began to fear that the country was at risk of being overrun, in Henry James's words, by a growing herd of "vociferating women." With all of the talk of suffragists being the worst offenders in an already "womanized . . . feminine, nervous, hysterical, chattering, canting age," mainstream feminists sought to differentiate themselves by adopting the rational speech of citizenships.[199]

By the 1870s, Spiritualists no longer occupied the center of the movement for women's rights. It was at this historical moment that suffrage leaders began to distance themselves from their Garrisonian roots and their radical past and to relegate Spiritualism to the fringe of the women's movement. Part of this move involved a reconstruction of female citizenship, shorn of the mystical, irrational, utopian politics of the antebellum era. What was lost in this remaking of the women's rights movement was a place in American feminism for the transformative politics of the body imagined and enacted by Spiritualists.

Spiritualists were in the mainstream of their culture while also embodying certain values and qualities associated with the margin. Both feminized and largely female, the movement embraced a range of ways of inhabiting female gender and sexuality. At the same time, many Spiritualists identified more broadly with the "other": male Spiritualists with femininity, white Spiritualists with Native Americans. These affinities sometimes caused the movement to be cast as other by the broader culture. Yet Spiritualists were the other within: nineteenth-century American Protestants, mostly white and middle-class. These believers claimed mysticism for white America, creating a spiritual practice out of a communion with difference. Opening themselves to other voices and other bodies, they turned to the "vanished" Indian as a model for spiritual fulfillment.

TWO

Indian Guides

Haunted Subjects and the Politics of Vanishing

In 1853 Charles Partridge, the editor of the *Spiritual Telegraph*, received news from one of his readers that a spectral Indian had spoken through a thirteen-year-old medium in Lebanon, New Hampshire. This was no nameless ghost. Powhatan, "the once proud chief of a fallen nation[,] now comes to speak to his pale faced sister," with the message of a beneficent afterlife from a departed "once powerful race."[1] Echoing the cadences of the many vanished Indians who haunted American literature, Powhatan's lament was not unique to this particular spirit circle or to American culture. But if the tenor of Spiritualist Indian messages echoed the melancholic tones of their antebellum literary counterparts, the "liveness" of these Indian ghosts also carried an uncannily different charge. In these years, legendary as well as unnamed Indians would deliver words from beyond the grave at séance circles, rendering the mythological manifest. Indians spirits began to appear as guides to the afterworld, as healers, and as disembodied envoys of American historiography. Relying on a cultural understanding of Native Americans as highly spiritual, and mapping onto the spirit world the colonial relationship of the Indian as a guide for the white man, Spiritualists positioned Native Americans as a vital link between this world and the next. It was the Indian guide who could bring Spiritualists through the veil, tracing the invisible footprints beyond.

This chapter situates the cultural processes by which American subjects conjured Indian ghosts as central and particular to the practice of Spiritualism.

The prevalence of Indian manifestations at Anglo-American séance tables foregrounds a complicated politics of transtemporal and cross-racial connection which was at once in keeping with a larger nineteenth-century cultural imaginary and also specific to a Spiritualist cosmology and reform ethos. On the one hand, Spiritualists saw Native Americans as powerful spiritual predecessors, evincing romantic attachments to an ideal or imagined Indian that sometimes translated into unexamined cultural appropriation. On the other hand, some Spiritualists called for the protection of native lands and sovereignty, laboring to right the wrongs of white colonists while also salvaging the spiritual life of non-Indian Americans. Neither wholly appropriative nor simply reformist, the history of Anglo Spiritualists' ambivalent affiliations with American Indians raises questions about the importance of a specifically religious worldview to the construction of secular politics.

Scholars have traced Anglo-Americans' vexed identifications with colonized natives through myriad literary and parodic cultural practices. From nostalgic portrayals of dying warriors and lost tribes to what Philip Deloria has termed "playing Indian," nineteenth-century subjects produced themselves as Americans through an engagement with national fantasies of a "white man's Indian."[2] As Indians were being literally erased from the national landscape through ongoing dispossession and removal acts, the figure of the "vanishing Indian" often took on an apparitional, if metaphorical, form. As Renée Bergland has argued in her work on spectral Indians in American literature, "the figure of the Indian ghost is profoundly ambiguous. Although the ghosts register dissatisfaction with the European conquest of the Americas, the fact that they are ghosts testifies to the success of that conquest."[3] Spiritualists' materialization, as opposed to representation, of Indian spirits complicates this logic of absention and abstraction.

While often overwriting the specificities of native cosmologies, Spiritualists' contact with Indians in the afterworld at once illuminated the contours of their own Summerland and transformed their worldly understanding of the politics of place. Robert S. Cox's recent study finds white Spiritualists' "sympathy" with Indians, extending to the point of "being Indian" through channeling Indian spirits, limited by the "ethnological dilemma" of the day, wherein "race was the spiritual core of identity."[4] As a result, Cox argues, negotiating the terrain of the afterlife amounted to an extension of a colonial project, the forging of "an apartheid of the spheres."[5] Yet this projection of racial difference into the ethereal realm often deflected back onto national political life, making some nineteenth-century Spiritualists newly aware of the presence and plight of living Native Americans. Far from vanished,

Indian spirits directed reform-minded Spiritualists from the séance table to political action.

The 1853 New Hampshire case of communication by an Indian spirit is among the earliest recorded. This account is emblematic both of standard antebellum cultural representations of Native Americans and of early séances, yet the crossing of the two practices complicates the political and historical impulses of each. The fact that the speech was written through a young female medium and attributed to the spirit of a powerful man was by no means unusual for Spiritualist channeling. As the previous chapter discusses, the putative youthful innocence and guileless femininity of girls made them ideal mediums and guaranteed the authority of those who spoke through them. Nor was it unusual for a magisterial figure like Powhatan, commonly heard through the pages of nostalgic fiction in this era, to deign to visit a humble parlor in rural New England. Although Spiritualists, for the most part, wanted to reunite and communicate with their own deceased relatives, patriots and inventors like Ben Franklin were also very popular apparitional advisers.[6] Whereas messages from Franklin commonly lauded devices like the spiritual telegraph as an advance on his discovery of electricity, the messages of dead Indians were much more ambiguous and, indeed, haunting.

Given that what spirits "said" revealed most about whom they said it to, séance revelations provide a unique window into what a segment of nineteenth-century Americans might have wanted to know from both their own ancestors and from the other actors who peopled America's past. At the same time, Spiritualist conjuring functioned as a collective construction of certain personages and moments in the American past *as* historical. While the mid-nineteenth-century United States was rife with images and voices of an Indian past, the words of Powhatan channeled through rural white girlhood suggest an urgency and specificity of presence that belies broader cultural narratives of Indians as vanished and vanquished.

Powhatan's ambivalent and ambiguous address from beyond begins: "There are but few left to lament the departure of a once powerful race, none to sit by the council fire, to seek friendship or to plot revenge. No daring footsteps now climb the hills and precipices of our native land. And where is now the Indian maiden, who roamed through the glens and valleys, or skimmed o'er the lake in her swift canoe? All, all are gone! What is the cause of this downfall of a whole nation? Look to your brothers for an answer."[7] While Powhatan confirms a succession narrative in which Indians have already ceded to the onslaught of civilization, the rhetoric also deploys a set of familial terms that complicate the political stakes of his message. Whereas the reference to "your brothers" marks a racial separation and casts blame on white men as the cause of Indian downfall, the evocation of a "pale faced sister" suggests a larger filial affinity that may offer a détente among the families of man and perhaps also an invitation to a unified afterworld. Moreover, the pointed gendering of the active Indian maiden relative, to the genderless "few," "none," and even "footsteps," implies the young female medium's cross-cultural, cross-temporal identification with a form of subjectivity unavailable to her.

Powhatan's speech opens with a damning testimony of massive loss but ends with contented resignation: "We are at peace with all. . . . The Indian grew sad when your brothers took possession of his lands; vengeance became the object of his soul, the rest you know; suffice it to say, we are happy now. Heaven is ours. Powhatan has finished."[8] Finished with earthly battles, Indians could be happy in heaven—where, presumably, they would cease to make claims on white America. Yet the phrase "The rest you know" suggests at once Powhatan's collusion with an Anglo historiography of vanishing and an ambiguous and expansive history in which the genocidal realities and knowledge of this past frame white guilt as an ongoing problem for the supposed victor.

Powhatan's presence two hundred years after his death in an Anglo Spiritualist drawing room reflects nineteenth-century Americans' limited knowledge of native history as well as the desire for a connection to a colonial past. Powhatan, or Wahunsenacawh, was the leader of the thirty to thirty-five Algonquian-speaking tribes located in the tidewater region of what is now Virginia from approximately 1572 to 1617, when the English colonized Jamestown.[9] Spiritualists, like other Americans, would have known of Powhatan from the tales of Captain John Smith, which were published and read as travel narratives.[10] By the middle of the nineteenth century, romantic poets and nationalist narrators had created a mythical Powhatan, noble but inevitably defeated. In many ways he was eclipsed by his daughter, Pocahontas, who allegedly loved John Smith, the English, and the Christian faith, and intervened to save English lives.[11] Storytellers who have depicted both Powhatan and Pocahontas, not surprisingly, elide the complications of the history, including the original charter of Jamestown, which included the conversion of the Indians as one of the "most pious and noble" goals of the colony and also stipulated that the colony "procure from them some convenient number of their children to be brought up in your language and manners."[12] The appeal of Pocahontas, from her reception in the Court of King James as Lady Rebecca Rolfe to her nineteenth-century representation in poetry and primer (and a twentieth-century Disney film), is that of the difficulties of transcultural contact resolved through a romantic marriage plot.[13]

That a young white medium would channel an Indian chief—whose own young daughter had been married to a white man after being kidnapped and held in captivity by the English colonists—speaks not only to the power of the interlocking myths animating this particular spirit but also to a series of telling displacements. When this medium searched for an Indian guide, she did not look nearby, either to the native tribes inhabiting the area or to neighboring Dartmouth College. A few miles from Lebanon, New Hampshire, Dartmouth was chartered in 1769 "for the education and instruction of youth of the Indian tribes in this land in reading, writing, and all parts of learning which shall appear necessary and expedient for civilizing and christianizing children of pagans . . . and also of English youth and others."[14] Yet this unfulfilled charter—Dartmouth graduated only nineteen Native Americans in the two hundred years following its founding—produced more mythological natives than Native American students: the mission transformed the Indian into mascot.[15] When the figure of Powhatan appeared in New Hampshire, he did so not only as an Indian from another time but also, and perhaps more important, from another place.

The manifestation of Powhatan reflects the way in which many white Americans of the 1850s understood Indians: as the group of people who lived on the East Coast in the earliest years of the nations' founding. Whereas Indian spirit voices of the 1860s and on increasingly echoed the militant rhetoric of Plains Indians and other Western tribes doing battle with the U.S. government and individual settlers, Indian spirits first appeared at séance gatherings in the 1850s as members of a vanished people. Hailing from a geographic and temporal elsewhere, these Indian ghosts were dispossessed and displaced from this world and replaced in the next.

The Spiritualist embrace of unwieldy Native American spirits, many of whom insisted that peace was not the equivalent of justice and that Indians had passed but had not been contained in a worldly past, complicates the monolithic myth of the vanished Indian. Popularized during the Jacksonian age of Indian removal, and circulated through an emergent national literature, the vanishing Indian was heroic, yet doomed.[16] Although this figure increasingly became a construction of what Renato Rosaldo has termed "imperialist nostalgia," Anglo Americans' earliest relationship to the figure of the doomed Indian found its roots in Calvinist providence.[17] John Winthrop's chilling statement, "For the natives, they are neere all dead of small

Poxe, so as the Lord hathe cleared our title to what we possess," indicates the foundational centrality of Indians, and indeed Indian death, to an American vision of the City on a Hill.[18] Winthrop's triumphant confirmation of spiritual space and literal lands cleared constructs the Indian as fodder for God's intention. Perhaps more striking is his blank acknowledgment of disease as both an effect of white settlement and a means of dominion.

Later, Christian missionaries would write elegies to vanished Indians, using increasingly pastoral metaphors that mystified both the fact of disease and the effect of warfare. The earliest of these, as Laura M. Stevens has documented, were written by eighteenth-century English missionaries.[19] Employing naturalized language to efface the ravages of disease and starvation among the Iroquois, Thoroughgood Moore, a missionary from the Society for the Propagation of the Gospel in Foreign Parts, wrote in 1705: "They waste away, and have done so ever since our arrival among them (as they say themselves) like snow against the sun, so that very probably forty years hence there will scarce be an Indian seen in our America."[20] Though melancholic, this image demands no more accountability than the melting of snow in spring. Early nineteenth-century literary culture adopted such metaphors, at once trumping the religious origins of Anglo-Indian relations and troping them as implicitly secular.

The production of the vanishing Indian took on new force in antebellum America. Between the War of 1812 and the Civil War, American literary romanticism and cultural nationalism converged to produce a New World folk tradition in which both the noble and the savage Indian were central. Romanticism conjured Indians, who roamed the sublime landscape of a pre-contact utopia, only to stage their disappearance. The American forest, wilder and less tame than its European counterpart, provided the perfect backdrop for the march of progress and civilization. Sentimental literature incorporated romanticism's production of a literary counterhistory, relegating Native Americans to a safely historical, typically precolonial, past.

Distanced from the antebellum present, the passing of the Noble Indian could thus arouse pity in a middle-class white public. The vanishing Indian, often the last of his tribe, became a staple of American literature and popular culture. James Fenimore Cooper's *Last of the Mohicans* (1826), Henry Wadsworth Longfellow's *Song of Hiawatha* (1855), and John Augustus Stone's play *Metamora; Or, the Last of the Wampanoags* (1829) moved antebellum audiences to sentimental tears as they lamented the fate of a dying race. In *Metamora,* in which the famed actor Edwin Forrest toured for forty years, theater spectators could cheer the proud Metamora without ever acknowledging that his death was the result of the onslaughts of their own white ancestors.[21]

So persistent was the cultural power of the vanishing Indian that, even when whites encountered real Native Americans, the referent was always the fictional. In 1877 the *New York Times* reported on the return from exile of the Sioux chief Sitting Bull by noting, without a trace of irony, that "one could not help thinking of the late Edwin Forrest in the character of Metamora, when he used to stalk upon the stage (with that peculiar slap with the bottom of his feet). . . . Sitting Bull was quite as melodramatic as the 'Last of the Wampanoags' ever was on the Bowery stage."[22] In this elision, Sitting Bull's political efficacy and urgency are contained by the stage and rendered merely performative. In nineteenth-century representations of Indians, fictional melodrama eclipsed real tragedy and muted real resistance.

This national popular culture effectively renarrated the destruction of Indian lands and forced subjugation of native people as a story of the inevitable fall of a savage population, necessary to make room for a civilized one. Its ideological weight lay in the occlusion of the historical actors who actively "vanished" Native Americans. As Deloria has argued, "In conjunction with Indian removal, popular American imagery began to play on earlier symbolic linkages between Indians and the past, and these images . . . which proclaimed it foreordained that less advanced societies should disappear in the presence of those more advanced. Propagandists shifted the cause-and-effect of Indian disappearance from Jacksonian policy to Indians themselves, who were simply living out their destiny."[23] The ubiquity and power of metaphors representing colonization as a natural process was such that even U.S. lawmakers mouthed them, eschewing even the need for legal justification of Indian removal. "By a law of nature," asserted Chief Justice Joseph Story in 1828, "they [Native Americans] seemed destined to a slow, but sure extinction. Everywhere, at the approach of the white man, they fade away. We hear the rustling of their footsteps, like that of the withered leaves of autumn, and they are gone forever. They pass mournfully by us, and they return no more."[24]

INDIAN BLESSINGS FROM THE BEYOND

Spiritualists joined nineteenth-century culture in romanticizing Native Americans as a people at one with nature, untainted by civilization, and blessed by an innate spirituality untouched by modernity. Indians, however, spoke uniquely to Spiritualists, precisely because they literally spoke through them. Although no less nostalgic than their contemporaries, Spiritualists' calling of bygone tribes to the séance tables of the present inherently destabilized the disappearance of Indians so central to Anglo-American justifications of succession. Borrowing from American culture's vague, secular constructions of Indian spirituality, Spiritualists infused their own religion with the once and future power of the (un)vanished Indian.

It is precisely because Spiritualist cosmology resisted the idea of the dead as vanished that Spiritualists professed special access to Indian ghosts. In the Boston-based *Banner of Light,* Jane M. Jackson claimed particular knowledge of Native Americans' worldly vanishing as well as an otherworldly wilderness: "They are fading away like dreams of the past; we shall see no more of their fine forms. Accounts of their strength, agility, and bravery will soon appear as fables to coming generations. Beyond the grave we now turn our attention, for Spiritualism has opened its portals, giving us power to hail the return of the lost Indians, who come to us for good."[25] Seemingly unaware of a deep American lore of Indians noble, doomed, and imagined, Jackson's referring to "fading" Indians in the present tense resists labeling them as already vanished while framing Spiritualism as the means of their future manifestation. Constructing Spiritualists as veritable explorers on a new ethereal frontier, Jackson's subtle "turning" to the "return" of the undead native both evokes and departs from the logic of U.S. westward expansion by offering a portal through which Indian spirits could freely travel, both temporally and geographically, for the good of all.

Rather than overtly acknowledge the ongoing removal of Native Americans to the Western territories, early Spiritualists brought the vanished Indian back to life—but only in an afterworld. One Spiritualist commented: "This true, native soul-grandeur of theirs will shine out more clearly in the hunting-grounds of heaven."[26] As Spiritualists appropriated Native Americans as ancestors, precursors, and spiritual teachers, they consistently projected these spirits into an afterworld that both rationalized and validated Indians' passing from this world. This writer's insidious implication—that it is better to be dead if red—at once reflects a general cultural ambivalence toward the concept of living Indians and marks the spectral Indian's instrumental status in an emergent Spiritualism.

Like the adherents of many incipient movements, Spiritualists saw the construction of a usable history as an important part of legitimating their own new, and often embattled, practice. Some white Spiritualists were anxious to document Native Americans' long-held relationships with the spirit world, but they typically relegated this practice to a distant past. In an article titled "Spiritual Manifestations among the Indians," one amateur historian quotes

Figure 6. "Mrs. S. A. Floyd," with Indian spirit, ca. 1861. William H. Mumler (photographer, American, 1832–84, active Boston, Massachusetts). Catalog no. 84.XD.760.1.31. The J. Paul Getty Museum, Los Angeles.

Cotton Mather and other writers to assert that American Indians were central to a long line of Spiritualist forebears stretching back into the early history of the New World. While claiming indigenous Americans as brethren who had regular "intercourse with Spirits," this Spiritualist also sets "primitive" Indians radically apart from modern white subjects. "All primitive nations, during their simplicity, and while uncorrupted by the sensualisms of artificial life, have believed in, and professed to enjoy, intercourse with supramundane intelligences."[27] The universalizing impulse of "all nations" is nevertheless structured by a historical narrative in which "simplicity" is a developmental stage, and corruption by "sensualisms" and artificiality a looming inevitability.

Even as Spiritualists understood Native Americans as sharing a spirituality roughly equivalent to their own, they saw these "premodern" people as bereft of other traits of civilization. Whereas Spiritualists spoke of their own religion as a science, they described Native American spirituality as "magic."[28] One Spiritualist, noting the similarities between Spiritualist practice and Native American spirituality, marked the difference in anthropological terms: "The Indians believe that the souls of the deceased employ themselves in much the same manner in the country of the spirits as they did on earth. They send messages by the dying to those that have previously gone to the brighter hunting-grounds of the Great Spirit, and by a sort of magic they profess to bring back their departed to deliberate in the proceedings held around the council fires."[29] If Indian religious beliefs and practices seemed too close to those of Spiritualists, then reifying primitivism would seemingly reinforce the separation between the white modern and the racially devolved Indian.

Yet if it was the primitivism of Native Americans that distinguished them from and doomed them in the eyes of much of white America, it was precisely this quality that made them ideal guides for Spiritualists. Spiritualist collecting of "Indian" history mirrored the nationally validating impulses of other Anglo-Americans.[30] Yet Spiritualists were interested in more than a secular conjoining of Indian and white American heritage: their transhistorical and transcultural religious syncretism specifically deployed the idea of Native Americans' inherent spirituality, if not their actual religious practices, in the production of a new cosmology. Invoking a variant of the Noble Savage, the San Francisco Spiritualist editor Herman Snow hailed these "simple, unsophisticated sons of the forest" and their spirituality untouched by modernity, which could offer something both more powerful and more beneficent than technology or civilization.[31] Nineteenth-century Spiritualist newspapers regularly listed advertisements in their back pages for books and illustrated newspapers detailing and describing "Indian Religion."[32] While such encyclopedic gatherings were more a popularizing gesture than a scholarly project, the present Indian would find its way from the séance table to the everyday Anglo-American home as an otherworldly apothecary.

One of the unique gifts of Indian spirits was the power to restore physical health. This "primitive" medicinal knowledge was used less to supplant the ethos of modernity than to compensate for its failures and add to its advances: it was a turning backward as a means to move forward. Anglo herbalists and homeopaths could thus deliver cures coded as "Indian." By the 1860s, Spiritualists like Jane Jackson were describing the many spectral Indians guiding Anglo mediums "to heal the sick, and comfort the afflicted. Medicine men from different tribes lead their mediums into the forest to hunt for herbs and roots, teach them to prepare medicines, and administer them with good effects. Filled with the desire of returning kindness for ill-treatment, they bury the hatchet, and bring peace instead of discord."[33] Another Spiritualist described Indian spirit guides "receiving and taking sympathetic charge of the spirits of persons who have just died in hospitals, by accident, or on the field of battle. They exhibit the finest shades of sympathy and brotherly love."[34] In these séance narratives, Indian spirits appear as doubly useful: they give succor to individual ailing Anglo-Americans while relieving them of genocidal guilt. As Robert S. Cox argues, Indians "proliferated in death because they performed a vital function for the living within a racial system that facilitated an adjustment to a universe of constrained sympathetic reach, becoming as much the healers of sympathy as they were sympathetic healers."[35]

The sympathetic reach of Indian spirits, however, sometimes proved more unwieldy than Cox details. Rather than simply confirming that vanquished natives had finally buried the hatchet, their brotherly love from beyond could lead to problems for Anglo mediums in the material world. An unnamed correspondent wrote to the *Herald of Progress* in 1860 about a Mrs. Caroline A. Batchelder of Danvers, Massachusetts, who had been influenced by Indian spirits. In language redolent of both possession and mesmerism, he wrote: "It is clear from her present condition that certain parties of the Better World desire to employ her sympathies and hands for the sake of 'poor mortals here below.' Her principle of fraternal justice is much unfolded. This unfits her for society. Love and justice, alas! are strangers in many neighborhoods." Suggesting that Mrs. Batchelder had become the virtual avatar of a vengeful Indian, he warned that "if the Indian influence continues to be urgent, the restorative course lies through a complete magnetization of her nervous system."[36]

Two years later, Batchelder's militancy seems to have subsided, as a follow-up letter reports her still working as an "Indian healing medium," "being possessed of extraordinary magnetic powers to tranquilize the excitement of the insane, and restore the unbalanced mind to its normal state."[37] If Mrs. Batchelder's Indian-induced insanity eventually morphed into a curative magnetism for the (presumably white) insane, without an intervention involving "a complete magnetization of her nervous system," then both the racial and technological fields of sympathy that attend this incident appear less conclusive than complicated.

More than sympathetic healers, Indian spirits would trouble Spiritualists even as they aided them. After the 1853 report in the *Spiritual Telegraph* of Powhatan's visitation to the young New Hampshire medium, other Spiritualists submitted similar accounts to the newspaper. In these narratives, Indian spirits were less articulate and even further distanced from Anglo Spiritualists' own worlds than Powhatan was. "We have another lady medium, whose guardian spirit represents himself to have been an Indian chief, who left the American hunting-grounds before the advent of the pale faces," wrote a correspondent from Buffalo, New York, to the *Spiritual Telegraph*. "He speaks Indian through her organs with great fluency; but no one here in the normal state can understand a word of it."[38] Indians may have been Spiritualist forebears, but they did not speak the same language as white Americans. The lack of a lingua franca at once authenticated the visitation and marked the Indian spirit as a nonthreatening, precolonial subject.

Others jumped into the fray, arguing that Natives, at least in their spirit form, could adopt modern language as they saw fit. James Stott of Carbondale, Pennsylvania, wrote to the *Spiritual Telegraph* with "the case of an excellent medium in that place who is influenced to speak in the most eloquent manner by an Indian Spirit, who says that during his life in the flesh he knew little or nothing of English. As a peculiarity of his operation upon the medium, Mr. Stott mentions that in private conversation he uses broken English just as a *living* [italics in original] Indian might be expected to; but that when speaking in public his diction is in the purest English, which he pours forth in an eloquent manner." The writer describes this public speech as a sort of enthusiastic collaboration such that "in public addresses" the Indian spirit guide "has control only of the young man's mind, leaving the thoughts thus vividly excited to clothe themselves in words with which the medium is familiar."[39] Rather than authenticate the speech by reproducing "Indian" (i.e., broken) English in a public setting, here the Indian spirit's "thoughts" are mediated, clothed in "familiar" words, yet more eloquent than the medium's own. This linguistic channeling works more in the logic of incarnation than translation; the spirit speaks as the medium rather than through him, raising questions about the politics of who might speak for whom.

In at least one antebellum séance report, the specter of captivity and its narrative conventions structured the tale. From Keokuk, Iowa, considerably farther west than the other spirit gatherings, came the news that two mediums had been developed in January of 1854. "One of them was influenced to speak Latin and translate the same into English," and "speak in an Indian tongue.... The Indian spirit claimed to be a Chippewa. The other medium was made to deliver an oration on bad treatment the Indians had received from white people, after which the spirits, through the two mediums, held an earnest and lengthy interview, closing with a majestic anthem."[40] The expression *made to* marks both passivity and a lack of consent on the part of the medium that is unusual in these accounts. Yet the Indian-induced oration and interview on "bad treatment" seem to have ended on a celebratory note, as Anglo Spiritualists and Indian spirits concluded the evening together in song.

As chapter 1 argues, the dialectic of innocence and eloquence attending female mediums provided a productive tension for Spiritualist practice. Inasmuch as Spiritualists bridged the domestic and public spheres by bringing séance missives to the pulpit and podium, many nineteenth-century subjects were willing, if not also charmed, to see women and girls hold forth about the afterlife and call for reform, even of their own gendered conditions. Indians, by contrast, were rarely allowed to speak for or of themselves. Yet their powerful presence as channeled would eventually compel certain mediums to speak for them both in and out of trance. Later in the 1850s, some began to argue that the spirits of dead Indians had present-day descendants to whom Spiritualists owed a great deal. Pointing to the importance of Indian guides in Spiritualist practice, these believers urged others to organize on behalf of the living and embattled Indian.

THE CAUSE OF THE INDIAN

In April 1859, the medium Emma Hardinge lectured in Philadelphia on the "cause of the Indian." At the end of her speech, she urged Spiritualists in the audience to recall "the beneficent character of the Indian spirits, who returned to earth to bring gifts of healing and goodwill to those who had despised and oppressed them." Spiritualism, she maintained, could embrace all causes and all people. "This blessed Spiritualism! reviled and scoffed at by the many, what glorious reforms does it not advocate? It forms no narrow circle around its own firesides, seeking to draw its heavenly benefits alone unto its adopted children, but worldwide, boundless, all-embracing, it reaches every wrong, and by its earnest exponents of truth and justice, co-operating with every effort of reform, strives for the poor, neglected Indian, driven from his home and hunting-grounds by the arrogant usurpations of his unjust white brother. God speed the Indians' cause, for it is a just one."[41] The medium Cora Wilburn closed her report on Hardinge's speech by directing those interested to a meeting on the "condition of the Indian" to be held on the subject later in the week.[42]

When Wilburn guided Spiritualists to this meeting in Boston in 1859, they joined a cause embraced decades earlier by New England reformers.[43] During the 1830s, white abolitionists linked the causes of Native and African Americans in campaigns opposing Cherokee removal in the Southern states. "The same despotic, cruel, and diabolical spirit that oppresses the African race," wrote John Greenleaf Whittier in the *Pennsylvania Freeman* in 1838, "acts in all its unearthly force and virulence against the poor Indians."[44] Indeed, many white abolitionists and intellectuals—Whittier, James Russell Lowell, and Lydia Maria Child among them—were involved in both Indian reform and abolitionist work. Petitions protesting Cherokee and Seminole removal came to the nation's capitol from the same regional groupings that opposed slavery: reform-minded New Englanders, Protestant missionary societies, and Northeastern colleges and benevolent organizations.[45]

Abolitionists like William Lloyd Garrison, the Grimké sisters, and Lucretia Mott mobilized national shame to defend the rights of the Indian. Arguing that the United States government had entered into a contractual relationship with Native Americans, reformers insisted that broken treaties undermined the integrity of the American state. These individuals also believed that Indian removal, like slavery, denied Natives and African Americans the "benefits of civilization" to which they might aspire. Moreover, as Ralph Waldo Emerson argued at a meeting on Indian affairs in 1861, Indians could be understood as a unique American treasure. Any caring person could see "the peculiar genius of the Indians as a people, the purity and the nobleness of their native character, of their unmatched skill in their own arts, of their history, dating far back into the forgotten ages, marking them as the primitive people of the earth, all of which commended them to our peculiar affection and watchcare."[46] Emerson's call for stewardship over Indians anticipated the rhetoric of the conservation movement of a later generation, also concerned with preserving and protecting. While New England reformers effaced or ignored native histories in the Northeast, they nonetheless also insisted on a temporally present, if geographically distant, living Indian. The nineteenth-century cultural work of erasing the legacy of indigenous peoples subsumed local histories into a national imaginary that at once pointed to the future and pointed west, implicitly endorsing the ideology of manifest destiny. Even if New Englanders, interested in the cause of live Indians, did not fully relegate a romanticized Indian to the past, they similarly projected the Indian problem onto a regional elsewhere.

This logic of displacing Indians to the western United States parallels the logic of "disowning" slavery in the north that the historian Joanne Pope Melish finds at the core of antebellum New Englanders' relationship to race. She argues that, following the abolition of slavery in New England in 1820, white Northerners succeeded in constructing "a triumphant narrative of a historically free, white New England in which a few people of color were unaccountably marooned."[47] Actively forgetting their own recent history of slavery, white citizens could cast it as a peculiar problem of the Southeast, creating new constructions of race and forms of racism in the process. In the same way, New Englanders projected their own history of the dispossession of Indian lands onto the West. New England reformers would be moved to protect Native Americans through a justice buttressed by a constructed innocence: they could feel righteous about the Indian question as long as they did not look too close to home.

Spiritualists' relationship to this issue was a complex one. On the one hand, they were part of a broader white American culture that variously romanticized, erased, and appropriated Indian history, rituals, and land. Spiritualists, like other reformers, spoke in paradoxical ways about the Indian question, oscillating between the language of civilization and that of savagery, invoking paternalism as well as a discourse of rights and brotherhood. At the same time, many Spiritualists labored for progressive reform and took part in concrete work undergirded by a commitment to ameliorating the damage done by white colonists. As Gail Bederman has argued, the dialectic between savagery and civilization structured American reform politics from the nineteenth century to the early twentieth.[48] Spiritualists' relationship to that dialectic, however, was a somewhat countercultural one. If, for example, Theodore Roosevelt and others appropriated an idealized "savagery" to masculinize white men while also actively endorsing colonialism to combat the less exalted savagery in others, Spiritualists often engaged in the first cultural gesture but subverted the latter. Their romantic attachment to Native American spirituality and primitivism became a foundation not for colonialism but for anticolonialism.

What was distinctive about Spiritualist reform was the enmeshment of spectral Indians in Spiritualist practice. Whereas abolitionists saw the United States' broken treaties with native nations as a breach of the social contract inherent in America's enlightened vision of itself, Spiritualists extended this contract as an ongoing negotiation between this world and the next. While the expansion of the American nation-state into western territories challenged the range of progressive politics situated in New England, Spiritualists imagined that they were charting an otherworldly wilderness with the consent and aid of Indians, whose welfare must also be attended to in this world. Many abolitionists saw slavery and the oppression of Indians as equally corrosive to Anglo-Americans' Christian souls; by contrast, Spiritualists' will to protect native lands and sovereignty was self-serving inasmuch as they needed Indian spirit guides to illuminate their own evolving cosmology. Individual Spiritualists varied in their views on the issue, and those stances, in turn, changed over time. However, the relationships between Anglo Spiritualists and American Indians reveal a tangled history of colonialism and nineteenth-century progressive reform.

Among the antebellum abolitionists and coreligionists who constituted nineteenth-century reformism, Quakers held a privileged place.[49] By forging a genealogy of spiritual and political affinities with the Quakers, Spiritualists not only provided their movement with a usable past but also, crucially, challenged the historical myopia of New England reformers and provided an alternative historiography of Anglo-American colonialism. In contrast to the popular circulating myth of the vanishing Indian, which functionally absolved colonists of responsibility, Spiritualists would write a revisionist history, lauding Quakers as colonists exceptionally benevolent in their treatment of the Indian. Recovering this Quaker past at once provided a pragmatic political model for Indian relations and defined the Spiritualist project as both honorable and exceptional.

Since the late seventeenth century, Quakers had sought to establish respectful relations with Native Americans. As one Spiritualist maintained, when white people cooperated with Indians, as did "William Penn and his followers, there were no Indian wars, and not a drop of Quaker blood shed by an Indian has ever moistened the soil of this continent."[50] Another wrote, "Had we always treated them as Penn did, paying them fairly for what they got from him, and refusing to take under force of any temptation, what was not our own, we should not have known of the troubles which have perplexed and disgraced us."[51] This model of "respectful cooperation" to avoid national "disgrace" was championed in the Spiritualist press and best represented by John Beeson, a Methodist minister and farmer, who was prominent among the organizers of national conventions on the Indian question from 1859 through the early 1860s.[52]

In pointing to the Quakers as ideal colonists, white supporters of Indian rights could tell a particular story about the contemporary problem of Indian removal: the vicious frontier whites were at least as responsible for the Native Americans' plight as was the federal government. Lawless settlers had committed numerous outrages against the native peoples they displaced. John Beeson and others outlined a vision in which Indians should have land set aside for them, which could be shared only with a respectful subset of white Americans. "The object," Beeson argued in a speech from Boston's Old South Chapel, "should therefore be to consider the propriety of designating a territory which shall be exclusively Indian, with such settlers only as will voluntarily co-operate with them in the development of their resources, and in sustaining such laws and government as will be best adapted for their improvement and protection."[53] By drawing a firm distinction between good and bad white people, Spiritualists, like other New England reformers, could remain unimplicated in U.S. Indian policy while placing blame on presumably less-civilized frontier whites.

Spiritualist campaigners assumed that all reformers who constituted their imagined community would embrace the cause of the Indian. Yet even among those who supported the movement, there was a great deal of disagreement not only over the best solution but also as to the nature of the problem. In the *Herald of Progress,* Beeson, a Spiritualist fellow traveler, penned his tales of fighting the good fight, lamenting that there were many white Christians who refused to act on their "duty to the Indian." In 1860, he described an unhappy visit to Boston. "I went to Tremont Temple, which was then crowded with thousands. People of all kinds and classes were prayed for—the slave, the infidel, those who disregarded the Church and broke the Sabbath. I stepped upon the platform and said in a whisper to the conductor of the meeting, 'Will you allow me to offer a word for the Indians, that this audience may pray for them?' and the presiding elder answered, 'It will be an intrusion.'"[54]

This exchange demonstrates that the dichotomy of putatively good versus bad whites was neither a problem of the past nor one inherent to the Western frontier. If the Indian question was one too many for Tremont Temple's politics of universal inclusion, then the "intrusion" of Indian spirits in the daily realities of Spiritualist circles was singularly pressing. Denied the pulpit, Beeson and other Spiritualists relied on their own proven forms of dissemination and organization. A report from a "meeting to consider the condition of the Indians in our territories" concluded: "The measures necessary to stop Indian wars are the same as are used to stop other evils: Agitation through the press, public discussions, but above all a national convention."[55]

Whether or not Indians needed Spiritualists' prayers, Spiritualists needed Indians. Their religious practice was structured by an indebtedness to their borrowed Indian guides. Allying themselves in a uniquely personal way with the cause of the Indian, many Spiritualists claimed that it was inextricably linked with their own. As Thomas Griffin of Worcester, Massachusetts, wrote to the *Banner of Light* in 1860, "The cause of Spiritualism and of the Indians, as Mr. Beeson presents them, are almost one and the same, for the noble spirits of that race are the most active to help our cause with their magnetic forces. And certainly we as a people cannot progress, morally or spiritually, until a feeling of kindness and brotherhood is generally awakened, at least high enough to give them human sympathy and the protection of the law."[56]

With the evocation of the "magnetic forces" at their disposal, the Spiritualists' claims on behalf of Native Americans surpassed the language of rights deployed by many of their reformist contemporaries. If rights rhetoric typically relies on analogies of equality and parity, Spiritualists saw Indians as beneficially different: Their savagery could civilize; their spirituality could save. Indians' special qualities, therefore, entitled them to special protections. Spiritualists needed the "magnetic forces" of spectral Indians for séance communion and relied on them as spiritual forebears and teachers. In this line of argument, it was only right to reciprocate the help of Indian spirits by helping living Native Americans. The very least the Spiritualists could offer was the return of the "sympathy" and protection that spectral Indians had offered spiritual seekers.

Spiritualists seemed to mark both Indian difference and sameness, to invoke the language of help and compassion for the less fortunate while also gesturing to a reciprocity born of "brotherhood." These incongruities underline the instability of Spiritualist political thought on the Indian question; ultimately, most Spiritualists labored for the cause of the Indian while disavowing a horizontal relationship between Native Americans and themselves. While pious white women took the lead, and the stage, in Spiritualist practice, Indians were rarely invited to the podium. Seemingly, to be spiritual, Indians had to be spirits.

As antebellum Spiritualists increasingly drew Indian ghosts near, while keeping live Indians at a physical distance, some Spiritualists turned to race to account for these impersonal intimacies. After the flurry of speeches, writings, and organizing on the Indian question in the early 1860s, many Spiritualists entered the debate to remind their coreligionists of the innate differences between Native Americans and themselves. "Indian spirits are robust, healthy, and sympathetic; but they seldom confer *wisdom* upon their mediums," wrote a Massachusetts Spiritualist to the *Herald of Progress*. Returning native spirits to their mythic role as guides for white settlers, the writer continued, "In the Spirit Land they are exceedingly officious and useful in many ways ... but are rarely wise and prudent in the employment of their powers." For this Spiritualist, although Indians were helpful, they were not to be fully trusted and certainly not considered equals. He ended his letter with a description of the spirit world as divided "into classes, as in a school; and thousands of illustrious wise men, once so called on earth among men, delight in appointing themselves to the office of monitors and teachers among the classified red men who are so grouped in the celestial spheres."[57] This paternalistic vision conjures nothing less than a celestial Indian boarding school.

Another Spiritualist observed, "The distinctive character of the three grand races are the Negro, with his warm impulses, beating and bounding to the spirit of kindness, making him happy, even in his bonds; the Indian, with his strong instinct, and pure, free soul, jealous and watchful of its liberties even unto death; and the white man, with his cold intellect, compressing soul and spirit into forms of wisdom, forms of beauty."[58] The happy Negro, instinctive Indian, and intellectual white man in this schema are inherently different and unequal, even though this writer attributes to the Indian those most American of qualities—freedom and liberty "unto death." Others invoked the racial language of science to mark the inferiority of Native Americans, both embodied and in spirit form. The prominent Spiritualist Hudson Tuttle reminded others that "in our zeal for their welfare we must not overlook the cardinal, all-important fact of race."[59] Asking rhetorically why the Indians have not become Christianized, he answered, "Christianity is the outgrowth of the Caucasian mind, is the ultimate of its moral and intellectual consciousness, and belongs to that race only, as inseparably as its predominant intellectual brain."[60]

Many white reformers, including Spiritualists who worked on behalf of Native Americans, believed in the importance of Protestant missionary work among the tribes. The 1859 convention on behalf of "the Indians on the Western Frontier" proposed to set aside land for Native Americans "where they could be reached by the missionaries, and where they could be inspired with hope and love."[61] Tuttle, in contrast, criticized the missionary impulses of most white reformers, but he did so by invoking a racial hierarchy in which Christianity, whiteness, and civilization stood in contrast to the pagan sloth of the red man, who should not, because he could not, be converted to "white ways." Tuttle continued, "But here I tread on the other question, 'Why have they faded from the land?' Simply because they cannot be Christianized—which means Caucasianized—because the mass of brain behind the Indians' ears cannot be placed in front—or, in other words, because no training can convert a red man into a white. . . . He will not work: for his subsistence three thousand acres of forests are required. He abuses the earth, which is required for the support of a race that will labor, and hence must disappear."[62] In Tuttle's formulation, Indians' unwillingness to be civilized into the rules and rituals of property-respecting laborers marked them as beyond the pale.[63] Tuttle's rendering of Indians as wasting the land, and thereby wasting away, is another noxious variant of Emerson's conception of Indians themselves as natural resources.

Tuttle represents a reactionary, and indeed reactive, stance in the spectrum of Spiritualist thought. The range of rhetoric from Griffin's fraternal embrace to Tuttle's racist will to disappearance signals the unwieldy nature of the Indian question. Spiritualists seemingly could not live without Native American spirits but were unsure as to how to live with existing native nations. Spiritualist speech on behalf of the Indian, like that of other reformers, did not allow Native Americans to speak for themselves in the debates of the early 1860s. Indians nonetheless spoke to Spiritualists in increasingly militant voices from beyond the realm of worldly politics. Although the privileging of the Indian cause may appear as a sublimation of white guilt for these subjects, many Spiritualists sensed an obligation where other sympathetic Anglo-Americans felt only regret. Indebted to Indian spirits for their tangible blessings, advice, and healing, Spiritualists embraced the Native American cause in an economy of exchange and debt rather than through sublimation of guilt.

MANIFESTING MILITANCY

As some Spiritualists responded in reactionary ways to the ubiquity of Indian manifestations at séances and the growing importance of the Indian question to reform efforts, spectral Indians also began to change their tone. This transformation illustrated Spiritualists' own new relationships to Native

Americans, in some cases born of their involvement with Indian spirit guides. In contrast to Powhatan's 1853 speech, in which he reassured listeners that "we are happy now. Heaven is ours," by 1863 Powhatan and other guides were making it clear that there was much earthly work left to do. Beginning in the 1860s, Indian spirits came to white mediums to demand Indian rights. As the veteran Spiritualist James M. Peebles described this shift, the spiritual realm paralleled the political exigencies of the material world. "Humanity is waking; all races are demanding their rights, and no nation can long live, unless its foundation be based upon Justice, Equity and Equality, but cemented by those diviner principles of human brotherhood and universal love."[64] By the later 1860s, Indian spirits spoke less of universal love than of broken vows. Spectral healers offering blessings were largely overshadowed by warriors issuing increasingly militant warnings.

Yet some Indian spirits continued to offer help to Spiritualists. Typically, it was Indian "maiden" spirits who carried on this tradition from the antebellum years: they blessed weddings, protected travelers, and took special care of the spirits of children in the afterlife.[65] Dohomey, "an Indian Maid," spoke through Mrs. J. H. (Fannie) Conant, the medium of the *Banner of Light* "free circle" for seventeen years. Dohomey did triple spiritual duty, blessing spirit circles, speaking on behalf of "her people," and affirming white women's "brilliance": "White man, say through your great talking sheet, that the Indian maid Dahomey *[sic]*, who passed on many years ago at Manhattan, would be glad to speak to the white squaw, . . . that she, in turn, with her brilliant talk, may talk to the white man. Tell her, Dohomey blesses her in the Hunting-ground of the Great Spirit."[66] This Indian maid continued to speak in sentimental tones, stilted language, and in great admiration of both female mediums and the enchanted media of "the great talking sheet."

The larger transformations in spirit speech between 1853 and 1868 reflect the dramatic political changes during this period. Throughout the 1850s, colonists flooded west. Spiritualists, like other Americans, were involved and implicated in westward migration and the dispossession of the American Indian. Many prominent Spiritualists headed to California, passing through the Great Plains, the site of a massive Indian removal. The lure of gold and silver and new land annexations invited further immigration. California and Oregon became states, and nearly all the rest of the land west of the Missouri River was reorganized into territories. Between 1848 and 1860, settlers beyond the ninety-fifth meridian had multiplied more than threefold. According to the 1860 census, Texas alone claimed a population of 604,215 and California 379,994.[67]

In 1861, a *New York Times* correspondent described the "startling character" of this expansion, focusing not on the great white land grab but on the Indian "massacres" that stood in its way. "It is now something more than ten years since our frontier line has been thrown from the western limit of the great valley of the Mississippi, to those regions known as the rocky mountain slopes, bounded by British possessions on the north and by Mexico on the south. During the early period of the California emigration, when emigrants in large bodies rushed across the country, we heard little of Indian depredations. But later, when civilization attempted to make a stand in sections of the intermediate countries, and emigrants in small bodies wound their slow and weary way over a variety of routes, the wild Indian commenced his systematic course of plunder and butchery." Ignoring all Indian losses, the *Times* correspondent estimated the number of settlers killed by Indians in the frontier region at "one thousand per annum."[68]

Although the *New York Times* could in no way be considered the newspaper of record during this era, it was typical in its coverage of Indian issues. Before the Civil War, the *Times* used most of its ink to decry the military's inability to stop the supposed Indian butchery of white settlers, particularly those crossing the Great Plains to the West Coast. Between 1858 and 1861, the *Times* ran articles and editorials on "Indian depredations of the most frightful character in Arizona and New Mexico" on an almost weekly basis. The disgrace to a "civilized nation," as one *Times* editorialist termed it, could be heard in "the dying shrieks and groans, and the bleaching bones of thousands and thousands of our murdered pioneers" and the inability of the War Office to stop it.[69] As the Civil War waged on, Native Americans were represented even less sympathetically by the mainstream press. The Northern press in particular observed that the Southern tribes assisted the Confederacy, while the Western tribes created another front on which the beleaguered Union army needed to fight.

Although the Civil War distracted many of the reformers who had once engaged with the Indian question, many Spiritualists remained committed to the cause and increasingly turned to their own press as a vehicle for political agitation. Referring to the silencing of Beeson among Boston's reformists, one supporter placed particular faith in the power of the printed word: "Could Mr. Beeson's efforts be backed by the press of the country as they deserve, it would not be long before a new feeling would come over our people upon this important subject."[70] This new feeling was not forthcoming. If anything, the Spiritualist press seemed further distanced from dominant American opinion during the war years than it had been in the past, exposing the corruption in the Office of Indian Affairs and giving rare voice to an "Indian side" in the military conflicts of the early 1860s.

The Sioux wars marked a significant turning point. In 1862, as fewer and fewer of the annuities promised by treaty were paid to the Western tribes, the Sioux of Minnesota, led by Little Crow, attacked white settlers, killing close to four hundred. A military commission found 303 Sioux guilty and condemned them to hang. President Lincoln stepped in to assess what reformers charged were a vast number of convictions with little or no evidence. Ordering the trial transcripts, Lincoln reduced the number of death sentences from three hundred to thirty-eight, much to the outrage of Minnesota's white citizenry.[71]

Following the Sioux uprising, the Spiritualist press was a lone voice calling for justice for Native Americans. As one editorialist opined in the *Banner of Light,* "There never was a time when more people were thoroughly misrepresented and misunderstood than are our aboriginal tribes at the present day." Having exposed the dealings of Senator Morton S. Wilkinson of Minnesota (who had been profiting from moneys diverted from the Indians and was charged, and later cleared, by the Senate) in previous editions of the *Banner,* the Spiritualist press took him on again. When Wilkinson made a speech before the Senate in which he affirmed that in the late outbreak in Minnesota "more than a thousand white people were brutally massacred by savages," and that it was done "savagely and without any pretext, without any cause, and apparently without any motive," the *Banner* noted that "no witnesses were called to testify to the Indians side." The article, by John Beeson, blamed white settlers and the Indian Bureau for the massacre. Beeson wrote: "I am prepared to furnish authentic testimony to the following points: 1. That the crimes which were charged upon the Indians in the late outbreak in Minnesota, and for which thirty eight of them have been hung, are of common occurrence committed by white settlers in the Territories upon the Indians, against which they have no redress to protection. 2. That the Indian Department, as practically carried out, is at once a fraud and a swindle, both upon the Indians and upon the people of the United States, and that the first step in reform is an impartial investigation from the Indian's standpoint."[72] A notice inside the same issue urged readers to "Read Mr. John Beeson's letter in regard to the Indians. . . . . When *justice* is done to our red brethren, we shall hear of no more massacres, such as have lately occurred in the West. The Indian is a man, and should, in his present weak condition, be protected in his rights by the strong arm of the General Government."[73]

Supportive letters to the *Banner* poured in. S. C. Simonds wrote from

Foster's Crossing, Ohio, to praise Beeson: "I am glad, *heartily* glad, that there is a man to write such a proposition, and a paper which will allow it to reach the eyes of the people."[74] Peebles compared the condemned Indians to John Brown. "Last December, at Mankato [Minnesota], they hung thirty-eight condemned Indians.... Virginia hung John Brown. Today the rope is around the neck of Virginia. How perfect the law of compensation. I justify no Indian outrage. They terribly erred; but who were the first aggressors? In nearly every border outbreak, the causes were ultimately traced to the treachery of whites, who had not only corrupted and deceived them, but through dishonest 'Indian agents,' defrauded them of their governmental funds. Many of the Congressional Treaties proved but nuclei for organized villainies."[75] Far from regarding the Indian wars as secondary in importance to the Civil War, Peebles linked radical abolition with the uprising of the Sioux.

As Spiritualist politics regarding the Indian question became more radical and more directly policy-oriented, the vague language of universal brotherhood became more personal and urgent. Peebles, a hard-hitting critic of U.S. policy, waxed sentimental about the ubiquitous "Indian Chief Powhatan, of Pocahontas memory." In 1863, he wrote: "Powhatan, long in spirit-life, came to me over five years since—came when wanted—and I have no truer friend on earth, or in realms immortal, than he—honest, truthful, sympathetic, and genial as the warmth that ever streams from their council fires of peace. I love him—I love the Indian character—I love the peace language that now rings from the eloquent Powhatan, Red-Jacket, Black Hawk, Logan, King Philip and others, and shall rejoice when freed from mortality to roam with them as brothers, blessed of the same 'Great Spirit,' through the Celestial Hunting Grounds of Immortality."[76] Peebles's fraternal longing, romantic as it is, marks an affective connection with Indians, spectral and real, that bolstered an increasingly identificatory politics of dissent.

It is also possible to see such effusive statements as a compensation for the increasingly frustrated and militant language of Indian spirits themselves in these years. In an extraordinary 1863 letter to the editor in the *Banner of Light,* signed by "King Phillip, Tecumseh, Osceola, and Billy Bowlegs," this coalition of spectral warriors united across time and space to speak directly to Spiritualists: "Now look to this, dear White brothers, for our people, and to you, noble Chief Beeson, we would say we will stimulate you on in your good work, until victory shall have given you her crown.... We will come to you again at some future time.... We now bid you an affectionate farewell, and though we may not at present commune with you again very soon, we would have you know and realize that we shall be with you and around you, and urge you on to do your destined part."[77] This letter is remarkable for a number of reasons, not least of which is that it is a *letter*. When other spectral Indians spoke through white mediums, both medium and messenger were identified by name. Here the messengers need no medium except the Spiritualists' own press. Giving a nod to "noble Chief" Beeson, the spirits urge the Spiritualists to do their "destined part" beyond the séance table. Seemingly, these Indians also issue a warning; they will not speak directly or "commune" again until the "good works" of the present have been done. There would be no good Indian guides until these Spiritualists proved themselves worthy of the gifts already bestowed.

As if in answer, Spiritualists intensified their rhetoric and organizing work. Cora Wilburn again voiced the sentiment that the cause of the Spiritualist and the cause of the Indian were one and the same. She lambasted the national Spiritualist convention, held in Chicago in 1864, for not properly attending to the plight of Native Americans. "We, as Spiritualists, pledged against all forms of slavery, benefited as we are by the ministrations of Indian spirits, who, returning good for the evil received at our hands, come from the blessed souls-lands with missions of healing and beneficence, with messages of encouragement and consolation, owe them in their present need the returns of gratitude and just dealing." She challenged that "the voice of the united body of Spiritualists go forth to the world in earnest protest against further infringement of the Indians' rights, in solemn vindication of those rights, side by side with our own."[78]

Three years later, Dr. H. T. Childs presented a resolution to the Fourth National Convention of Spiritualists resolving that "as Spiritualists, we owe more to the Indians than to any body of men or women on this continent. These people have been driven from their homes in this country, pillaged of their means and cheated by the treachery of white traders, have come to us from their homes in the happy hunting grounds and I do not know a medium of all the many thousands through which the developments of Spiritualism has come to bless us, that does not owe much to the strength and influence that the red man brings to them."[79] Two resolutions were adopted by the convention; one issuing "our firm and unqualified condemnation" of the government of the United States, "assured, as we are, that said war is without just cause," the other resolving "to endeavor, by every means in our power," to secure a permanent and "inviolate" peace, home, and "equal chance in the race of nationalities."[80]

During the height of Radical Reconstruction, as Spiritualists adopted resolutions condemning the U.S. government, Osceola, the Seminole warrior, came from the "swamps of the Floridas" to a Northeastern spirit circle in 1867 with ominous warnings and bitter indictments. "Osceola, with many chiefs and warriors, returns from the hunting-ground where the Great Spirit gives justice to all his children; and he would rather see peace than war. But if the white man's feet grow so large that they want all the hunting-grounds, then the Indian Osceola would sharpen his knife and cut them off. . . . The white man cannot teach the red man, for the red man knows that the white man has no justice in his heart."[81] Not only were Indian curses beginning to outstrip Indian blessings, but some specters were issuing pointed condemnations from which Spiritualists could not imagine themselves immune.

In 1868, the Indian spirit Sagoyewatha (Red Jacket, a Seneca warrior who fought in the Revolutionary War) returned with an alleged last word, and a warning, on behalf of the Plains Indians. "This is the last time that the warriors on the plains will listen to words from the white man. If these vows are broken now, they never can be mended. If they are not kept, the red man will wage an eternal war against the white man, and it will not be easy to exterminate him. . . . Sagoyewatha from yonder hunting-grounds pleads the cause of his people, but he pleads no more for them than for the white man, for he knows that the white man will suffer as the red man will if the white man's vows are broken. Good moon. Sagoyewatha is done."[82] In a decade and a half, Indian spirits had changed from content to militant.[83]

Spiritualists hinted that it might be in their interest, even imperative, to right the wrongs of this world for the sake of the Indians who protected them from beyond. As one Spiritualist opined in 1867: "We should make haste to set this wrong right, and there are symptoms of it being done in due time. No matter if it is interest or necessity that leads to it; only let it be accomplished in time to repair, in some small degree, the wrongs, the outright crimes with which we stand chargeable."[84] Beyond the ritual performance of white guilt, some white Spiritualists were implicating themselves in "out right crimes."

At the same time, the Spiritualist press could be strikingly self-congratulatory, crediting itself with moving the country forward through its early and sustained stance opposing war against the Indians. "But now we witness a general eruption of serious talk on the subject of Indian wars and the general treatment of the Indians, which promises to lead to the best results," one editorialist wrote. "For ourselves, we took hold of this discussion because it was an act of justice to see that a downtrodden race had their wrongs righted."[85] The Spiritualist press had, indeed, been one of the earliest and often the lone progressive voice on the Indian question, while also regularly taking on the New York *Tribune, Times, Sun,* and *Herald* for their unfair reporting.[86] Spiritualists with roots in abolitionism went beyond demanding abstract justice, now connecting the cause of the Indian with the cause of Reconstruction. In 1868, Cora (Scott Hatch) Daniels wrote to the *Antislavery Standard,* urging the cessation of Indian wars not only for the sake of "justice" but also to protect the Reconstructed South "in this their most perilous crisis."[87] Some Spiritualists explicitly linked these struggles. As one wrote simply: "Let us have justice for all—whether they be white, back, or red."[88]

The Spiritualists' renewed call for Indian rights throughout the 1860s was primarily a product of their twenty-year relationship with Indian spirit guides. However, as they became increasingly active in campaigns on behalf of Native Americans, some Spiritualists began to encounter Indians outside séances. If an imagined debt toward Native spirits produced one politics and the confrontation with increasingly militant spirit guides another, engaging with real Native Americans would challenge Spiritualists in entirely new ways.

Along with conversing in the Spiritualist press, which constituted a kind of community in print, Spiritualists met regularly at conventions and camp meetings. The best-known and longest-lasting of the camps, Lily Dale on Cassadaga Lake in western New York, gathered Spiritualists, mediums, and reform speakers for séances, lectures, picnics, and boat rides on the lake.[89] A resort that still attracts curiosity seekers and believers to the town of North Collins each summer, Cassadaga showcased Indians in the summer of 1868.

Asked to lecture on the "Indian question" to a supportive audience of Spiritualists, Dr. P. Wilson began the summer series. Described as "an Indian originally descended from the famous Six Nations," Wilson had graduated from the Geneva Medical College and resided on a "very near 'reservation.'" He began his talk by playfully criticizing the tone and content of several of the Spiritualist speeches that preceded his own before launching into a synopsis of the "native Indian's theology." "Indians all believe in one Great Spirit, and that human spirits come right from this Great Spirit. . . . We neither know of nor believe in any death, for we live right on. . . . Spirits continually come back. We all believe this. I expect when I get through with this world to go to the hunting-grounds of my ancestors." Having begun by marking the similarities in the two belief systems, Wilson concluded by differentiating native theology from Spiritualist Christianity and himself from white Spiritualists. "None of us desire to go to the Christian's Heaven! Why should we? They'd turn us out if possible." The Spiritualist supporters of the cause of the

Indian who had invited Wilson to speak were initially delighted about "the intensified diversity by the appearance upon the rostrum of a native American."[90] Yet, having realized their fantasy of a Native American Spiritualist, they were quickly disabused of the notion that their causes were "one and the same."

After the 1868 summer camp season, Spiritualists brought the issue of Indian rights to their national conventions and to their work in the peace movement.[91] Yet they continued to discount living Native Americans in favor of Indian spirit guides. As one Spiritualist grappled with the knotty problem of Native American history, he concluded that perhaps Indians were better off as spirit guides than as living beings. "How weird their history—so full of hopes, romance and mystic charms! How bright their future in the spirit world! Upward they will progress toward the highest angel band, never failing to send from the sparkling fountains of their nature, jets of pure spiritual magnetism to assist struggling humanity in earth-life. God bless the Indian spirits in the summer-land, for Spiritualism would not stand where it does today had it not been for their influence!"[92]

Still, Spiritualists believed that material reform work was necessary lest white people be punished in the great hunting grounds. "It is useless for any man or woman to say, 'It is nothing to me. I cannot help these outrages,'" wrote a *Banner of Light* editorialist about the Plains Indian massacres. "You can every one of you do something. You can exercise your kindly thoughts. You can send out a magnetic influence, to change the great tide that is threatening to overwhelm justice. You can all do something, and rest assured that if you do not, the consequences you cannot escape hereafter. Rest assured of it. You cannot escape it. Die you must; and because you must die you will enter the spirit-world; and what then? Those oppressed ones, black and red, may come to you, individually, asking what you have done for their people here. See to it that you can give them a good answer."[93]

Whether because of these dire warnings or their own worldly political commitments, Spiritualists continued to organize for Indian rights and other reforms throughout the 1870s. As the political climate shifted to one of Reconstruction, retrenchment, and backlash, Spiritualists stood out as radicals in this new era. During the 1870s, moral crusaders like Anthony Comstock would find in Spiritualism an ideal target for the political and sex wars of the day.

THREE

Spectral Sexualities

Free Love, Moral Panic, and the Making
of U.S. Obscenity Law

In 1873, Anthony Comstock, a young clerk from New York City, went to Washington, DC, to present Congress with his personal collection of abominations.[1] He brought with him racy playing cards, contraceptive "rubber goods," and such salacious dime novels as *The Lustful Turk,* all acquired from Manhattan booksellers, Bowery newsdealers, and mail-order sellers.[2] Comstock saw this work as central to his new appointment as special agent for the New York Committee for the Suppression of Vice, a group sponsored by the Young Men's Christian Association. Relying on the influence of a few well-placed friends, Comstock secured the office of Vice President Schuyler Colfax to stage the first official exhibition of obscene matter in the Capitol. Comstock delivered his horrors to the Senate chambers with a dire warning of a deadly contagion which had "succeeded in injecting a virus more destructive to the innocence and purity of youth . . . than can be the most deadly disease to the body."[3] By his own account, Comstock's powers of persuasion moved Congress to act. As he confided to his diary, "All were very much excited, and declared themselves ready to give me any law I might ask for, if it was only within the bounds of the Constitution."[4]

Comstock's unlikely welcome in Washington owed much to the political climate of the 1870s. When Comstock made his trip to Washington, Colfax and a number of other high-ranking politicians were in the middle of a scandal involving bribes and kickbacks paid through the Credit Mobilier, a joint-stock company that financed the construction of the Union Pacific Railroad. Colfax himself had been named by the Democratic newspaper *The New York Sun* as a prime offender. When Comstock proposed the display of new and unrelated horrors in Colfax's office, it must have been a welcome distraction from the vice president's own troubles.[5]

Comstock's condemnations drew on a language that resonated in a nation still consumed with Spiritualism, speaking as he did of obscene images as "vile phantoms" and visions that return to "haunt the mind."[6] Moreover, he explicitly crafted his law to stop the distribution of one Spiritualist free-love newspaper. The histories of Spiritualism and Comstockery are mutually entangled in the fascination and fright produced by the new presence of sexualized bodies—such as that of the notorious free-love advocate Victoria Woodhull—stalking the public sphere, as well as a new flow of texts and images into the private home through the U.S. mail. Spiritualist affinities and the logic of Spiritualism itself provide a means of tracing the fears surrounding obscenity, gender, and sexuality and the motives behind the enactment of national obscenity regulation. Restoring Spiritualism to the history of censorship illuminates the complicated workings of this formative moral panic, arguably America's first sex war.

As a result of Comstock's lobbying, the scandal-ridden Forty-second Congress passed the first national obscenity law on March 1, 1873.[7] A gleeful Comstock pasted a clipping into his diary from the conservative New York *Journal of Commerce,* which read: "Something will be forgiven a Congress which thus powerfully sustains the cause of morality."[8] Although there was almost no debate or comment on it at the time it passed, this seemingly innocuous piece of postal legislation, later known as the Comstock Law, governed traffic in sexual literature and information for nearly a century afterward.[9] The Comstock Law marked a new federal involvement in the fight against vice and the beginning of a particular brand of state-sponsored censorship. It expanded the category of obscenity to include all printed matter, and, for the first time in history, criminalized the circulation of information and advertisements about contraception and abortion.[10]

Comstock targeted the mail as the site of his campaign, and Congress appointed him an official agent of the U.S. Postal Service. With the adoption of the new law, he and all other willing local postmasters were granted the right to inspect mail and seize material they deemed obscene. The United States now had both a national obscenity law and a means to police the circulation of sexual texts, images, and information.

The Comstock Law marks not only a founding moment in the history of censorship but also the culmination of a national moral panic in which Spiritualism and Spiritualists were central. Focusing either on vice reformers or on the objects of their wrath (sexually explicit texts and images), historians have sought to explain why this new concern emerged when it did, and why it did so at the national level.[11] As two legal historians have summed up the quandary, "Little of value in terms of legal historical background can be found to show why, just after the Civil War, Protestant leaders in New York City became so aroused over obscenity."[12] Shifting attention to the terrain on which Comstock battled might help answer such questions. What was it about the mail that Comstock and, more important, Congress sought to police? How did the transmission of sexual information heighten modern fears about the movement of ideas and bodies? Might middle-class anxieties over the increasingly permeable boundary between public and private speak to more amorphous concerns about new media of circulation, as well as a potentially contaminated, deviant public culture, leaking into the presumed sanctity of the private, middle-class home? These questions are central to the making of the Comstock Law.

Gayle Rubin, following an important formulation by the historian Jeffrey Weeks, has argued that moral panics are staged in characteristic ways. They channel widespread cultural fears, but rather than further a search for the "real causes" of such anxieties, they instead displace popular passions onto convenient (and typically unpopular) targets. Of course, such nebulous concepts as "cultural anxieties" are notoriously hard to track and even harder to historicize. Moral panics form a moving target precisely because they are wars conducted as a series of displacements: They recirculate old fears and project them onto new demons. They are conducted with misplaced passions and fought at oblique angles; they are aimed at scapegoats and directed at phantasms.[13]

Although often lost in modern accounts, the link between Spiritualism and Comstockery was quite explicit in the 1870s. Indeed, it was a Spiritualist, Victoria Woodhull, who became Anthony Comstock's own personal demon and ultimately drove him to Congress to appeal for stronger obscenity laws.[14] Although Woodhull was better known as a feminist than a Spiritualist, both belief systems placed her squarely at odds with the vice-fighting Comstock. Her use of the podium as a Spiritualist—a claim of public space that was a violation of middle-class gender norms—combined with her own brand of noisy, free-love feminism made Woodhull a perfect target. The public conversation about sex that she initiated produced a host of powerful enemies.

Woodhull had long known how to use a stage to further her own political goals. In 1871, two years before Comstock's trip to Washington, she had been elected president of the American Association of Spiritualists, a result that surprised and upset many of the group's leaders, who saw her as opportunistic and unrepresentative of the movement. Some suspected that Woodhull, who had never before attended a Spiritualist convention, showed up solely to be elected president. Her appearance at the Spiritualist conference came in the wake of a number of high-profile appearances at other political events. She attended the National Woman Suffrage Association (NWSA) convention, where she managed to upstage all other participants by securing an audience with the House Judiciary Committee to appeal for women's suffrage. Presenting a suffrage memorial to the committee in January 1871, Woodhull became the first woman to testify before Congress. She was also involved in organizing and promoting the first English-speaking section of the International Workingmen's Association, the first international socialist organization in the United States. In 1872, she was elected for a second time to head the American Association of Spiritualists. Although she declined the position, the convention would not accept her refusal.[15]

Despite rumblings that Woodhull was only using the Spiritualist movement for self-promotion, she was a lifelong Spiritualist.[16] She got her start by performing as a medium in her family's traveling medicine show. As little girls, Victoria and her sister Tennessee (sometimes "Tennie C.") Claflin, billed as the Claflin Sisters, performed acts of faith healing while their father, Buck, sold nostrums to the sick. Married at fourteen to an alcoholic doctor named Canning Woodhull, Victoria supported the family as a medical clairvoyant. In 1866 Woodhull met, magnetized, and married Colonel James Harvey Blood after obtaining a speedy divorce from the doctor, who nevertheless remained a part of the extended household. Soon after, the spirits urged Woodhull to relocate her clan to Manhattan. By 1868, the sisters were ensconced in New York, billing themselves as "Professors of Magnetic, Mental, and Spiritual Science."[17] Their access to the spirit world, coupled with a decided personal magnetism, won them the backing of the financier and Spiritualist dabbler Cornelius Vanderbilt. He backed their brokerage house, Woodhull, Claflin & Company, making the two sisters the first women on the New York Stock Exchange.[18]

Like many Spiritualists, Victoria Woodhull was an advocate of free love. Not every Spiritualist was a free lover, explained one who had been "behind the scenes" in both camps, "yet it may be said that all Free Lovers, with rare exceptions, are spiritualists."[19] The free lover and Spiritualist Thomas Nichols went even further, proclaiming that "the truth is, and it is well known to those who know anything, that the Free Love Doctrine, rightly understood, is the Great Central Doctrine of Spiritualism."[20]

Few Spiritualists would have made this strong a connection between the two movements. Indeed, nearly every Spiritualist newspaper published during the 1860s and 1870s printed heated debates on the relationship between Spiritualism and free love. According to one editorialist for the *Banner of Light* in 1862, free love "is not admitted by Spiritualism, and forms no part of, and is not connected in the least with, the philosophy developed by spiritual teachings."[21] "How the perverted term 'free love,' in any possible way became connected with Spiritualism, is to us a mystery," wrote another. "The tendency of the more spiritually minded is complete celibacy. . . . Spiritualism and perpetual chastity is the only pathway that leads into the heaven of heavens."[22]

When women wrote to join the debates, they tended to present the problem a bit differently, focusing on marriage rather than on sexuality per se. In response to a stridently anti-free-love column written by the prominent Spiritualist James M. Peebles, one woman responded, "Marriage, to most women, is little more than an honorable servitude; and those who are fitted for this situation and for nothing higher, take pride and pleasure in their housekeeping. . . . To a woman whose spirit is stirred by poetry, art, or perhaps wisdom, to which her husband has no claim, and for which he has no appreciation, obedience would be difficult."[23]

Spiritualist communities, particularly those with strong female leadership, literally married Spiritualism and free love. The 1865 Chicago Spiritualist Convention included a free-love marriage ceremony officiated by Mrs. H. F. M. Brown, which began with a sermon condemning marriage laws. Brown pleaded for the equality of wife and husband "before the law as before God," arguing that current laws robbed the wife of her child, her property, her name, and her individuality. The ritual itself concluded with the declaration "Man has no right to woman . . . by the linking of your hands we infer your hearts are already united, and that you only ask public recognition of the marriage already registered in heaven."[24] Each month, the Spiritualist *Religio-Philosophical Journal* listed couples joined in this manner. For many, this antiauthoritarian marriage meshed neatly with their spiritual beliefs.

The connection between free love and Spiritualism turned on the importance for each of a radical individualism, coupled with a sometimes-shared doctrine of "spiritual affinities." Some versions of this belief maintained that for each person there was a single spiritual mate, to be revealed either in the world beyond or through communications with spiritual messengers. Other interpretations stressed the need to find one's true spiritual mate in the present, even if that meant dissolving the earthly bonds of marriage to do so. In either version, such spiritual affinities ran counter to, and outweighed, the conventions of nineteenth-century bourgeois marriage, sanctioned by either church or state. Nineteenth-century Spiritualists dissolved their marriages with greater frequency than most of their middle-class contemporaries: Woodhull herself had three husbands and many more lovers.[25]

While often construed by the general public as untrammeled sexual license, free-love ideology, in its various manifestations, constituted an individualistic, antiauthoritarian attack on the sexual, economic, and legal inequities of marriage. These inequities included the sexual double standard for men and women as well as men's legal control over women's bodies, property, and reproductive lives. Free-love advocates, who often had ties to the abolition movement, frequently invoked comparisons between marriage and chattel slavery to emphasize—however hyperbolically—the coercive, bodily bonds of marriage.[26] As an advocate of free love, Woodhull crossed the guardians of public morality, using the press and the post to attack bourgeois marriage and expose the hypocrisies of powerful men.[27]

Woodhull used the stage at both the 1872 Spiritualist convention and that year's NWSA convention as well as her newspaper, *Woodhull & Claflin's Weekly*, to divulge Henry Ward Beecher's affair with a married parishioner, Elizabeth Tilton.[28] Beecher, one of the best-known and most highly respected ministers in the nation, was the pastor of the Plymouth Congregationalist Church in Brooklyn. A prominent Republican and antislavery advocate as well as a theologian, Beecher reached an unusually wide audience with his writings. It was noted that he "published his lectures in the weekly press almost as fast as he spoke them."[29] He also toured widely on the lecture circuit. In fact, Beecher spoke in Europe on behalf of the Union during the Civil War and has been credited with influencing Great Britain's refusal to recognize the Confederacy. He was an esteemed leader in suffragist circles and served as the figurehead president of the American Woman Suffrage Association.[30] He was also the brother of Catherine Beecher and Harriet Beecher Stowe, women who had little respect for the radical stances and putative publicity-mongering of Victoria Woodhull.

In *Woodhull & Claflin's Weekly* of November 2, 1872, Woodhull created the Beecher-Tilton scandal, charging that Reverend Henry Ward Beecher practiced free love in private while hypocritically upholding monogamous marriage in public. She did not condemn the adulterous conduct of either Beecher or Elizabeth Tilton but rather used the occasion to pillory both the eminent divine and polite society for their hypocrisy. Woodhull's exposé, which occupied eleven and a half double columns in her newspaper, took as its authority Theodore Tilton, the wronged husband. Yet Woodhull's interest was not in righting the wrongs that befell cuckolded men; she evinced little patience for Tilton, accusing him of "bogus sentimentality, pumped in his imagination, because our sickly religious literature, and Sunday school morality, and pulpit phariseeism had humbugged him all his life into the belief that he ought to feel and act in this harlequin and absurd way on such an occasion."[31]

New Yorkers grabbed for the scandal sheet, and the paper sold out almost immediately on newsstands across the city. Woodhull described the rush to her offices of readers desperate for a copy and told tales of subscribers renting their copies to others for "dollars per day."[32] In spite of the barrage of publicity, Beecher's loyal congregation at Plymouth Church ignored the accusations (at least for a while) and stood behind the right reverend. Yet the scandal dogged Beecher for the next six years, and he was eventually forced to defend himself in church hearings and a criminal trial.

The same issue of *Woodhull & Claflin's Weekly* contained two other inflammatory articles, naming—or threatening to name—additional infamous New York cads. Tennie C. Claflin threw down the gauntlet: "We know who they are and what they are, and shall not hesitate to write and publish their history so definitely that all men shall know them."[33] Claflin singled out Luther C. Challis, a Wall Street broker, who, she claimed, had seduced and deflowered a young virgin at a "French Ball" that she and her sister had attended in disguise.[34] Together the Beecher exposé and Claflin's jeremiad formed a full frontal assault on the New York elite's hypocrisy and its sexual double standard. Tennessee Claflin modestly explained the stunningly countercultural project she and her sister were undertaking: "We have tried to make 'rake' as disgraceful as 'whore.' We cannot do it. And now we are determined to take the disgrace out of whore."[35]

Woodhull's and Claflin's sensationalism placed some suffragists in a bind. Both Theodore Tilton and Henry Ward Beecher were prominent movement leaders, whereas Victoria Woodhull was something of an outside agitator. The pro-Republican, suffragist *Woman's Journal* attempted literally to bridge this ideological divide on the printed page. Its publishers, Lucy Stone and Henry Blackwell, ran a "disclaimer" of the connection between free love and Spiritualism in the issue of January 4, 1873, alongside a defense of Victoria Woodhull, which was itself printed opposite a short story by Henry Ward Beecher: a sentimental morality tale about a little girl and her doll.[36] A few prominent feminists applauded Woodhull's efforts. Paulina Wright Davis, a suffragist and historian of the women's rights movement, congratulated Woodhull on her triumph, and in particular the way she "took hold of those men whose souls are black with crimes and should be torn from their thrones of the judgement of woman's morals and made to shrink from daring to utter one word against any woman so long as they withhold justice from her."[37]

Anthony Comstock was so outraged by the public airing of sexual gossip that he used an alias to acquire a copy of the paper. He then sought a warrant for the arrest of Woodhull and Claflin, charging them under a federal statute that prohibited sending obscene literature through the U.S. mail. Marshals arrested the sisters, who spent four weeks in the Ludlow Street jail before they were tried and acquitted. The trial of the flamboyant duo provided weeks of entertainment for New York newspaper readers, but Comstock failed to get a conviction.[38] Judge Samuel Blatchford, who heard the case, instructed the jury not to convict because the postal regulation that Comstock had relied on did not apply to newspapers.[39] Comstock's new law, the national obscenity ordinance that would bear his name, was a direct result of Woodhull and Claflin's having slipped his grasp.

If Victoria Woodhull is the explicit link between Comstockery and Spiritualism, there are ultimately deeper and more telling links that brought these two movements together. As Comstock rushed to the Capitol to stop the flow of sexual information leaked by two scandalmongering women, other sexualized female bodies were creating another sensation. The summer after Comstock went to Washington, Americans in Boston and New York, and at least as far west as Michigan, were taken up with the craze of materialization séances. No longer content with the raps, knocks or levitating tables which marked the manifestation of spirits in the early years of the movement, Spiritualists of the 1870s witnessed the appearance of a spirit in bodily form rather than by auditory signs or through the voice of the medium. These séances were popular and sensational enough to warrant coverage in the tabloid press almost every week, and sometimes every day, through the summer and fall of 1874.[40] During these spiritualistic performances, mediums conjured phantasmic bodies—literally materialized spirits—that moved through the air and landed, fully formed, in the Victorian parlor. Although materializations never entirely supplanted hearing the voices of the dead, this second wave of Spiritualism can be seen as a shift from sound to vision: communication through raps, much like the telegraph, gave way to the materialization of wraithlike bodies, paralleling new developments in photography.

Figure 7. Materialization séance by flash-light, ca. 1890s. Photographer unknown, Collection of the author.

Many Americans who saw materialized spirits at séances across the country found in them a "proof palpable" of their spiritual beliefs.[41] On the twenty-fifth anniversary of Spiritualism's founding, the *New York Daily Graphic,* a Manhattan-based tabloid, heralded its growing popularity. Rebuffing critics who might have imagined Spiritualism as a short-lived "impostuture," which would "pass away as all other delusions have that have visited the world," the writer instead found growing faith in the movement: "The faith in the power of the dead to make their identity manifest to the living by means of certain physical phenomena has grown and strengthened until Spiritualists abound in every clime, and have so increased in this country that the late Judge Edmonds ventured to claim that there were eleven millions of believers avowed and unavowed here."[42]

Part of Spiritualism's ability to attract new followers, while holding the attention of the old, lay in the power of the spirits to constantly better their tricks. Materializations, in the words of one witness, "beat everything that has gone before." Materialization involved "the restoration of a spirit to flesh, blood, & bones, as in life. Sometimes the materializations are partial only, and no more than a hand, arm, or head appears. At other times, the entire form appears, stalks around the room, converses, allows itself to be felt and embraced, and vanishes into nothingness before the eyes of the amazed beholders."[43] During these séances, the medium sometimes remained in view of the audience, though she often disappeared behind a curtain or into a closed cabinet.

The first reported "full-form materialization" occurred as early as 1860 at a séance conducted by the medium Leah Fox Fish Underhill, the eldest of the Fox sisters.[44] By the 1870s, accounts of materialization séances filled the tabloid press. Having attracted a multitude of new readers to the *New York Sun* with his first round of coverage, the peripatetic New York attorney Colonel Henry Steel Olcott was engaged by the *Daily Graphic* to cover the materialization séance beat. Prominent among his stories were the Eddy family's materializations in Chittenden, Vermont, which were attracting pilgrims from all over the world. The Spiritualist Jesse Shepard wrote in his memoirs of arriving from Europe and being invited by two friends, one from New York, the other from Houston, to accompany them to the Green Mountains of Vermont. When the train arrived in Chittenden, he recalls "a carry-all waiting to take us into the mountains. Then we began a slow ascent from the hum-drum old town to a region of medieval magic and hocus-pocus never depicted in the mysterical pages of Edgar Poe or the opium dreams of Thomas DeQuincey." Although Shepard and his fellow Spiritualists were unimpressed by the Eddy brothers' performance—"the boarders," he joked, "were plainly bored"—Shepard was struck by another visiting spiritual pilgrim, Helena Petrovna Blavatsky. Blavatsky, whom Shepard termed "the being with the cold, steely eyes," then "fixed her mesmeric gaze on the unsuspecting Colonel [Olcott], and with one swift gesture closed her hypnotic tentacles on the personality of the man who had neither the time nor the wit to realize what was happening. Then and there the hieroglyphs of Modern Theosophy were written as by an invisible hand on the scroll of the mystical future."[45] A year later, Henry Steel Olcott and Madame Blavatsky founded the Theosophical Society out of their shared investigations.[46]

To at least some, a materialization séance's appeal was the thrill of being literally touched by a spirit. The Spiritualist writer and editor Mary Dana Shindler recalled being drawn to materialization séances, attending again and again just to feel "those singular touches." She wrote in her autobiography: "Wishing to feel once more those singular touches of fingers which were certainly neither mine nor the medium's, I visited Mrs. D. the morning after the séance at Mrs. Boothby's. Again those mysterious touches thrilled through my soul."[47]

Indeed, in the darkened room of a séance circle, spirits could be seductive. A report from an 1868 materialization emphasized the erotics of spiritual intercourse: "The spirit beckons to someone; and . . . presently shows that a young man is wanted who goes forward nearly to the curtain and is whispered to, embraced, and very audibly kissed; and the spirit then goes back behind the curtain, but reappears again for a moment to exchange some more kisses. Then a similar performance is gone through with another sitter, a young woman, who is so excited that she nearly faints away, the kissing being very animated and prolonged."[48] The séance offered the possibility of multiple boundary crossings: As easily as a spirit could move back and forth through the barrier of the curtain, a young man could receive public kisses, and a woman attract enough "animated" attention that she nearly fainted away. Both propriety and traditional gender dichotomies dissolved in the dark as spirits bestowed their touch on willing men and women alike. Part of the allure of this form of spiritual contact was physical contact itself.

The most captivating spirit of the era was Katie King. In 1874, the *Daily Graphic* charted "the return" of a lovely and diaphanously clad female phantom who had previously charmed a host of London Spiritualists. Katie and her father, John King, the ghost of a dead swashbuckler, had made appearances at a number of British séances and were mainstays at the materializations held by the Holmeses of Philadelphia and Florence Cook, the mediumistic doyenne of London's East End.[49]

Katie King arrived in Philadelphia, fresh from her tour of Europe, "without the aid of a steamer . . . in order to delight Philadelphians who prefer spiritual to real women."⁵⁰ At a moment in history when middle-class white women in the United States were becoming less associated with the spiritual values of the vaunted cult of true womanhood, who better to take that mythic spiritual place than a ghostly translucently white woman who was, herself, a spirit? As real women found new sites of public power and stretched the boundaries of bourgeois propriety, they also highlighted the supernatural status of true womanhood itself, bringing it into focus as both an ideal and as something unreachable by ordinary means.

Katie King was a source of endless fascination to East Coast newspaper readers. The *Daily Graphic* featured daily, often illustrated, coverage, complete with eyewitness accounts of her sightings. One witness provided this account: "On the evening of the 9th of May, Katie King led me, at my own request, into the room with her beyond the curtains, which was not so dark that I could not distinguish surrounding objects, and then made me kneel down by [the medium]'s prostrate form and feel her hands and face . . . [while Katie] held my other hand in hers and leaned against my shoulder, with one arm round my neck. I have not the slightest doubt that upon that occasion there was present with me two living, breathing intelligences perfectly distinct from each other. . . . If Katie King who grasped and embraced and spoke to me, is a projection of thought only—a will-power, an instance of unknown force—then it will no longer be possible to know who's who in 1874, and we should hesitate to turn up the gaslight lest half our friends should be mere projections and melt away beneath its glare."⁵¹

Spirits like Katie King and, indeed, Spiritualism as a practice toyed with a number of telling nineteenth-century cultural anxieties. As historians have argued, middle-class Americans at midcentury were becoming increasingly ill at ease in a new urban culture.⁵² In such a setting, where individuals were surrounded by strangers and class differences were often difficult to read, the fear of not knowing "who's who" transcended the séance circle. The shadowy borders between classes of people, between public and private, between the living and the dead, could no longer be illuminated by gaslight.

Before her 1874 U.S. tour, Katie King had been embroiled in two controversies which turned on whether she was a spirit or a Spiritualist in disguise. In London in December 1873, during one of her appearances at the séances of the famed British medium Florence Cook, Katie was "grabbed" by a Mr. Volckman, who became convinced that the ghost and the medium were one and the same. Volckman wrote an exposing letter to the Spiritualist newspaper *The Medium and Daybreak*. Prominent supporters came to Katie's aid, among them the scientist William Crookes (who discovered the element thallium, an essential chemical for the later development of the cathode ray tube, and went on to head the British Royal Society).[53] This esteemed scientist attested to the authenticity of the specter after a number of public tests in which Crookes photographed her during materialization séances. While Florence Cook was collapsed on the floor inside a closed cabinet, Crookes took photographs of the spirit Katie both to prove her existence and to disprove that she and Cook were the same person. Whether or not they persuaded nonbelievers (Katie and Florence had remarkable physical similarities), the photographs were widely reprinted at the time, and Crookes's scientific reputation convinced many of their veracity.[54] However, Crookes himself found photography an inadequate medium for capturing Katie's allure. He wrote: "Photography is as inadequate to depict the perfect beauty of Katie's face, as words are powerless to describe her charms of manner. Photography may indeed give a map of her countenance; but how can it reproduce the brilliant purity of her complexion, or the ever varying expression of her most mobile features?"[55]

Despite, or perhaps because of, her allure, scandal followed Katie King across the Atlantic. A little over a year later, the utopian socialist Robert Dale Owen, who had himself been duly charmed and convinced by Katie King at séances held by the Holmeses in Philadelphia, met the woman who had impersonated the spirit Katie. She came forward and offered apologies to Owen. Unfortunately, he had already attested to the spirit's authenticity in an article for the *Atlantic Monthly*. Its editor, William Dean Howells, ran the piece with the postconfession disclaimer, and Owen's children had him temporarily committed to an insane asylum.[56]

Although one might expect that the exposure of such a high-profile specter would spell the end of materializations, Spiritualists had always battled accusations of fraud. Another deceptive medium would not taint the honorable whole; indeed, exposés often had the effect of buttressing the reputation of principled mediums rather than discrediting them all. As self-styled investigators, Spiritualists prided themselves on their skeptical gaze; hence the attraction for scientists like Crookes. Yet quizzical doubt did not simply vanquish belief. Even in a culture wary of hoaxes and humbugs, in which materializations looked to some like "rank fraud," for many nineteenth-century Americans, seeing was still believing.[57]

The fundamental appeal of materializations was the physical proof they provided of the existence of the departed. The fact that the medium and the ghost could be felt and experienced as "two, living, breathing intelligences" offered evidence that spirits moved among the living. Spiritualists prided themselves on the modernity and rationality of their religion. Its appeal to factual evidence and its reliance on the production of positive knowledge of spirit life represented a uniquely nineteenth-century modernization of post-Calvinist Protestantism updated with the methodologies of natural science. This reliance on evidence linked Spiritualism to positive science at a point in history when the magical and the technological were often seen as one and the same. New technologies were often greeted with a sense of wonder; mysterious science produced spectacular magic. In turn, Spiritualists relied on the language of science to endow their revelations with the authority of recent inventions and called on scientists to attest to spiritual phenomena. Crookes was not alone in acting as an investigator and, eventually, a Spiritualist spokesman. Materializations, one Spiritualist wrote, "have been thoroughly investigated and demonstrated by Prof. Wallace, Prof. Crooks [sic], Col. Olcott, Epes Sargent, and thousands of the best informed persons of our day. No phenomenal fact of the manifestations of Modern Spiritualism is better attested than that of the materialization of spirit forms."[58]

Spiritual investigators similarly relied on photography as a technological support for a new positivism. Photographs, which captured images of the material world on a chemically treated plate, could provide uniquely scientific evidence of the existence of spirits.[59] At the same time, from the earliest years of the new technology, photography was associated with magic and even necromancy. At least metaphorically, the photograph was a form of technology that could stop time and confer a form of immortality by which the living could be held indefinitely before the eye. The *Daguerreian Journal* reported an incident from 1851 that reveals the extent of the association between photography and magic: "A lady and gentleman called in, and wished to be 'Daguerrotyped together.' When our arrangements were made, and they were about to 'take a seat,' the lady remarked, that she had lost a child about three months previous, and desired me to take them with her child upon her lap."[60]

The notion that a photographer could image the dead or insert a ghost into the family portrait was probably not widely held. However, those who first experienced the daguerreotype repeatedly characterized it as magical, perhaps even more magical than the conjuring of spirits. The poet Elizabeth Barrett Browning wrote in 1843 that the "Mesmeric disembodiment of spirits strikes one as a degree less marvelous" than imaging and imagining "a man sitting down in the sun and leaving his facsimile in all its full completion of outline and shadow, steadfast on a plate, at the end of a minute and a half."[61]

Figure 8. Portrait of Katie King, 1874. Albumen silver print. Courtesy Keith de Lellis Gallery, New York. From the original plate with handwritten inscription by William Crookes.

Figure 9. Portrait of William Crookes and Katie King, 1874. Albumen silver print. Courtesy Keith de Lellis Gallery, New York. The inscription reads: "Around her she made an atmosphere of life; the very air seemed lighter from her eyes. They were so soft and beautiful, and rife with all we can imagine of the skies; her overpowering presence makes you feel it would not be idolatry to kneel."

Photographers soon realized that their medium could produce a range of marvelous results. A whispery, ghostlike figure would appear if a subject moved during the long period necessary for an exposure. A double exposure could produce a spirit double in a traditional photographic portrait. One writer, describing the wonders of this new invention, advised his readers that "for the purposes of amusement the photographer might carry us even into the realm of the supernatural," as it was possible to give a spectral appearance to figures and to exhibit them as "'thin air' amid the solid realities of the . . . picture."[62] Before these magical effects and manipulations of photographic processing became widely understood, Spiritualists turned to the camera for evidence of the other world.

William H. Mumler is considered the first, and is without question the best-known, nineteenth-century spirit photographer (see figures 2, 5, 6, and 10). Beginning his career as an engraver for a Boston jewelry firm, Mumler announced in 1861 that he had not only made a successful photograph of a spirit but had been able to obtain repeatable results. Clients began to pour in. Aided by his clairvoyant wife, Hannah, Mumler opened himself not only to the spirit world but also to the capitalist market. He became so successful that he moved his business to New York, opening a studio on lower Broadway. The procedure for spirit photography was not substantially different from a normal portrait sitting: the person desiring a photograph of a deceased friend or relative simply posed as if for his or her own picture. The spirit "extra," as it was called, did not appear in the studio but was visible in the negative and the subsequent print. Mumler charged ten dollars for his service, roughly five times the going rate for a standard photographic portrait.[63]

In 1869, Mumler was arrested and charged with two felonies and one misdemeanor for public fraud, larceny, and obtaining money under false pretenses. The press followed his trial closely.[64] Objective experts, including photographers who could attest to studio practices, were called to testify alongside Spiritualist believers like Judge Edmonds, who stated to the court that he believed that "the camera can take the photograph of a spirit, and I believe also that spirits have a materiality . . . enough to be visible to the human eye, for I have seen them."[65] The testimony from numerous Spiritualists, including prominent New Yorkers who lent their social and professional respectability to the cause, contributed to Mumler's defense. As an expert on hoaxes and humbugs, P. T. Barnum fittingly appeared as a witness for the prosecution. In the end, the judge found in favor of Mumler, ruling that the prosecution had "failed to make out the case." The verdict was reported under the headline "The Triumph of the Ghosts."[66]

The case of Mumler demonstrates more than a charlatan taking advantage of a new technology. The advent of the daguerreotype and photograph both troubled and titillated nineteenth-century Americans. More important, it moved them. So great was Americans' belief in the transporting power of the photograph that Mumler encouraged clients to send him pictures of themselves to serve as surrogates if they were unable to come in person for sittings. Among his most affecting works are those in which a spirit appears next to a photograph of an absent client. Many commentators have noted the imbrication of death and photography, the camera's seemingly uncanny ability to preserve an image of the lost in an unparalleled mimesis. Inasmuch as a photograph functioned as a copy of the real, the materialized spirit was also received as a kind of copy or spirit double.

A method for making a direct positive image on a silver plate was announced in 1839 by a French painter named Louis Jacques Mande Daguerre. He gave his name to the process, enraging the British scientist William Henry Fox Talbot, who had been simultaneously working on this technology. In 1847, the introduction of the glass-plate process, involving a single negative from which innumerable positive copies could be printed on paper, fundamentally transformed the nature of the photographic image. The notion that a copy could trouble the original ran through a number of stories that appeared in the American popular press beginning at midcentury. These tales revolved around an unruly copy, typically a daguerreotype or photograph, depicted as the technological embodiment of absolute lifelikeness.[67] In these narratives, the photograph acted as a character, an embodied double or ideal other of a human character. In "The Inconstant Daguerreotype," a short story published in *Harper's*, a woman becomes enamored of her lover's portrait, eventually leaving him for his image. In a similar plot from *The Daguerreotype Miniature*, an 1846 novel by Augustine Duganne, a daguerreotype saves the hero's life, only to steal his girl.[68] Running through these stories was the fear that a dangerous technological double could compete for the status of the original and displace the real thing. In these narratives, the double has a unique ability to disrupt an ordinary, heterosexual love plot. In this sense, the copy encodes a certain kind of sexual transgression, troubling marriages and redirecting female desire in inappropriate directions.

Perhaps this anxiety about doubles accounts for Anthony Comstock's otherwise puzzling concern with the mischief caused not only by pornographic photographs but also by artistic reproductions of all kinds. Among the themes to which Comstock repeatedly returned in his writing was what he referred to as "artistic traps," artworks that were obscene precisely because

Figure 10. "Mr. Chapin oil merchant—& his spirit wife & babe recognized," ca. 1861. William H. Mumler (photographer, American, 1832–84, active Boston, Massachusetts). Catalog no. 84.XD.760.1.3. The J. Paul Getty Museum, Los Angeles. When clients were unable to come in person to his studio, Mumler asked that they send photographs of themselves to be photographed. A framed picture of Mr. Chapin is on the table at left, pictured with his dead "spirit wife and babe," whom he recognized in this print.

they were reproductions rather than originals. In *Morals versus Art*, published in 1887, Comstock distinguished between original works of art, which he claimed to hold in high esteem, and their copies, which he saw as capable of mischief. After raiding Herman Knoedler's gallery in New York, Comstock explained that his project was to suppress "not French art, but . . . cheap lewd French photographs."[69] Comstock had first broached this topic four years earlier in his book *Traps for the Young*, presenting a bizarre argument that "art," presumably painting, imparts beauty, whereas photography "unmasks" this beauty in the copy. Comstock elaborated: "So with a work of art as compared to a copy; in the first there are things which call for a division of attention; the artist has spent much time to bring his picture to perfection. The lines of beauty, the mingling of colors, tintings, and shadings, all seem to clothe the figures by diverting attention from that which, if taken alone, is objectionable, with a surrounding which protects its offensive character. In other words, that which, if taken alone, is offensive to good morals, is unmasked in the copy."[70]

Comstock's distinction between high and low art involved the oft-repeated distinction between true artistry, which involved human craft, and photography, which merely employed a technological process wherein the hand of the artist presumably exerted no role. However, Comstock's concerns moved beyond slippery distinctions between art and mechanical reproduction and revealed themselves to be, at base, a fear of the masses. High art, unlike mass-produced photography, could remain safely in the sacred spaces of museums or elite homes. A photograph, by contrast, might be bought and sold to anybody. It could appear before untutored eyes, which might see in a nude not a masterful painterly representation but something more akin to a naked body. Photographic copies could move out of upper-class hands and circulate in public. For Comstock, this possibility conjured new dangers.

Walter Benjamin, writing over a half century later, found radically democratic possibilities in the very phenomenon that Comstock feared. The work of art in the age of mechanical reproduction would "put the copy of the original into situations which would be out of reach for the original itself." It would enable "the original to meet the beholder halfway, be it in the form of a photograph or phonograph record. The cathedral leaves its locale to be received in the studio of a lover of art; the choral production, performed in an auditorium or in the open air, resounds in the drawing room."[71] Mass-produced art would forever alter the sacred spaces of high culture. Freed from the spatial locations of privilege, the reproduced art object would be available to all and, in Benjamin's words, "reactivated."

To Comstock, photographs were menacing precisely because they were public. To avoid seeming the complete Philistine, he defended the art of museum lovers, but he fervently distinguished this brand of art from the street traffic in photography, writing: "If we must have 'works of art' that are shocking to modesty, or offensive to decency," the public should be protected by "restricting those products to the galleries of art, and not permitting counterfeits of the vile in them to be disseminated indiscriminately before the public."[72]

Like the "lewd" photographs Comstock so assiduously confiscated, Katie King was a copy both more compelling and more troublesome than the real thing.[73] She was the ideal woman who ghosted the real, and as a copy, she stirred up trouble that the original could not. If the division between public and private was always a construct designed to falter, Spiritualism reveals the parlor wall as something more akin to a trick door.[74] The ghostly creatures conjured at materialization séances could traverse the shadowy wall separating public and private and protecting the bourgeois home from the dangers beyond. Materializations provided proof to believers of the existence of spirits, but they also worked to dissolve boundaries between this world and the next, between the domestic spirit circle and the public world of strangers. Even if the actual presence of ethereal bodies was suspect, this cultural phenomenon created a community of worldly bodies willing to engage in a kind of haptic contact in the darkened séance room.

Comstockery was structured by the fear of (and fascination with) sexualized information and images traveling out of cities, spreading into the hinterlands and across state lines, and bringing a contaminated public culture into the sanctity of the private sphere. Moral reformers like Comstock battled to keep the vices of the streets at a remove from "proper" homes at a moment when those homes were seen as needing protection. Despite his single-minded zealotry, Comstock was not alone in his campaign against obscenity. The term *Comstockery* lends undue importance to the influence of one man: the Comstock Law passed only because legislators sensed that there were constituencies that would back moral-purity campaigns. The New York Society for the Suppression of Vice included some of the city's most prominent citizens: the philanthropist Morris K. Jesup, a founder of the Young Men's Christian Association of New York, who also went on to found the Museum of Natural History; the soap heir Samuel Colgate; and the millionaire banker J. P. Morgan.[75] Comstock's warm reception in Washington was made possible through these wealthy men's connections with politicians such as the Republican congressman Clinton L. Merriam of New York, who shepherded what would soon be termed the Comstock Law through Congress.

The antivice movement also extended beyond Comstock's circles in New York, claiming a national appeal. Cincinnati had its own Western Society for the Suppression of Vice, modeled on New York's association, as did St. Louis, Chicago, Louisville, and San Francisco. Boston had a comparable group of vice fighters in the Watch and Ward Society, with a number of prominent Congregationalist ministers rounding out the group of Anglo-American bank presidents and businessmen. Middle-class white women swelled the ranks of a related array of grassroots antivice campaigns. All were part of a larger reform movement, sometimes termed the "social purity" movement, which coalesced in the United States in the decades following the Civil War.[76]

Beginning in the 1860s, in a multitude of local campaigns, reformers attempted to protect the nations' private homes by policing the public sphere. Thus temperance advocates urged controls on establishments serving liquor in order to keep husbands and fathers from bringing their drunken vices home to wives and children. In a parallel logic, reformers, including many nineteenth-century feminists, fought the physical and moral "contamination" of and by prostitutes with the argument that disease contracted in public would eventually infect the family. Accordingly, middle-class women and children needed protection from male vice.[77] The influence of these moral-reform movements led to widespread changes in American society in the postwar years, including a new policing of urban vice districts and restrictions on taverns and liquor licensing. Additionally, a number of states passed obscenity statutes that policed the expressions of sexual dissidents. By 1885, twenty-four state legislatures had passed "little Comstock Laws" modeled on the federal statute or on a more stringent New York obscenity law passed shortly after the federal one.[78]

Antiobscenity campaigns are relatively recent phenomena. Until the middle of the nineteenth century, neither Great Britain nor the United States had laws or legal precedents banning sexually explicit images or texts. An eighteenth-century English vagrancy statute enforced in a few colonies punished "obscene exhibitions," and three New England states legislated against the circulation of "indecent prints and books." In these statutes, however, indecency was never defined and was typically equated or elided with blasphemy. Eighteenth-century courts tended to prosecute the indecent or blasphemous behavior of individuals, rather than the purveyors of texts or images that represented such behavior. Common-law cases involved prosecutions for blasphemy, lewd behavior, or indecent exposure. Cases were prosecuted under juridical categories like breaches of the peace, or "public wrongs," in Blackstone's formulation, rather than under obscenity proscriptions.[79]

In the first decades of the nineteenth century, American legislatures began to shift from circumscribing sexual acts to banning representations of them as a means of controlling behavior.[80] The logic behind this move was that, in the wrong hands, such representations might lead to—or actually produce—illicit sexual acts. In part, this view reflected a fear of the uncontrollable impulses of a newly literate working class. Universal free education dramatically increased literacy in the United States. This fact, combined with the boom in partisan and commercial presses beginning in the 1830s, and the rise of the "penny press" a decade or so later, created a new reading public consisting of large numbers of workers and, crucially, women and children.[81]

The growth of literacy was met with a network of new obscenity laws. In 1821, the year that the country's first public school was established in Boston, the Commonwealth of Massachusetts initiated the first American case of prosecution of the publisher of an "obscene" book, *Fanny Hill; Or, Memoirs of a Woman of Pleasure.*[82] In the same year, Vermont enacted the country's first antiobscenity law. Connecticut passed a similar statute in 1834, and Massachusetts followed in 1836.[83] An older tariff law, enforced through the customs service, prohibited the importation of foreign obscene material into the United States. However, advances in printing and photographic technology, combined with the mobilization of thousands of young men during the Civil War, produced the first significant supply of and demand for domestic pornography, as well as pressure on legislatures to close the mails to such material. The earliest federal legislation criminalizing the use of the mails to transport obscene material (described as "a book, pamphlet, picture print or other publication . . . of a vulgar and indecent character") was passed in 1865 explicitly to protect soldiers. The United States Christian Commission, a YMCA-affiliated evangelical organization ministering to Union fighters, crafted a provision in the Postal Act of 1865 to shield soldiers from sexual materials sent through the U.S. mail.[84]

In 1866, more than a decade before Anthony Comstock joined the fray, the New York YMCA became concerned with the supposed depravity of clerks.[85] These junior employees in New York's rapidly expanding mercantile world constituted a new bachelor subculture.[86] Typically living outside the protection and purview of families, many of these men, like Comstock himself, had come of age during the Civil War. Whether working as lonely clerks or serving as soldiers away from home, some had developed a taste for prostitution and pornography. Comstock claimed that New York boasted a teeming market in "vile newspapers" and "licentious books," which any resourceful young man could purchase cheaply.[87] Reformers crafted organizations and legislation to fight this supposed tide of pornography. Indeed, legislation much like Comstock's own had already been introduced in Congress by the secretary of the YMCA in Washington, DC.[88]

This activism was a response to a new geography of circulation of sexuality in the public sphere. In the eighteenth century, an older libertine tradition had accorded—at least to upper-class white men—some license for the public discussion of sex. Mid-nineteenth-century urban sexual culture, by contrast, included women as well as men, and the respectably genteel as well as the rakish.[89] Similarly, while there was nothing new about saloons, brothels, or even small purveyors of racy books and drawings, these establishments had traditionally been confined to vice districts in a few large American cities. Economic and technological developments after the Civil War created faster and more efficient means of distributing sexually explicit material. Mail order could bring the wares of the vice districts of New York into any unsuspecting small town through the magical, national workings of the U.S. Postal Service.[90]

There was nothing accidental about the Comstock Law's focus on the mail. A national interest in obscenity prohibition called for a national means of control. Because the mail transported goods and information across state lines, it represented an ideal target for reformers interested in constructing a unified national culture in the decade following the Civil War. Concentrating on the mail offered both federal policing powers and a new terrain of control.[91]

The mail service represented a liminal space between the public and the private spheres. Of course, bookstores, newsstands, and brothels were still subject to older, more direct forms of policing.[92] Indeed, moral-purity campaigners sought increasing control of the defiled public sphere to prevent it from seeping into the private. But Comstock was convinced that the mail was a unique conduit. In his reports to the New York Society for the Suppression of Vice, he argued that "the mails of the United States have been the channel above all others through which hundreds of thousands of insidious and corrupt publications have gone out to schools, seminaries, male and female colleges and the homes of our land."[93] Comstock saw the mails as at once "great arteries of communication—mighty thoroughfares leading up to all our homes and institutions of learning" and a dangerously clandestine passage, which "goes everywhere and is secret." In keeping with Comstock's metaphors for obscenity, the mail is figured here as an avenue of both secrecy and vulgar public display.

The passage of the Comstock Law marked the power and effect of a national moral panic. Following the fracture of the Civil War, vice fighting was a goal that many middle-class reformers could agree on as crucial to establishing a shared national culture. The year 1873, when Comstock went to Washington, is perhaps better known to historians for the onset of the worst industrial depression the country had ever seen. Reconstruction was waning, and at least some middle-class Americans saw vice as a more tractable problem than economic crises, class conflict, or race relations. Fighting vice could produce safe streets and clean consciences for middle-class reformers. During the obscenity trial of the free-love advocate D. M. Bennett, the prosecuting district attorney pontificated: "This case is not entitled 'Anthony Comstock against D. M. Bennett'; this case is not entitled 'The Society for the Suppression of Vice Against D. M. Bennett.' . . . It is the United States against D. M. Bennett, and the United States is one great society for the suppression of vice."[94]

Comstockery is typically understood as a panic about the spread of sexualized texts and images. Indeed, the urge to control information about sexuality, especially concerning contraception and abortion and other representations of nonreproductive sexuality, was central to it. However, the linkages between Spiritualism and Comstockery elucidate a logic of displacement. Fear of actual bodies—overtly sexual feminists and vice peddlers of all kinds—was displaced onto the channels through which information travels. The way into the home for sexualized bodies (at least the ones that were not materialized spirits) was through the mail.

Prior to Comstockery, the only other time that the U.S. mail became a battleground in a national panic was during the height of the abolitionist movement. An 1810 law made it illegal for African Americans to carry the U.S. mail, presumably because they could also carry news of revolts. During the 1830s, as the antislavery movement gained strength, Southern politicians moved to block the circulation of antislavery tracts and appealed to Congress to police the mail to do so. In 1835, after a midnight break-in at the Charleston, South Carolina, post office, a local mob set fire to a sack of abolitionist publications as an enthusiastic and supportive crowd of the city's finest citizens looked on. The fear of seditious publications was intimately related to fears of the movement of actual bodies: the mail could transmit dangerous ideas, but it could also provide a passage for dangerous bodies. The Virginia slave Henry "Box" Brown, as if fulfilling the possibility embodied in that fear, mailed himself in a box from Richmond to Philadelphia, securing his freedom when he arrived in the offices of an abolitionist organization.[95] Brown later made a career of reenacting his confinement and liberation from the very same box on stages on both sides of the Atlantic. According to Daphne

A. Brooks, his spectacular performances of freedom anticipated and increasingly mirrored the use of cabinets and enclosed spaces in materialization séances. By the end of his career, "the magic of his boxing seemed to have transmogrified into full-blown spiritualist demonstration."[96]

Perhaps the most crucial link between Spiritualism and Comstockery, and one elucidated by the 1830s race panic, is the way in which fear symbolically transformed ideas into bodies. The anxieties structuring Comstockery slid from the circulation of information to the ability of troubling bodies to penetrate supposedly separate spheres, thereby finding new sources of power. Policing the mail became a way to ward off public vices and to protect white women and children from pornography peddlers, free-love feminists, and the "vile and depraved" of the streets.[97] Like the spirits who floated through walls in the summer of 1874, the public mails were, in the words of a Massachusetts judge who upheld that state's "little Comstock Law," the "flow" that could "override the barrier that protects the home, and reach to the young girls sheltered there."[98] But, more than that, as this judge elaborated, the mail was the means for what he referred to as "the lechers of the street" to enter the home. Contrasting the filth of the streets with the sanctity of the home, the judge argued for a strengthened obscenity law:

> The moral worth of every community rests with the family. . . . It is there that the youth are taught [that] honesty and virtue are above price. It is there that the girls in the innocence and purity of their youth, are nurtured and guarded against the wiles and intrigues of the wicked and the seducer. If they may be approached and insulted on the streets with impunity by the vile and depraved, or if the same class may . . . through the public mails, by letters sent to them which teach, or attempt to teach, them that voluptuousness is more to be desired than true womanhood, and that virtue better be exchanged for sexual dissipation, then indeed, there is a crying necessity for further legislation.[99]

Protecting the bourgeois home is typically reformers' first line of defense in times of moral panic. Comstock inaugurated the national campaigns against obscenity and led the way for a long line of smut hunters who similarly mobilized the language of child protection. In the pages of the New York vice society report, he railed: "If we had the ear of all the teachers, parents, and guardians in our land we would plead with them, 'Guard with ceaseless vigilance your libraries, your closets, your children's and wards' correspondence and companionships, lest the contagion reach and blight the sweetness and purity of your homes."[100]

This national fear of bodies that can penetrate the home through the mail and through the air continues. New technologies are met with new restrictions. Many Americans worry that child molesters will infiltrate their homes over the Internet, materializing from AOL chat rooms into children's bedrooms. And again we find Americans in dimly lit rooms, communing with other spirits and bodies, this time in front of a flickering computer screen. This "public sex" occurs, as did the "singular touches" of materialization séances, in private, suggesting that the real dangers have been in the home all along.

Just as nineteenth-century moral reformers sought to protect the middle-class home from vice, and found in Spiritualism a fitting target for their project, another group of professionals built their careers battling this new religious practice and social movement. Beginning as early as the 1840s and culminating, like Comstockery, in the 1870s, medical doctors discovered in mediums new symptoms of a social disease.

FOUR

Mediomania

The Spirit of Science in a Culture of Belief and Doubt

One year after the first raps were heard in Hydesville, the spirits requested through the Fox sisters that Rochester's largest hall be rented for three consecutive nights, specifying that members of the public be charged seventy-five cents each to witness the girls' mediumship. On November 14, 1849, four hundred people filled Corinthian Hall, gazing at the raised stage framed by the majestic columns that gave the building its name. The well-known abolitionist Amy Post, who had taken the Fox sisters into her home in Rochester, sat nearby to lend both moral support and the respectability conferred by her age and station. Eliab W. Capron, a Quaker lawyer from nearby Auburn, New York, had been chosen to address the crowd as to the meaning of the messages. The gathering surely included mourners and believers, as well as debunkers and plain curiosity seekers, eager either to hear the Fox sisters' spirit communications or to witness their failure.[1]

The "long address" by Capron, as a reporter from the *Auburn Daily Advertiser* described it, "contained much abstract truth and but little that related to the business that had called the audience together." By contrast, this reporter—like the rest of the audience—was quite taken with the two stars of the show. "Yes," he attested, "the "knocking' commenced forthwith, and continued during the entire evening, to the great astonishment of those who had gone hither, with gaping ears to catch the mysterious sounds."[2] Yet for many in attendance, hearing was not equivalent to believing. The assembly appointed a committee of skeptics to investigate and report back to the group on the following night. The committee duly announced that they had heard the raps, and that although the answers to audience questions were "not altogether right nor altogether wrong," they were unable to discover any fraud or trick by which the girls produced the noises. They confirmed that "these raps came on walls and doors some distance from the girls, causing a sensible vibration" and admitted that the committee "entirely failed to find any means by which it could be done."[3] That evening's crowd demanded a new committee of skeptics.

Although Kate and her sister Maggie were the two Fox sisters made famous by their channeling of a restless spirit in Hydesville, it was Maggie and her older sister Leah Fox Fish (later Underhill) who appeared at Corinthian Hall. With a lawyer present for certification and a doctor's stethoscope aimed at the girls' heads, hands, and feet, and at the floor, the second committee concluded that "the sounds were heard, and thorough investigation had conclusively shown them to be produced neither by machinery nor ventriloquism."[4] Again, when the committee reported their conclusions to the newly assembled crowd, the latter demanded a new group of avowed skeptics. This third group included one man who "vowed that if he could not find the trick he would throw himself over the falls of the Genesee River."[5]

For reasons of decorum, the river jumper was not privy to the third investigation, which was conducted by a group referred to as the Ladies Committee.[6] The ladies of Rochester searched the clothes, shoes, and undergarments of the mediums. On the hypothesis that electricity might have something to do with the magic, they undressed the girls and had them stand on pillows, on sheets of glass, and in bare feet to see whether electrical currents might pass more freely through these substances. The committee bound the girls' ankles, tied and untied their arms, and announced that, in all of these states, "we all heard the rapping on the wall and floor."[7] No trick could be found, and the group produced a certificate attesting to their findings. The sincerity literally embodied by the mediums exempted them from verbal interrogation. Yet if the girls were seen as too innocent to defraud the public through speech, their bodies were not beyond scrutiny.

The communal body search performed on the Fox sisters fixed a moment in the history of public interest in female mediums. More important than confirming the truth claims of the mediums themselves was the egalitarian confirmation of the investigators' own powers of perception. Except for a Dr. Langworthy, who provided the stethoscope to rule out charges of ventriloquism, the citizens who tested Maggie and Leah Fox for signs of fraud made no claims to expert knowledge. The people of Rochester, like the people of Hydesville who witnessed the first spirit raps, believed implicitly in their own authority and innate abilities of observation and verification.[8] If the naked-eye science of Rochester's investigating citizens had failed to find any trickery, it was not for lack of trying.

Although native-born, rural white girls like the Fox sisters would have seemed unlikely hucksters to their contemporaries, Americans were becoming increasingly watchful of suspected hoaxes. As the historians Karen Halttunen and Ann Fabian have argued, the figures of the huckster, the gambler, and especially the confidence man ran through antebellum literature as warnings of the dangers of men who might deceive the unaware in this new world of strangers.[9] The penny press and widely circulating dime novels told tales of unsuspecting youths led astray by shady urban characters—men who might cheat them out of money and women who would taint their virtue. Advice manuals warned middle-class Americans of the dangers of hypocrisy, regulating class and gender by prescribing a culture of sincerity and conscious social marking, as seen in the era's mourning culture.

The confidence man, whose skill lay in artifice and deception, stood in stark contrast to the woman of sensibility who was seen as constitutionally incapable of disguising her true feelings. Middle-class white women were thought to be creatures of the heart, acting from felt emotion; they stood as the antithesis of white middle-class men, figured as paragons of mind and reason. An unscrupulous man could betray his birthright by deceiving through false appearance, but the woman of sensibility could not help but express her true feelings through fainting, illness, trances, ecstasies, and tears. The public reaction to the Fox sisters was governed by the expectation that, as with other middle-class white women, their transparency of emotion would make outright deceit unthinkable. At the same time, the public demonstration of their spirit channeling took place in a world in which hoaxes and humbug abounded.[10]

The occasion of the Fox sisters being poked and prodded by groups of curious laypeople marks the spectacular debut of the movement that would come to be known as Modern American Spiritualism. Yet it also anticipates the dime museums and freak shows of P. T. Barnum and Robert L. Ripley, whose patented phrase "Believe it or Not" encapsulated the commodification of "wonder" and the term's double evocation of skepticism and delighted mystification. In fact, Barnum later featured the Fox sisters as one of the sideshows in his burgeoning business.[11] More than indicating the overlap of religion and entertainment incumbent to this era, the sisters' careers also delineated a less obvious convergence of science and magic. That a dissipated and broke Maggie Fox went on tour almost forty years later to debunk Spiritualism, by admitting to the very manipulations of bone and joint of which doctors had earlier accused her and her sisters, does not confirm the triumph of science over superstition.[12] Indeed, Maggie Fox later recanted her own admissions of trickery. Throughout the history of the public's willingness to indulge the Foxes, science and magic were intertwined and equally manipulable discourses.

Spiritualism complicates the relationships among confidence, wonder, and skepticism that nineteenth-century Americans brought to the imbricated cultures of medicine, religion, and spectacle. This chapter resists the reductive dichotomies between science and religion, mediumship and madness, men of medicine and women of the spirit that often attend histories of religion and secularism in the nineteenth-century United States. Rather, it examines unique manifestations arising out of a triangular relation between gendered somatic experience, the professionalization of science, and emergent religious discourses. The scenes of egalitarian examinations attending the Fox sisters at their home in Hydesville and later at Corinthian Hall gave rise to Spiritualism's ethos of democratic skepticism and its radical redefinition of the congregant as "spiritual investigator." The disparate currents of authority circulating around the bodies of mediums and the voices of the dead reveal a transitional period in the history of science and religion.

Rather than thrive in spite of a mounting scientific secularism, Spiritualism would bridge the gap between the dying dogmatism of institutional Protestantism and incipient technologies of modern knowledge. Yet doctors and mediums would compete for this terrain in distinctly gendered modes. The production of scientific expertise offered a system for understanding and explaining the world in terms of the body and a material universe stripped of older theological and metaphysical cosmologies. Doctors' midcentury preoccupation with the relationship between mind and body, and between perversity and normality, defined both disease and the parameters of their own authority.[13] Nineteenth-century "heroic" medicine produced bodily changes in the patient through treatments like bloodletting and laxative purges, treatments which were often at least as dangerous as the diseases they were intended to cure. Medical experts gained stature and professional status less by proving their ability to cure the ill than by claiming that they alone could describe and explain certain phenomena.[14] They could offer themselves as a new and different breed of confidence men in which the public might place their trust, for better or worse. The phenomenon of mediumship was one area in which doctors staked an explanatory and professional claim, and this impulse says much about the status of science and religion in nineteenth-century understandings of secularism and modernity.

From its earliest manifestations, Spiritualism was debunked by scientists. In particular, the bodies of mediums, and later their brains and psyches, were examined and probed by doctors looking for scientific explanations of meta-physical phenomena. Doctors pointed to the minds of mediums and their followers as evidence of both individual and cultural insanity. From the early 1850s onward, both lay and medical commentators published books and articles linking Spiritualism and disease. One respondent wrote that "these phenomena never appear spontaneously, or can be evoked, except in persons more or less diseased, or in weak women and impressionable children."[15] Although firmly disavowing any connection between spirit phenomena and disease, Spiritualists would not deny the frequency with which spirits spoke to women and children. Indeed, a Spiritualist might reclaim the supposed weakness of women as the openness that allowed spirits to speak through her. The impressionability of children might be understood as innocence and purity enabling manifestations of a higher truth.

In the 1870s, the New York neurologist Frederic Marvin coined the term *mediomania*, linking Spiritualism and insanity, and siting pathology in the body of the female medium.[16] Although he argued that mediomania could, in theory, affect men, in his practice he found the disease only among women. The reason, he believed, lay in the disorder of the female body. Using the term *utromania*, Dr. Marvin, like many of his nineteenth-century contemporaries, posited a scientific connection between disordered female biology and disor-derly acts. In the tilt of the uterus, Marvin purported to discover the cause of a disease that he argued was "epidemic" among American women. He wrote: "Utromania frequently results in mediomania. . . . The angle at which the womb is suspended in the pelvis frequently settles the whole question of san-ity or insanity. Tilt the organ a little forward—introvert it, and immediately the patient forsakes her home, embraces some strong ultraism—Mormonism, Mesmerism, Fourierism, Socialism, oftener Spiritualism."[17]

Marvin's nomination of mediomania says as much about the futures and past of medical sciences as it does about the connections between the status of femininity and allegedly irrational religious and utopian practices in his own historical present. The condition Marvin described was later subsumed under the rubric of hysteria. Yet nineteenth-century notions of hysteria differed from those of the Hippocratic school of the fifth century B.C.E.—the belief that the specifically female "hysterical" condition, deriving from the Greek word for *uterus,* resulted from a pathological wandering of a restless womb from its normal position in the body.[18] Nineteenth-century U.S. doctors expanded the connections between female physiognomy and hysterical behavior in an attempt to diagnose religious affect, contain "ultraisms," and justify their own profession.

Late nineteenth-century hysteria and mediumship do bear certain resemblances. The various states of mediumistic performance—trance, rigidity, catalepsy, and ecstasy—mirrored the stages of hysteria as it was being diagnosed and codified at the time in asylums and symposiums throughout the United States and Europe. By the late 1860s and early 1870s, specialists in diseases of the mind began to associate mediumship with a range of pathological symptoms. Comparing pathologizing diagnoses to appreciative recognitions reveals national biases and disciplinary anxieties as well as a range of secular and spiritual attitudes about gender norms.

Mediums and hysterics, women ventriloquized by spirits or by disease, expressed bodily what could not be vocalized by the rational, speaking, and implicitly male self. Constructed through dominant notions of female frailty and hyperreceptivity, hysteria and mediumship might be seen as distinct yet parallel responses to the limited options for female expression and subjectivity in Western society. Each phenomenon produced a kind of psychic double play of fractured subjectivities that blurred the boundaries between active, speaking subject and passive object. Both mediums and hysterics performed and produced bodily states that at once confounded and informed men of science. Each performance remained tainted both by its supposed link to femininity and female passivity and by a suspicion that it belonged to the realm of the imaginary.

The spiritual trance state was a kind of out-of-body experience that at once reflected and inverted the hysterical fit, the most characteristic and dramatic of hysterical symptoms. There were two main variations of a hysterical fit: falling into a fainting trance, sometimes called catalepsy, and uncontrolled thrashing, jerking, or trembling. Sometimes mimicking an epileptic seizure in its suddenness of onset, at other times coming on gradually, the hysterical fit, according to many case studies, began with "pain and tension, most frequently in 'the uterine area.' The sufferer alternately sobbed and laughed violently, complained of palpitations of the heart, clawed her throat as if strangling, and at times abruptly lost the power of hearing or speech. A deathlike trance might follow, lasting hours, even days. At other times, violent convulsions—sometimes accompanied by hallucinations—seized her body."[19] Wild fluctuations between activity and passivity in these female patients led medical scientists to conclude that expected social and sexual dichotomies were out of order, and indeed, at war within these pathological subjects. Mediums were often "developed" through similarly unexpected episodes of seizure or trance. Anglo-American Protestant culture had long been home to what the historian Ann Taves has termed "fits, trances, and visions," and it is not surprising that Spiritualists would interpret such speech attending these episodes as revelations rather than signs of disease.[20] Because they did not believe trance states to be pathological, and perhaps because they both expected and hoped for them to manifest, the writers for the Spiritualist press provided little detail of the bodily transformations of women experiencing these states. The scientific press, however, was loquacious in defining the detailed stages of transfiguration.

Frederick Simpson, a doctor in Hartford, Connecticut, who began practicing medicine in the 1880s, remembered the first "hysterical fit" he saw in his practice:

> On a Sunday-school picnic a young lady was noticed by her friends to act queerly. She stopped talking, became absent-minded, stared about her in a dazed way, began to walk off in an automatic fashion, turning now this way and that. . . . We led her on board the steamboat and got her to lie down in a berth in the stateroom. She was only half conscious of her environment. She soon began to get rigid and her face flushed. Then she commenced to go through various irregular movements of the body. She thrashed with her arms and kicked with her legs, threw her head from side to side, arched up her back and rolled about with such force that several of us had to hold her to keep her in the berth.[21]

The young woman eventually recovered consciousness and could remember nothing of the incident.

Whether in sickness, ecstasy, or revelation—often overlapping categories—the extremity of these female manifestations reflects the cultural limitations on bodily performance for nineteenth-century women. For women understood by certain sub- and dominant cultures as mediums, convulsions, hallucinations, and trance opened up the possibility of revelation. For those understood as hysterics, these acts represented a different kind of mastery and control, variously construed as either attention-getting behavior or real illness.

The new professions of the mind, as they developed in the United States in the last third of the nineteenth century, were constructed on, and by, the diagnosis of hysteria and the figure of the hysteric. The etiology of hysteria, in turn, depended on transatlantic understandings of the phenomenon of Spiritualism and the female medium. Retelling the history of medicalization of female mysticism in the United States demands taking religion seriously and reveals a complex interplay between patient and doctor, medium and scientist.

HATCHING A BROOD OF WONDERS

The notion that spiritual states and psychic disorder might bear some relationship to one another predated American Spiritualism. In 1847, a year before the Fox sisters inaugurated the movement, an article in the British medical journal *Lancet* proclaimed that "all the malingering of the age has a natural determination toward mesmerism."[22] Mesmerism, which was in many ways the precursor to Spiritualism, produced the same outward signs in its subjects: trance states, suggestibility, and clairvoyance.[23] While not overtly accusing mesmeric subjects of "actual deceit," the *Lancet* writer suggests that the issue might be "merely a morbid desire to parade these disorders, real or imaginary, before the public eye." Believers, then, were also tainted by their willingness to absorb and mirror this morbid desire. This writer goes on to connect "the sensations, disorder, credulity, and cunning, and self-deception of this class of subjects, and the simplicity of the great number who believe in them," positioning followers as "the other great division of the mesmeric array."[24] The *Lancet* writer seems unsure where malingering and mesmerism, deception of self and other, begin and end. But perhaps these questions struck too close to home for a newly professionalized class of healers seeking to shed associations with quackery.

In contrast to the general public, which was quickly intrigued by Spiritualism at midcentury, most scientists, and especially doctors, were immediately dismissive of the phenomenon. Spirit manifestations challenged scientific skepticism, questioning where productive disinterest ended and reactive lack of interest began. The American Association for the Advancement of Science refused to discuss Spiritualism at its annual meetings in the 1850s, and several years later an investigating committee of Harvard faculty, including Louis Agassiz, the celebrated professor of natural history, rejected such beliefs as spurious.[25] Yet scientists' interest mounted as Spiritualism claimed a number of converts from within their own ranks. In 1856, a respected chemist from the University of Pennsylvania, Robert Hare, announced his conversion to Spiritualism. He was soon joined by John B. Fairbanks, the editor of *Scientific American*. The British scientist William Crookes became a partisan and influenced a number of prominent British physicists during the 1870s, including William Barrett, Lord Raleigh, and Oliver Lodge, all of whom became active in psychical research through the London Theosophical Society and the Society for Psychical Research.[26] Spiritualism itself invoked the language and tools of popular science in its reliance on tests and investigation, material proof and evidence. An interest in Spiritualism ostensibly allowed some scientists to retain their professional identity as empirically based investigators while rejecting the stark materialism to which many of their colleagues subscribed. Rather than science vanquishing religion, as in the classic secularization narrative, here science and religion worked as mutually constitutive knowledges, together producing a materialist belief system to explain the immaterial world.

The medical community, trying to differentiate itself from other healing practices of the nineteenth century, was much less divided in its views on Spiritualism than was the larger scientific community. Medical experts at first tried to explain spirit channeling as conscious deception. After hearing the first knocks and raps of nineteenth-century spirits, a group of doctors theorized that the Fox sisters produced the noises by cracking their bones to simulate spirit communication. A trio of doctors, led by Austin Flint of the University of Buffalo, published an article in the February 1851 issue of the *Commercial Advertiser,* and later in medical journals, in which they advanced the theory that the spirit raps were produced by a partial dislocation of the knee joint, the relocation of which produced the snap or rap of the ghostly communication.[27] This "joint and tendon" theory was taken up by a number of other doctors in the 1850s. In 1855, the editors of the *American Journal of Insanity* reported on the investigations of a doctor from Frankfurt who, rather than "closely observing a young girl endowed with the power of rapping," had meticulously analyzed a human skeleton and discovered the secret in the "sudden escape of a tendon." The learned Dr. Schiff reproduced this phenomenon by snapping his own ankle tendon and joint. He reportedly finished the demonstration by rapping out the "Marseillaise" by tendon snap, much to the delight of all the doctors assembled.[28]

As Spiritualism expanded into a nationwide movement, doctors' early attempts to expose fraudulent mediums shifted to a broader explanatory rubric. Deploying their exclusive biomedical knowledge, physicians and medical researchers diagnosed spiritual manifestations, and Spiritualists themselves, as pathological. One of the first to adopt this approach was Dr. Edward C. Rogers of Boston. He argued in 1853 that the ability of mediums to manipulate objects could be understood using Baron von Reichenbach's newly discovered theory of odylic force.[29] This force, sometimes called "odic force," was akin to both electricity and magnetism and thought to be particularly powerful in persons with an abnormal nervous constitution. It was supposed that magnetism resided in the human body and that some people were particularly sensitive to magnets and the magnetism exuded by others. Reichenbach's theories were used to explain mesmerism, or animal magnetism, as well as hypnotism and thought transference. Midcentury science was just beginning to make sense of electricity and the other invisible "powers of the air," some made newly visible by the camera and the microscope.[30]

At this point, the line between science and what would come to be called pseudoscience was barely visible. In 1857, Dr. Stanley Grimes propounded the theory that mediumship was a disease and that the disorder could best be explained by reference to phrenology. Specifically, he argued that mediumistic trances and associated states simply represented abnormalities in "the conforming social organs in the upper front part of the cerebrum."[31] Grimes referred to the mental state into which mediums slipped as "credo-mania," a condition contagious to séance-goers with a similar deficiency of the nervous system. Using an idiom familiar to their professional contemporaries, scientists made Spiritualism mundane. In place of the supernatural, readers were presented with an explanation couched in the vocabulary of medical science and based on the reorganization of Reichenbach's odylic force and phrenological neurophysiology. These concepts would have been familiar to physicians in the 1840s and 1850s. That they would be largely abandoned and debunked by medicine before another decade passed is irrelevant; for the time being, the profession had examined, explained, and dismissed the claims of Spiritualism.

That doctors would align themselves with materialism against supernaturalism is less significant or surprising than the means by which they did so. Mediumship as practice was not available to the man of reason, the educated thinker, or the strong of will. Yet these men of medicine could, and did, take on the role of "operator," imbued with the power to induce trance states in more passive subjects. Grimes argued in an 1857 treatise that he himself was responsible for creating the first medium through his own powers of suggestion and thereby, unknowingly and unintentionally, concocting the belief system of Spiritualism. Drawing a link between nineteenth-century mesmerism and Spiritualism, Grimes contended that "modern spiritualism originated at ... [his] lectures in Poughkeepsie in 1843."[32] These lectures on phrenology and the nervous system included demonstrations of mesmeristic trance or what Grimes termed "credencive induction." Grimes brought twenty volunteers from the audience, "mesmerized" them, and gave them a series of verbal commands. All twenty were successfully mesmerized and controlled. Two of the twenty had the clairvoyant power to receive telepathically communicated messages. One of the two was Andrew Jackson Davis, who later became one of the most famous mediums of the nineteenth century, known in the annals of Spiritualism as "the Poughkeepsie Seer."

Dr. Grimes's fantasy that he birthed what he considered a kind of Frankenstein's monster in Spiritualism speaks at once to the failure of medical diagnosis as a strategy of containment and to the protean quality of Spiritualist practice, even as doctors positioned themselves as critics or debunkers. Grimes imagined himself as both critic and creator, commenting that "though my lectures in Poughkeepsie gave birth to modern spiritualism, and first caused A. J. Davis to come into notice, I distinctly protested at the time, and always since, against the principles and the practices which grew illegitimately out of my labors, and finally resulted in producing a motley brood of pretended spirit mediums."[33] This vexed scene of creation provides an even more distinct instance of "reverse discourse" than the example Michel Foucault privileges in his explication of the "tactical polyvalence of discourses" attending the birth of the homosexual "species" from the sexological clinic.[34] Grimes inadvertently "developed" Davis as an unlikely medium, one who literally spoke back to pathologizing authority in a voice not his own.

Whereas both believers and debunkers evoked women's innate passivity as a cause of mediumship, it was literacy—an acquired quality central to the man-of-reason mythos—that accounted for Andrew Jackson Davis's unique position as a medium. Davis wrote more than thirty books by "spirit guidance," and his *Principles of Nature, Her Divine Revelations, and a Voice to Mankind* is considered the first Spiritualist book. Davis was barely a man when he began his spiritual work. Young, poor, and hailing from a rural area, he was, in Dr. Grimes's words, "notoriously ignorant and illiterate."[35] For believers, this lack of formal education was what made Davis's prodigious production truly miraculous. For Grimes, Davis's "gifts" had to be denigrated in essentialist, feminizing terms: he noted that Davis had "neither wit, nor words, natural nor acquired preeminence," and that it was only his "masterly passiveness of mind which enabled the spirits to nest in his brain and hatch a brood of wonders."[36] Grimes's mixed rhetoric of mastery and passivity, including a complicated "nest" metaphor about male procreation that seems to validate spirit channeling more than debunk it, indicates an unease with the distinctions between reason and religion that cannot be separated from an anxiety about proper gender roles.

As the next chapter details, there were a number of nineteenth-century male mediums with the passiveness of mind befitting their spiritual calling. In the United States at midcentury, however, women of any class or background would have been understood as having the attributes of a potential medium. The very qualities that modern scientific culture found least valuable—unreason, passivity, susceptibility, femininity—became ideal qualifications for mediumship. Although Spiritualism often reified essentialist distinctions between male and female ways of being, the movement also complicated gender roles through its openness to immaterial realms. The otherworldly strivings of Spiritualists in some ways transcended social restrictions. Invoking "blankness" as the quality most befitting a medium, Arthur Conan Doyle explained that "it has been the habit to say that great intellect stands in the way of personal psychic experiences. The clean slate is certainly most apt for the writing of a message."[37] This clean slate allowed certain subjects to establish alternative identities on a tabula rasa addressed to a higher order.

Spiritualism employed the middle-class discourses of purity, passivity, and sickliness to buttress female mediums' spiritual practice. Sickliness itself, thought to be ubiquitous among mid-Victorian women, was recoded by Spiritualists as a state of possibility. Catherine Beecher, surveying her upper-class acquaintances in 1855, commented on the "terrible decay of female health all over the land."[38] One Spiritualist writer imagined that the same delicate constitution and nervous excitability that engendered invalidism might also open a space of revelation. "Women in the nineteenth century are physically sick, weak and declining," he maintained. "But if the functions depending on force and muscle are weak . . . the nerves are intensely sensitive. . . . Hence sickness, rest, passivity, susceptibility, impressionability, mediumship, communication, revelation!"[39] The spiritual, the expressive, the undisciplined became the means by which female mediums claimed a kind of religious power. At the same time, this spiritual and feminine coding of mediumship allowed it to be recoded by doctors as disease. As the nineteenth century progressed, the specifically female practice of mediumship came to be consistently linked with the gendered rise of hysteria. In the intervening years, however, multiple etiologies infected medical diagnoses, as older, explicitly religious narratives troubled modern secular science and its diagnostic hegemonies.

The nineteenth-century U.S. medical community was by no means univocal, but many of its practitioners asserted their own authority over the otherworldly assertions of mainly female Spiritualist mediums. Western medical professionalization is enmeshed with parallel histories of women's public speech and extrainstitutional religious utterances. The containment of "spirit" voices by materialist medicine moved from debunking spiritual manifestations to pathologizing their generally female mediums to analyzing women's words in the emergent field of psychoanalysis. As these techniques of scientific analysis shifted, the spirits faded, and these women came to speak for and about themselves.

Famously, the methodology eventually named by the female patient Anna O. as the "talking cure" began when another hysterical patient, Emmy von N., commanded Sigmund Freud to stop interrupting her and "let her tell me what she had to say."[40] Psychoanalysts reappropriated this specifically female command to listen by making the very negotiation between analyst and analysand a new material for scientific inquiry. Founding its practice as a response to female hysterics, psychoanalysis resisted reducing bodily symptoms to preexisting scientific models or even attempting to relieve them. Psychoanalysis, as one American historian has argued, was "the child of the hysterical woman."[41]

Yet how does this well-rehearsed story of the birth of psychoanalysis in Europe inform histories of illness and medicine in the United States, where relations between male doctors and female patients were arguably more contentious, and where the residuum of religious discourse never fully yielded to a dominant scientific one? Looking to European historiographies linking secularization and the medicalization of religious experience informs understandings of parallel moments in U.S. history. Inaugurating his genealogy of a specifically Continental history of sexuality, Foucault's lectures at the Collège de France in 1974 and 1975 center the body of the female mystic in a secularization narrative that moves from the witch to the possessed to the hysteric. For Foucault, it was the movements of the body, as opposed to the speech act, that mattered to inquisitors and confessors, and later to doctors: "The mark or signature of possession is not the spot, for example, that was found on the witch's body. It is something very different, an element that will have fundamental importance in Western medical and religious history: the convulsion."[42]

Contrasting the ability of the premodern witch's body to "be transported and made invisible" with "a new detailed body taking the place of or arising from that body, a constantly agitated and shaking body," Foucault indicates that disturbing transits between mortal bodies and immortal forces would be expressed, and consolidated, in the movements of the convulsive hysteric.[43] Medicine's vanquishing of the mystical depended on a relocation of confounding occurrences from the ether and otherworldly to a gendered body. Foucault here anticipates and parallels his rejection, in *The History of Sexuality, Volume 1,* of the "repressive hypothesis" in lieu of a more complex reading of how Victorian culture counterintuitively proliferated multiple forms of sexuality instead of hiding or denying them. In these earlier lectures, published under the title *Abnormal,* Foucault suggests that scientific engagement with possession did less to contain religious phenomena than to narrativize them, to reproduce the "devil's signature" as an equivalent to the "author function" he theorized earlier.[44] The move from the literal mark on the body to the body's convulsive performance designates a shift from an imperative location of the possessed to the production of a narrative of possession readable through a somatic text.

Foucault observes that "the convulsive flesh of the possessed will come to serve, in the history of psychiatry, as "the neurological model of mental illness.'"[45] Convulsion, "this immense spidery notion that extends its web over both religion and mysticism on one side and medicine and psychiatry on the other," allows Foucault to "establish connections between psychiatry and medicine through the interstitial or liminal discipline of neurology, rather than through the formal organization of psychiatric knowledge and discourse."[46] Inasmuch as neurology informs Foucault's renarration of psychiatric hegemony and the process of secularization, it is worth examining the chaotic history of neurology in the United States and its specific relationship to American Spiritualism in order to understand how the production of modernity, medical professionalization, and gender codes reads differently in the American context.

Before taking up the distinctly sexist nature of U.S. neurology, I want to examine the mixed discourses informing both feminist and medical histories of this era. Foucault, perhaps inadvertently, reifies gender roles in his account of the transformation of broad spiritual concourse into contained bodily experience by neglecting to foreground the gendered nature of this shift.

Feminist readings of the ceding of religious affect before a discourse of disease see active medicine men pitched against female patients who, however violent their conniptions, are rendered passive objects of inquiry.[47] In the nineteenth-century U.S. context, constructions of a battle between the sexes, distinctions between expertise and illness, and negotiations between the religious and the spiritual tangle in ways that cannot be reduced to the mark of "the devil's signature," the triumph of scientism over religious thought, or male versus female ways of being. Although it is easy to reproduce a "repressive hypothesis" over the agonistic struggles between American neurologists and their predominantly female patients, closer analysis demonstrates how these male subjects and female objects circulate and are produced as gendered through multiple vectors of power.

In an 1860 article titled "Case of Mania with the Delusions and Phenomena of Spiritualism," an unnamed doctor discusses the case of a patient named "C.," a twenty-six-year-old, unmarried seamstress, hospitalized in an asylum in Utica, New York. It is perhaps a coincidence that this case is situated in the notorious "Burned-Over District," only about one hundred miles and a decade away from the insistent knocks heard by the Fox sisters.[48] Yet it is certainly significant that the "case of mania" was published in the *American Journal of Insanity*. Founded in 1844 by Amariah Brigham, superintendent of the Utica State Hospital, this journal was the first and most august psychiatric periodical in the nation.[49] Brigham was among the thirteen superintendents from the nation's twenty-four mental hospitals who established the first association of American alienists: the Association of Medical Superintendents of American Institutions for the Insane. Brigham's central interest in the relation between religion and madness informed his book *Observations on the Influence of Religion upon the Health and Physical Welfare of Mankind* in 1835.[50]

Twenty-five years later, this new Utica case was termed a "possession." The narrative begins: "Again the possession commences. The manner is suddenly changed, the eyes fixed, and the utterances commence. At first they are delivered in a broken manner, as in reading from a blurred sheet; then become continually louder and more hurried." A spirit then enters the case record as the doctor continues in the third person. "The spirit directs the doctor to remove 'the girl' to the convalescent ward, to the garden, and to the next room in a single breath. Part of a sentence is here interjected, as from another source, when the first spirit upbraids her for being the medium of the devil.... During a brief interval, she is permitted in her own person, to speak a few words, which, the reality of mediumship being allowed, do not give the slightest evidence of insanity." The doctor breathlessly continues, "Through the copious notes of her previous trance-speakings and oracular sayings are the fact that an urgent and repeated command of the spirits was, that she should leave the Asylum and return home."[51]

Throughout this case history, science and religion, madness and the demonic are enmeshed. The asylum doctor begins by referring to the patient as *possessed,* a term that invokes both the older language of New England witchcraft and a European Catholic tradition of otherworldly control. That demonic possession would have been among the etiologies available to a doctor at midcentury—in one of New York's foremost asylums, in a predominantly Protestant region of the United States—speaks to the imbrication of nineteenth-century science in a residual transatlantic religious language as well in as the newer discourse of Spiritualism. The doctor seems to take at face value that it is a "spirit" who "upbraids" the patient for "being a medium of the devil." And he allows that within the "reality of mediumship," the patient does not "give the slightest evidence of insanity."[52]

That the asylum doctor allowed for the "reality" of mediumship as medical explanation, given his prior diagnosis of mania and insanity, suggests a cultural context shared by doctor and patient, one that was fast unraveling by the 1860s. That he permitted her worldview to influence his own, or relaxed his authority enough to allow for the possibility of a reality beyond science, is atypical of American doctors who wrote on Spiritualism. This case study seems to speak in the multiple voices of science and religion much in the same way that the "possessed" woman speaks intermittently in the voices of the rational and the irrational, self and spirit.[53] Significantly, the doctor himself appears silenced as he observes a chaotic triangular conflict between the patient, a spirit, and the devil. "C" herself seems to channel a polyvocal history of demonic possession that was flagging before the progress of modern science and the beneficent specters whom Spiritualists valued as personal and political guides.

The chiasmic quality of this case study points to the transitional moment in which it occurred. A few years later, "alienist" asylum keepers—who were more likely to posit holistic connections between body and mind—would find themselves battling with neurology's incipient claims of pure materialist science. In 1860, however, it was rare for doctors to accept spirit possession as anything but a pathological symptom. In other words, this case is the exception that proves the rule of American scientific receptions of mediumship. But it is precisely the ways in which this case study calls into question terms like *science, mediumship,* and *reception* —and, implicitly, *American* and its incumbent *exceptionalism*—that allow us to see how dominant historiographies reproduce both secular and Continental European narratives of progress as a universalizing mode of medicalization "rewriting the soul."[54] That this specialist in insanity would cede his own diagnostic expertise before wild spirit manifestations underwrites both an alternative vision of medicine in the United States and the imperative for the medical profession to reassert secular scientism.

Circulating throughout nineteenth-century American as well as the French and British medical literature was the notion that hysteria was actively performed. Of particular interest to these theorists was the trance or "death spell," ubiquitous among mediums and not uncommon among hysterics. Physicians such as Silas Weir Mitchell, the founder of the infamous "rest cure," would attribute it to recalcitrance in his female patients. As he theorized it, placing oneself in a trance state required a great deal of bodily control on the part of the performer, a control seized from the physician who had no means by which to cease, cure, or explain it. In an extraordinary case study from his private practice, Mitchell described one patient's inducement of a death spell: "She said to me, 'I am going to have an attack; feel my pulse. In a few minutes I shall be dead.' Her pulse, which just before was about 100, was now racing and quite countless, while the irregularity and violence of the heart's action seemed to me inconceivable. With the interest of an hysterical woman in her own performances, she said to me, 'Now watch it; you will be amazed.' This certainly was the case. Within a few minutes the pulse began to fall in number, and . . . in some fifteen minutes was beating only 40. Then a beat would drop out here and there; the pulse meanwhile growing feebler, until at last I could neither feel it, nor yet hear the heart. In this state of seeming death, white, still, without breathing or perceptible circulation, this girl lay for from two to four days."[55]

Blurring the lines between consciousness and unconsciousness, life and death, trance was viewed as the ultimate act of bodily control. It also brought with it attendant dangers. The Spiritualist press began to run articles beginning in the 1850s warning of the dangers of being buried alive, presumably while in a spiritualistic trance. This particular fear circulated widely, finding early expression in Gothic tales like Edgar Allen Poe's 1839 "The Fall of the House of Usher." Spiritualists felt themselves in particular danger of accidental burial because of the unmistakable resemblance of death and trance. One article from the *Banner of Light* warned that "trances resembling the postmortem state are becoming more frequent than ever before, and constant watchfulness is required lest we unbar the tomb to the living."[56] The article went on the tell the story of "a Miss J. R. Hough, sixteen years of age, of Ashtabula, Ohio," who was buried and later unburied because her family feared that her warm skin at the time of burial signified a state other than death. (The article did not reveal whether a true mistake had been made.) Publications like *Popular Science Monthly* responded with articles such as "The Extreme Rarity of Premature Burial," arguing that the public need "place renewed confidence in the ability of the *ordinary* [emphasis in original] general practitioner of medicine to recognize the distinction between a state of trance and a state of death, and . . . disregard the idle stories of ignorant and superstitious persons upon premature burials."[57] At least one enterprising nineteenth-century businessman cashed in on the fear, advertising a coffin rigged with a bell inside, which the undead could ring to call for rescue.[58]

Hysterical death-spells and mediumistic trances were bodily performances that would continue to ghost one another as the frequency of each escalated in American culture. The critic Elaine Showalter has deemed the nineteenth century "the golden age of hysteria."[59] In the United States, Great Britain, and France, and perhaps most notably in Vienna, where hysterics provided the material with which Sigmund Freud and Joseph Breuer devised the rudiments of the psychoanalytic method, incidents of hysteria reached remarkably high levels at the end of the century, tapering off and eventually disappearing by the mid-twentieth century. The dramatic, polysymptomatic forms of the disease found in Jean-Martin Charcot's writings of the 1870s and 1880s and the gross, florid motor and sensory somaticizations displayed in the case reports of Freud and Breuer's 1895 *Studies on Hysteria* are regarded today as extreme rarities. The classic diagnosis of hysteria, born in the nineteenth century, has since been fragmented and distributed among other disease categories.[60]

That hysteria nonetheless remains a culturally salient category of psychic dysfunction underscores both the continuing influence of classical psychoanalysis and the resistance inhering in the disease itself. It is precisely a disease that haunts death itself through its own imagined, or even realized, morbid states. Hysteria was a disease that at once defied neat classification and presented a serious problem for nineteenth-century medicine's privileging of diagnosis over cure. Yet it was also the urge to classify that led physicians to look for and, not surprisingly, to find female hysterics in unprecedented numbers.[61]

From Freud to feminist historians, observers of hysteria have most typically looked to the private lives of women for clues to its causes and frequency.

Freud argued that hysteria was the somaticization of repressed sexual desires. He pointed to the social and cultural factors that encouraged and enforced the regulation of highly charged desires to the unconscious and thus spread the disease. Freud lumped these factors together under the heading " 'civilized' sexual morality."[62] The historian Carroll Smith-Rosenberg, studying middle-class American women, has proposed that the contradiction between the relentless stress of their domestic life and the prevailing feminine idea of frailty, docility, and subordination to men made the "flight into illness" through hysteria an appealing form of indirect dissent. The symptoms of hysteria, really parodies of femininity, enabled women to take to their beds, thus defeating both their husbands, whose households they left untended, and their male physicians, whose medications they showed to be useless.[63]

In an overtly misogynistic reading, S. Weir Mitchell, in his book *Fat and Blood,* likened female neurasthenics to vampires sucking the life out of their families and attendants.[64] In all of these analyses, nineteenth-century hysteria was figured as a sort of unconscious bodily dissent by middle-class white women, who had so thoroughly accepted a hegemonic value system that they could neither admit their discontent to themselves nor speak it to others. Through hysteria, the body itself spoke. Although feminist historians have seen hysteria as a kind of bodily protest by mid-Victorian women, American medical professionals often saw it as a manifestation of an atavistic resistance to secular modernity. Nineteenth-century doctors regularly listed "religious excitement" as a prime cause of insanity. As early as the 1830s, during the religious fervor of the Second Great Awakening, medical journals began to publish articles linking religious ecstatic experience with insanity.[65] Amariah Brigham wrote about this connection over almost two decades.[66] Followers of Millerism, Shakerism, and other revivalist religions that burned through the Northeastern United States in the 1830s and 1840s were considered fanatics by mainstream Protestants and lunatics by the burgeoning medical profession.[67]

Early in the history of nineteenth-century Spiritualism, both medical journals and the popular press found in this new belief system both the cause and effect of insanity. A great deal of space in the Spiritualist press was taken up with defending its believers against charges of lunacy. Yet even defenders of Spiritualism began to adopt the language of rationality as they warned their fellow believers to "be reasonable." One editorialist for the *Banner of Light* drew on the language of popular science in urging Spiritualists to "be reasonable and calm in whatever you undertake. . . . Fanaticism, whether this be found in Spiritualism, Mormonism, Millerism, or any other ism, only serves to show a weak or disorganized brain."[68] Complaining of inequitable treatment, another writer for the newspaper protested that all religions have their lunatics. He proceeded to tell the tale of a "renewal of religious excitement" among the Methodists in his town, "and, as one of the fruits, a young and beautiful girl was last week carried to the hospital for the insane at Worcester, a raving maniac."[69] In 1858, the editors of the *Banner* maintained that the "lunatic asylums are not more plentifully populated now than they ever were; and careful inquiry will satisfy anyone, that, out of all who receive the care of the attendants at those places, a very, *very* small fraction are taken from the ranks of true Spiritualists."[70]

By contrast, to demystify the belief system of Spiritualism on the grounds of pathology rather than fraud, scientific experts would have to construct it as ubiquitous. Frederic Marvin found himself overwhelmed by cases in which, as he understood it, "tilted" uteruses produced noxious social and religious fanaticism. William Alexander Hammond, Marvin's colleague in the medical department at New York University and a former surgeon general of the United States Army, similarly discovered hundreds of "hysterical" women "suffering from mediumship."[71] "At most of the spiritualistic meetings which I have attended," Hammond wrote, "there have been hysterical phenomena manifested."[72] Dr. Forbes Winslow, a London alienist, toured the United States in the 1870s, repeating the assertion that there were "ten thousand lunatics in the United States who were made insane by Spiritualism."[73] Although the medical press came to question the accuracy of Winslow's numbers, they agreed strongly that "the Superintendents of American and foreign asylums for the insane will bear out this . . . statement—that spiritualism makes many lunatics, and the counter statement—that lunacy makes spiritualists."[74] This 1888 article from the *Alienist and Neurologist*—a journal committed to combining research from public asylums and private neurological practices and, implicitly, to bridging what were often perceived as conflicting clinical epistemologies—quite starkly produces indeterminacy, or at best a kind of Möbius strip of lunacy and spiritualism, suggesting that medical skepticism toward embodied spiritual experience trumped scientific differentiations between cause and effect.

NEUROLOGY AND ITS DISCONTENTS

William James, the chair of the first academic psychology department in the United States, at Harvard, gave a series of lectures in Edinburgh in 1901 that were later compiled as *The Varieties of Religious Experience*. The first was titled "Religion and Neurology." In it, James decried the influence of what he termed "medical materialism." James was central among many scientists and psychologists who were critical of thinking that wrenched science from religion and pathologized certain varieties of religious experience. Indeed, these lectures can be read as a detailed refutation of the strand of scientific thinking that classified religious experience as illness such that "Fanny's extraordinary conscientiousness is merely a matter of overly-instigated nerves. William's melancholy about the universe is due to bad digestion—probably his liver is torpid. Eliza's delight in her church is a symptom of her hysterical constitution."[75] That James felt compelled to begin his lectures by rescuing religious believers from the realm of the pathological says a great deal about the age in which he was writing and about the particular cultural battles that had been raging throughout the preceding decades between science and religion and over contested meanings of the rational.

Although physicians staking their ground against holistic healers were interested in Spiritualism in its initial manifestations, their interest waned after 1860, then revived with the emergence of the new science of neurology. From 1870 to the mid-1880s, a group of the most prominent Anglo-American medical men took up the question of Spiritualism. The neurologists William Hammond, Silas Weir Mitchell, and George M. Beard; the British physiologist William B. Carpenter; and prominent alienist Henry Maudsley all launched a polemical attack on Spiritualism. Their views were shared by a number of lesser medical authorities, as well as eminent Continental colleagues such as Wilhelm Wundt, Jean-Martin Charcot, and Cesare Lombroso.[76] A reading of their publications suggests that these doctors' concerns with clinical and epistemological issues, were directly connected to questions of medical professionalization.

In the late nineteenth century, medical doctors were in the process of forming a profession for the care of the diseased spirit or psyche, a duty traditionally left to religion. Medical doctors' claim to jurisdiction over insanity rested on an effort to minister to the body rather than to the mind. In a Cartesian universe, where the concepts of mind and soul were conflated, a patient with a psychic illness would be better served by ministrations of the clergy than of the medical profession. Indeed, medical doctors were in a sense competing directly with clergymen. As one historian has noted, the "extraordinarily rapid proliferation of religiously-based mental healing cults (of which the most notable was Christian Science) had prompted a growing exodus of patients from the doctor's waiting room to the minister's study."[77] By the beginning of the twentieth century, prominent physicians like Charles

L. Dana were publicly wringing their hands over Americans' growing choice of alternative and overtly spiritual cures and their rejection of scientific medicine. Calling on the medical profession to reverse the tide of converts to psychic healing, he wrote:

> There ought to be some definite form of psychotherapeutics approved by the profession so that people would not go after "soul massage" or other faked forms of psychotherapeutics. What are we going to do with the large number who won't come to us and will go to anyone who will raise his psychic standard? We must find out the good behind these false methods and organize it into some wise scientific measure which we will prescribe. Until we do this there will be a continual succession to new cults, Christian Science, osteopathy, etc., to the discredit of medicine and more especially of psychiatry and neurology.[78]

Physical medicine, at least as nineteenth-century doctors practiced it, failed to soothe the soul or ease the mental pain of many Americans. But if doctors could not always console, they could classify. Nineteenth-century physicians almost universally asserted that mental disease had an entirely somatic basis and was thus accessible to physical remedies. This somatic emphasis brought those who in another era might have been classified as mystics under the purview of science.

These struggles were embedded in what the historian Robert Young calls the "fragmentation of a common context."[79] Yet this fragmentation produced not a schism between religion and science but an aggregation of diagnostic and healing regimes, variously infused with the remains of a putatively diluvial secular split. By the 1880s, through the development of intellectual disciplines and delineated professions, the study of the mind, brain, soul, and nature had become discrete fields of knowledge.[80] Neurologists laid claim to the brain while debunking and explaining the outer fringes of religious experience as pathology.

Nineteenth-century neurology was particularly imbricated in the shearing of brain from mind and in the project of explaining the soul as a physical function. To think otherwise would bring doctors into territory that at least one of them imagined as frightening and bewildering—indeed, supernatural. Frederic Marvin wrote that "were I obliged to prescribe for the mind as an entity, I should throw up my arms in despair; I should as soon think of prescribing for an apparition or of administering drugs to a shadow."[81] Hammond, the most prolific of the neurologists writing on Spiritualism and insanity, dismissed Spiritualism as well as ecstatic religious behavior throughout the ages with the broad strokes of a man convinced that his new discipline, neurology, could account for a broad range of psychic and bodily experiences with reference to the diseased nervous system. At this formative moment, the female medium became a site of cultural struggle over the meanings of the soul, brain, and psyche.

Neurology was an invention of the 1860s, and Hammond was among its American founders. In 1866, the Philadelphia College of Physicians and Surgeons created a special position for Hammond so that he could lecture on the new field. Bellevue Hospital created a professorship of "diseases of the mind and nervous system" in 1867, and Hammond published the first comprehensive English-language textbook on neurology in 1871.[82] In the same year, he opened the New York State Hospital for Diseases of the Nervous System at the corner of Second Avenue and St. Mark's Place. Its objective was "to afford an opportunity for physicians and medical students for clinical observation and instruction in the . . . diseases of the nervous system." Although the hospital closed in its third year, for a brief time it offered instruction, treatment, and even a museum of "the normal and the pathological anatomy of the nervous system."[83]

Hammond and a number of other neurologists developed an industry devoted to debunking, explaining, and classifying Spiritualist phenomena.[84] Hammond's monumental *Physics and Physiology of Spiritualism* included detailed case studies of mediums that illustrated the various stages of hysteria, especially catalepsy and ecstasy. Among the case studies, and somewhat typical of them, is the story of a Spiritualist medium through whom two spirits spoke: "a good spirit called 'Katy,' and a 'bad one,' she asserted to be a sailor-boy." The sailor-boy eventually took over, ventriloquizing the medium with "loud laughter, hoarse and profane jokes" and "preternatural state of agility and strength." Hammond concludes this account, which bears a remarkable similarity to many of his others, with the rhetorical question: "Can any person familiar with the vagaries of hysteria doubt for an instant that this girl was suffering from it, and that her condition was aggravated by the notoriety which she gained by her performances?"[85] The blurring of male and female, self and other, and related questions of subjectivity are unexamined in these case studies. Mediums are simply diagnosed as hysterics, women possessed of a disordered nervous system, necessitating a trained neurologist.

Hammond diagnosed nineteenth-century female mediums as well as long-dead "religious hysterics," including Saint Catherine of Siena, Joan of Arc, Saint Theresa of Avila, and Joanna Southcott, as "celebrated cataleptics and ecstatics."[86] In constructing the genealogy of the religious hysteric, of which the medium was thought to be only the newest version in a long tradition, pre-Freudian doctors like Hammond relied not only on a collection of endlessly repeated and elaborated case studies but also on the evidence provided by the religious hysteric's continuous presence in history.[87]

The Catholic Middle Ages was the customary home of these hysterics, newly pathologized by the putatively secularized, dispirited Protestant nineteenth century.[88] Examples of self-flagellation and religious ecstasy were repeated alongside examples of trance speaking and hallucinations. This particular coupling inadvertently threw into relief the dangerous ease with which religious devotion could give way to the erotic, thereby exposing the fragile epistemological division between religion and sexuality, normal and perverse desire.[89] Women were imagined to be particularly vulnerable to this blurring of boundaries.

Hysteria, especially religious hysteria, was thought to worsen and spread when susceptible women were gathered together. In his much-circulated and often-reprinted essay "Epidemic Delusions," William Carpenter invoked a language of contagion, filtered through a neurological model, to explain why women are prone to both hysteria and religious belief. He followed the logic of Victorian gender ideology, explaining that women are subject to hysteria because "in the female the feelings are more easily excited, while the male generally has a less mobile nervous system, his feelings being less easily moved, while he is more influenced by the intellect." Carpenter argued that because of the weak female nervous system, women were highly suggestible, and hysteria, like ecstatic religious belief, was spread by the contagion of imitation. Theorizing from his own work in a Bristol asylum, he advised that hysteria could be halted by either separating women from each other, to avoid the pathological problem of "imitation," or by "curative" measures:

> I remember perfectly well, when I happened to be a resident pupil, having to go and scold these girls well, threatening them with some very severe infliction. I forget what was threatened, perhaps it would be a showerbath, for any one who went off into one of these fits. Now, here the cure is effected by a stronger emotion, the emotion of the dread of—we will not call it punishment—but of a curative measure; and this emotion overcame the tendency to what we commonly call imitation. It is the suggestion produced by the sight of one, that brings on the fit in another.[90]

Linking the behavior of medieval nuns, female flagellants, nineteenth-century hysterics, and Spiritualist mediums, Carpenter hoped that the "contagious influence of Mental Epidemics" could be stemmed by keeping suggestible females away from one another, a precaution that says as much about cultural fears of feminism as it does about hysteria. Carpenter also believed strongly in the triumph of "Science": "There is absolute truth in Science," he wrote, "which if not at present in our possession, is within our reach; and that, the nearer we are able to approach it, the clearer will be our habitual perception of the difference between the real and the unreal, the normal and the hysterical."[91]

George Miller Beard was arguably even more renowned in neurological circles than either Carpenter or William Hammond. He has since secured a place for himself in the canon of American medical history. In the typical telos of the history of psychiatry, where all roads that matter lead to Freud, Beard is the American neurologist most consistently acknowledged as having "prophetic psychiatric insights."[92] The author of *American Nervousness,* he created the disease category of neurasthenia and is considered a pioneer in the study of neuroses.[93]

George Beard had attended séances in the 1870s and even made pilgrimages to the famous Eddy Homestead in Vermont in 1874 to test the powers of materialization mediums. There, as Beard wrote some years later, he "joined circles the members of which developed the phenomena both of trance and hysteria, and some of whom were already nearly, if not quite, insane."[94] Beard brought his scientific knowledge of electricity and circuitry to the investigation of what he perceived as cultural insanity. He read Hermann Helmholtz, worked with Thomas Edison, and gained a working knowledge of physics and electricity. These models gave Beard a paradigm in which he could imagine the mind as a function of the nervous system, one which could be overheated, overstimulated, and short-circuited. His training in neurology, supplemented by his own mechanistic model, led Beard to argue that trance was a disease of the nervous system in which the cerebral activity was concentrated in "a single part of the brain, the activity of the rest of the brain being for a time suspended."[95] For those with inadequate nervous force, improperly loaded circuits would produce a "dimming." This suspension of nervous power could produce neurasthenia, a nervous exhaustion in those men and women who were overly civilized and overly stimulated by life's demands; in others, it manifested a parallel, altered consciousness.

Under the rubric of trance, Beard lumped the symptoms of neurasthenia as well as the phenomena of Spiritualism: "somnambulism artificial and spontaneous, mesmerism, animal magnetism, hypnotism, Braidism, catalepsy, ecstasy."[96] Leaving aside the question of why, when nervously taxed, some nineteenth-century Americans took to the fainting couch while others were driven to the séance table, Beard offered a neurological explanation for both. Those with nervous systems weakened by heredity and made worse by civilization were susceptible to nervous malfunction. For Beard, it was not just civilization, but a particularly nineteenth-century American variant of it, that was to blame. "American Nervousness" was, he argued, "as peculiar a product of the nineteenth century as the telegraph." Beard cited five factors particular to nineteenth-century civilization that increased the everyday demands on Americans' nervous systems and, thus, created neurasthenia: "steam power, the telegraph, the periodical press, the sciences, and the mental activity of women."[97] The rhetorical momentum of Beard's first three technologies subsumes the latter two—at once suggesting that female "mental activity" is as powerful an influence as modern technology while also mystifying the modern science of his own neurological practice. Beard's implicit separation of medicine from damaging "sciences" is perhaps informed by the fact that his practice was founded on the experience of upper-class subjects and middle-class neurasthenic professional men and their domesticated women. As opposed to the working classes, who would find their bodies maimed and lives taken by the machines of industrial capitalism, the exhausted businessman, the neurasthenic writer, the hysterical housewife, and the Spiritualist medium were all more abstract victims of an incipient technological age.

Beard's theories fit squarely within an emergent nineteenth-century social Darwinism. They also provided him with one explanation of why so many intelligent, wealthy urbanites in his New York practice suffered from neurasthenia. Nervous disease was, in Beard's view, the unhappy outcome of America's natural superiority. The "best" Americans had the highly evolved nervous systems and intelligence necessary to create a complex civilization. Yet it was precisely these highly evolved nervous systems, with their concomitant "fineness of organization," which were most vulnerable to the tensions inherent in the civilization human evolution had made possible.[98] Beard was certain that nineteenth-century Americans were being made sick by the very society that only they were highly evolved enough to create.

Some Americans, however, were excluded from Beard's catalog of sufferers. Neurasthenia, as Gail Bederman has argued, was a disease category that named a cultural problem, and the culture in question was "civilized" white America.[99] As a racial disease, indeed a disease of whiteness, neurasthenia was unknown "among savages or barbarians, or semi-barbarians or partially civilized people."[100] Neither the "Negro nor the South Sea Islander" suffered from nervous disorders, and Beard found them neither likely neurasthenics nor adept trance subjects.[101] Yet both nervous disease and Spiritualist trance could, in effect, return middle-class white Americans to the primitive. Beard, like Herbert Spencer, believed in a concept of "dissolution" (Spencer's coinage) in which insanity "makes us children, makes us savages, makes us animals."[102] Unlike neurasthenics, Spiritualist mediums, who were also mostly middle-class white Americans, embraced this experience. Rather than view it as an unwanted atavism, as Beard would have it, Spiritualists valorized it as heightened consciousness. Indeed, as one critic of Beard's work on trance put it: "The 'abnormal' conscious life in these [case studies] is not a one-sided, sick life, but is generally heightened—is altogether richer and fuller than the common life."[103]

Neurology overlapped with the broader discipline of psychological medicine: neurologists competed with alienists for preeminence in the study and care of the mind. The professional rivalry between alienists and neurologists partly explains why the most prominent neurologists in the United States in the last third of the nineteenth century engaged with the phenomenon of mediumship.[104] As Hammond explained in a review of a work by John P. Gray, who succeeded Amariah Brigham as head of the Utica asylum, "the modern science of psychology . . . is neither more nor less than the science of the mind considered as a physical function."[105] Neurologists like Hammond stood in active opposition to those doctors, alienists prominent among them, who held to the more metaphysical position that the mind might be considered a spiritual entity of which the brain was an instrument. If the supernatural, metaphysical phenomena of trance speaking, telepathy, and clairvoyance could be explained with reference to the physical, neurologists would have come a long way toward debunking a notion of the mind as anything more than brain matter, enlightened or deranged by a nervous system. Within this explanatory system, neurologists held the key to the human mind.

By contrast, William James and many of the psychologists who paved the way for Freud's famous 1909 visit to the United States understood that psychoanalysis might bridge the distance between brain and soul through a turn to mind. The U.S. scientific community's cool reception of Freud's theory of the unconscious, which complicated rather than narrowed this divide, indicates not only the prevalence of materialist scientism in America at this time but also its discomfort with the morally neutral centering of sex in psychoanalysis.[106] While Freud described his own therapy as a modification of S. Weir Mitchell's "rest cure" and had favorably reviewed many of his writings, Mitchell himself mocked mind-oriented approaches like Freud's and purportedly threw a psychoanalytic text into the fire, demanding, "Where did this filthy thing come from?"[107] It perhaps provides easy psychoanalytic fodder to note that this fireside scene and Mitchell's infamous "rest cure" for neurasthenic women were preceded by his more unorthodox techniques and bedside manners: in one case Mitchell "cured" a woman understood to be dying by igniting her bed sheets and stating to the concerned outside her room, "She will be coming out in a few minutes . . . A clear-cut case of hysteria!" In another, Mitchell threatened to rape an invalid if she did not rise from her bed.[108] Determining whether the convergence of fires, beds, and sex in Mitchell's "practice" suggests professional hypocrisy, circumstantial coincidences, or unconscious repression is less important than marking his clearly violent intolerance for somatic experience that was irreducible to physiological explanation.

Mitchell's rejection of psychological explanations in favor of still-unproven neurological "facts" implicitly conflated his rejection of the "talking cure" with his consistent resistance to hearing his patients' speech, personal histories, and self-explanations. That psychoanalytic practice, by contrast, would form itself over and through the latter is no coincidence. Rejecting such methodology would be the very means by which American neurology would isolate itself as native, pure, and scientifically objective. Yet inasmuch as we accept Freud's thesis that every iteration of confidence belies a repression and that the repressed always returns, then it is clearly narrative itself that returns to Mitchell. In addition to publishing his own poetry and fiction, Mitchell famously inspired Charlotte Perkins Gilman—after treating her through his rest cure and refusing to read her letter to him describing her condition—to write *The Yellow Wallpaper*.

There is a large body of literature on the gender issues attending Gilman and Mitchell's intertextual and interdisciplinary relations. Yet, as the critic Jane F. Thrailkill notes, Mitchell merely extrapolated his experience with the wounded men of the Civil War to female subjects. His tour of duty as a Union doctor and experience with "the damaged bodies of soldiers during the Civil War primed him to take seriously maladies of the nerves dismissed by the medical community."[109] Mitchell drew on the haunted language of Spiritualism to name the phenomenon of pain or feeling from an amputated limb: he called it "phantom limb" syndrome.

In his short story "The Case of George Dedlow," anonymously published in the *Atlantic* in 1866, Mitchell tells the tale of a Union doctor who loses all four limbs on a Civil War battlefield.[110] Dedlow finds cold comfort in the "stump hospital" of wounded men and turns to Spiritualism for solace. In the final scene, a medium conjures Dedlow's limbs from the Army Medical

Museum where they are preserved in alcohol, and the reconstituted hero staggers on ghostly legs into the community of the séance circle. The story, which satirizes Spiritualism, nevertheless points to its importance after the Civil War as a means of reconstituting a wounded nation and re-membering lost bodies, if only fantastically. Indeed, the fact that his *Atlantic* readers sent contributions to this fictional character at the Stump Hospital in Philadelphia indicates that the pathos of the story may have exceeded Mitchell's satiric intent.[111] Like the feeling of a phantom limb, the conjuring of a ghost is a form of recovering the lost, of returning the dead to the living, the part to the whole. Spiritualism was a technology of memory, fundamentally collective in its gathering of bodies and souls to reconstitute and remember the past.

THE BROOKLYN ENIGMA

Women's bodies were always implicitly and abstractly the ground over which secular science and spiritual subjects battled. Yet the most direct engagement between these camps occurred neither at the séance table nor in the clinic, but at a domestic bedside and in the pages of the popular press. The most celebrated case of the era involved two of New York's leading neurologists, William A. Hammond and George M. Beard, and a mystical medium: Mollie Fancher, whom the press dubbed the "Brooklyn Enigma." A "dyspeptic schoolgirl" turned fully empowered clairvoyant, Fancher vexed these men of science. New York newspapers covered the case in remarkable detail, splashing "The Extraordinary Case of Miss Fancher of Brooklyn" across front pages for much of the fall of 1878, along with the comments of skeptics and believers.[112] One article from the New York *Sun* described Fancher as a "puzzle for the psychologists." "Stranger than any fiction, . . . this blind woman, lying in a darkened chamber, in some ways sees persons, scenes and events, not only immediately around her but miles away, and describes them with photographic minuteness and accuracy. How does she do it? Let the scientific men answer—if they can."[113] The scientific men returned the media's rhetorical volley with their own diagnoses.

Mollie Fancher was an unlikely media sensation. Born in 1847, a year before the Fox sisters heard their raps and knocks, Mollie was raised by her aunt following the death of her mother and the remarriage of her father. She attended the elite Brooklyn Heights Seminary. One of her teachers there attested that "rarely ha[d] he seen a brighter or more interesting miss."[114] Yet, in a pattern typical of many bourgeois Victorian girls, by age sixteen Fancher's health began to fail: "Her trouble was pronounced nervous indigestion, her stomach rejecting most kinds of food: She had wasted away and become weak, and was the subject of frequent fainting spells."[115] Complaints that began with mild dyspepsia were coupled with serious injuries that rendered her a complete invalid by the time she was eighteen. Two accidents, one in which she was thrown from a horse and a second, in June 1865, in which she was dragged by a streetcar, resulted in spinal injuries. From the streets of Brooklyn, Mollie Fancher was carried unconscious, to her bed, "where she has never been removed since, save for a few minutes at a time."[116] It was then that her powers began to manifest themselves.

Fancher's gifts seemed to develop in direct correlation with her medical symptoms. As she lost her eyesight, she developed the gift of "second sight." She described the onset of her powers to her biographer, Abram Dailey, himself a Spiritualist, as a kind of transmutation of the senses: as she lost one sense it would wander and become more powerful. Her second sight emerged, by her own account, in the spring of 1866, three months after her blindness set in.[117] It was sometimes reported that she could not hear, but she could reconstruct conversations that took place miles away and could even guess the contents of sealed letters placed beneath her pillow. She read "letters that were enclosed in envelopes" and "books whose covers were closed."[118] As accounts of the case took great pains to assert, Fancher was not the entrepreneurial type, nor was she pleased at the possession of her particular gift, but lived in "strict seclusion as the only means of protection against the visits of the curious and incredulous."[119] A representative of P. T. Barnum was even said to have visited Fancher's bedside, offering her "an independent fortune would she put herself in the great showman's care."[120] Mollie, of course, refused.

Although the 1870s saw a number of cases of trance, clairvoyance, and even second sight, Fancher's true "gift," and the behavior that ultimately drew the attention of Hammond and Beard, was her miraculous ability to live without food. In one six-month period she was said to have taken only four teaspoons of milk punch, two teaspoons of wine, one small banana, and a piece of cracker. Her Brooklyn physician, Dr. Spier, who treated her first for her spinal injuries and then for the manifold symptoms that followed the accidents, assured a New York *Herald* reporter that no food "that is, solids— ever passed the woman's lips since her attack of paralysis, consequent upon her mishap." He concluded: "The case knocks the bottom out of all existing medical theses, and is, in a word, miraculous."[121] Termed anorexia mirabilis in the medical literature, as well as in medieval historical and religious writings, here was yet another example of nineteenth-century girls claiming power through forgotten feats of bodily transcendence.[122]

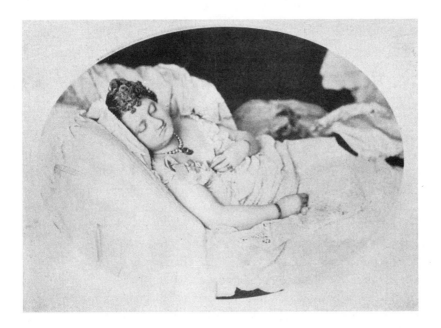

Figure 11. Mollie Fancher in a spirit trance, 1887. Frontispiece to Abram Dailey, *Mollie Fancher, The Brooklyn Enigma* (1894). Collection of the author.

William Hammond, not surprisingly, showed little respect for either the saints of the Catholic Middle Ages or their nineteenth-century mystical counterparts. "Strange to say the ability to live on the eucharist and resist starvation by diabolical power, died out in the middle ages, and was replaced by 'fasting girls' who still continue to amuse us with their vagaries."[123] "I have read the article on Miss Fancher published in today's *Sun*," Hammond told a reporter in 1878. "It's all a humbug. Why my dear fellow, she isn't the first girl that has deceived learned and good men. . . . There are plenty of cases of simulative hysteria, and Miss Fancher's case is one."[124]

George Beard also dismissed the miracles, writing, "The stories that periodically arise of young girls who live without food, may probably be explained partly by fraud, and partly by ignorance."[125] Living wholly without food is not something George Beard would have been able to either fathom or much sympathize with. He himself spent a great deal of time thinking and writing about food, privately struggling throughout his life to control his appetites and keep his weight in check. Beard kept copious notes about his own daily habits and continually made resolutions to "observe due moderation in my meals," confessing in his journal, "My great temptation is to over-eat—I do not know when to stop."[126] Given his own predilections for overindulgence, Beard would not have been disposed to empathize with the self-imposed starvation of a teenage girl.

Both Hammond and Beard consistently linked fasting to hysteria and to femininity more broadly. "Fasting girls," Hammond's coinage, were always girls no matter what their age. Their disease was a product of the untruthfulness of women and the public's pathological will to maintain the image of inexorable feminine innocence. Hammond wrote: "I am not aware that this power has been claimed to its fullest development for the male of the species. When he is deprived of food he dies in a few days, more or less, according to his physical condition as regards adipose tissue and strength of constitution: but if a weak or emaciated girl asserts that she is able to exist for years without eating, there are at least certificates and letters from clergymen, professors, and even physicians in support of the story. The element of impossibility goes for naught against the bare word of such a woman."[127]

Both George Beard and William Hammond diagnosed Fancher without ever visiting her. Despite their lack of direct clinical knowledge, their summations of the case and accusations of deceit appeared in both the medical literature and the popular press. Hammond even offered Fancher a "reward" for a public test of her clairvoyance. A check for one thousand dollars was to be placed in a sealed envelope, its contents known only to Hammond and his helpers. If Mollie could "completely and accurately" describe the check, its contents would be hers to have or distribute as she saw fit. Fancher declined, explaining that her powers would be diminished in the company of "someone as 'gross and materialistic' as Dr. Hammond."[128] Hammond attacked Fancher in the pages of the New York *Sun,* stating: "I can read you case after case where they [hysterics] have deceived thousands."[129] He then refers to another group of doctors who had recently overseen the death by starvation of a fasting girl who had perished during one of their tests, thereby proving herself deceptive.[130]

To Hammond, Mollie Fancher was one of many deceitful hysterics, a problem to be excised. To Spiritualists, she was one of their own and deserving of their support. Spiritualists refused to concede that their own science of direct sensory experience was somehow less accurate than that of the neurologists' abstract conclusions. As mediums and their believers increasingly became patients and case studies, Spiritualists entered the public conversation about Fancher, claiming their own expertise and attempting to chart a shared ground between debunkers and believers. As one believer wrote to George Beard, "Your assumption too that the testimony of experts stands in contrast with the testimony of eyes and ears is false and unscientific. The only difference between experts and nonexperts is that the former have more eye and ear testimony than the latter to give, and more time to do so."[131]

Spiritualists wrote Beard suggesting that he actively investigate incidents like the Fancher case rather than "coarsely denounce them."[132] One correspondent sent Beard a *New York Herald* clipping of "The Case of Miss Fancher" with a list of pointed questions scrawled at the bottom: "Does Dr. Beard consider himself the only scientist in the world? Is his dictum to be the law for others equally as well able to have an opinion on the above case, and with intellect far superior to his?"[133] Putting aside questions of intellect, Beard tautologically offered expertise itself as his evidence. "I claim that people are divided into two classes—experts, and non-experts. A non-expert has no right to pretend authority."[134] The *Sun* placed Beard's quote in a banner headline: "The Case of Miss Fancher: 'If She Can Do All This, Then All Science Goes For Naught.'"[135] Whether because of Spiritualists' urgings or merely the continuation of his own interests, by the early 1880s, Beard began to conduct experiments with subjects in "artificially-induced trance" and on phenomena associated with Spiritualism.[136]

Spiritualists were figured as causes and effects central to a nineteenth-century American culture perceiving, and perhaps producing, shattered nerves and spiritual emptiness. Refusing the desiccating effects of modernity, Spiritualism posited instead a direct correspondence between bodies and spirits, individuals and their affective communities. The Beards and Hammonds and other "specialists without spirit, sensualists without heart," found Spiritualists sometimes insane, sometimes laughable. Yet scientists and Spiritualists were not so far apart. Both used the language of empiricism to establish the truth claims of their respective belief systems. Born of the same wellspring of culture, they were both searching for ways to ease themselves into the end of the old century and the beginning of the new.

FIVE

Secular Spirits

A Queer Genealogy of Untimely Sexualities

[handwritten margin note: Spiritualism as offering new forms of embodiment]

For nineteenth-century Spiritualists, the experience of seeing ghosts—of being taken up, with, and by another body—became a means of understanding subjectivity both around and away from the séance table. For many, the mediumistic process of channeling differently gendered bodies produced another way of being in the world. Performing or speaking "out of body" segued with material and political reform causes, such as alternative healing and dress reform, to create a religious and social movement based on a reimagining of the corporeal. Spiritualist practice, in the form of trance speaking and mediumship, was understood as the possibility of disembodiment and a kind of purifying transfiguration and release from the earthly, gendered body. In offering new forms of embodiment, Spiritualism held enormous appeal for women and men who inhabited gender and sexuality in transgressive ways. These nineteenth-century subjects let us make contact with a history that troubles easy divisions between the religious and the secular, the spiritual and the sexual.

Spiritualism as a practice offered historiographic techniques of remembrance and theories of time that challenge secular history itself. The history of sexuality, as it has been written and theorized over the past three decades, is entangled with the history of secularism. More typically a powerful, unspoken assumption than a meaningful historiographic description, *secularism* names the product of a forward-moving modernity that swept magic from the world to make way for the capitalist market and the reign of reason.[1] Following Foucault, many scholars have taken for granted that the process of secularization occasioned the birth of the modern sexual subject. As clinics and courtrooms emerged over the long nineteenth century as privileged sites from which to identify and name deviance, social-scientific ways of knowing came to eclipse older theological forms. In this narrative, then, secularization and sexual identity formation seem to march forward together, each ushered in by capitalism.

This chapter untangles these twined progress narratives to examine how histories of secularism structurally underwrite histories of sexuality and function to elucidate some forms of sexual subjectivity while occluding others. Assuming a binary divide between the secular and the religious likewise masks the religious residuum of a post-Calvinist Protestantism that inheres in such putatively secular discourses as Anglo-American sexual science. Turning to the spiritual subcultures of the late nineteenth and early twentieth centuries reveals a world in which religious utopians and grassroots theologians understood themselves as scientists, many of them particularly interested in theorizing gendered embodiment. Spiritualism was one of many responses to the vaunted Victorian crisis of faith. Like secularism, it arose from a shared font of specifically Calvinist thought; but, rather than extend the promise of the "worldly asceticism" of the market, Spiritualists imagined another world entirely.[2]

When Michel Foucault published *The History of Sexuality, Volume 1,* it became a map for a new field of study.[3] For many who have followed Foucault's initial outline, secularization remains both the unnamed process and the context within which the fundamentally Christian duty of "passing everything having to do with sex through the endless mill of speech" was transformed from the solitary and semiprivate religious task of confession into the garrulous and often public act of speaking truth about the self. Beginning in the nineteenth century, the originators of an emergent scientific discourse forced new truths from old mouths, making science the preeminent way of knowing about sex. In the now-famous Foucauldian formulation, *scientia sexualis* discovered varied perversions and sexual heterogeneities and labeled the myriad types that would become modern sexual subjects.[4] Dominant understandings of same-sex desire shifted from sin to crime to sickness, each codification supplementing but not supplanting the one before. Religious sin was transmuted into secular morality, concomitant with the medical profession's construction of homosexuality as a medical condition alongside other anomalous sexualities.

Secularization, then, was the process by which the sodomite was transformed from a "temporary aberration" into the species of the homosexual.[5]

The trajectory from sin to crime to illness, from aberration to species, is a history of secularization. More often, though, this story and the subjects whose story it tells are made to stand under the sign of the "modern," as in the "creation of modern sexual subjects."[6] In this model, secularism and modernity are at best conflated, losing the historical specificity of Foucauldian genealogy.

Since the publication of Foucault's sweeping work, scholars have critiqued and augmented his narrative while simultaneously forwarding their own. Whereas some find continuities in same-sex sexuality and gender nonconformity across time, others hold fast to the notion of a "Great Paradigm Shift" that introduced the discursive categories of homosexuality and heterosexuality at the end of the nineteenth century.[7] The field has evolved in such a way that even those theorists most closely associated with social constructionism would now critique a catechism that creates a diluvial divide between premodern subjects, who performed sexual acts, and modern people, who were named and claimed by sexual identities.[8] In a different intervention, a generation of European and U.S. historians have detailed the ways that sexual subjects, far from being passive recipients of medical and juridical labels, crafted their own identities by renegotiating the terms under which they lived.[9] Social and community historians have stressed the importance of subculture over science, reversing the trajectory of subject formation from the discourse of experts to the lived experience of collective social worlds.[10] Historians have debated dates and origin stories and specified differences in national histories. New work on global sexualities and queer diasporas has focused on the situational nature of sexualities, detailing the importance of space and place, colonialism and global capitalism, in producing identities and desiring bodies.[11]

These important contributions have reoriented studies of sexuality to encompass expanded categories of difference. The historian David M. Halperin describes the project as a search for "different historical forms of sexual experience—different ways of being, different sets of relations to others and to oneself, different articulations of pleasure and meaning, different forms of consciousness."[12] At least syntactically, all of these multiple differences fall under the rubric of historical difference. Temporality functions here as the difference most difficult to bridge, the ultimate otherness. Indeed, Halperin points out elsewhere that writing a history of sexuality that respects the radical alterity of the past may have the paradoxical effect of eliminating the category of sexuality altogether.[13] Yet this commitment to marking the pastness of the past, a historicist strategy to avoid misrecognition or mistaken presentism, is necessarily belated, as it is occasioned by an initial sexual or gendered recognition. Like Spiritualists channeling the past, historians of sexuality ineluctably look for dead ancestors.

Because Euro-American studies of sexuality have subscribed to the dictum that homosexuality is an invention of Western urbanity, birthed at the moment of consolidation of capitalism and wage labor and subtended by the discourse of experts at the end of the nineteenth century, particular spaces and practices have been privileged sites of investigation.[14] Scholars have unearthed a modern and premodern history of sexuality by digging into the records of courts and prisons to locate sex criminals and sodomites; they have delved into diaries and letters for traces of lost relationships and the communities built around them and turned to the records of sexologists to find the invert, the pervert, and the deviant. Yet these optics have a tendency to obscure other ways of being—and feeling—beyond the secular taxonomies that produced the so-called modern sexual subject. I would like to ask how some varieties of religious experience may have been a marker for an incipient, not yet materialized, sexuality, a sexual dissidence outside the medico-juridical matrix and beyond the expected spaces of subculture. This past might also reveal alternative secularisms alongside alternative modernities, not one secularism but many, incomplete and necessarily so.[15]

An alternative history of nonsecular sexualities in nineteenth-century Anglo-America, one that restores a connection to histories of religion, also challenges the Continental secularization narrative in which the (French) Catholic confessional sits in a genealogical relationship to the psychoanalyst's couch. If the confessional is one culturally specific site for producing speech about the self, the Protestant evangelical tent, the revival meeting, and the Spiritualist séance may be among its American corollaries. Foucault's reliance on confessional speech as the privileged mode for the production of discourse on and about sexuality makes bodily knowledges secondary to linguistic ones.[16] By contrast, certain Anglo-American spiritualities uniquely fostered emergent sexualities precisely because spiritual embodiment—from hearing the voices of the dead to being moved bodily by the spirit—grounded religious experience, which in turn shaped social and sexual subjectivities.[17]

This imbrication of the spiritual and the sexual suggests more than the well-established connection between enthusiastic religion and ecstatic experience.[18] In an important caveat and implicit critique of certain postmodern writers who regard "all religion as an unrecognized form of sexuality," Michael Warner writes: "You can reduce religion to sex only if you don't especially believe in either one."[19] Religion is more (and other) than sublimated, displaced sexuality; it is also a system that has not been particularly kind to sexual deviants. Conjoining a history of sexuality to a history of religion must avoid both casting spirituality as false consciousness and reviving it in an implicit apologia that fails to acknowledge its place in the history of bodily regulation of queer subjects. Each of these seemingly oppositional gestures does the same ideological work in failing to take seriously either religion or sexuality.[20]

THE ALCHEMY OF SCIENCE AND MAGIC

There is an extensive literature detailing the ways in which women have been able to access power and authority through religion. As discussed in chapter 1, Spiritualists reappropriated the characteristics that had been used to deem women unfit for public life, transforming them into ideals of spirituality and sources of power and authority. There was also, however, a small number of male mediums who found the belief system similarly suited to their temperaments and tendencies. Engaging this related history of male mediumship furthers an understanding of Spiritualist theory as a radical philosophy of gender. As a gendered religious practice, Spiritualism was structured by a cosmology of balanced opposites. Séances took place in a "sacred circle," a kind of geometric symbol of order and communion. Uriah Clark's 1863 *Plain Guide to Spiritualism* recommended that a spirit circle contain an equal number of each sex to "balance" a gathering.[21] This attention to equilibrium was sometimes expressed in the language of science: the flow of negative and positive charges was thought to be as essential for a séance as it was for electrical circuitry. Positive, masculine and negative, feminine subjects were directed to sit opposite each other for "maximum effect": positive forces should sit on the medium's left, negative forces on the right. Persons of strong intellectual, positive, temperament were as necessary for a spirit circle as those of a more receptive, emotional or passive presence.[22]

The positive and negative forces that were needed to balance spirit circles, harmonize bodies, and equalize society were carefully and consciously gendered. Yet, remarkably, spiritual gender did not always correspond to biological sex. As Andrew Jackson Davis explained it, the "distinction of *male* and *female*" was "not so essential with regard to *sex*" as it was to a balancing of "the feminine attributes of character which are *negative* and *affectionate*" and the "*masculine* or *positive* and *intellectual* temperament" (italics in original).[23] Spiritualist practice, then, created a space for a range of femininities and masculinities, many of which would have violated the gendered proscriptions of Victorian culture.

The gendered modes in which Spiritualists claimed religious authority provided the means by which the practice was demonized and marginalized by nonbelievers. It was precisely the negative, feminine coding of mediumship that shaped a cultural understanding of Spiritualism as irrational and connected it with excessive, uncontrolled sexuality that later allowed doctors to recategorize the medium as the hysteric. The tropes they employed became familiar in the latter part of the century as they were appropriated by the emergent discourse of sexology.

Spiritualism flourished at a time when the dominant culture, informed by science and medicine, was working overtime to fix the boundaries of maleness and femaleness (and later, homosexuality and heterosexuality) and solidifying those binaries as natural, essential, and immutable. It is not surprising that Victorian women, cast as both pious and passive, could claim mediumship as a natural calling. Quite different questions and connections are raised by the fact that a significant number of men would find a parallel power in receptivity, crafting an unconventional model of masculinity through spiritual mediumship and trance speaking. That both Spiritualist men and women could reimagine their gender through practices ranging from cross-dressing to defying the vocal ranges equated with sexual difference, as shown below, suggests yet another world of transformations.

Spiritualist practice reveals social formations that even in their time were considered transgressive. From a twenty-first-century standpoint, Spiritualism seems rather queer in at least three ways: as gender deviance and resistance to gender binarism; as sexual deviance both in the form of free love, which defied the regulatory structure of heterosexual marriage, and in corporeal same-sex connections that belie easy divisions between the homosocial and the homosexual; and as a language of gendered practice and erotic attachment that directly influenced the seemingly secular consolidation of these categories in the name of sexological science.

At first glance, these queer elements most obviously involve transgressive sexual encounters and gender formations. Yet the amorphous sexual matrix offered by Spiritualism so emphatically blurred contemporary categorical distinctions that the sexual couplings of Spiritualists may be the least strange thing about them. In historicizing Spiritualist practices, one must resist severing the connections between religion, politics, sexuality, gender, and less easily named modes of experience whose very connectedness informed Spiritualist philosophy. The boundaries that Spiritualists crossed—or momentarily bridged—produced a unique set of affinities through a radical collapse of temporality. Crossing the boundary of life itself worked to unsettle a whole

Figure 12. "Planchette," albumen print mounted on stereopticon card,
ca. 1880. Wm. B. Becker Collection/American Museum of Photography
© MMVII The American Photography Museum, Inc. Viewed through a
stereopticon, the doubled image appears three-dimensional. Stereoscopes
were widely available in the United States beginning in the 1860s; this image
of two girls, a planchette (or Ouija board), and a conjured spirit likely dates
from the 1880s.

series of earthly boundaries, and this unsettling provided both a creative opportunity for believers and a disturbing set of paradoxes for debunkers.

SPIRITUAL AFFINITIES

Mediums often began their dealings with the dead from the borderland of childhood. Andrew Jackson Davis, who became a leading Spiritualist philosopher, like many mediums discovered his spiritual powers in early adolescence.[24] The apprentice of a rural shoemaker, Davis had skills of healing and diagnosing illness that far surpassed his formal education, of which he had had no more than a few years. His clairvoyance and otherworldly knowledge soon earned him the designation the "Poughkeepsie Seer."[25] Emma Hardinge described his bearing and manner as unusual, given his station: "Of a slight and delicate temperament, the young physician possessed a degree of intuitive refinement which in some sense compensated for his total deficiency of educational culture, and an artificial grace which could not be expected from his exceedingly humble origin."[26] What is notable in Hardinge's account is that she cannot seem to decide on which of Davis's multiple differences to focus—his age, class, effeminacy, or rhetorical refinement.

As befitted one with effeminate refinement and delicate grace, Davis soon proved himself an adept submissive. At the age of fourteen, he was "magnetized" by William E. Levingston, of Poughkeepsie, an itinerant mesmerist who discovered that the shoemaker's boy had wonderful clairvoyant powers. Levingston gradually drew him from his trade into association with the world of mesmerism, and the two performed together as "operator" and "subject." In 1845, under the sway of another masculine influence, Davis traveled to New York City to give a series of "trance lectures."[27] Davis's "harmonial philosophy" and heralding of a new dispensation, emanating as it did from a boy with only a "slender stock of village scholasticism," attracted curious crowds eager to witness these mysterious ministrations.[28]

Though Davis began his career magnetized by stronger spirits and guided by eminent men, his passive adolescence gave way to a more active, albeit somewhat atypical, manhood. After leaving his male operators, Davis convinced a wealthy admirer, Catherine DeWolf Dodge, to divorce her husband and marry him. As well as being more affluent than Davis, Mrs. Dodge was also quite a bit older, making her a "strong spirit" and an appropriate guide for the young medium.[29] Within the Spiritualist community, erotic and spiritual attachments that transgressed differences in sex, age, and status were equalized through a belief in free love or "spiritual affinities."

The *Spiritual Telegraph* editor Samuel B. Brittan delineated the deceptively simple principle behind "spiritual" marriage. "To constitute a true spiritual marriage two congenial souls must be irresistibly attracted and perfectly conjoined . . . by the spiritual natural law of affinity; and when the marriage falls short of this ideal, if the married pair cannot possibly agree to live together, they should do the next best thing, which may be to separate by mutual consent."[30] After the death of his first wife, Davis married a second previously married woman, Mary Fenn Love, and then divorced her for Della Markham, a third.[31] Far from a marriage made in heaven, the connection between the free-love and Spiritualist movements inspired regular and heated commentary in Spiritualist and mainstream newspapers throughout the 1860s and 1870s.[32]

Free lovers were not the only sex radicals publicly allied with Spiritualism. Dr. Mary Walker, who was dubbed "the most distinguished invert in the United States" in a 1902 medical journal article, had been singled out more than twenty years earlier by a fellow reformer as an example of the "Follies of Spiritualists."[33] Known for her bloomers, top hat, "neatly fitting frock coat," and "gold-headed cane, which she handled with the dexterity of a city dandy," Walker was a dress reformer, surgeon, and the only woman to receive the Congressional Medal of Honor for Meritorious Service during the Civil War.[34] Walker, who volunteered as an army doctor and insisted on wearing the standard male Union Army officer's uniform, also refused to return her medal when Congress revised the criteria for awarding it to include only "actual combat with an enemy."[35]

In 1878, she attracted the attention of both the police and the tabloid press when she was arrested "for breaking the law, which forbids members of one sex from wearing the attire of the other." The *New York Sun* ran the arrest as a color story about an obviously well-known downtown character. "Dr. Mary Walker walked up Broadway shortly after noon yesterday, wearing trousers, as usual, and carrying her cane. The customary crowd followed her." At Franklin Street, Patrolman Lawrence Flannery stopped her, asking, "Are yez man or woman?" Refusing to answer, Walker shook off the officer's hand and told him to "mind your own business." After her arrest, she threatened to "carry a pistol" next time. The *Sun* reporter clearly sided with Walker, rebuking the officer for his "illegal" arrest, which Walker termed "the most enormous of the many outrages perpetrated upon her by 'Jacks in office.'" Sharing the enthusiasm of the swelling crowd that followed her from the precinct to the superintendent's office, the *Sun* delights in reporting that Superintendent Walling and Walker greeted each other as "old friends," concluding: "As her trousers were not worn for the purpose of disguise, in order to commit a felony, [Walling] ruled that her wearing them did not come within the statute prohibiting women from attiring themselves as though they were men."[36] The *Sun* ran a bit of doggerel about the incident the next day, entitled "Dr. Mary Walker's Protest":

> In a bifurcated Walker suit
> I take my customary walk
> Regardless of the mob's pursuit
> And careless of the common talk.

If hardly a paean to Walker's "protest," it did celebrate her bravado with the closing line, "Beware! She shoots!"[37]

Walker's dress-reforming dandyism was part of a larger political movement, but it was also intimately connected to her belief in Spiritualism.[38] In 1878, twelve years after Walker had been elected president of the National Dress Reform Association, one editorialist of a leading Spiritualist newspaper pointed to her as an example of the "odd set," a "small proportion" of Spiritualists who are "generally the most noisy." He continued: "They carry all their hobbies to extremes, and are perpetually forcing their eccentric notions upon the people who do not care to hear them. . . . Nature never designed that a woman should be a man, nor a man a woman, and these efforts at transposition, especially in the part of the male sex who seek to appear as feminine as possible, is an evidence of a weak, unbalanced or disordered mind."[39] This writer tellingly slips from confronting "noisy" notions that "people" do not want to hear to attacking the gender that nature did not intend, ending with a particularly pointed assault on effeminate men in an article about a gender-transgressive woman. These tendencies would become increasingly joined in descriptions of a certain set of Spiritualists. Spiritualist circles overlapped with American decadents, dandies, and other denizens of urban subcultures; but what is important here is that when mediums wrote about their gender embodiments and, in some cases, same-sex partnerships, they explicitly employed the language of Spiritualism. Walker's "transposition," later termed *inversion,* was not occasioned by Spiritualist practice, but it was clearly not anomalous in Spiritualist communities.[40]

For some Spiritualists, gender transposition was more central to the phenomenon of mediumship. Decades after Henry Steel Olcott and Helena Petrovna Blavatsky joined forces to found modern Theosophy, Olcott remembered their first fateful meeting and the anxious letters that soon ensued. He portrays "her very first letter to me, written from New York within a week after she left me . . . addressing me as 'Dear Friend' and signing herself 'Jack,' and . . . her second one, dated six days later and signed 'Jack Blavatsky.'"[41] Blavatsky's transgendered self-nomination, while seemingly playful in these epistles, would haunt her career.

After their initial meeting, Blavatsky and Olcott traveled together to India, establishing a world headquarters for their newly founded Theosophical Society first in Bombay, and then at Adyar, and later in London.[42] Blavatsky's reputation as the "Divine Hermaphrodite" signaled an appreciative understanding of her syncretic fusion of diverse religious traditions and a mixing of the gender codes presumed to attend them. Yet these mutual crossings also drew phobic and mocking critique. The well-known Spiritualist William Emmette Coleman wrote that Blavatsky's Theosophy amounted to a "mongrel mixture of Brahmanism, Buddhism, Christianity, Rosicrucianism, Kabbalism, European mediaeval magic, the hermetic philosophy, Kardecian re-incarnation, astrology, modern Spiritualism, and Eliphas Levi's Parisian system of magic, with a little morsel of modern science and philosophy thrown in to give it a slight coloring in conformity to 19th-century modes of thought." After this breathless paratactic recitation, Coleman concludes: "And this hotch-potch of rubbish fabricated by Madame Blavatsky, the product of the mind of one old woman, has been and is being accepted by a number of other old women of both sexes, some of them being those who were formerly Spiritualists."[43]

Coleman's 1888 complaint is made in the defense of Spiritualism as the proper "philosophical system," in opposition to "the crude unscientific speculations of the mystagogues of ancient mediaeval, and modern times."[44] Years earlier, Blavatsky had understood herself as one such defender of Spiritualism. Olcott reported in his diary: "'I speak to you,' she tells me, "as a true friend to yourself and (as a) Spiritualist anxious to save Spiritualism from a danger.'"[45] This clear and present danger was Jesse Shepard, the medium who portrayed the boarders of the Vermont Eddy materializations as "bored," even as he found himself fascinated with the way Blavatsky "mesmerized" Olcott when they first met. Blavatsky entreated Olcott "not to praise the mediumistic musical performance of one Jesse Sheppard [sic], whose pretence to having sung before the Czar, and other boasts she had discovered to be absolutely false."[46] Blavatsky herself would fight charges of charlatanism, but her pique over Jesse Shepard seems to have less to do with his credibility as a musical trance medium than with his faked society credentials and his involvement with the Russian demimonde.

Blavatsky tended to travel in tonier circles. Olcott reports her comments on Shepard: "Led by his unlucky star, Sheppard—she writes—had brought her a lot of his St. Petersburgh credentials, in Russian, to translate. Among them she found a Police license to sing at the Salle Koch, a low-lager bier saloon and dance hall, resorted to by dissipated characters of both sexes, and a music-master's bills for 32 roubles, for teaching him certain Russian songs— which we heard him sing at Eddy's *in a dark séance when he was ostensibly under control of Grisi and Lablache!*" (italics in original).[47] Shepard's own memoir attests that he felt deprived of both aesthetic and spiritual inspiration. He writes: "There were séances every evening at about eight o'clock in the great kitchen of barn-like proportions . . . the room being so dark that nothing could be plainly distinguished. At these séances there was no music, and what with the strain of trying to see the 'forms' and the continuous nerve tension many were glad when the séance was over."[48]

Jesse Shepard and Helena Blavatsky's mutual animus was clearly the effect of having one too many divas in a room. But theirs was also a turf war fought by two mystical masters whose differently bent gender would mark their future careers. Shepard was already something of a Spiritualist superstar by the time he met Blavatsky and Olcott. Beginning in the 1860s, he captured fans from St. Petersburg to Paris with his extraordinary vocal range. Neither falsetto nor castrato, when Shepard entered a state of trance he channeled a an uncannily high voice that he credited to the spirits who sang through him. The Spiritualist press pronounced him "an extraordinary musical genius." One 1868 reviewer wrote: "It seems impossible to distinguish him from a female soprano." And, like a blurb from *Playbill:* "Critics are unanimous in pronouncing [Jesse Shepard] the 'greatest male soprano living.'"[49] It was Shepard's ability to channel female spirit voices that most impressed his Spiritualist audience.

After his sojourns in Europe, Shepard landed in boomtown San Diego in 1886, where he fell into a Spiritualist circle that included the wealthy ranchers William and John High. Shepard seemingly enchanted the High brothers, who offered to build Shepard and his longtime companion, Lawrence Tonner, a magnificent mansion. The result, Villa Montezuma, a Victorian manor with a stained-glass window featuring the poet Sappho, still stands in San Diego. Writing under the name Francis Grierson, Shepard was also a prolific author: his most notable works were a mystical biography of Abraham Lincoln, *The Valley of the Shadows,* and his final book, 1921's *Psycho-phone Messages,* which gathers the words of famous persons delivered from beyond the grave. Shepard's career ended in Los Angeles, where he lectured, performed, and accompanied himself on piano as a "World Famous Mystic." Los Angeles newspapers reported that he died at age seventy-nine while performing an Egyptian arabesque at his beloved piano.[50] Marking his late career more than his international status as a musician and medium, the *Los Angeles Times* subtitled his obituary "Francis Grierson Declared Victim of Starvation Here after Pawning Watch Presented by King."[51]

The famous medium and Spiritualist theologian, Wilberforce J. Colville, born a generation after Jesse Shepard, styled himself after the famed nineteenth-century trance speaker Cora L. V. Scott Hatch, known for her radiant beauty. Colville, who burst onto the American scene and packed lecture halls across the country, was best influenced by one operator, a young gentlemen of "extraordinary psychological powers" and "very attractive personal appearance" to whom Colville devoted himself from the first moment of their meeting.[52] Colville was typical of mediums in that his receptivity was occasioned by a strong male operator. A certain Cornelius Throgmorton gets special praise in Colville's autobiography as "a gentleman who knows more about [my] real history and character than perhaps any other one individual now living."[53]

Colville began his long career at sixteen and chronicled his life and work in numerous writings, including a book-length autobiography in which he tells the story of how, in 1874, he found Spiritualism. A religious teenager, an active Unitarian, and a choir singer much in demand in area churches, Colville had never been interested in Spiritualism until one day, walking through his native Brighton, England, he spotted a notice advertising a lecture to be held that night by the famed American trance speaker Cora Hatch. Colville described feeling himself strangely drawn to Hatch and went to hear the medium speak. Recalling his first sight of her, he remembered feeling "under a most agreeable spell, as though some very pleasant change were about to take place."[54]

The change began as soon as Colville got home. Sitting down with his family and their boarders, who spent the dinner hour making fun of his new interest in Spiritualism, he felt his body undergo "a complete transformation, and in a girlish voice of very peculiar tone, expressed his readiness to improvise on any suitable theme."[55] In his account, the boarders just stared. He described the sensation as being "suddenly lifted in the air. . . . I seemed to have an enormous head and a very small body. My lips seemed to be moving mechanically, under the pressure of some influence over which I could exert, and could will to exert, no power whatever."[56] His dinnertime trance speech concluded with the words: "We thank you for the opportunity afforded us tonight of commencing a work through this instrument which will spread over Europe, America, and the antipodes."[57] This moment marked the beginning of Colville's career as a Spiritualist, the time-honored process of being "developed" as a medium. From this point, it was female spirits who spoke through him.

Spiritualist trance, though it sometimes came unannounced, could also be reproduced in public settings and performances. Colville, like Andrew Jackson Davis before him, was easily put under sway and worked with a series of strong male operators. Accounts of Colville often mentioned that his chosen companions were "vigorous young men," and that "he seemed entirely destitute of appreciation of wedded bliss, and though thoroughly domesticated from childhood, [was said to be] utterly unfit to enter the married state." Colville himself wrote that he could not understand the attraction between the sexes, except only "very theoretically."[58] Though not attracted to the opposite sex, he was a tireless campaigner for women's suffrage and often spoke of the importance of "the female principle" to spirituality. He wrote, "The degradation of women is always supported most strongly when the belief is regnant that only males are fit to officiate at sacred altars."[59]

Observers commented on Colville's receptivity, but they also paid excessive, almost obsessive, attention to his body, often remarking on his delicate and unnaturally youthful appearance: "Mr. Colville is beardless, boyish, *spirituelle* looking"; he is "small of stature, but with mighty powers. He has a large and remarkably shaped head, almost all intellect and spirit, with only base enough to anchor him to the earth."[60] The recurring fascination with the shape of his skull suggests that his difference, which ultimately was not physical at all, needed to be rooted and fixed in the body. Phrenology provided the means to do so.

THE POETICS OF ATTACHMENT

The popular mid-nineteenth-century science of phrenology, a precursor to sexology and other emergent sciences of the mind, offers valuable contexts for understanding how Spiritualism persisted as a residual discourse both in the emergent cultures of science and secularism and in twentieth-century notions of sexuality and gender. As Raymond Williams has defined it, the residual is a cultural element that "has been effectively formed in the past but is still active in the cultural process, not only and often not at all as an element of the past, but as an effective element of the present."[61] The residual persists as an active strain in culture, experienced and practiced in an alternative or even oppositional relation to the dominant. Spiritual science had a particular power in this moment when the emergent values of the science of sex had yet to coalesce as dominant. The history of phrenology reveals that modern psychological sciences are by no means the product of a Copernican revolution that secularizes the prior terrain of the soul, converting it into the mind or brain. It also shows that this now-debunked science, for all its other regulatory deployments, presented a discourse that sought to integrate the emergent discourses of sexuality with emotional states and spiritual propensities.

Phrenologists postulated that discrete areas of the brain governed specific human characteristics, which could be read through the shape and texture of the skull. Phrenology's assertions that degeneracy and devolution could be correlated with cranial measurements made it an easy partner to racial science and criminology. It was also a sort of first draft of sexology. As late as the 1880s, commentators used phrenological terms when describing Colville. As one biographer noted in 1886, his "leading phrenological indications of character seem to be conscientiousness, benevolence, ideality," whereas he found "amativeness and some others—conspicuous by their absence."[62] Before sexology or the first psychiatric case studies of homosexuality were published, phrenologists identified a region at the base of the brain that was said to govern "amativeness." Individuals in whom this area was underdeveloped experienced, like Colville, "little conjugal love" or "desire to marry" and "were cold, coy, distant and reserved toward the opposite sex." According to Fowler's phrenological guide, this faculty, when "perverted[,] . . . depraves all other propensities."[63] Walt Whitman invoked another area on the phrenological chart, adhesiveness, when he used the term "adhesive love" to describe the attraction and "fervid comradeship" he felt for other men.

Michael Lynch has done groundbreaking work on the critical role of phrenology in Whitman's interventions (poetic and otherwise) in nineteenth-century notions of sexuality and gender.[64] Lorenzo Fowler, who was the publisher of the leading work on phrenology as well as the distributor of the first edition of *Leaves of Grass* and the publisher of the second, personally read Whitman's skull.[65] This moment purportedly produced a "psychic transformation" in Whitman. In the language of science, this reading offered confirmation of the young writer's potential, allowing him to transform himself into a "bold prophet of a rich and new life."[66] More than this, Lynch argues that Whitman's utilization of the phrenological language of adhesiveness was a way to "admit the bodily experience of male-male love," to "create or make possible new developments in that experience," and to produce new modes of literary expression.[67]

Phrenology, which offered no category for the homosexual, made itself available for reinterpretation, as the diagnosis of disease was secondary to its broader purpose of revealing character. Adhesiveness was a moral faculty, associated with friendship and sociability, "manifested regardless of sex"; Whitman reinterpreted it as a term to describe his relationships with other men.[68] This designation stands in contrast to *amativeness,* which was applied to queer young men negatively, connoting only a lack of conjugal love, as in Colville's case. Although Whitman's creative intervention does indeed reclaim a language of science, it is not the same as the function of reverse discourse that Foucault uses to describe the way homosexuals could "speak" collectively after being thus defined by sexology. Rather, Whitman's ability to exploit the language of phrenology points to a transitional moment in the history of science in which the diagnostic was not automatically collapsed into the punitive or curative.

If *adhesiveness* describes Whitman's connection with men, it also describes something of his connection to the world. Literary scholars since the early 1990s have reinterpreted Whitman's poetics and his personal attachments to men as a kind of queer world-making project: as Michael Warner contends, "Whitman wants to make sex public."[69] Peter Coviello argues that "virtually every strand of Whitman's utopian thought devolves upon, and is anchored by, an unwavering belief in the capacity of strangers to recognize, to desire, and to be intimate with one another."[70] Michael Moon takes this will to connection and frames it as the form and mode of Whitman's literary project, his desire "to disseminate affectionate physical presence from (author) to the (audience), fervently and directly."[71] These readings center the enmeshing of the social and the sexual, but it is also important to put these associations on the same plane as the spiritual.[72] Situating Whitman in the same context as Davis and Colville reveals sexuality as an emergent discourse of attachment rising out of a subcultural cosmology of spiritual connectedness.

The "poet of attachment," who wanted both to connect with and channel the other, published the first edition of *Leaves of Grass* in 1855 and a second edition in 1856.[73] Between the publication of these two editions, he became interested in the phenomenon of trance mediumship. Whether to gain the magical ability to extemporize on any subject or to connect with the Other Side, Walt Whitman tried for a full year to train himself as a medium, taking as his model Cora Hatch, the trance speaker who had first inspired Colville. Whitman revealed his metaphysical failure at a meeting of the New York Conference of Spiritualists, which he attended to discuss the question of the day: "What Makes a Medium?" According to the meeting minutes, Whitman "had observed that mediums were of every variety physically, intellectually and morally. One was delicate, frail and of nervous constitution, another was robust, healthy and vigorous. One was ignorant and imbecile, while another was intelligent and learned. He wished to come at the knowledge of what peculiar constitution, temperament, quality or condition is requisite to constitute a medium." Whitman asked a phrenological question and received a spiritualist answer. Cora Hatch, who was leading the discussion, explained to him that it was really not about him, his constitution, or temperament: what was required was a corollary "medium-spirit on the other side of the line." This answer could only have been frustrating to the poet who prided himself on his uncanny skills of connection.[74] Whitman's porosity enabled him to move horizontally, imagining laterally shared social worlds. Whitman's unrealized spiritual communion may have driven him to seek connection more intently through his writing. Regardless, his forays into Spiritualism provide a crucial context for understanding Whitman's urge to forge intimate bonds with spiritual and embodied strangers.

The history of sexuality as a secular discipline allows the recovery of Whitman as a queer ancestor. This practice, however, has effaced his status as a fellow traveler in a culture in which the scientific was shot though with the spiritual, which together were theorizing the sexual. By the beginning of the twentieth century, Whitman's "adhesiveness" would be termed *inversion*, taking its place in the taxonomies of sexological science. The Spiritualist (and musical) transgendering of a Shepard or Colville would take on specifically scientific, secular inflections.

By the early twentieth century, stories like Shepard's channeling of female sopranos faded from the Spiritualist press. Yet, in the decades after the Civil War, Spiritualists had embraced Colville, Shepard, and others who voiced and embodied a range of fluid genders and sexualities that countered the dictates of dominant nineteenth-century culture. Moving across and between genders, Spiritualists claimed a language and experience of disembodiment and reembodiment before other discourses emerged to give new meaning. One of these new discourses was sexology.

TRAPPED SOULS

Turning to the documents of sexology, one finds that even the annals of science prove haunted. During the late nineteenth century and well into the twentieth, both sexologists and the narrators of their case studies use the language of inversion, of women's souls trapped in men's bodies and vice versa. Historians, like many of the sexual scientists before them, have typically read through or past this language of the trapped soul, seeing it as somehow arbitrary or as merely metaphorical.[75] Yet attending to the historical specificity of this language reveals a world in which spirituality functioned not only as a powerful residual discourse, in Raymond Williams's formulation, but also as a function of emergent discourse itself.[76] Returning sexology to its original context illuminates the spiritual and the scientific as inextricably linked.

A number of sexologists employed spiritual, and in many ways explicitly Spiritualist, language when describing the new subjects of sexual deviation. Interestingly, they are the sexologists who have been seen as somewhat less stigmatizing of their subjects. In early sexological writing, especially the work of Richard von Krafft-Ebing, "sexual inversion" was characterized as a sickness, a manifestation of "functional degeneration" that sometimes took the form of a gendered self trapped in a differently sexed body.[77] By the turn of the century, two alternative sexological approaches had become increasingly influential; both rejected the notion that same-sex attachment was simply an illness. One was the "third-sex model" put forward by Karl Heinrich Ulrichs and widely circulated in Britain by Edward Carpenter as the concept of the "intermediate sex." Carpenter, who counted himself among the intermediate sex, attributed a spiritual power and occult knowledge to these subjects, who "through their double nature, command of life in all its phases, and a certain freemasonry of the secrets of the two sexes . . . may well favor their function as reconcilers and interpreters."[78] The other was the model of sexual inversion popularized by Havelock Ellis, which was similar to Krafft-Ebing's idea of souls trapped in the wrong bodies but without his notion of degeneracy.[79] Although he used different terminology from either Ulrichs or Carpenter, Ellis shared similar beliefs, among them that homosexuality was neither an "illness that needed to be cured" nor a freely chosen "vice," that "inversion was not pathological, it was not a hideous anomaly or an acquired vice, and it was not the result of an 'execrable seduction.'"[80] Part of Ellis's sympathy for his subjects is revealed in the degree to which he reproduces their own words in his case studies. At least some of these narratives are steeped in the language of Spiritualism through its British descendant, Theosophy.

Preserved in sexological texts is a historical crossing, marking a moment when the extrapolations of Spiritualist thought met with the emergent discourses of sexual science. At the beginning of the twentieth century, sexology was less an incipient science that a stew of the mystical and mundane. As the historian Joy Dixon has argued, "Sexology may have triumphed as an academically respectable way of knowing about sex in the twentieth century but, at the time of its creation, it by no means held the field uncontested." Dixon frames her study of British Theosophy's presence in the discourse of sexology as an attempt "to explore an alternative trajectory in which—as psychics, mystics or theosophists—men and women . . . influenced, assimilated, and reworked new sexological and psychoanalytic claims regarding gender and sexuality into and through an elaborate constellation of spiritual beliefs, beliefs that they claimed were also scientific, even though their occult science might not be universally (or even widely) recognized as such."[81] Belying the notion that the practice effectively taped sexological labels over the mouths of its silenced subjects, at least some sexological narrators were actively engaged in shaping the new discourse and brought to it their particular knowledge of spiritual and occult science. Like Spiritualism in the United States, Theosophy was a site for a sophisticated struggle over some of the most vexing issues of the day: questions about the nature of scientific knowledge and its place in late Victorian society and the possibilities (and the limits) of the scientific method in understanding phenomena like mediumship. It was also a spiritual and political organization that attracted some of the most prominent freethinkers in the United States and Britain.[82] Radclyffe Hall, Havelock Ellis, E. M. Forster, William James, and Edward Carpenter were all part of a large, cosmopolitan Theosophical circle.

Theosophy differed from Spiritualism in important ways. A belief in reincarnation, a concept not widely endorsed by Spiritualists, made Theosophy an unlikely, but ready, partner to sexology. In the face of new sciences that were inevitably typologizing, if not also pathologizing, Theosophy posed the incarnation of past lives as a mode of subjectivity that offered an alternative to the material conditions of turn-of-the-century British culture. Theosophy offered a theory in which one's embodied person might differ from one's "individuality" as a matter of course; this bifurcation need not be pathological but merely the spiritual residuum of past lives. This distinctive understanding of reincarnation was a highly debated and esoteric tenet that held that "a person is never reincarnated, yet from a higher point of view, an individuality is."[83] This curious distinction between personhood and individuality mirrors the distinction between soul and body that undergirds the logic of sexology.

Unlike Theosophy, Spiritualist theories of embodiment never meshed quite so neatly with sexology's typological regime. Both the theosophical theory of reincarnation and the sexological notion of a soul trapped in a particular body depend on an idea of fixity, whereas Spiritualist embodiment turned on a notion of flux, both in subjectivity and time. A Spiritualist medium would not have described souls trapped inside her. When female spirits spoke through male mediums (or vice versa), the phenomenon was a product of the mediums' own receptivity to other, external presences, not the expression of a spirit trapped in the wrong body. Spiritualism's grounding but elusive category of "receptivity"—the quality that frustrated Whitman in the answer he received to his question about what kind of person can become a medium—speaks of connectedness without identity.

By the 1920s, however, Theosophy had become so tangled and tied to a particular type of transgressive sexuality that it almost stood as an identity in itself. Not coincidentally, Radclyffe Hall, the quintessential invert of the era, who used her fiction to narrate the entrapment of gender and asked Havelock Ellis, the architect of inversion, to write the preface to her novel, publicly embraced Theosophy. The author of *The Well of Loneliness,* Hall is perhaps less well known as a prominent member of London's Society for Psychical Research. More than merely a curious dabbler in the practice, as many leading intellectuals were at the time, she was steeped in the ritual. Hall went so far as to employ a medium to contact her deceased lover, seeking a blessing for a new relationship.[84]

Although it was a 1928 obscenity trial that cemented Hall's reputation as London's best-known literary lesbian, she had also faced magistrates eight years earlier in a less secular, if no less scandalous, affair.[85] In an effort to block Hall's election to the Society for Psychical Research, a member of the society, Saint George Lane Fox Pitt, told two prominent fellow members that Hall was a "grossly immoral woman" who had lived for many years with a "most objectionable person," Mabel Batten, before "influencing" Lady Una Troubridge, "coming between her and her husband" (Fox Pitt's friend Admiral Sir Ernest Charles Troubridge), and "wrecking the Admiral's home."[86] Hall, like Oscar Wilde in 1895, sought to clear her name through the courts, bringing an action for slander. In the midst of the trial, Fox Pitt rescinded his accusations. But the press coverage of the case raises fascinating questions about the relationship between the psychical and the sexual.

The London press hinted at the cause of the alleged slander, naming it "as horrible an accusation as could be made against any woman in this country . . . [that she was] addicted to unnatural vice."[87] Yet the truly sensational language and the bigger typeface were left to the headline writers, who gave the spirits bigger billing than the sapphists.[88] As reported in the trial transcript, Lady Troubridge left her husband not for Hall's mythic mannishness but for the spirit world. She allegedly told her husband that "this 'spirit' business was now her life and that she had no further concern in his views, interests or occupations."[89] A London *Times* editorialist took the occasion to attack spiritual circles more generally, writing: "A slander action of a very simple nature has attracted a great deal of attention, because the evidence revealed to a wondering public something of what goes on in the regions of psychical research."[90] If the love that dare not speak its name was muffled during the trial, the noisy ruminations about the occult effectively stood in for that name in the press. Indeed, the speculation raised by the *Times* as to "what goes on in the regions of psychical research" suggests the extent to which the British public was already wondering about the queer conjurings of mediums in the dark.

The press coverage of the Hall scandal illustrates a forward-moving, secularizing tendency in which both believers in the spirit world and sexually deviant subjects attracted censure, not only for their marginal subjectivity but also for their marginal relation to history. The Spiritualist faced backward, threatening the new, secularizing order. The invert, though often described as atavistic, loomed as a new, frightening creature who would haunt the future. Hall's story reveals these seemingly new secular sexualities to be not very secular after all.

Spiritualism did not die with the end of the nineteenth century. It found its way not only into related spiritualities, like Theosophy, but also functioned as a residual discourse in the science of sexology, one that was critical to the making of modern subjects. For nineteenth-century Spiritualists, communing with spirits was a process by which the lost and departed made themselves known through unsettling occurrences. Hall's conjuring of her ex-lover in the middle of a new relationship need not be literal for readers to understand what it means to be haunted by the past. Certainly there is something about spectral metaphors, of ghosts and hauntings, that has been particularly compelling to queer theorists.[91] Film and literary scholars have elaborated multiple connections between the ghostly and the queer and, more specifically, between the apparitional and the lesbian in nineteenth- and twentieth-century texts. As Terry Castle writes: "The lesbian remains a kind of 'ghost effect' in the cinema world of modern life: elusive, vaporous, difficult to spot—even when she is there in plain view, mortal and magnificent, at the center of the screen."[92] This mode of analysis turns on a notion of visibility and invisibility, a kind of phantom force wherein certain embodied sexualities make themselves visible only to those who have the ability to see. Queer theorists are not alone in using the figure of the ghost as a way to explain the apparitional social status of marginalized subjects; indeed, the ghost is a powerful way of understanding memory and identity.

Radclyffe Hall suffered from living at the threshold of a new era in which an ascendant discourse of science and identity clashed with what seemed to be an anachronistic belief in magic. Her character Stephen Gordon suffers, among other things, a desiccated world in which her gender figuratively haunts her, and her disavowed deviant community quite literally haunts her at the end of the novel. In fact, Radclyffe Hall was part of another community that understood spirits not as unwelcome guests but as, precisely, an otherworldly community. Yet Hall seems to stage the impossibility of either transtemporal or transgender communion as if to sacrifice Stephen as a martyr to the future. In the phantasmic last scene of the *Well of Loneliness,* Gordon is visited by a throng of spirits. Some she recognizes: "Wanda, And someone with a neat little hole in her side—Jamie clasping Barbara by the hand; Barbara with the white flowers of death on her bosom." They call her by her name, and gape at her with their phantom faces, "the haunted melancholy eyes of the invert." They point accusingly with their "shaking, white-skinned, effeminate fingers." In a final *Night of the Living Dead* moment, the damned rise up and proclaim, "We are coming, Stephen—we are still coming on, and our name is legion—you dare not disown us!" In the last line in the book, they demand: "Give us also the right to our existence!"[93] Stephen is possessed by the voices of the past, which return to entreat her not to disown them or, by extension, herself and the future.

One way to read this scene is as an inversion of the presentist urge to find queer ancestors before there was anything like a queer history to recover them. Yet the very literalness of Hall's final pages conjures the more uncanny, the more spectral sexualities that haunt the queer past. In this final scene, in which past, present, and future are collapsed, the "quick, the dead, and the yet unborn" all call on Stephen to give them voice. And finally, "There was only one voice, one demand, her own voice into which those millions had entered."[94] The undead of *The Well of Loneliness* do not offer themselves simply as metaphors. Rather, they insist on their very materiality in a world that does not recognize anything of their presence—in life or in death. Stephen is not so much haunted as forced to become a kind of unwilling medium for untimely sexual subjectivities. Hall's fantasy scene stages the radical dissolve of time, of the possessor and possessed, of the medium and the messengers. Nineteenth-century Spiritualism was an embodied technique of remembrance, born of a century that invented multiple forms of memory: from the technology of photography to history, the secular discipline of memory. Yet mediums, when they channeled spirits of the dead, literally—if momentarily—became the past for the sake of those left in the present. The séance erased divisions in time and space as it did distinctions between bodies and genders. This performance and practice, then, allowed connectivity without fixity, and occasioned "touches across time" made possible not by a particular type of person but by the quality of receptivity.[95] If the history of sexuality has been receptive to the inclusion of a Walt Whitman or Radclyffe Hall, it is because they have been assumed to be secular, sexual subjects, moderns in search of an identity and ripe for reclamation. Yet their "modern" worlds were not merely littered with the residuum of religion. These subjects made sense of their own queer time through spiritual theories of embodiment and forms of memorialization that offered what secular science refused: transfigurative affiliation, consolation, and connection.

NOTES

INTRODUCTION

1. The term *spiritual telegraph* was quickly taken up by nineteenth-century Spiritualists and even used as the title of one of the earliest Spiritualist publications, founded by Samuel Byron Brittan and Charles Partridge in 1852. For early accounts of the Fox sisters' discovery, see *Report of the Mysterious Noises, heard in the house of Mr. John D. Fox in Hydesville, Acadia, Wayne Co. Authenticated by the Certificates and Confirmed by the Statements of Citizens in that Place and Vicinity* (Rochester, NY: D. M. Dewey, 1850) and Eliab Wilkinson Capron, *Singular Revelations: Explanation and History of the Mysterious Communion with Spirits* (Auburn, NY: Finn & Rockwell, 1850).

2. *A Memorial to the Honourable Members of the Senate and House of Representatives of the United States in Congress Assembled* (without signatures), reprinted in S. B. Brittan, *Telegraph Papers,* annual compendium of the *Spiritual Telegraph* 5 (1855): 401. See also "Rappers in Congress," *Mobile [Alabama] Evening News,* reprinted in *Telegraph Papers,* 401, which urges a Congressional investigation of the subject.

3. In 1898, Harrison Bennett, the president of the National Association of Spiritualists, addressed the meeting of the yearly convention "earnestly pleading" for Spiritualists to "make some declaration with regard to the question of Imperialism," as "great standing armies and large standing navies are menaces to the peace of the world." "Report of the President, Harrison D. Barrett, for the Year Ending October 18, S.E. 51," *Banner of Light,* October 22, 1898, 1.

4. On Theosophy in California, see Emmett A. Greenwalt, *California Utopia: Point Loma, 1897–1941* (San Diego, CA: Point Loma Publications, 1978); Bruce F. Campbell, *Ancient Wisdom Revived: A History of the Theosophical Movement* (Berkeley: University of California Press, 1980); and Erik Davis, *The Visionary State: A Journey through California's Spiritual Landscape* (San Francisco, CA: Chronicle Books, 2006).

5. Emma Hardinge Britten, *Modern American Spiritualism: A Twenty Years' Record of the Communion between Earth and the World of the Spirits* (1869; reprint, New York: University Books, 1970), 13.

6. Marvin writes: "I am informed there are four million men and women in America who believe in spiritualism and whose minds are never lifted from its delusion" (*The Philosophy of Spiritualism and the Pathology and Treatment of Mediomania: Two Lectures Read before the New York Liberal Club* [New York: Asa K. Butts & Co., Publishers, 1874], 18). He contrasts his own numbers with those of the eminent barrister and Spiritualist, Judge John Worth Edmonds, who, in a letter to the *Spiritual Magazine* of London dated May 4, 1867, estimated the number of Spiritualists in the United States at "ten millions."

7. The historian Catherine L. Albanese, who has done the most thorough accounting of Spiritualists in the United States, writes that even a figure of one million, "this pared-down version for the mid-1850s," in a population of twenty-eight million is "still impressive" (*A Republic of Mind and Spirit: A Cultural History of Metaphysical Religion in* America [New Haven, CT: Yale University Press, 2007], 221).

8. John Weiss, ed., *Life and Correspondence of Theodore Parker*, vol. 1 (London: Longmans, Green, and Co., 1863), 428, quoted in R. Laurence Moore, *In Search of White Crows: Spiritualism, Parapsychology and American Culture* (New York: Oxford University Press, 1977), 4.

9. Albanese, *Republic of Mind and Spirit*, 6. Albanese's magisterial remapping of American religious history is more complex than I can do justice to here and should change utterly what historians call "American religion."

10. The National Association of Spiritualists was founded in 1893, and the formal record keeping of the organization began in that year.

11. On the séance circle as the "structure of Spiritualist practice," see Bret E. Carroll, *Spiritualism in Antebellum America* (Bloomington: Indiana University Press, 1997), 120–51.

12. The Spiritualist newspaper *The Banner of Light* regularly ran advertisements for "rooms for mediums." One, in the edition of January 23, 1858, advertised "two parlors, furnished in handsome style. Also an office on the first floor, suitable for a healing medium."

13. Gerrit Smith, *Lectures on the Religion of Reason* (Petersboro, NY: C. A. Hammond, 1864), 39–40.

14. This history is well documented in Ann Braude, *Radical Spirits: Spiritualism and Women's Rights in Nineteenth-Century America* (Boston: Beacon Press, 1989).

15. The nineteenth-century Spiritualist press was vast. I rely most heavily on the newspapers *Banner of Light*, the *Spiritual Telegraph*, the *Religio-philosophical Journal*, and, to a lesser extent, the *Shekinah* and the *Carrier Dove* (see bibliography for details of publication). Many of the contributors to these publications also published longer works in book or tract form.

16. Hardinge's *Modern American Spiritualism* was probably the first full treatment. Also useful is Julia Schlesinger, *Workers in the Vineyard: A Review of the Progress of Spiritualism* (San Francisco: By the Author, 1896). Earlier works include John W. Edmonds and George T. Dexter, *Spiritualism*, 2 vols. (New York: Partridge & Brittan, 1853); Eliab Wilkinson Capron, *Modern Spiritualism; Its Facts and Fanaticisms, Its Consistencies and Contradictions* (Boston: Bela Marsh, 1855); and Uriah Clark, *Plain Guide to Spiritualism: A Hand-Book for Skeptics, Inquirers, Clergymen, Believers, Lecturers, Mediums, Editors...* (Boston: W. White & Company, 1863). For histories by contemporary skeptics or ex-Spiritualists, see Frank Podmore's somewhat unreliable *Modern Spiritualism: A History and a Criticism, in Two Volumes* (London: Methuen and Company, 1902) and Joseph McCabe, *Spiritualism: A Popular History From 1847* (London: T. Fisher Unwin, 1920).

17. Arthur Conan Doyle, *The History of Spiritualism*, vol. 1 (London: George H. Doran Company, 1926); Robert Dale Owen, *The Debatable Land between This World and the Next* (New York: G. W. Carleton & Co., 1872); and Robert Dale Owen, *Footfalls on the Boundary of Another World* (Philadelphia: J. B. Lippincott & Co., 1860).

18. Dissertations include Burton Gates Brown Jr., "Spiritualism in Nineteenth-Century America" (Ph.D. diss., Boston University, 1973); Mary Farrell Bednarowski, "Nineteenth-Century American Spiritualism: An Attempt at a Scientific Religion" (Ph.D. diss., University of Minnesota, 1973); and Ernest Joseph Isaacs, "A History of Nineteenth-Century Spiritualism as a Religious and Social Movement" (Ph.D. diss., University of Wisconsin, 1975). Books include Howard Kerr, *Spirit Rappers and Roaring Radicals: Spiritualism in American Literature, 1850–1900* (Urbana: University of Illinois Press, 1972); Ruth Brandon, *The Passion for the Occult in the Nineteenth Century* (Chicago: University of Chicago Press, 1973); Moore, *In Search of White Crows;* Braude, *Radical Spirits;* Carroll, *Spiritualism in Antebellum America;* Robert S. Cox, *Body and Soul: A Sympathetic History of American Spiritualism* (Charlottesville: University of Virginia Press, 2003); and John J. Kucich, *Ghostly Communion: Cross-Cultural Spiritualism in Nineteenth-Century American Literature* (Hanover, NH: Dartmouth College Press, 2004).

19. Braude, "Introduction to the Second Edition," *Radical Spirits: Spiritualism and Women's Rights in Nineteenth-Century America,* 2nd ed. (Bloomington: Indiana University Press, 2001), xxii. Since the initial publication of Braude's book, Bret E. Carroll and Robert S. Cox have engaged the politics of Spiritualism, focusing instead on the reactionary undertones of Spiritualist reformism: see Carroll, *Spiritualism in Antebellum America;* and Cox, *Body and Soul.*

20. The year 1877 marks an end point because it was then that President Rutherford B. Hayes pulled federal troops out of the South to use against striking railroad workers in the North. The years 1873 and 1875 are also crucial, marking legislative retreats from the inclusive interpretations of citizenship found in the Reconstruction amendments.

21. Daniel Walker Howe, "Victorian Culture in America," in *Victorian America* (Philadelphia: University of Pennsylvania Press, 1976), 13.

22. On the failures of Radical Reconstruction, see Eric Foner, *Reconstruction: America's Unfinished Revolution, 1863–1877* (New York: Harper & Row, 1988). On the aging of the Civil War generation and the ordering of America, see George Fredrickson, *The Inner Civil War* (New York: Harper and Row, 1965); Robert Wiebe, *Search for Order, 1877–1920* (New York: Hill and Wang, 1967); John Higham, *From Boundlessness to Consolidation* (Ann Arbor: University of Michigan Press, 1969); and Alan Trachtenberg, *The Incorporation of America: Culture and Society in the Gilded Age* (New York: Hill and Wang, 1982). Histories of the "Gilded Age" tend to omit mention of utopianism and religious reform cultures, focusing instead on party politics, labor radicalism, and the seeds of Progressivism and Populism. See, for example, Sean Dennis Cashman, *America in the Gilded Age* (New York: New York University Press, 1993).

23. Wiebe, *Search for Order*, 4. John L. Thomas, in his classic essay on nineteenth-century American reform movements, similarly casts the post–Civil War years as a time of intellectual and political "counterrevolution": see Thomas, "Romantic Reform in America, 1815–1865," in *Intellectual History in America*, ed. Cushing Strout (New York: Harper & Row, 1968).

24. *Banner of Light*, September 21, 1872.

25. Douglas Crimp, "Mourning and Militancy," in *Melancholia and Moralism: Essays on AIDS and Queer Politics* (Cambridge, MA: MIT Press, 2002).

26. Michael Moon, "Memorial Rags," in *Professions of Desire*, ed. George E. Haggerty and Bonnie Zimmerman (New York: Modern Language Association of America, 1995); David L. Eng and David Kazanjian, eds., *Loss* (Berkeley: University of California Press, 2003); George E. Haggerty, "Love and Loss: An Elegy," *GLQ: A Journal of Gay and Lesbian Studies* 10, no. 3 (2004): 385–404; and Judith Butler, *Precarious Life: The Powers of Mourning and Violence* (London: Verso, 2006)

27. Philippe Ariès, *L'homme devant la mort* (Paris: Éditions du Seuil, 1977); Philippe Ariès et al., *Death in America*, ed. David E. Stannard (Philadelphia: University of Pennsylvania Press, 1974); Philippe Ariès, *Images of Man in Death* (Cambridge, MA: Harvard University Press, 1985); and Philippe Ariès, *The Hour of Our Death*, trans. Helen Weaver (Oxford: Oxford University Press, 1991).

28. Peter Homans, "Introduction: The Decline of Mourning Practices in Modern Western Societies; A Short Sketch" in *Symbolic Loss: The Ambiguity of Mourning and Memory at Century's End*, ed. Peter Homans (Charlottesville: University Press of Virginia, 2000), ix. See also Alessia Ricciardi, *The Ends of Mourning:*

Psychoanalysis, Literature, Film (Stanford, CA: Stanford University Press, 2003), and William Watkin, *On Mourning: Theories of Loss in Modern Literature* (Edinburgh: Edinburgh University Press, 2004).

29. Ricciardi, *Ends of Mourning,* 3.

30. James Baldwin, *The Evidence of Things Not Seen* (New York: Holt, Rinehart & Winston, 1985); Toni Morrison, "Unspeakable Things Unspoken: The Afro-American Presence in American Literature," *Michigan Quarterly Review* 28 (Winter 1989): 1–34; Patricia White, "Female Spectator, Lesbian Specter: *The Haunting,*" in *Sexuality and Space,* ed. Beatriz Colomina (Princeton, NJ: Princeton Papers on Architecture, 1992), 131–61; Terry Castle, *The Apparitional Lesbian: Female Homosexuality and Modern Culture* (New York: Columbia University Press, 1993); Jacques Derrida, *Specters of Marx: The State of the Debt, the Work of Mourning and the New International,* trans. Peggy Kamuf (New York: Routledge, 1994); Joseph Roach, *Cities of the Dead: Circum-Atlantic Performance* (New York: Columbia University Press, 1996); Patricia White, *Uninvited: Classical Hollywood Cinema and Lesbian Representability* (Bloomington: Indiana University Press, 1999); Sharon Patricia Holland, *Raising the Dead: Readings of Death and (Black) Subjectivity* (Durham, NC: Duke University Press, 2000); Russ Castronovo, *Necro Citizenship: Death, Eroticism, and the Public Sphere in the Nineteenth-Century United States* (Durham, NC: Duke University Press, 2001); and Carla Freccero, "Queer Spectrality: Haunting the Past," in *A Companion to LGBT/Q Studies,* ed. George E. Haggerty and Molly McGarry (London: Blackwell Publishing, Inc., 2007).

31. Avery F. Gordon, *Ghostly Matters: Haunting and the Sociological Imagination* (Minneapolis: University of Minnesota Press, 1997), 8.

32. See for example, Epes Sargent, *The Proof Palpable of Immortality; Being An Account of the Materialization Phenomenon of Modern Spiritualism* (Boston: Colby & Rich, 1876).

33. "Concerning Things Spiritual," *Nation,* January 17, 1867, 53.

34. On mourning in American sentimental culture, see Ann Douglas, *The Feminization of American Culture* (New York: Doubleday, 1977); Karen Halttunen, *Confidence Men and Painted Women: A Study of Middle-Class Culture in America, 1830–1870* (New Haven, CT: Yale University Press, 1982); Carol Mavor, *Pleasures Taken: Performances of Sexuality and Loss in Victorian Photographs* (Durham, NC: Duke University Press, 1995); and Mary Louise Kete, *Sentimental Collaborations: Mourning and Middle-Class Identity in Nineteenth-Century America* (Durham, NC: Duke University Press, 2000).

35. I take this term from Talal Asad, *Genealogies of Religion: Discipline and Reasons of Power in Christianity and Islam* (Baltimore, MD: Johns Hopkins University Press, 1993), 46.

36. Jon Butler, *Awash in a Sea of Faith: Christianizing the American People* (Cambridge, MA: Harvard University Press, 1990), 225–56.

37. Sydney E. Ahlstrom, *A Religious History of the American People* (New Haven, CT: Yale University Press, 1972), 475.

38. Mechal Sobel, *Trabelin' On: The Slave Journey to An Afro-Baptist Faith* (Westport, CT: Greenwood Press, 1979) and Butler, *Awash,* 152–53. On the persistence of Spiritualism in nineteenth- and twentieth-century African American culture, see Cynthia D. Schrager, "Both Sides of the Veil: Race, Science, and Mysticism in W. E. B. Dubois," *American Quarterly* 48, no. 4 (December 1996), 551–86; Victoria W. Woolcott, "Mediums, Messages, and Lucky Numbers: African-American Female Spiritualists and Numbers Runners in Interwar Detroit," in *The Geography of Identity,* ed. Patricia Yaeger (Ann Arbor: University of Michigan Press, 1996), 273–306; and Daphne A. Brooks, *Bodies in Dissent: Spectacular Performances of Race and Freedom, 1850–1910* (Durham, NC: Duke University Press, 2006).

39. See, for example, "Priestcraft at Work," *Banner of Light,* March 10, 1866.

40. Edmonds and Dexter, *Spiritualism,* 1: 44, quoted in Howard Kerr and Charles L. Crow, "Introduction," *The Occult in America: New Historical Perspectives* (Urbana: University of Illinois Press, 1983), 3.

41. Max Weber, *The Protestant Ethic and the Spirit of Capitalism,* trans. Talcott Parsons (New York: Dover Publications, Inc., 2003), especially "The Religious Foundations of Worldly Asceticism."

42. On religious materialism, see Colleen McDannell, *Material Christianity: Religion and Popular Culture in America* (New Haven, CT: Yale University Press, 1995).

43. Vanessa D. Dickerson, "A Spirit of Her Own: Nineteenth-Century Explorations of Spirituality," in *That Gentle Strength: Historical Perspectives on Women in Christianity,* ed. Lynda L. Coon, Katherine J. Haldane, and Elisabeth W. Sommer (Charlottesville: University Press of Virginia, 1990), 243.

44. Barbara Welter, "The Feminization of American Religion, 1800–1860," in *Religion in American History,* ed. Jon Butler and Harry S. Stout, 58–78 (New York: Oxford University Press, 1998).

45. Welter, "Feminization," 160.

46. G. S. Rousseau and Roy Porter, "Introduction: Toward a Natural History of Mind and Body," in *The Languages of Psyche: Mind and Body in Enlightenment Thought,* ed. G. S. Rousseau (Berkeley: University of California Press, 1990), 9.

47. Keith Thomas, *Religion and the Decline of Magic* (London: Redwood Press, 1971), ix.

48. E. P. Thompson, "Anthropology and the Discipline of Historical Context," *Midland History* 1 (1972): 53–54.

49. See Alex Owen, "'Borderland Forms': Arthur Conan Doyle, Albion's Daughters, and the Politics of the Cottingley Fairies," *History Workshop Journal* 38 (1994): 48–85; Joy Dixon, *Divine Feminine: Theosophy and Feminism in England* (Baltimore, MD: Johns Hopkins University Press, 2001); and Alex Owen, *The*

Place of Enchantment: British Occultism and the Culture of the Modern (Chicago: University of Chicago Press, 2004).

50. Hildred Geertz, "An Anthropology of Religion and Magic, I," *Journal of Interdisciplinary History* 6, no. 1(Summer 1975): 71–89.

51. Weber, *Protestant Ethic,* 105, 95–154.

52. Dipesh Chakrabarty, "Radical Histories and Questions of Enlightenment Rationalism: Some Recent Critiques of *Subaltern Studies,*" *Economic and Political Weekly,* 8 April 1995, 752.

53. Talal Asad, *Genealogies of Religion,* 46, quoted in Guari Viswanathan, *Outside the Fold: Conversion, Modernity, and Belief* (Princeton, NJ: Princeton University Press, 1998), xv–xvi.

54. Viswanathan, *Outside the Fold,* xiv–xv.

55. Bryan Wilson advances this argument in "Secularization: The Inherited Model," in Butler and Stout, *Religion in American History,* 336–44, though it is hardly his alone.

56. Pierre Macherey, "Marx Dematerialized, or the Spirit of Derrida," in *Ghostly Demarcations,* ed. Michael Sprinker (London: Verso, 1999), 19.

1. MOURNING, MEDIA, AND CONJURING THE DEAD

Epigraph: William James, "Sargent's Planchette," a review of Epes Sargent, *Planchette; Or the Despair of Science,* originally published in the *Boston Daily Advertiser,* March 10, 1869, reprinted in James, *Collected Essays by William James* (London: Longmans, Green and Co., 1920), 1–2.

1. Alfred R. Wallace, epigraph to Epes Sargent, *The Proof Palpable of Immortality; Being an Account of the Materialization Phenomenon of Modern Spiritualism* (Boston: Colby and Rich, 1876).

2. See John William Draper, *The History of the Conflict between Science and Religion* (New York: D. Appleton and Company, 1875); Josiah P. Cooke Jr., *Religion and Chemistry: A Re-statement of an Old Argument* (1864; reprint, New York: Charles Scribner's Sons, 1880); Henry James [Sr.], "Faith and Science," *North American Review* 101 (October 1865): 335–78; George Frederick Wright, *Studies in Science and Religion* (Andover, MA: Warren F. Draper, 1882); and Andrew Dickson White, *A History of the Warfare of Science and Religion within Christendom* (New York: D. Appleton and Company, 1896). On the secularization debate in American historiography, see especially Charles Rosenberg, *No Other Gods: On Science and American Social Thought* (Baltimore, MD: Johns Hopkins University Press, 1961); Bryan Wilson, "Secularization: The Inherited Model," in *Religion in American History,* ed. Jon Butler and Harry S. Stout (New York: Oxford University Press, 1998), 336–44; and Steve Bruce, ed., *Religion and Modernization: Sociologists and Historians Debate the Secularization Thesis* (Oxford: Oxford University Press, 1992).

3. Always described as more peaceful and lovely than anything in this world, the Summerland often bore an uncanny resemblance to New York's new Central Park.

4. Ann Braude, *Radical Spirits: Spiritualism and Women's Rights in Nineteenth-Century America* (Boston: Beacon Press, 1989), 2.

5. Ibid.

6. In an important recent study, John J. Kucich intervenes in the historiography "by pushing the temporal boundary of spiritualism beyond the beginnings of European settlement in what would become the United States, and the cultural boundary beyond the narrow spectrum of European American religion." Kucich, *Ghostly Communion: Cross-Cultural Spiritualism in Nineteenth-Century American Literature* (Hanover, NH: Dartmouth College Press, 2004), xi. For the purposes of this study, I retain the more clearly delineated boundaries.

7. Lyman C. Howe, "The Past of Spiritualism," in H. D. Barrett and A. W. McCoy, eds., *Cassadaga: Its History and Teachings with Histories of Spiritualist Camp Meetings and Biographies of Cassadaga Pioneers and Others* (Meadville, PA: Gazette Printing Company, 1891), 78–79.

8. See Patricia C. Phillips, "Close Encounters," *Art Journal* 62, no. 3 (Autumn 2003): 3.

9. Samuel F. B. Morse conceived of an electromagnetic telegraph in 1832 and constructed an experimental version in 1835. In 1844, he constructed the first practical system, building a line from Baltimore to Washington, DC.

10. "A Spiritual Telegraph," *Banner of Light,* April 27, 1861, 3.

11. On Thomas Watson's use of the telephone to contact the dead, see Avital Ronell, *The Telephone Book: Technology—Schizophrenia—Electric Speech* (Lincoln: University of Nebraska Press, 1989).

12. As Frank Podmore wrote in 1909: "Of those who assisted at the birth of the *Revelations* [a book by Andrew Jackson Davis] and afterwards united in editing the *Univercoelum,* many in the course of the next two or three years became editors of papers devoted to one aspect or another of the new movement." Podmore, *Mediums of the Nineteenth Century* (1909; reprint, New Hyde Park, NY: University Books, Inc., 1963), 203–4.

13. For a comprehensive guide to the nineteenth-century Spiritualist press, see Ann Braude, "News from the Spirit World: A Checklist of American Spiritualist Periodicals, 1847–1900," *Proceedings of the American Antiquarian Society* 99 (October 1989): 399–462.

14. "The Messenger" first appeared in the *Banner of Light* on Saturday, May 29, 1858.

15. Soon after his conversion, Edmonds cowrote a history of the movement: John Worth Edmonds and George T. Dexter, *Spiritualism* (New York: Partridge and Brittan, 1853).

16. "The Comforter," *Shekinah* 3 (1853): 25–37. Edmonds is never listed by name, but it is clear from certain biographical details that he is the Comforter.

17. Jeffrey Steele, "The Gender and Racial Politics of Mourning in Antebellum America," in *An Emotional History of the United States,* ed. Peter N. Stearns and Jan Lewis (New York: New York University Press, 1998), 92.

18. Letter of 8 July, *Shekinah* 2 (1852): 29.

19. On nineteenth-century cultures of sentiment, see Jane Tompkins, *Sensational Designs: The Cultural Work of American Fiction* (New York: Oxford University Press, 1985); Shirley Samuels, ed., *The Culture of Sentiment: Race, Gender, and Sentimentality in Nineteenth-Century America* (New York: Oxford University Press, 1992); and Glenn Hendler, *Public Sentiments: Structures of Feeling in Nineteenth-Century American Literature* (Chapel Hill: University of North Carolina Press, 2001).

20. Nancy Isenberg and Andrew Burstein, eds., introduction to *Mortal Remains: Death in Early America* (Philadelphia: University of Pennsylvania Press, 2003), 1.

21. Charles Rosenberg, *The Cholera Years: The United States in 1832, 1849, and 1866* (Chicago: University of Chicago Press, 1962); Sheila M. Rothman, *Living in the Shadow of Death: Tuberculosis and the Social Experience of Illness in American History* (Baltimore, MD: Johns Hopkins University Press, 1995); and Robert V. Wells, *Facing the "King of Terrors": Death and Society in an American Community, 1750–1990* (Cambridge, MA: Harvard University Press, 2000).

22. Garret Stewart, *Death Sentences: Styles of Dying in British Fiction* (New York: Cambridge University Press, 1984). On cultures of death in Anglo America, see Ann Douglas, *The Feminization of American Culture* (New York: Knopf, 1977), 200–226; Karen Halttunen, *Confidence Men and Painted Women: A Study of Middle-Class Culture in America, 1830–1870* (New Haven, CT: Yale University Press, 1982), 124–52; Carol Mavor, *Pleasures Taken: Performance of Sexuality and Loss in Victorian Photographs* (Durham, NC: Duke University Press, 1995); and Russ Castronovo, *Necro Citizenship: Death, Eroticism, and the Public Sphere in the Nineteenth-Century United States* (Durham, NC: Duke University Press, 2001).

23. Douglas, *Feminization of American Culture,* 200.

24. Little Eva's deathbed scene in *Uncle Tom's Cabin* is the classic in this genre. For a Spiritualist deathbed narrative, see Lizzie Dotten's account of her friend Achsa Sprague's passing in "The Lamented Miss A. W. Sprague," *Banner of Light,* May 2, 1863.

25. "Mourning," *Godey's Ladies' Book* (February 1854), quoted in Halttunen, *Confidence Men,* 136.

26. Thomas Bender, "The Rural Cemetery Movement: Urban Travail and the Appeal of Nature," *New England Quarterly* 47 (1974): 196–211; Stanley French, "The Cemetery as Cultural Institution: The Establishment of Mt. Auburn and the 'Rural Cemetery' Movement," in Philippe Ariès et al., *Death in America,* ed. David E. Stannard (Philadelphia: Temple University Press, 1975), 69–91; and David Charles Sloan, *The Last Great Necessity: Cemeteries in American History* (Baltimore, MD: Johns Hopkins University Press, 1991).

27. Ralph Houlbrooke, "Introduction," *Death, Ritual, and Bereavement* (New York: Routledge, 1989), 5.

28. Halttunen, *Confidence Men,* 124.

29. Steele, "Gender and Racial Politics of Mourning," 97.

30. Nehemiah Adams, *Agnes and the Little Key: Or, Bereaved Parents Instructed and Comforted* (Boston: S. K. Whipple and Co., 1857) and Reverend Theodore Cuyler, *The Empty Crib: A Book of Consolation* (New York: R. Carter and Brothers, 1868.

31. Halttunen, *Confidence Men,* 145.

32. Letter of July 8, *Shekinah* 2 (1852): 29.

33. *Shekinah.* 3 (1853): 28.

34. Philippe Ariès, *Images of Man in Death* (Cambridge, MA: Harvard University Press, 1985), 241–60. Ariès connects the emergence of individuality in death directly to the rise of individual burial.

35. David E. Stannard, "Where All Our Steps Are Tending: Death in the American Context," in *A Time to Mourn: Expressions of Grief in Nineteenth-Century America,* ed., Martha Pike and Janice Gray Armstrong (Stony Brook, NY: Museums at Stony Brook, 1980).

36. "Disguising Death," *Banner of Light,* March 17, 1866.

37. *Banner of Light,* September 8, 1866.

38. "The Departure of Children," *Banner of Light,* September 8, 1866.

39. "Disguising Death."

40. Victor Turner, *The Forest of Symbols: Aspects of Ndembu Ritual* (Ithaca, NY: Cornell University Press, 1967), and Robert Hertz, *Death and the Right Hand,* trans. Rodney and Claudia Needham (Aberdeen: University Press, 1960) and Peter Homans, ed., *Symbolic Loss: The Ambiguity of Mourning and Memory at Century's End* (Charlottesville: University Press of Virginia, 2000), 2.

41. Daniel T. Rogers, "Socializing Middle-Class Children: Institutions, Fables, and Work Values in Nineteenth-Century America" in *Growing Up in America: Children in Historical Perspective,* ed. N. Ray Hiner and Joseph M. Hawes (Chicago: University of Illinois Press, 1985) and Viviana A. Zelizer, "From Useful to Useless: Moral Conflict over Child Labor," in *The Children's Culture Reader,* ed. Henry Jenkins (New York: New York University Press, 1998).

42. Emma Hardinge Britten, *Autobiography of Emma Hardinge Britten* (Manchester, U.K.: John Heywood, 1900), 218–19.

43. Emma Hardinge [Britten], *Modern American Spiritualism: A Twenty Years' Record of the Communion between Earth and the World of the Spirits* (1869; reprint, New Hyde Park, NY: University Books, 1970), 13.

44. Although Leah Fox was much older, in one of the first histories of Spiritualism written by a noted Spiritualist, she is grouped with the "young" sisters.

45. Harrison D. Barrett, *Life Work of Mrs. Cora L. V. Richmond* (Chicago: Hack & Anderson, Printers, 1895), 4.

46. Britten, *Modern American Spiritualism*, 33.

47. My account of the story is taken from *Report of the Mysterious Noises, heard in the house of Mr. John D. Fox in Hydesville, Acadia, Wayne Co. Authenticated by the Certificates and Confirmed by the Statements of Citizens in that Place and Vicinity* (Rochester, NY: D. M. Dewey, 1850); Julia Schlesinger, *Biographical Sketches, Lectures, Essays, Poems* (San Francisco: By the Author, 1896), 19; and Britten, *Modern American Spiritualism*, 32–33. Mr. Splitfoot also makes an appearance in Arthur Conan Doyle's *History of Spiritualism*, vol. 1 (London: George H. Doran Company, 1926), 66. In different versions of the story, however, the girls are variously called Catharine, Cathie, or Kate, and Margaret, Maggie, or Margaretta.

48. According to Doyle's account, when a human skeleton, supposedly belonging to the murdered peddler, was discovered in the cellar of the Fox house in 1904, the (non-Spiritualist) *Boston Journal* reported on November 23: "The skeleton of the man supposed to have caused the rappings first heard by the Fox sisters in 1848 has been found in the walls of the house occupied by the sisters, and clears them from the only shadow of doubt held concerning their sincerity in the discovery of spirit communication." *Report of the Mysterious Noises*, quoted in Doyle, *History of Spiritualism*, 1: 73. Among the remarkable things about this article is that it assumed a reading public's familiarity with the events of 1848 more than a half century later.

49. Leah Underhill, quoted in Julia Schlesinger, *Workers in the Vineyard: A Review of the Progress of Spiritualism* (San Francisco: By the Author, 1896), 19.

50. Statement of Mrs. Margaret Fox, April 11, 1848, reprinted in "Record of Facts: Early Manifestations," *Banner of Light*, April 11, 1857, 6.

51. E. E. Lewis, Esq., of Canandaigua, New York, recounted in Britten, *Modern American Spiritualism*, 29, published as *Report of the Mysterious Noises Heard in the House of Mr. John D. Fox*.

52. Schlesinger, *Workers in the Vineyard*, 20, and Braude, *Radical Spirits*, 10–11.

53. Braude, *Radical Spirits*, 12.

54. On various attempts to debunk the Fox sisters, see chapter 4.

55. Luther Colby to J. Gowen, "The Trouble with Mediums," *Banner of Light*, April 16, 1859, 4.

56. Britten, *Modern American Spiritualism*, 61.

57. Born Cora Linn Victoria Scott, she took the married names Hatch, Daniels, Tappan, and Richmond. She made her career in her teens and early twenties as Cora L. V. Hatch.

58. "N. P. Willis on Spiritualism," an account by Willis from the *Home Journal*, reprinted in the *Banner of Light* (April 11, 1857, 4), includes descriptions of the "flaxen ringlets" and Hatch's "self-possession." "A Remarkable Young Lady," *Banner of Light*, October 10, 1857, 5, describes Hatch as "charming," "childlike," and "profound."

59. Britten, *Modern American Spiritualism*, 149.

60. "History of Mediums," *Banner of Light,* Saturday, July 17, 1858, 6, and Barrett, *Life Work,* 8–9.

61. "History of Mediums," 6 and Barrett, *Life Work,* 14–15.

62. See, for example, "A Medium's Charges," *Banner of Light,* July 31, 1858, 7, which argues that "in the present condition of life, it cannot be denied that it is proper and necessary for mediums, who devote their whole time to the subject, to receive compensation for their services." See also "Women's Employment," *Banner of Light,* September 22, 1860, 3.

63. Emma Hardinge Britten, *Nineteenth Century Miracles* (Manchester, U.K.: John Heywood, Inc., 1900), 5.

64. "The Mission of Woman," *Banner of Light,* April 11, 1857, 4.

65. "Portrait of Mrs. Cora L. V. Richmond," *Carrier Dove* 2, no. 9 (September 1886): 1. Barrett, *Life Work,* 6.

66. Barrett, *Life Work,* 11.

67. Ibid., 30.

68. "History of Mediums," 6. In Spiritualist parlance, a "regular speaker" is one who is not in trance; it is not clear from the above source whether, while in Buffalo, Scott spoke to the group regularly (at set intervals) or without trance. My guess is the former.

69. "History of Mediums," 6; Barrett, *Life Work,* 32; and Britten, who wrote that "through the joint mediumship of Miss Sarah Brooks and Miss Cora Scott [afterwards Mrs. Hatch the celebrated lecturer], these young ladies, both of them mere children in age, shortly after the visit of the Misses Fox, became mediums and frequently held trance séances" (*Modern American Spiritualism,* 156).

70. Sources are vague on the dating of her marriage to B. F. Hatch. Her official biography, Barrett's *Life Work,* omits him altogether. See also B. F. Hatch, *Spiritual Iniquities Unmasked, and, the Hatch Divorce Case* (New York: B. F. Hatch, 1859).

71. Quoted in Laurence R. Moore, *In Search of White Crows: Spiritualism, Parapsychology and American Culture* (New York: Cambridge University Press, 1977), 122.

72. Hatch, *Spiritual Iniquities Unmasked,* 32–41.

73. Hatch, *Spiritual Iniquities Unmasked,* 41.

74. "A Metropolitan Free Lover," *New York Daily Tribune,* September 13, 1858, 6. "Trouble among the Spiritualists," *New York Daily Tribune,* September 14, 1858, 7; "Separation of Cora L. V. Hatch and her Husband," *New York Daily Tribune,* September 15, 1858, 7.

75. The *Banner of Light* ran a weekly column titled "The Movements of Mediums," as well as reports from Dodsworth's Hall. On Greeley and Spiritualism, see Barbara Weisberg, *Talking to the Dead: Kate and Maggie Fox and the Rise of Spiritualism* (New York: HarperCollins Publishers, 2004), 113–17.

76. "A Remarkable Young Lady," *Banner of Light,* October 10, 1857, 3.

77. Descriptions of Cora Hatch's lectures and trance behavior are numerous:

see especially "Spiritualism in New York—Concluded" in Britten, *Modern American Spiritualism,* 149; "New York Conference, Stuyvesant Institute, December 19, 1857," *Spiritual Telegraph* 9 (1857): 156; "Mrs. Cora L. V. Hatch," *Banner of Light,* October 24, 1857, 3; "Christianity in America: A Lecture Delivered by Cora L. V. Hatch at Dodsworth's Hall, New York," *Banner of Light,* August 11, 1860, 5.

78. For example, see "Mrs. Cora L. V. Hatch," *Banner of Light,* October 24, 1857, 2, which reports that the "subject in the afternoon was 'Science,' selected by the controlling spirit, and is said to have been most ably and beautifully elucidated. In the evening, the following subject was selected by a committee:—For what purpose did Christ come into the world to die? How many, and who, are saved, or to be saved, through his death?"

79. An 1886 study by the British Society for Psychical Research estimated that 63 percent of the spirit agents were male and 37 percent female. Quoted in Vieda Skultans, "Mediums, Controls, and Eminent Men," in Pat Holden, ed., *Women's Religious Experience* (New York: Pantheon, 1987), 17.

80. "N. P. Willis on Spiritualism," *Banner of Light,* April 11, 1857, 4.

81. Ibid.

82. On Willis and Jacobs, see Jean Fagan Yellin, *Harriet Jacobs: A Life* (New York: Basic Civitas Books, 2004); on Jacobs and Spiritualism, see Kucich, *Ghostly Communion,* 1–35.

83. Mrs. T. C. Gaston, quoted in Barrett, *Life Work,* 34.

84. See "Christianity in America, a Lecture Delivered by Cora L. V. Hatch at Dodsworth's Hall, New York," *Banner of Light,* August 11, 1860, 11.

85. "A Talented Lecturess," letter to the editor from "J.S.," Tiogaboro, Pennsylvania, August 27, 1860, in *Banner of Light,* September 15, 1860, 2.

86. Britten, *Modern American Spiritualism,* 149–50.

87. *Banner of Light,* September 25, 1858, 3. For a response that mediums make good marriage partners, see Warren Chase, "B. F. Hatch and the Mediums," *Banner of Light,* October, 2, 1860, 4.

88. B. F. Hatch, "Marriage and Divorce," *Banner of Light,* August 31, 1858, 3, and B. F. Hatch, "Obsession of Evil Spirits," *Banner of Light,* September 25, 1858, 2.

89. "Women and Men," *Banner of Light,* September 8, 1860.

90. The editorialist (probably Luther Colby) wrote: "Though there remain thousands of Spiritualists living happily with their companions, as happily and circumspectly as can be found among any others[,] ... [i]t is true that development as a medium exposed one to serious dangers, as it sensibly lays him open to impure as well as pure spiritual influences; in the same manner that all on the physical plane are open to influences both pure and impure. It is also true that Spiritualism, in a certain sense, unless carefully guarded, opens the door to great and reprehensible freedom of action" (*Banner of Light,* September 25, 1858, 3).

91. Cora L. V. Richmond, *My Experiences While out of My Body and My Return after Many Days* (Boston: Christopher Press, 1915).

92. "History of Mediums—Anna M. Henderson," *Banner of Light,* Saturday, June 5, 1858, 7.

93. Anna M. Henderson, letter to the editor, *Banner of Light,* Saturday, June 5, 1858, 5.

94. Ibid.

95. Barbara Welter, "The Feminization of American Religion, 1800–1860," in *Religion in American History,* ed. Jon Butler and Harry S. Stout (New York: Oxford University Press, 1998), 159. For an important contemporary account, see Charlotte Perkins Gilman, *His Religion and Hers: A Study of the Faith of Our Fathers and the World of Our Mothers* (1923; reprint, Westport, CT: Hyperion Press, 1976).

96. Welter, "Feminization," 158.

97. Alice Felt Tyler, *Freedom's Ferment: Phases of American Social History to 1860* (Minneapolis: University of Minnesota Press, 1944), 2; Arthur Schlesinger, *The American as Reformer* (Cambridge, MA: Harvard University Press, 1950); and Ronald G. Walters, *American Reformers, 1815–1860* (New York: Hill and Wang, 1978).

98. Ralph Waldo Emerson, *Collected Works,* vol. 1 (Cambridge, MA: Harvard University Press, 1982), 237.

99. Luther Colby, "What Spiritualism Calls For," *Banner of Light,* September 3, 1857, 2. See also G. W. Holliston, "Mass Reform Convention, Report," *Banner of Light,* August 4, 1860, 9.

100. J. Hoke, letter to the editor, *Banner of Light,* September 1, 1859, 2.

101. The *Banner's* masthead claimed, "No weekly Paper in the Country furnishes so great a variety of Reading matter" (*Banner of Light,* July 30, 1859, 16).

102. "Reform Resolutions 1858, Free Convention at Rutland Vermont," reprinted in *Banner of Light,* July 3, 1858, 1. The public speakers included: A. J. Davis, Mrs. Mary F. Davis, S. B. Brittan, Joel Tiffany, H. B. Newton, Geo. Sennett Esq., Henry C. Wright, Mrs. Ernestine Rose, Dr. H. F. Gardener, Julia Branch, and Mrs. Frances Gage. The trance speakers were Miss A. W. Sprague, H. B. Storer, Mrs. H. F. Huntley, Sarah Horton, Mrs. F. O. Hyzer, A. E. Simmons, and Flora Temple.

103. Sydney E. Ahlstrom, *A Religious History of the American People* (New Haven, CT: Yale University Press, 1972), 475.

104. "Their Meaning," *Banner of Light,* October 24, 1857, 4.

105. The Union [Universalist] Association contended that Rev. Clark was dismissed from his charge for "unministerial conduct." On this controversy see, "A Premature Discharge," and "Response," *Spiritual Telegraph* 5 (1855): 369.

106. William J. Broadway, "Universalist Participation in the Spiritualist Movement," *Proceedings of the Unitarian Universalist Historical Society* 19 (1980–81): 1–15, quoted in Braude, *Radical* Spirits, 48.

107. My work in this chapter builds on two groundbreaking books on women

and Spiritualism in the United States and England: Ann Braude, *Radical Spirits,* and Alex Owen, *A Darkened Room: Women, Power and Spiritualism in Late Victorian England* (London: Virago, 1990).

108. The passage from the King James translation reads: "Let your women keep silent in the churches; for it is not permitted unto them to speak. And if they will learn anything, let them ask their husbands at home; for it is a shame for women to speak in the church."

109. The first wave of scholarship on women and religion was concerned with analyzing the exclusion of women from positions of authority, documenting the sexism of mainstream religious traditions, and constructing or reclaiming a feminist spirituality. See Mary Daly, *The Church and the Second Sex* (New York: Harper & Row, 1968); Mary Daly, *Beyond God the Father: Toward a Philosophy of Women's Liberation* (Boston: Beacon Press, 1973); Rosemary Radford Reuther, ed., *Religion and Sexism* (New York: Simon and Schuster, 1974); and Carol P. Christ and Judith Plaskow, eds., *Womanspirit Rising: A Feminist Reader in Religion* (San Francisco: Harper & Row, 1979). Major academic journals produced a number of special issues on women and religion during the 1970s: see especially Janet Wilson James, ed., *American Quarterly* (Winter 1978) and *Signs: Journal of Women in Culture and Society* (Winter 1976).

110. Doyle, *History of Spiritualism,* 1: 50.

111. This subject has been extensively studied cross-culturally for the nineteenth century as well as other periods. General studies include Rosemary Radford Reuther and Rosemary Skinner Keller, eds., *Women and Religion in America,* vol. 1: *The Nineteenth Century* (New York: Harper & Row, 1981); Janet Wilson James, ed., *Women in American Religion* (Philadelphia: University of Pennsylvania Press, 1980); Pat Holden, ed., *Women's Religious Experience* (London: Croom Helm, 1983); Amanda Porterfield, *Feminine Spirituality in America: From Sarah Edwards to Martha Graham* (Philadelphia: Temple University Press, 1980); Susan Starr Sered, *Priestess, Mother, Sacred Sister: Religions Dominated by Women* (New York: Oxford University Press, 1994); and Lynda L., Coon, Katherine J. Haldane, and Elisabeth W. Sommer, eds., *That Gentle Strength: Historical Perspectives on Women in Christianity* (Charlottesville: University Press of Virginia, 1990). On white women in religious communities in the Northeast, see Mary P. Ryan, *Cradle of the Middle-Class: The Family in Oneida County, New York, 1790–1865* (New York: Cambridge University Press, 1981) and Teresa Anne Murphy, *Ten Hours' Labor: Religion, Reform and Gender in Early New England* (Ithaca, NY: Cornell University Press, 1992). On African American women in the South, see Evelyn Brooks Higginbotham, *Righteous Discontent: The Women's Movement in the Black Baptist Church, 1880–1921* (Cambridge, MA: Harvard University Press, 1992). Especially helpful to me have been Mary Farrell Bednarowski, "Women in Occult America," in *The Occult in America: New Historical Perspectives,* ed. Howard Kerr and Charles L. Crow, 177–95 (Urbana: University of Illinois Press, 1985), and Barbara Taylor,

Eve and the New Jerusalem: Socialism and Feminism in the Nineteenth Century (New York: Pantheon Books, 1983).

112. On the problems of defining mainstreams and margins, see R. Laurence Moore, "Insiders and Outsiders in American Historical Narrative and American History," in *Religion in American History,* ed. Jon Butler and Harry S. Stout, 199–221 (New York: Oxford University Press, 1998).

113. On women in nonmainstream religions, see Mary Farrell Bednarowski, "Outside the Mainstream: Women's Religion and Women Religious Leaders in Nineteenth-Century America," *Journal of the American Academy of Religion* 48, no. 2 (June 1980): 207–31, and the essays collected in *Women's Leadership in Marginal Religions: Explorations outside the Mainstream,* ed. Catherine Wessinger (Chicago: University of Illinois Press, 1993).

114. Robert S. Ellwood, Jr. *Alternative Altars: Unconventional and Eastern Spirituality in America* (Chicago: University of Chicago Press, 1979), 68. On the Shakers, see Stephen J. Stein, *The Shaker Experience in America: A History of the United Society of Believers* (New Haven, CT: Yale University Press, 1992). On Seventh-Day Adventists, Christian Scientists, and New Thought, see Ronald L. Numbers, *Prophetess of Health: Ellen G. White and the Origins of Seventh-Day Adventist Health Reform* (Knoxville: University of Tennessee Press, 1992); Stephen Gottschalk, *The Emergence of Christian Science in American Religious Life* (Berkeley: University of California Press, 1973); and Beryl Satter, *Each Mind a Kingdom: American Women, Sexual Purity, and the New Thought Movement, 1875–1920* (Berkeley: University of California Press, 1999). On Mormonism, see Jan Shipps, *Mormonism: The Story of a New Religious Tradition* (Chicago: University of Illinois Press, 1985). On sexual and gender relations in communitarian religions, see Barbara Taylor, *Eve and the New Jerusalem,* and Lawrence Foster, *Women, Family, and Utopia: Communal Experiments of the Shakers, the Oneida Community, and the Mormons* (Syracuse, NY: Syracuse University Press, 1991).

115. Quakers, Shakers, members of the Oneida community, and other antebellum religious utopianists would have found points of convergence in this model of thought: see Lawrence Foster, *Women, Family and Utopia;* Louis J. Kern, *An Ordered Love: Sex Roles and Sexuality in Victorian Utopias, The Shakers, the Mormons, and the Oneida Community* (Chapel Hill: University of North Carolina Press, 1981); and Robert Abzub, *Cosmos Crumbling: American Reform and the Religious Imagination* (New York: Oxford University Press, 1994).

116. Margaret Fuller, *Woman in the Nineteenth Century, and Kindred Papers Relating to the Sphere, Condition, and Duties of Woman,* ed. Arthur B. Fuller (New York: Tribune Association, 1869), 17.

117. S. B. Brittan, "Woman and Her Rights," *Spiritual Telegraph* 1 (1853): 43–45; Cora Linn Daniels, *As It Is to Be* (Franklin, MA: Cora Linn Daniels, 1892); "Woman," *Banner of Light,* July 28, 1860, 6; "Active Women," *Banner of Light,* November 14, 1857, 4; and "Spiritual Culture," *Banner of Light,* October 31, 1857, 3.

118. "Mrs. Amanda M. Spence at Ordway Hall, Boston, Sunday, December 11th," *Banner of Light,* December 24, 1859, 4.

119. Emma Hardinge [Britten], *The Place and Mission of Women* (Boston: Hubbard W. Sweet, 1859), 3 and Owen, *A Darkened Room,* 13–14. One letter to the editor of a Spiritualist newspaper opined that "two theories are entertained by Spiritualists; the one that God is a personal Being; the other that he is a principle," in "God a Principle," *Banner of Light,* February 20, 1859, 4.

120. W. J. Colville, *Ancient Mysteries and Modern Revelations* (New York: R. F. Fenno, 1910), 342.

121. Catharine A. F. Stebbins, in Elizabeth Cady Stanton, Susan B. Anthony, and Matilda Joslyn Gage, eds., *History of Woman Suffrage,* vol. 3 (Rochester, NY: Charles Mann, 1887), 530.

122. Ibid.

123. Ibid., 3: 531.

124. The *Religio-philosophical Journal* editor J. C. Bundy is quoted as saying: "Although not especially published in the interests of woman, this journal is a stalwart advocate of woman's rights, and . . . has done much to encourage women to renewed and persistent effort for their own advancement." November 22, 1884, quoted in Stanton, Anthony, and Gage, *History of Woman Suffrage,* 3: 531.

125. *Banner of Light,* April 16, 1859, 4. See, among others, "The Rights of Woman," *Spiritual Telegraph* 1 (1853): 351; and "Let Them Be Heard," *Spiritual Telegraph* 2 (1853): 285.

126. *Religio-philosophical Journal* 1 (1865): 1.

127. On the male "body reformers," see Abzug, *Cosmos Crumbling,* 163–82, and Stephen Nissenbaum, *Sex, Diet, and Debility in Jacksonian America: Sylvester Graham and Health Reform* (Westport, CT: Greenwood Press, 1980).

128. Rufus Elmer to S. B. Brittan, Springfield, Mass., September 10, 1853, *Telegraph Papers* 3 (1853): 287–89.

129. "Diet, Given through the organism of Mary E. Frost, of Philadelphia, by S. Graham," *Banner of Light,* June 4, 1859, 7.

130. Nissenbaum, *Sex, Diet, and Debility,* 79–99, 119–27.

131. "Diet," 7.

132. Cora Wilburn, "My Religion," *Agitator,* March 15, 1860, 90.

133. "Report of the President, Harrison D. Barrett, for the Year Ending October 18, S.E. 51," *Banner of Light,* October 22, 1898, 1.

134. "The Times," *Banner of Light,* January 5, 1861, 2.

135. "The Government Policy," *Banner of Light,* April 13, 1861, 1.

136. "Disunion," *Banner of Light,* February 9, 1861, 1.

137. "The Voice of the People," *Herald of Progress,* April 27, 1861, 2.

138. "Ten Years," *Banner of Light,* March 23, 1867, 3.

139. Emma Hardinge [Britten], "Spiritualism—Its Growth and Status," *Banner of Light,* February 25, 1865, 7.

140. *Banner of Light,* February 25, 1865, 7.

141. S. C. Case, "Religion Based on Science," *Banner of Light,* May 27, 1865.

142. "Call for a Peace Convention," *Banner of Light,* February 10, 1866, 1.

143. "What Does the Radical Peace Movement Mean?" *Banner of Light,* June 20, 1868.

144. Ibid.

145. "On the Body," *Banner of Light,* July 19, 1862, 9.

146. Thomas R. Hazard, "The Three Great Problems of the Nineteenth Century," *Banner of Light,* July 4, 1868.

147. Payton Spence, "Spiritualism Always Radical and Revolutionary," *Banner of Light,* March 2, 1867, 2.

148. A significant exception and historiographic reformulation is Robert S. Fogarty, *All Things New: American Communes and Utopian Movements, 1860–1914* (Chicago: University of Chicago Press, 1990), which maps a larger utopian movement paralleling postwar Spiritualism.

149. Alan Trachtenberg, *The Incorporation of America: Culture and Society in the Gilded Age* (New York: Hill and Wang, 1982), 180.

150. William Dean Howells, *Impressions and Experiences* (1896; reprint, Freeport, NY: Books for Libraries Press, 1972), 21.

151. William Dean Howells, *Years of My Youth* (1916; reprint, Freeport, NY: Books for Libraries Press, 1972), 106.

152. I am assuming that Howells, born in 1837, is referring to the antebellum years.

153. Robert Wiebe, *The Segmented Society* (New York: Oxford University Press, 1975), 19.

154. Nancy Fraser, "Rethinking the Public Sphere: A Contribution to the Critique of Actually Existing Democracy," in *Habermas and the Public Sphere,* ed. Craig Calhoun (Cambridge, MA: MIT Press, 1992), 116.

155. Spence, *Banner of Light,* March 2, 1867, 2.

156. E. L. Godkin, *Nation,* February 1867.

157. On these developments, see especially Tera W. Hunter, *To 'Joy My Freedom: Southern Black Women's Lives and Labors after the Civil War* (Cambridge, MA: Harvard University Press, 1997).

158. Christopher Clark, Nancy A. Hewitt, and Roy Rosenzweig, *Who Built America? Working People and the Nation's History,* vol. 2 (Boston: Bedford/St. Martin's 2007), 19.

159. "American Anti-slavery Society," *Herald of Progress,* May 19, 1860, 4, and Emancipation Proclamation, *Banner of Light,* October 4, 1862, 1.

160. "A New Labor System," *Banner of Light,* February 6, 1864, 2.

161. See for example, "Seeing Face to Face," *American Spiritual Magazine* 1 (1875–1876): 6, which counterposes an "intelligent" Spiritualist to "certain wild-eyed, long-haired reformers."

162. "Dr. Hall on Women, Infants, and Idiots," *Herald of Progress,* March 10, 1864, 4.

163. *Herald of Progress,* March 10, 1866, 4.

164. "Lank, Long-haired and Cadaverous," reprinted in the *Banner of Light,* April 13, 1869.

165. Waisbrooker's novels include *Alice Vale: A Story for the Times* (Boston: W. White and Company, 1869); *Mayweed Blossoms* (Boston: W. White and Company, 1871); *Nothing Like It; Or, Steps to the Kingdom* (Boston: Colby & Rich, Publishers, 1875); *Perfect Motherhood; Or, Mabel Raymond's Resolve* (New York: Murray Hill Publishing, 1890), all of which were sentimental novels with didactic plots to which "voluntary motherhood" was central. Waisbrooker also published numerous treatises on free love.

166. Waisbrooker, *My Century Plant* (Topeka Kansas: Independent Publishing Company, 1896).

167. Waisbrooker, "Gleanings," *Banner of Light,* May 20, 1865, 6.

168. Fred Folio [pseud.], *Lucy Boston; or Woman's Rights and Spiritualism* (New York: Alden and Beardsley, 1855).

169. On the bachelor narrator as "representative man," see Eve Kosofsky Sedgwick, *Epistemology of the Closet* (Berkeley: University of California Press, 1990), 188.

170. Luther Colby, "Revivals of Failure," *Banner of Light,* May 5, 1866.

171. Britten, "Spiritualism—Its Growth and Status," 7. See also "Seeing Face to Face," 6.

172. W. J. Colville, "The Relation of Spiritualism to Social and Political Reforms," in Barrett and McCoy, *Cassadaga,* 169.

173. Warren Chase, "Health of American Women and Children," *Banner of Light,* August 24, 1867.

174. For a similar argument linking women's power to civilize with their right to suffrage, see "Woman Suffrage," *Banner of Light,* April 27, 1867, which argued that "the adoption of so broad a principle as this would at once elevate the character of our politics, and raise Woman to at least a level with the ruder sex who owe to her their civilization."

175. W.S.P., "Uses of the Physical Body," *Banner of Light,* September 6, 1868, 5.

176. "Can the Spirit of the Medium Leave Her Body Temporarily?" *Banner of Light,* July 26, 1862, 3.

177. "How to Balance Brain and Body," *The Herald of Progress,* April 7, 1860, 5; "Weight of the Spirit Body," *Herald of Progress,* May 19, 1860, 1; "Can Spirits See Material Objects?"; "Do Spirits Wear Clothing?"; and "Reproduction in the Spirit Land," *Herald of Progress,* March 31, 1860, 3.

178. Richmond, *My Experiences,* 7, 73, 75.

179. Schlesinger, *Workers in the Vineyard,* 23 24.

180. Margaret Booth, "Letter from California," *Banner of Light,* September 6, 1862.

181. A. C. Stowe, "Letter from California," *Banner of Light,* April 7, 1866.

182. Boaz W. Williams, "Letter to the Editor," *Banner of Light,* February 9, 1867.

183. See especially Booth, "Letter from California"; "Spread of Spiritualism in California," *Banner of Light,* March 17, 1866; "Letter from California"; and "Spiritualism in California," *Banner of Light,* February 10, 1866. In the issue of February 10, 1866, the *Banner of Light* announced the establishment of a "Western Department."

184. "Spiritual Movement in San Francisco," *Banner of Light,* June 20, 1866.

185. Schlesinger, *Workers in the Vineyard,* 24.

186. Remarks of Mr. Dyott, *Proceedings of the Fourth National Convention of Spiritualists, Held at Cleveland, Ohio, September 3rd, 4th, 5th, and 6th, 1867. Fourth Day—Friday, Sept. 6, Morning Session,* 26.

187. *Banner of Progress* 1, no. 1 (1867).

188. Lisle Leslie, San Francisco, December 17, 1867, *Banner of Light,* February 1, 1867, 4.

189. The first Spiritualist paper published on the West Coast was the *Family Circle,* published in San Francisco in 1859. Then followed the *Golden Gate,* started by Fanny McDougall in Sacramento, which "starved to death before it had time to make its merits known." That failure served as a warning against further attempts until 1867, when Benjamin Todd, a lecturer, and W. H. Manning, a printer, issued the *Banner of Progress,* headquartered in San Francisco. This was a large, well-run paper, and publication continued for nearly two years. The next paper to appear was *Common Sense,* started in 1874 by W. N. Slocum and Amanda M. Slocum. In May 1875, the *Philomathean,* a pamphlet-shaped weekly, was started by Prof. W. H. Chaney but also passed away after a brief existence. *Light for All* had a brief career. See Schlesinger, *Workers in the Vineyard,* 26–27.

190. Schlesinger, *Workers in the Vineyard,* 25.

191. Luther Colby, "Social Reform 'Communities,'" *Banner of Light,* January 28, 1865, 2.

192. Laura De Force Gordon, letter to the editor, *Banner of Light,* July 4, 1868.

193. On nineteenth-century spiritual pilgrimages to the West, see Sarah Sitzer Frankiel, *California's Spiritual Frontiers: Religious Alternatives in Anglo-Protestantism, 1850–1910* (Berkeley: University of California Press, 1988). On the relationship of "cures" to westward migration, see Nissenbaum, *Sex, Diet, and Debility.*

194. Harrison D. Barrett, "Spiritualist Camp Meetings," in Barrett and McCoy, *Cassadaga,* 34.

195. Anita Clair Fellman and Michael Fellman, *Making Sense of Self: Medical Advice Literature in Late Nineteenth-Century America* (Philadelphia: University

of Pennsylvania Press, 1981), 6–7. On nineteenth-century health reform, see Nissenbaum, *Sex, Diet, and Debility;* Abzub, *Cosmos Crumbling;* William Leach, *True Love and Perfect Union: The Feminist Reform of Sex and Society* (New York: Basic Books, 1980); and Donald Meyer, *The Positive Thinkers: A Study of the American Search for Health, Wealth and Personal Power from Mary Baker Eddy to Norman Vincent Peale* (Middletown, CT: Wesleyan University Press, 1988).

196. Fellman and Fellman, *Making Sense of Self,* 7.

197. Cridge died in Riverside, California, in 1873 of pneumonia. Alfred Cridge, "Annie Denton Cridge," *Carrier Dove* 3 (1886): 263, and Braude, *Radical Spirits,* 195.

198. Schlesinger, *Workers in the Vineyard,* 30–31.

199. Claire Kahane, "Hysteria, Feminism, and the Case of *The Bostonians,*" in *Feminism and Psychoanalysis,* ed. Richard Feldstein and Judith Roof (Ithaca, NY: Cornell University Press, 1989), 287.

2. INDIAN GUIDES

1. The writer, identified only as C.B.G. of Lebanon, New Hampshire, sent this spirit speech to the New York editors Charles Partridge and Samuel Byron Brittan on March 14, 1853. It was published as "An Indian Spirit's Speech," *Spiritual Telegraph* 1 (1853): 20–21.

2. Philip J. Deloria, *Playing Indian* (New Haven, CT: Yale University Press, 1998) and Robert F. Berkhofer Jr., *The White Man's Indian: Images of the American Indian from Columbus to the Present* (New York: Vintage Books, 1979). There is an extensive literature on this issue, which I discuss below.

3. Renée L. Bergland, *The National Uncanny: Indian Ghosts and American Subjects* (Hanover, NH: University Press of New England, 2000), 2.

4. Robert S. Cox, *Body and Soul: A Sympathetic History of American Spiritualism* (Charlottesville: University of Virginia Press, 2003), 191, 193.

5. Ibid., 196. In contrast to Cox, Daphne A. Brooks has recently claimed: "Yet one could argue that, despite its putative social divisions, spiritualism's emphasis on metamorphosis posed an ideological resistance to the cultural politics of segregation . . . spiritualism continually flirted with the disruption of presumably arbitrary racial, class, and gender boundaries. In this regard, perhaps no cultural performance ritual figuratively and corporeally encompassed the turbulence of 1850s American culture and reflected the dissonant landscape of nineteenth-century transatlantic popular culture more than spirit-rapping." Brooks, *Bodies in Dissent: Spectacular Performances of Race and Freedom, 1850–1910* (Durham, NC: Duke University Press, 2006), 15–16.

6. Werner Sollors, "Dr. Benjamin Franklin's Celestial Telegraph, or Indian Blessings to Gas-Lit American Drawing Rooms," *Social Science Information* 22, no. 6 (1983).

7. "An Indian Spirit's Speech," 20.

8. Ibid., 21.

9. Paula Gunn Allen notes: "Wahunsenacawh is usually identified as Powhatan—his title not his name—by historians and the English records of the seventeenth century and also wrongly identified as Pocahontas's biological father" (*Pocahontas: Medicine Woman, Spy, Entrepreneur, Diplomat* [New York: Harper-SanFrancisco, 2003], 21). She continues: "Because of the law of mother-right . . . it is impossible to say with any confidence that Pocahontas was Wahunsenacawh's daughter, eldest or otherwise" (75). See also Stephen R. Potter, "Early Effects on Virginia Algonquian Exchange and Tribute in the Tidewater Potomac," in *Powhatan's Mantle: Indians in the Colonial Southwest,* ed. Peter H. Wood, Gregory A. Waselkov, and M. Thomas Hatley (Lincoln: University of Nebraska Press, 1989); Karen Ordahl Kupperman, *Indians and English: Facing Off in Early America* (Ithaca, NY: Cornell University Press, 2000); and Camilla Townsend, *Pocahontas and the Powhatan Dilemma* (New York: Hill and Wang, 2004).

10. John Smith, *The True Travels, Adventures and Observations of Captain John Smith* (London: Thomas Slater, 1630) in Philip Barbour, ed. *The Complete Works of Captain John Smith,* 3 vols. (Williamsburg, VA: Institute for Early American Culture, 1986), and William Stratchey, *The Historie of Travell into Virginia Britania,* ed. Louis B. Wright and Virginia Freund (1612; reprint, London: Hakluyt Society, 1953).

11. The English colonized Jamestown in 1607 and, after a brief period of trade, entered into a decades-long war. In 1614 relative peace was obtained through the marriage of Pocahontas and the colonist John Rolfe. The English continued to expand far into Powhatan's territory, and after a series of uprisings, culminating in the Powhatan Uprising of 1644, all Virginian Algonquian groups were made tributaries of the crown.

12. Instructions prepared for Sir Thomas Gates in 1609, quoted in Frederic W. Gleach, *Powhatan's World and Colonial Virginia: A Conflict of Cultures* (Lincoln: University of Nebraska Press, 1997), 69.

13. Pocahontas continues to be a vexed historical figure precisely because of the power of the myths surrounding her life story, rendered as it was entirely through English sources. She has recently been recovered as a figure of hybridity by Paula Gunn Allen, whose *Pocahontas* is dedicated to America's "first boarding-school Indian, and the first to walk two paths in a balanced manner."

14. Charter of Dartmouth College, December 13, 1769, www.dartmouth. edu/~govdocs/case/charter.htm. Accessed 5/30/2006.

15. Marcella Bomardieri, "A Show of Respect Urged at Dartmouth College: Native Americans Allege College Racism," *Boston Globe,* November 23, 2006, B1. My thanks to Darren J. Ranco of Dartmouth College for bringing this article, and the number of pre-1970s graduates, to my attention. The New Hampshire tribes now recognized by the federal government include the Abnaki and the Pennacook.

16. On the ideology of the vanishing Indian and the political and cultural context within which it has circulated, see Deloria, *Playing Indian;* Bergland, *National Uncanny;* Shari M. Huhndorf, *Going Native: Indians in the American Cultural Imagination* (Ithaca, NY: Cornell University Press, 2001); S. Elizabeth Bird, *Dressing in Feathers: The Construction of the Indian in American Popular Culture* (Boulder, CO: Westview Press, 1996); Berkhofer, *White Man's Indian,* 86–96; Linda K. Kerber, "The Abolitionist Perception of the Indian," *Journal of American History* 62 (September 1975): 271–95; and Michael Paul Rogin, *Fathers and Children: Andrew Jackson and the Subjugation of the American Indian* (New York: Knopf, 1975).

17. Renato Rosaldo, "Imperialist Nostalgia," in *Culture and Truth: The Remaking of Social Analysis* (Boston: Beacon Press, 1989).

18. Quoted in Noble David Cook, *Born to Die: Disease and New World Conquest, 1492–1650* (Cambridge: Cambridge University Press, 1998), 199.

19. Laura M. Stevens, "The Christian Origins of the Vanishing Indian," in *Mortal Remains: Death in Early America,* ed. Nancy Isenberg and Andrew Burstein, 17–30 (Philadelphia: University of Pennsylvania Press, 2003). On seventeenth-century Anglo-Indian spiritual dramas, see Ann Kibbey, *The Interpretation of Material Shapes in Puritanism: A Study of Rhetoric, Prejudice, and Violence* (London: Cambridge University Press, 1986), especially chapter 5, "1637: The Pequot War and the Antinomian Controversy," 92–120; and Mary Beth Norton, *In the Devil's Snare: The Salem Witchcraft Crisis of 1692* (New York: Alfred A. Knopf, 2002).

20. Quoted in Stevens, "Christian Origins," 18. As Stevens points out, "vanishing" was complicated, as these missionaries "thought themselves in a race to save heathens from a damnation that would be forever sealed by death." Stevens, "Christian Origins," 18–19.

21. Kerber, "Abolitionist Perception," 271–72.

22. "The Exile's Return," *New York Times,* December 21, 1877.

23. Deloria, *Playing Indian,* 64.

24. Joseph Story, "Discourse Pronounced at the Request of the Essex Historical Society, Sept. 18, 1828 in Commemoration of the First Settlement of Salem, Mass.," quoted in Brian Dippie, *The Vanishing American: White Attitudes and U.S. Indian Policy* (Middletown, CT: Wesleyan University Press, 1982), 1.

25. Jane M. Jackson, "Facts Concerning the Indians," *Banner of Light,* March 3, 1866, 4.

26. "Sumner and the Indian," *Banner of Light,* January 26, 1867, 8.

27. "Spiritual Manifestations Among the Indians," *Telegraph Papers* 4 (1854): 116.

28. On the disciplining uses of the term *magic,* see Randall Styers, *Making Magic: Religion, Magic, and Science in the Modern World* (Oxford: Oxford University Press, 2004).

29. "Indians' Conception of Death," *Banner of Light,* February 15, 1868, 2.

30. On collecting Indians and artifacts, see Deloria, *Playing Indian;* Johannes Fabian, *Time and the Other: How Anthropology Makes Its Object* (New York: Columbia University Press, 1982); James Clifford and George Marcus, eds., *Writing Culture: The Poetics and Politics of Ethnography* (Berkeley: University of California Press, 1986); Adam Kuper, *The Invention of Primitive Society: Transformations of an Illusion* (New York: Routledge, 1988); and Ivan Karp and Steven D. Lavine, eds., *Exhibiting Cultures: The Poetics and Politics of Museum Display* (Washington, DC: Smithsonian Institution Press, 1991).

31. Herman Snow, *Visions of the Beyond, by a Seer of To-Day; Or, Symbolic Teachings from the Higher Life* (Boston: Colby & Rich; San Francisco: Herman Snow, 1877), 91. Snow's bookstore and its publications formed an important movement center for California Spiritualists.

32. See, for example, advertisements for *Indian Arcana,* a monthly magazine published by the "Indian Medical Institute," devoted to "illustrations of Indian life, religion, medicine, customs &c." in the back pages of the *Banner of Light,* 1859–60.

33. Jackson, "Facts Concerning the Indians," 4.

34. E.P.H., "The Influence of Indian Spirits," *Herald of Progress,* August 25, 1860, 2.

35. Cox, *Body and Soul,* 191.

36. E.P.H., "The Influence of Indian Spirits," 2.

37. Advertisement for Mrs. Caroline A. Batchelder, "Indian Healing Medium": "Positive relief also given to all nervous diseases, and Rheumatism, and Headache cured." *Banner of Light,* November 15, 1862, 10.

38. "An Editor's Experience Continued," *Spiritual Telegraph* 3 (1854): 492.

39. Different Modes of Spirit Speech," *Telegraph Papers* 8 (1855): 31.

40. From a letter from Keokuk, Iowa, dated March 7, 1854, signed by William Wittinmyer, and published as "Spirits in Keokuk," *Telegraph Papers* 4 (1854): 409. Judge Edmonds (of New York) also reported that his daughter channeled Chippewa: "I knew the language, because I had been two years in Indian country" (John W. Edmonds, *Letters and Tracts on Spiritualism; also two inspirational orations by Cora L. V. Tappan; and particulars respecting the personal career and passing away of Judge Edmonds* [London: J. Burns Progressive Library and Spiritual Institution, 1875], 112).

41. "No Narrow Circle," *Banner of Light,* May 14, 1859, 1.

42. Cora Wilburn, "Lecture by Miss Emma Hardinge," *Banner of Light,* May 14, 1859, 1.

43. On white reformers and U.S. Indian policy, see Robert M. Utley, "The Vision of the Reformers," *The Indian Frontier of the American West, 1846–1890* (Albuquerque: University of Mexico Press, 1984), 203–26; Robert Winston Mardock, *The Reformers and the American Indian* (Columbia: University of Missouri

Press, 1971); Christine Bolt, *American Indian Policy and American Reform: Case Studies of the Campaign to Assimilate the American Indians* (London: Allen and Unwin, 1987); and Kerber, "Abolitionist Perception."

44. *Pennsylvania Freeman,* May 10, 1838, quoted in Kerber, "Abolitionist Perception," 273–74.

45. Bolt, *American Indian Policy,* 58.

46. "Meeting on Indian Affairs in Syracuse, N.Y.," *Banner of Light,* February 16, 1861, 3.

47. Joanne Pope Melish, *Disowning Slavery: Gradual Emancipation and "Race" in New England, 1780–1860* (Ithaca, NY: Cornell University Press, 1998), 3.

48. Gail Bederman, *Manliness and Civilization: A Cultural History of Gender and Race in the United States, 1880–1917* (Chicago: University of Chicago Press, 1995).

49. On the history of Quakers in Spiritualism, see Ann Braude, *Radical Spirits: Spiritualism and Women's Rights in Nineteenth-Century America* (Boston: Beacon Press, 1989), 12–25; 64–69.

50. "Indian Wars," *Banner of Light,* August 27, 1859, 8.

51. "Our Conduct with the Indians," *Banner of Light,* April 21, 1866, 4.

52. Beeson was described in 1861 as then of Oregon, "an Englishman by birth: came to the city of New York from England, in 1830; resided there awhile, and then removed on to a farm in Oregon, where he now resides" ("Meeting on Indian Affairs," 3; see also Bolt, *American Indian Policy,* 71).

53. "Report from a Meeting in the Old South Chapel to Consider the Condition of the Indians in Our Territories," *Banner of Light,* August 27, 1859, 6.

54. "Our Duty to the Indians," *Herald of Progress,* September 1, 1860, 5.

55. "Indian Wars," *Banner of Light,* August 27, 1859, 8.

56. Thomas Griffin, "Mr. Beeson and the Indians," *Banner of Light,* January 28, 1860, 5.

57. E.P.H., "The Influence of Indian Spirits," 4, 2.

58. "Convention for the Indians, Remarks of Mr. Emerson," *Herald of Progress,* January 12, 1861, 1.

59. Letter from Hudson Tuttle, Walnut Grove Farm, December 28, 1860, in "Correspondence," *Banner of Light,* January 19, 1861, 3.

60. Tuttle, letter, 3.

61. "Meeting on Behalf of the Indians on the Western Frontier," *Banner of Light,* October 1, 1859, 1.

62. Tuttle, letter, 3.

63. The ideological notion that Indians "abused the earth" by using too much of it was eventually turned on its head in the late twentieth century, as white Americans in general, and the 1970s ecology movement in particular, romanticized Native Americans as the original environmentalists. On this phenomenon, see Marianna Torgovnick, "New American Indian/New American White," in *Primi-*

tive Passions: Men, Women, and the Quest for Ecstasy (Chicago: University of Chicago Press, 1996), 135–55.

64. J. M. Peebles, "From Whence the Indians?" *Banner of Light*, October 24, 1863, 3.

65. See especially "A Test from Still-Born Children," *Banner of Light*, October 7, 1865, 8; "The Indian Maid's Greeting," *Banner of Light*, December 23, 1865, 8; "A Timely Spirit-Warning," *Banner of Light*, November 3, 1866, 1; and "Indian Songs," *Banner of Light*, October 5, 1867, 4.

66. Mrs. J. H. Conant, "Message Department," [through] Dohomey (An Indian Maid), *Banner of Light*, July 15, 1865, 8.

67. Utley, *Indian Frontier*, 37.

68. "Frontier Matters," July 3, 1861.

69. Ibid.

70. Griffin, "Mr. Beeson and the Indians," 5.

71. On the Sioux uprising, see Utley, *Indian Frontier*, 76–81.

72. John Beeson, letter to the editor, *Banner of Light*, February 7, 1863, 3

73. "The Indians," *Banner of Light*, February 7, 1863, 1.

74. S. C. Simonds, letter to the editor, September 2, 1863, *Banner of Light*, October 10, 1863, 5.

75. Peebles, "From Whence the Indians?" 3.

76. Ibid.

77. King Phillip, Tecumseh, Osceola, and Billy Bowlegs, letter to the editor, *Banner of Light*, October 10, 1863, 5.

78. Cora Wilburn, "The Convention Spiritual Séance—A Plea for the Indians," *Banner of Light*, September 3, 1864, 2.

79. "Official Report, Fourth National Convention of Spiritualists. Held at Cleveland, Ohio, September 3rd, 4th, 5th and 6th, 1867, Fourth Day, Morning Session," reported in *Banner of Light*, November 23, 1867, 1.

80. "Official Report," 1.

81. Mrs. J. H. Conant, "Message Department," [through] Osceola (an Indian chief), *Banner of Light*, July 27, 1867, 8.

82. "Message from an Indian Spirit," *Banner of Light*, April 25, 1868, 4.

83. For other militant Indian spirit guides, see "Message Department," *Banner of Light*, July 27, 1867, 8; "Indian Mediumship," *Banner of Light*, January 12, 1867, 3; "Message From an Indian Spirit," 4; and "The Red Man Again," *Banner of Light*, May 16, 1868, 8.

84. "The Indians," *Banner of Light*, March 30, 1867, 1.

85. "Discussing the Indians," *Banner of Light*, June 1, 1867, 6.

86. "The Indian Troubles," *Banner of Light*, May 25, 1867, 4; "Discussing the Indians," *Banner of Light*, June 1, 1867, 4; "The Indians—Their Treatment and Destiny," *Banner of Light*, August 24, 1867, 2; "The Indians," *Banner of Light*,

November 28, 1868, 8; and "The Destiny of the Indian," *Religio-philosophical Journal,* September 11, 1869.

87. Cora L. V. Daniels, letter to the *Anti-slavery Standard,* October 5, 1868, 3.

88. "Indian War Inaugurated," *Banner of Light,* November 14, 1868.

89. The North Collins (New York) Friends of Human Progress annual meeting grew into the Cassadaga Free Lake Association, founded in 1879. Its headquarters eventually became a Spiritualist summer resort, Lily Dale, in 1906. On Lily Dale, see H. D. Barrett and A. W. McCoy, eds., *Cassadaga: Its History and Teachings, with Histories of Spiritualist Camp Meetings and Biographies of Cassadaga Pioneers and Others.* Meadville, PA: Gazette Printing Company, 1891).

90. "Dr. P. Wilson, the Indian," *Banner of Light,* May 16, 1868, 8.

91. "What Does the Radical Peace Movement Mean?" *Banner of Light,* June 20, 1868, 2; "The Indian Question," *Banner of Light,* November 7, 1868; and Daniels, letter to the *Anti-slavery Standard,* October 5, 1868, 3.

92. "The Destiny of the Indian."

93. "Northwestern Massacres—Peace Changed to War," *Banner of Light,* December 19, 1868, 1.

3. SPECTRAL SEXUALITIES

1. For various versions of the Comstock story, see D. M. Bennett, *Anthony Comstock: His Career of Cruelty and Crime* (1878; reprint, New York: Da Capo Press, 1971), 1016; Heywood Broun and Margaret Leech, *Anthony Comstock, Roundsman of the Lord* (New York: Albert & Charles Boni, 1927), 128–44; Edward de Grazia, *Girls Lean Back Everywhere: The Law of Obscenity and the Assault on Genius* (New York: Random House, 1992), 4. The records of the New York Society for the Suppression of Vice (hereafter NYSSV) feature the "official" version of Comstock's fight against the traffic in "bad books, prints and instruments": see *The First Annual Report of the New York Society for the Suppression of Vice* (New York: February 11, 1875).

2. *The Lustful Turk; Or, Scenes in the Harem of an Eastern Potentate* (London: n.p., 1800).

3. *NYSSV, First Annual Report* (February 11, 1875), 10–11. The spread of disease continues to provide a powerful metaphor for sexual contagion, which late twentieth-century vice fighters exploited with particular potency in the context of the AIDS epidemic. Paradigmatic was Senator Jesse Helms's indictment of Robert Mapplethorpe's "sick" and "sickening" art in *Proceeding and Debates of the 101st Congress,* 1st sess., July 26, 1989, S. 8807; see also Kara Swisher, "Helm's 'Indecent' Sampler: Senator Sends Photos to Sway Conferees," *Washington Post,* August 8, 1989, B1.

4. Comstock's diary, quoted in Broun and Leech, *Anthony Comstock,* 153.

5. On the Credit Mobilier affair, see Morton Keller, *Affairs of State: Public Life in Late Nineteenth-Century America* (Cambridge, MA: Belknap Press of Harvard University Press, 1977).

6. NYSSV, *Third Annual Report of the New York Society for the Suppression of Vice* (New York, 1877), 8–9.

7. The official title of the Comstock Law is *Act for the Suppression of Trade in, and Circulation of Obscene Literature and Articles of Immoral Use,* 42nd Cong., 3rd sess., S.R. 1572, *Congressional Globe,* 3rd sess., 42nd Cong., March 1, 1873, 2004–5; *Appendix to the Congressional Globe,* 3rd sess., 42nd Cong., March 1, 1873, 2004–5.

8. Broun and Leech, *Anthony Comstock,* 144.

9. At least one congressional representative commented on the significance of the Comstock Law. Representative Michael C. Kerr (Democrat from Indiana) moved that the bill be sent back to the Committee on the Judiciary, arguing that "its provisions are extremely important, and they ought not to be passed in such hot haste." His motion was denied, and the bill passed on the second round of votes with a bare two-thirds majority. *Congressional Globe,* 3rd sess., 42nd Cong., March 1, 1873, 2005. A series of court cases—*Roth v. United States* (1957) and *Jacobellis v. Ohio* and *Miller v. California* (both 1964) significant among them—undid the last vestiges of the Comstock Law, though these cases did not test the constitutionality of the use of the postal service as censor, a position that was upheld in *Ex parte Jackson* (1877).

10. This law amended an older law, adding "lewd and lascivious" newspapers, as well as contraceptives, to the list of items prohibited from the mail. The relevant section of the bill (S. 1572) reads: "That no obscene, lewd or lascivious book, pamphlet, picture, paper, print, or other publication of an indecent character, or any articles or thing designed or intended for the prevention of conception or procuring abortion . . . shall knowingly be deposited for mailing" (*Congressional Globe,* 42nd Cong., 3rd sess., March 1, 1873, 2005).

11. On the vice-suppression movement, see Robert W. Haney, *Comstockery in America: Patterns of Censorship and Control* (Boston: Beacon Press, 1960); Paul S. Boyer, *Purity in Print: The Vice Society Movement and Book Censorship in America* (New York: Charles Scribner's Sons, 1968); David Pivar, *Purity Crusade: Sexual Morality and Social Control, 1868–1900* (Westport, CT: Greenwood Press, 1973). Feminist historians have tended to focus on the objects of Comstock's wrath: sexually explicit texts and images, and also sexual information, particularly about contraception and abortion. Janet Farrell Brodie, in *Contraception and Abortion in Nineteenth-Century America* (Ithaca, NY: Cornell University Press, 1994), argues that Comstock took advantage of an ambivalence among Americans about non-procreative sexuality, and an emergent middle-class ethos of privacy in sexual matters, to stop the flow of "obscenity" in the public sphere. Nicola Beisel, in *Imperiled Innocents: Anthony Comstock and Family Reproduction in Victorian*

America (Princeton, NJ: Princeton University Press, 1997) focuses on the concerns of the new middle class to protect children. Helen Lefkowitz Horowitz, in *Rereading Sex: Battles over Sexual Knowledge and Suppression in Nineteenth-Century America* (New York: Alfred A. Knopf, 2002) posits a four-part "sexual conversation" in which evangelical Christians, popular health reformers, free thinkers, and free-love advocates were competing over the contours and limits of sexual speech and knowledge in nineteenth-century America.

12. Morris L. Ernst and Alan V. Schwartz, "The Post Office as Censor," in James C. N. Paul and Murray L. Schwartz, *Federal Censorship: Obscenity in the Mail* (Westport, CT: Greenwood Press, 1961), 30.

13. Gayle Rubin, "Thinking Sex: Notes for a Radical Theory of the Politics of Sexuality," in *Pleasure and Danger,* ed. Carole S. Vance (New York: Routledge, 1984), 297; Jeffrey Weeks, *Sex, Politics, and Society: The Regulation of Sexuality Since 1800* (London: Longman Group, Ltd., 1981); and Jeffrey Weeks, *Invented Moralities: Sexual Values in An Age of Uncertainty* (New York: Columbia University Press, 1995).

14. Charles Gallaudet Trumbell, *Anthony Comstock, Fighter* (New York: Fleming H. Revell, 1913). Neither the NYSSV annual reports nor Comstock's official biography mention Woodhull or her sister, Tennessee Claflin.

15. Ann Braude, *Radical Spirits: Spiritualism and Women's Rights in Nineteenth-Century America* (Boston: Beacon Press, 1989), 170–71. Victoria Woodhull has had a wealth of biographers. Emanie Sachs, *The Terrible Siren: Victoria Woodhull* (New York: Harper & Brothers Publishers, 1928), is the formative narrative, which foregrounds scandal. Biographers since the second wave of feminism have recast Woodhull's life while retaining its more sensational moments. See Madeline B. Stern, *The Victoria Woodhull Reader* (New York: M & S Press, 1974); Lois Beachy Underhill, *The Woman Who Ran for President: The Many Lives of Victoria Woodhull* (Bridgehampton, NY: Bridge Works Publishing Co., 1995); Mary Gabriel, *Notorious Victoria: The Life of Victoria Woodhull, Uncensored* (Chapel Hill, NC: Algonquin Books, 1998); Barbara Goldsmith, *Other Powers: The Age of Suffrage, Spiritualism, and the Scandalous Victoria Woodhull* (New York: Alfred A. Knopf, 1998); and Amanda Frisken, *Victoria Woodhull's Sexual Revolution: Political Theater and the Popular Press in Nineteenth-Century America* (Philadelphia: University of Pennsylvania Press, 2004). On the new wave of Woodhull chroniclers, see Helen Lefkowitz Horowitz, "A Victoria Woodhull for the 1990s," *Reviews in American History* 87, no. 2 (September 2000): 403–34.

16. Hudson Tuttle was a particularly vocal critic, charging that Woodhull used the Troy convention as "the means whereby to prostitute spiritualism to the support of unparalleled selfishness." Hudson Tuttle, "A Protest," *Religio-Philosophical Journal,* December 16, 1871, 2, and Hudson Tuttle, "American Association of Spiritualists and the New Disgrace," *Religio-Philosophical Journal,* February 17, 1872, 3. The *Banner of Light* featured more measured coverage of Woodhull's election: see,

for example, "Victoria C. Woodhull," *Banner of Light*, October 28, 1871, 4, and "Meeting of the Trustees of the American Association of Spiritualists," *Banner of Light*, November 11, 1871, 1.

17. Anna Louise Bates, *Weeder in the Garden of the Lord: Anthony Comstock's Life and Career* (New York: University Press of America, Inc., 1995), 71–72. An advertisement in the back pages of the *Banner of Light* promoted "Mrs. Dr. Woodhull and Miss Tennessee (Formerly known as the Wonderful Child), Professors of Magnetic, Mental, and Spiritual Science." *Banner of Light*, November 12, 1869, 7.

18. In May 1870, supported by Vanderbilt, Woodhull used her earnings to found *Woodhull & Claflin's Weekly*.

19. John B. Ellis, *Free Love and its Votaries; Or American Socialism Unmasked, Being an Historical and Descriptive Account of the Rise and Progress of the Various Free Love Associations in the United States, and of the Effects of their Vicious Teachings on American Society* (New York: United States Publishing Co., 1870), 473.

20. Thomas Nichols, *Free Love: A Doctrine of Spiritualism. A discourse delivered in Foster Hall, Cincinnati, December 22, 1855* (Cincinnati, OH: F. Bly, 1856), 3. See also Andrew Jackson Davis, "Spiritualism, Socialism, and Free Love," *Social Revolutionist* 1 (April 1856): 124–25.

21. "Spiritualism vs. Free Love," *Banner of Light*, November 1, 1862, 2.

22. "The Beauty and Freedom of Love," *Banner of Light*, May 25, 1867, 2.

23. A.W., "An Answer to Mr. Peebles," *Banner of Light*, April 1, 1865, 6.

24. *Religio-Philosophical Journal* 1 (1865): 1, quoted in Braude, "Spiritualists Defend the Rights of Women: Spiritualism and Changing Sex Roles in Nineteenth-Century America," in *Women, Religion and Social Change*, ed. Yvonne Yazbeck and Ellison Banks Findley (Albany: State University of New York Press, 1985), 424–25.

25. Stern, *Victoria Woodhull Reader*, 33.

26. On feminist uses of the comparison between marriage and slavery, see Karen Sánchez-Eppler, "Bodily Bonds: The Intersecting Rhetorics of Feminism and Abolition," *Representations* 24 (Fall 1988): 28–59.

27. Woodhull's brand of free love was not entirely her own. Stephen Pearl Andrews was an important collaborator and likely ghostwriter. On Andrews, see Hal D. Sears, *The Sex Radicals: Free Love in High Victorian America* (Lawrence: Regents Press of Kansas, 1977).

28. On the Beecher-Tilton scandal, see Robert Shaplen, *Free Love and Heavenly Sinners* (New York: Alfred A. Knopf, 1954); Altina L. Waller, *Reverend Beecher and Mrs. Tilton: Sex and Class in Victorian America* (Amherst: University of Massachusetts Press, 1982); Richard Wightman Fox, "Intimacy on Trial: Cultural Meanings of the Beecher-Tilton Affair," in *The Power of Culture: Critical Essays in American History*, ed. Richard Wightman Fox and T. J. Jackson Lears, 103–32 (Chicago: The University of Chicago Press, 1993); and Richard Wightman Fox,

Trials of Intimacy: Love and Loss in the Beecher-Tilton Scandal (Chicago: University of Chicago Press, 1999).

29. Ann Douglas, *The Feminization of American Culture* (New York: Alfred K. Knopf, 1977), 84.

30. Tilton was elected president of the National Woman Suffrage Association. See Clifford E. Clark Jr., *Henry Ward Beecher: Spokesman for a Middle-Class America* (Urbana: University of Illinois Press, 1978), 202–4.

31. Victoria Woodhull, "The Beecher-Tilton Scandal Case," *Woodhull & Claflin's Weekly,* November 2, 1872, 14.

32. Victoria Woodhull wrote of the demand for this issue: "On Monday afternoon, however, the inquiry for the 'Weekly with the Beecher Scandal' began to be made at our office, it not being on the newsstands. This inquiry, small at first, by the close of the day grew to a rush, and from that time until Saturday November 2, . . . it continued to increase in volume and eagerness, two cylinder presses being incompetent to satisfy the city demand. . . . Since then, those who were so fortunate as to have copies readily loaned them to readers at dollars per day." Woodhull, "Moral Cowardice & Modern Hypocrisy," *Woodhull & Claflin's Weekly,* December 28, 1872, 10.

33. Tennie C. Claflin, "Beginning of the Battle," *Woodhull & Claflin's Weekly,* November 2, 1872, 2.

34. Tennie C. Claflin, "The Philosophy of Modern Hypocrisy—Mr. L. C. Challis the Illustration," *Woodhull & Claflin's Weekly,* November 2, 1872, 8.

35. Quoted by Austin Kent, *Mrs. Victoria C. Woodhull and her "Social Freedom"* (Clinton, MA: n.p., 1873), 13 in *Free Love in America,* ed. Taylor Stoehr (New York: AMS Press, 1979), 41.

36. Disclaimer, *Woman's Journal,* January 4, 1873, 6; J. Noble Jr., "Spiritualism Vindicated," *Woman's Journal,* January 4, 1873, 2; and Henry Ward Beecher, "Let Them Amuse Themselves," *Woman's Journal,* January 4, 1873, 3.

37. Paulina Wright Davis to Victoria Woodhull, May 1872, Woodhull Papers, University of Southern Illinois Library, quoted in William Leach, *True Love and Perfect Union: The Feminist Reform of Sex and Society* (Middletown, CT: Wesleyan University Press, 1989), 58.

38. Accounts of the trial and arrest include the *New York Times,* November 3, 5, and 10, 1872; December 4, 1872; and January 10 and 22, 1873; *New York Dispatch,* November 3, 1872; Victoria Woodhull, "The Progress of the Revolution," *Woodhull & Claflin's Weekly,* December 28, 1872, 9–11; Woodhull, "Moral Cowardice & Modern Hypocrisy or, Four Weeks in Ludlow Street Jail," *Woodhull & Claflin's Weekly,* December 28, 1872, 3–9; and "The Charge of Obscenity," *Woodhull & Claflin's Weekly,* February 15, 1873, 9–13.

39. Blatchford told the jury that "under the act of 1872 newspapers were not included, the act of 1873 [the Comstock Law] being specifically framed to cover the omission and meet the present case, and that therefore there was no evidence

to sustain the prosecution." Blatchford, quoted in "The Woodhull and Claflin Trial—Discharge of Defendants," *New York Times,* June 28, 1873, 2.

40. See "Katie King," *New York Daily Graphic,* August 5, 1874, 244; "The Ghost of Katie King," *New York Daily Graphic,* August 9, 1874, 247; "Topics of the Day," *New York Daily Graphic,* August 15, 1874, 313; "Spiritual Census," *New York Daily Graphic,* August 25, 1874, 546; "Personalities," *New York Daily Graphic,* September 14, 1874, 601; "Katie King Runs Away," *New York Daily Graphic,* September 28, 1874, 418; Henry S. Olcott, "From the Other World," *New York Daily Graphic,* September 29, 1874, 642, and Henry S. Olcott, "People from the Other World," *New York Daily Graphic,* October 6, 1874, 695.

41. I take this ubiquitous phrase from Epes Sargent's *The Proof Palpable of Immortality; Being An Account of the Materialization Phenomenon of Modern Spiritualism* (1876; reprint, Boston: Colby & Rich, 1876).

42. "Katie King," *New York Daily Graphic,* August 5, 1874, 244.

43. Ibid., 244.

44. Ruth Brandon, *The Spiritualists* (New York: Alfred A. Knopf, 1983), 98.

45. Jesse Shepard (Francis Grierson), 1872 entry, *Episodes and Interviews,* unpublished manuscript, San Diego Historical Society, Francis Grierson (Jesse Shepard) Collection, MSS 55, Box 1, folder 1, n.p.

46. Olcott's collected writings from the Eddy homestead appeared as Henry S. Olcott, *People From the Other World* (Hartford, CT: American Publishing Co., 1875.) On the history of Theosophy, see Joy Dixon, *Divine Feminine: Theosophy and Feminism in England* (Baltimore, MD: Johns Hopkins University Press, 2001).

47. Mary Dana Shindler, *A Southerner among the Spirits* (Boston: Colby & Rich Publishers, 1877), 32.

48. E. L. Godkin, "Among the Materializers," *Nation,* January 3, 1884, 9–10, in E. W. Fornell, *The Unhappy Medium: Spiritualism and the Life of Margaret Fox* (Austin: University of Texas Press, 1964), 145.

49. Katie was also said to have made appearances in the Western United States, and was even spotted in a woodshed in Adrian, Michigan. See "Katie King Runs Away," 418.

50. "Katie King," *New York Daily Graphic,* August 5, 1874, 244.

51. "The Ghost of Katie King," *New York Daily Graphic,* August 9, 1874, 247.

52. Karen Halttunen, *Confidence Men and Painted Women: A Study of Middle-Class Culture, 1830–1870* (New Haven, CT: Yale University Press) and Ann Vincent Fabian, *Card Sharps, Dream Books, and Bucket Shops: Gambling in Nineteenth-Century America* (Ithaca, NY: Cornell University Press, 1990).

53. Volckman's exposés appeared in *The Medium and Daybreak,* December 26, 1873, 618, and January 16, 1874, 39, after *The Spiritualist* ran an article on the episode titled "Gross Outrage at a Spiritualist Circle," *The Spiritualist,* December 12, 1873, 461. Crookes's supporting testimony includes letters to the editor of the *Ban-*

ner of Light, reprinted in the *Spiritualist* (London), April 17, 1874, 29, and William Crookes, *Researches in the Phenomenon of Spiritualism* (London: James Burns, 1874).

54. Crookes's photographs were reproduced in James Coates, *Photographing the Invisible* (Chicago: Advanced Thought Publishing Co., 1911). See also Arthur Conan Doyle, *The Case for Spirit Photography* (New York: George H. Doran, 1923).

55. Quoted in Trevor H. Hall, *The Medium and the Scientist: The Story of Florence Cook and William Crookes* (Buffalo, NY: Prometheus Books, 1984); Hall, *The Medium and the Scientist*, 86.

56. For Owen's "disclaimed" testimony, see Robert Dale Owen, "Touching Spiritual Visitants from a Higher Life: A Chapter of Autobiography," *Atlantic Monthly* 35 (January 1875): 247–48.

57. By the 1880s, the Spiritualist press was publishing debates about the "dangers" threatening Spiritualism, including "the prevalence of so-called materializations in our land, nearly all of which is rank fraud, destitute of the least particle of genuine mediumistic manifestation" (William Emmette Coleman, "The Dangers Now Threatening Spiritualism—Sensuous Ultra-phenomenalism and Hindu Theosophy," *Carrier Dove*, February 4, 1888, 82).

58. "Materializations," *Golden Gate*, July 18, 1885, 3.

59. On nineteenth-century photography and its relation to modernity and "evidence," see Michael Leja, *Looking Askance: Skepticism and American Art from Eakins to Duchamp* (Berkeley: University of California Press, 2004); Jonathan Crary, *The Techniques of the Observer: On Vision and Modernity in the Nineteenth Century* (Cambridge, MA: MIT Press, 1990); John Tagg, *The Burden of Representation: Essays on Photographies and Histories* (Amherst: University of Massachusetts Press, 1988); and Abigail Solomon-Godeau, "The Legs of the Countess," *October* 39 (Winter 1986): 66–108.

60. *Daguerreian Journal* 1, no. 5 (January 15, 1851): 149.

61. Elizabeth Barrett Browning, quoted in Betty Miller, ed., *Elizabeth Barrett Browning to Miss Mitford: The Unpublished Letters of Elizabeth Barrett Browning to Mary Russell Mitford* (New Haven, CT: Yale University Press, 1954), 208–9.

62. Sir David Brewster on the stereoscope in *Letters on Natural Magic, Addressed to Sir Walter Scott* (London: J. Murray, 1832).

63. William Mumler documented his own rise in William H. Mumler, *The Personal Experiences of William H. Mumler in Spirit Photography* (Boston: Colby & Rich, 1875). This work was followed by the testimony of believers, particularly James Coates, *Photographing the Invisible* (Chicago: Advanced Thought Publishing, 1911) and Doyle, *Case for Spirit Photography*. Recent scholarly accounts include Jennifer Tucker, "Photography as Witness, Detective, and Imposter," in *Victorian Science in Context*, ed. Bernard Lightman (Chicago: University of Chicago Press, 1997); Robert S. Cox, *Body and Soul: A Sympathetic History of American Spiritual-*

ism (Charlottesville: University of Virginia Press, 2003), 108–35; and Leja, "Mumler's Fraudulent Photographs," in *Looking Askance,* 21–58.

64. "A Wonderful Mystery. Ghosts Sitting for Their Portraits," *New York Sun,* February 26, 1869, 2; "'Spiritual' Photographs,'" *New York World,* April 13, 1869, 4; and "The 'Spiritual' Photography Case," *New York World,* April 17, 1869, 2.

65. Edmonds, quoted in Coates, *Photographing the Invisible,* 5–6.

66. "The Triumph of the Ghosts," *World,* May 4, 1869, 2, quoted in Leja, *Looking Askance,* 56.

67. A precursor of these tales is Edgar Allen Poe's short story "The Oval Portrait." In it, a painting steals the life from the original. The story was first published as "Life in Death" in *Graham's Magazine* in April 1842. It was shortened considerably in its final version and retitled "The Oval Portrait." This version first ran in the *Broadway Journal* on April 26, 1845.

68. "The Inconstant Daguerreotype," *Harper's New Monthly Magazine* 10, no. 60 (May 1855): 823–24; and A[ugustine]. J. H. Duganne, *The Daguerreotype Miniature; Or, Life in the Empire City* (Philadelphia: G. B. Zeiber, 1846).

69. Anthony Comstock, *Morals versus Art* (New York: J. S. Ogilvie and Co., 1887), 5.

70. Anthony Comstock, *Traps for the Young,* ed. Robert Bremner (1887; reprint, Cambridge, MA: The Belknap Press of Harvard University Press, 1967), 171–72.

71. Walter Benjamin, "The Work of Art in the Age of Mechanical Reproduction," in *Illuminations* (New York: Schocken Books, 1968), 220–21.

72. Comstock, *Traps for the Young,* 172.

73. Fraud is another link between these cases. Although he did not write about fraudulent mediums, Comstock's *Frauds Exposed* warned the public of common swindles, especially those involving mail fraud. See Anthony Comstock, *Frauds Exposed; Or, How the people are deceived and robbed, and youth corrupted. Being a full exposure of various schemes operated through the mails, and unearthed by the author in a seven years' service as a Special agent of the post office department and secretary and chief agent of the New York Society for the Suppression of Vice* (New York: J. H. Brown, 1880).

74. Patricia Cline Cohen has suggested that if "historians of sex . . . have long attended to a public/private dichotomy," then "the spirit world offers another metaphorical arena" for the historical study of sexuality. This is a particularly important point for studies of Spiritualism, in which the divide between public and private falters and the spirit world provides something of a counter–public sphere. Cohen, "Sex and Sexuality: The Public, the Private, and the Spirit Worlds," *Journal of the Early Republic* (Summer 2004): 310.

75. Boyer, *Purity and Print,* 3–8, and Robert Bremner, introduction to Comstock, *Traps for the Young,* xi. Helen Horowitz has a particularly careful analysis of moral reformers and the NYSSV in *Rereading Sex,* 144–58, 299–318.

76. On the various strands of the Anglo-American social-purity movement, see

Ellen Carol DuBois and Linda Gordon, "Seeking Ecstasy on the Battlefield: Danger and Pleasure in Nineteenth-Century Feminist Sexual Thought," in Vance, *Pleasure and Danger*, 31–49; Barbara Leslie Epstein, *The Politics of Domesticity: Women, Evangelism and Temperance in Nineteenth-Century America* (Middletown, CT: Wesleyan University Press, 1981); Judith R. Walkowitz, *Prostitution and Victorian Society: Women, Class and the State* (New York: Cambridge University Press, 1980); Linda Gordon, *Woman's Body, Woman's Right: A Social History of Birth Control in America* (New York: Viking, 1976); George M. Frederickson, *The Inner Civil War: Northern Intellectuals and the Crisis of the Union* (New York: Harper & Row, 1965); and Pivar, *Purity Crusade*.

77. Lisa Duggan charts this politics of displacement, in which, for example, temperance advocates fought alcohol as a proxy for more intractable problems in the family. See Lisa Duggan, "Feminist Historians and Anti-Pornography Campaigns: An Overview," in *Sex Wars*, ed. Lisa Duggan and Nan D. Hunter (New York: Routledge, 2006), 66–67.

78. Brodie, *Contraception and Abortion*, 257.

79. Blackstone describes this category of offenses as having the tendency "to create animosities, and to disturb the public peace." William Blackstone, *Commentaries on the Laws of England*, vol. 4: *Of Public Wrongs, 1765–1769* (Chicago: University of Chicago Press, 1979), 44.

80. I do not intend to argue here that sexual behavior was no longer scrutinized; if anything, the new scrutiny of sexual representations only widened the surveillance of (nonprocreative, nonheteronormative) sexual acts.

81. On these developments, see Daniel Czitrom, *Media and the American Mind from Morse to McLuhan* (Chapel Hill: University of North Carolina Press, 1982); Cathy Davidson, *Revolution and the Word: The Rise of the Novel in America* (New York: Oxford University Press, 1986); and Michael Denning, *Mechanic Accents: Dime Novels and Working-Class Culture in America* (New York: Verso, 1987).

82. John Cleland, *Fanny Hill: Memoirs of a Woman of Pleasure* (London: G. Felton, 1813).

83. de Grazia, *Girls Lean Back,* 695.

84. Cephas Brainerd, *The Work of the Army Committee of the New York Young Men's Christian Association, Which Led to the Organization of the United States Christian Commission* (New York: John Medole, Printers, 1866), 8–15.

85. The Committee for the Suppression of Vice separated from the YMCA and became the New York Society for the Suppression of Vice in 1874. The law establishing the Society and giving its agents special police powers was "An Act to Incorporate the New York Society for the Suppression of Vice," May 16, 1874, 96th session, chapter 527.

86. On this bachelor subculture in the antebellum years, see Patricia Cline Cohen, "Unregulated Youth: Masculinity and Murder in the 1830s City," *Radical History Review* 52 (Winter 1992): 33 and Patricia Cline Cohen, *The Murder of*

Helen Jewett: The Life and Death of a Prostitute in Nineteenth-Century New York (New York: Knopf, 1998).

87. NYSSV, *Second Annual Report* (January 27, 1876), 5.

88. The three bills were folded together by the lawyer Benjamin Vaughan Abbott, and Comstock's bill was substituted for all pending bills. Broun and Leech, *Anthony Comstock*, 131–32.

89. Here I follow an important formulation by Brodie in *Contraception and Abortion*, 7.

90. The years following the Civil War saw a boom in mail-order businesses, from corporations like Sears and Roebuck to small purveyors of specialty items. In 1866, a YMCA mission statement called its members' attention to "the traffic in bad books, prints and instruments, as a fruitful source of demoralization and crime" and the need "to prosecute, in all legal forms, a class of offenses so closely affecting young men." Quoted in NYSSV, *First Annual Report*, 6.

91. Comstock described himself as a humble servant of the nation: "The power possessed by Congress embraces the regulation of the entire postal system of the country. The right to designate what shall be carried necessarily involves the right to determine what shall be excluded ... Under the power to establish post-offices and post-roads, it must be held that Congress has the right to prescribe what it will carry ... as part of the mail, and what it will not carry, and to render this enactment efficient by punishing the offense of violating it" (Comstock, *Traps for the Young*, 218. On postal-service politics, see Richard John, *Spreading the News: The American Postal System From Franklin to Morse* [Cambridge, MA: Harvard University Press, 1995]).

92. U.S. police forces were an invention of the mid-nineteenth century and a direct response to increases in urban violence and a growing, sometimes militant, working class. Major American cities established full-time police forces, replacing relatively unorganized city "watch" forces, over a twenty-year period, beginning with New York City in 1845. Chicago followed in 1851, Philadelphia in 1855, and Detroit and Buffalo in 1865 and 1866. By the mid-1870s, most small cities had established police forces. See Sidney Harring, *Policing a Class Society: The Experience of American Cities, 1865–1915* (New Brunswick, NJ: Rutgers University Press, 1983).

93. NYSSV, *Second Annual Report*, 7.

94. Assistant District Attorney William P. Fiero, *U.S. v. Bennett* 16 Blatch 338 (1879), cited in Broun and Leech, *Anthony Comstock*, 89.

95. My thanks to Robin D. G. Kelley for suggesting this link. On the Charleston post-office action, see John, *Spreading the News*, 257–58; Paul and Schwartz, *Federal Censorship*, 7; and on Henry "Box" Brown, see Herbert Aptheker, *Abolitionism: A Revolutionary Movement* (Boston: Twayne Publishers, 1989), 24.

96. Daphne A. Brooks, *Bodies in Dissent: Spectacular Performances of Race and Freedom, 1850–1910* (Durham, NC: Duke University Press, 2006), 122–23.

97. *Thomas v. State of Massachusetts* 62 NE 808 (1875), in *Acts and Resolves Passed by the General Court of Massachusetts in the Year 1875* (Boston: Wright & Potter, 1875), quotation on 766.

98. *Thomas v. State of Massachusetts* 62 NE 808–820 (1875), 767.

99. *Thomas v. Massachusetts* (1875), 766–67.

100. NYSSV, *First Annual Report*, 9.

4. MEDIOMANIA

1. George Ellwood, *Some Earlier Public Amusements of Rochester, Read before the Rochester Historical Society, 1894* (Rochester, NY: Democrat and Chronicle, 1894); Emma Hardinge [Britten], *Modern American Spiritualism: A Twenty Years' Record of the Communion Between Earth and the World of Spirits* (1869; reprint, New Hyde Park, NY: University Books, 1970), 44–45; and Eliab Wilkinson Capron, *Modern Spiritualism: Its Facts and Fanaticisms, Its Consistencies and Contradictions* (Boston: Bela Marsh, 1855).

2. Quoted in Herbert Jackson Jr., *The Spirit Rappers* (New York: Doubleday, 1972), 51.

3. Report quoted in Arthur Conan Doyle, *The History of Spiritualism*, vol. 1 (1926; reprint, New York: Arno Press, 1975), 81.

4. Britten, *Modern American Spiritualism*, 44.

5. Doyle, *History of Spiritualism*, 82.

6. The Ladies Committee is mentioned in the major primary sources discussing the event, including Capron's 1855 and Emma Hardinge's 1869 accounts, but no details are given about the ladies themselves. My assumption is that the committee was a group of prominent women in the community, assembled, like the other committees of skeptics, by the organizers of the Corinthian Hall event.

7. Britten, *Modern American Spiritualism*, 45.

8. On Spiritualism and ventriloquism, see Steven Connor, *Dumbstruck: A Cultural History of Ventriloquism* (Oxford: Oxford University Press, 2000), 362–93.

9. Herman Melville, *The Confidence-Man: His Masquerade* (New York: Dix, Edwards, & Co., 1857). On the cultural anxieties embedded in fears of the hoax, see Karen Halttunen, *Confidence Men and Painted Women: A Study of Middle-Class Culture in America, 1830–1870* (New Haven, CT: Yale University Press, 1982); Ann Vincent Fabian, *Card Sharps, Dream Books, and Bucket Shops: Gambling in 19th-Century America* (Ithaca, NY: Cornell University Press, 1990); and Neil Harris, *Humbug! The Art of P. T. Barnum* (Boston: Little Brown & Company, 1973).

10. Halttunen, *Confidence Men*, 57. This notion of womanhood was associated only with white, middle-class women. By midcentury, there was already a large

(and growing) literature linking hypersexuality and criminality to nonwhite and working-class women.

11. In June 1850, Eliab Capron accompanied Mrs. Fox and her three daughters to Barnum's Hotel in New York, where they performed public demonstrations and private séances for New York notables, including the *New York Tribune* editor Horace Greeley, the Brook Farm founder George Ripley, and the writers James Fenimore Cooper and William Cullen Bryant. Ann Braude, *Radical Spirits: Spiritualism and Women's Rights in Nineteenth-Century America* (Boston: Beacon Press, 1989), 16.

12. Reuben Briggs Davenport, *The Death-Blow to Spiritualism: Being the True Story of the Fox Sisters, as Revealed by Authority of Margaret Fox Kane and Catherine Fox Johnson* (New York: G. W. Dillingham, 1888).

13. Ann-Louise Shapiro, "Disordered Bodies/Disorderly Acts: Medical Discourse and the Female Criminal in 19th-Century Paris," *Genders* 4 (Spring 1989): 69. See also Charles Rosenberg, *No Other Gods: On Science and American Social Thought* (Baltimore, MD: Johns Hopkins University Press, 1961); Julia Epstein, *Altered Conditions: Disease, Medicine, and Storytelling* (New York: Routledge, 1994); and Jennifer Terry, *An American Obsession: Science, Medicine, and Homosexuality in Modern Society* (Chicago: University of Chicago Press, 1999).

14. On this transformation in France, see Jan Goldstein, *Console and Classify: The French Psychiatric Profession in the Nineteenth Century* (Chicago: University of Chicago Press, 1987).

15. Catherine Crowe, *Spiritualism and the Age We Live In* (London: Colburn, 1859), 91.

16. Frederic R. Marvin, *The Philosophy of Spiritualism and the Pathology and Treatment of Mediomania: Two Lectures Read before the New York Liberal Club* (New York: Asa K. Butts & Co., Publishers, 1874).

17. Marvin, *Philosophy of Spiritualism*, 35–38.

18. Ilza Veith, *Hysteria: The History of a Disease* (Chicago: University of Chicago Press, 1965), 14.

19. Carroll Smith-Rosenberg, "The Hysterical Woman: Sex Roles and Role Conflict in 19th-Century America," in *Disorderly Conduct: Visions of Gender in Victorian America* (New York: Oxford University Press, 1985), 201.

20. Ann Taves, *Fits, Trances, and Visions: Experiencing Religion and Explaining Experience from Wesley to James* (Princeton, NJ: Princeton University Press, 1999); Ian Hacking, *Rewriting the Soul: Multiple Personality and the Sciences of Memory* (Princeton, NJ: Princeton University Press, 1995).

21. Frederick T. Simpson, "Hysteria: Its Nature and Treatment," *Psychotherapy* 3 (1909): 28–47; case, 32.

22. "Mesmeric Deceptions—The Whipton Prophetess," *Lancet* 1 (1847): 178.

23. On Victorian mesmerism, see Alison Winter, *Mesmerized: Powers of Mind in Victorian Britain* (Chicago: University of Chicago Press, 1998).

24. "Mesmeric Deceptions," 178–79.

25. S. E. D. Shortt, "Physicians and Psychics: The Anglo-American Medical Response to Spiritualism, 1870–1890," *Journal of the History of Medicine and Allied Sciences* 39, no. 3 (July 1984): 341.

26. On Theosophy and psychical research in Britain and America, see Joy Dixon, *Divine Feminine: Theosophy and Feminism in England* (Baltimore, MD: Johns Hopkins University Press, 2001), and Deborah Blum, *Ghost Hunters: William James and the Search for Scientific Proof of Life after Death* (New York: Penguin Press, 2006).

27. Austin Flint, M.D., "On the Discovery of the Source of the Rochester Knockings, and on the Sounds Produced by the Movements of Joints and Tendons," *Commercial Advisor* (February 1851) and *Quarterly Journal of Medical Science* 3 (1869): 417–46.

28. "Spirit Rappers; Physiological Explanation," *American Journal of Insanity* 11 (January 1855): 294–95.

29. Edward C. Rogers, *Philosophy of Mysterious Agents, Human and Mundane: Or, the Dynamic Laws and Relations of Man* (Boston: John P. Jewett, 1853), 131–43.

30. See Jennifer Tucker, *Nature Exposed: Photography as Eyewitness in Victorian Science* (London: Johns Hopkins University Press, 2006).

31. J. Stanley Grimes, *The Mysteries of Human Nature Explained by a New System of Nervous Physiology: To which is added, a review of the errors of spiritualism, and instructions for developing or resisting the influence by which subjects and mediums are made* (Buffalo, NY: R. M. Wanzer, 1857), 401.

32. Grimes, *Mysteries*, 346.

33. Ibid., 351–52.

34. Michel Foucault, *The History of Sexuality, Volume I: An Introduction,* trans. Robert Hurley (New York: Vintage, 1980), 100–102.

35. Grimes, *Mysteries*, 362.

36. Ibid., 361–62.

37. Doyle, *History of Spiritualism*, 2.

38. Catherine Beecher, *Letter to the People on Health and Happiness* (New York: Harper & Bros., 1855), 121.

39. *Banner of Light,* November 10, 1886, 2.

40. Josef Breuer and Sigmund Freud, *Studies on Hysteria,* trans. and ed. James Strachey (New York: Basic Books Inc., 1957), 63.

41. Smith-Rosenberg, "Hysterical Woman," 201.

42. Michel Foucault, *Abnormal: Lectures at the Collège de France, 1974–1975,* trans. Graham Burchell, ed. Arnold I. Davidson (New York: Picador, 2003), 212.

43. Foucault, *Abnormal,* 224.

44. Michel Foucault, "What Is an Author?" in *Language, Counter-Memory, Practice,* trans. Donald F. Bouchard and Sherry Simon, ed. Donald F. Bouchard (Ithaca, NY: Cornell University Press, 1977), 113–38.

45. Arnold I. Davidson, "Introduction," in Foucault, *Abnormal*, xviii.

46. Foucault, *Abnormal*, 213, 161.

47. Jana Sawicki, *Disciplining Foucault: Feminism, Power and the Body* (New York: Routledge, 1991). Also see the essays in *Feminism and Foucault: Reflections on Resistance*, ed. Irene Diamond and Lee Quinby (Boston: Northeastern University Press, 1988).

48. Utica is exactly 110 miles from Hydesville and marks an edge of the Burned-Over District, a place and idea that have held enormous explanatory power in histories of religion and regionalism in the nineteenth-century United States. See Whitney R. Cross, *The Burned-Over District: The Social and Intellectual History of Enthusiastic Religion in Western New York, 1800–1850* (Ithaca, NY: Cornell University Press, 1950).

49. "Case of Mania with the Delusions and Phenomena of Spiritualism," *American Journal of Insanity* 16 (1859–60): 1. In 1892, this journal became the official publication of the American Medico-psychological Association, which changed its name in 1922 to the American Psychiatric Association.

50. Amariah Brigham, *Observations on the Influence of Religion upon the Health and Physical Welfare of Mankind* (1835; reprint, New York: Arno Press, 1973).

51. "Case of Mania," 1.

52. Ibid.

53. Literary theorists have noted the fractured, doubled character of "hysterical narrativity," as well as the ways in which hysteria often infected the (male) narrative voice of case histories. See Claire Kahane, "Hysteria, Feminism, and the Case of *The Bostonians*," in *Feminism and Psychoanalysis*, ed. Richard Feldstein and Judith Roof (Ithaca, NY: Cornell University Press, 1989), 318, and Mark Micale, *Approaching Hysteria: Disease and its Interpretations* (Princeton, NJ: Princeton University Press, 1995).

54. For a complicated and nuanced revision of this history in France, see Hacking, *Rewriting the Soul*.

55. Silas Weir Mitchell, *Lectures on Diseases of the Nervous System, Especially in Women* (Philadelphia: Lea Brothers & Co., 1885), 179–80.

56. *Banner of Light*, April 7, 1860.

57. Professor William See, M.D., "The Extreme Rarity of Premature Burials," *Popular Science Monthly* 17 (1880): 530. See also Franz Hartmann, *Buried Alive: An Examination into the Occult Causes of Apparent Death, Trance, and Catalepsy* (Boston: Occult Publishing, Co., 1895).

58. Thanks to Katherine Ott, National Museum of American History, Smithsonian Institution, for bringing an advertisement for this device to my attention.

59. Elaine Showalter, *The Female Malady: Women, Madness, and English Culture, 1830–1980* (New York: Penguin Books, 1985), 5.

60. Mark Micale, *Approaching Hysteria*, 4.

61. Goldstein, *Console and Classify*.

62. Sigmund Freud, "'Civilized' Sexual Morality and Modern Nervous Illness" (1908), trans. James Strachey, *Standard Edition of the Complete Psychological Works of Sigmund Freud,* vol. 9 (London: Hogarth Press, 1959), 189–91.

63. Smith-Rosenberg, "Hysterical Woman," 209–10.

64. S. Weir Mitchell, *Fat and Blood: An Essay on the Treatment of Certain Forms of Neurasthenia and Hysteria* (Philadelphia: J. B. Lippincott, 1885).

65. Grant Powers, *Essay upon the Influence of the Imagination on the Nervous System, Contributing to False Hope in Religion* (Andover, MA: Flagg & Gould, 1828), Brigham, *Observations on the Influence of Religion;* and William L. Stone, *Letter to Doctor A. Brigham on Animal Magnetism* (New York: George Dearborn & Co., 1837).

66. See, for example Brigham, *Observations on the Influence of Religion,* as well as his *Remarks on the Influence of Mental Cultivation and Mental Excitement upon Health* (Edinburgh: Fraser, 1836); and *An Inquiry Concerning the Diseases and Functions of the Brain, the Spinal Cord, and the Nerves* (1840; reprint, New York: Arno Press, 1973).

67. Cross, *Burned-Over District;* see also David J. Rothman, *The Discovery of the Asylum: Social Order and Disorder in the New Republic* (Boston: Little, Brown and Company, 1971).

68. Lorenzo Dow, "Fanaticism," *Banner of Light,* January 30, 1858.

69. "Whence Comes This Insanity?" *Banner of Light,* February 20, 1859.

70. "More Insanity," *Banner of Light,* January 23, 1858.

71. William A. Hammond, *The Physics and Physiology of Spiritualism* (New York: Appleton & Co., 1871), 34.

72. Hammond, *Physics and Physiology of Spiritualism,* 34.

73. A Clergyman, "Insanity and Spiritualism," *American Journal of Insanity* 33 (1876–77): 594.

74. "A Case of Insanity," *Alienist and Neurologist* 9 (1888): 344.

75. William James, "Lecture I: Religion and Neurology," in *The Varieties of Religious Experience* (1902; reprint, New York: Modern Library, 1929), 21–38, quote on 27.

76. Wilhelm Wundt, "Spiritualism as a Scientific Question," trans. Edwin D. Mead, *Popular Science Monthly* 15 (1879): 577–93; J. M. Charcot, "Hysteria and Spiritism," trans. E. P. Hurd, *Medical Surgical Reporter* 59 (1888): 65–68; and Cesare Lombroso, *After Death—What?* trans. William Sloane Kennedy (Boston: Small, Maynard & Co., 1909).

77. Andrew T. Scull, "The Social History of Psychiatry in the Victorian Era," in *Madhouses, Mad-Doctors and Madmen: The Social History of Psychiatry in the Victorian Era,* ed. Andrew T. Scull (Philadelphia: University of Pennsylvania Press, 1981), 7.

78. Charles L. Dana, "Rest Treatment in Relation to Psychotherapy by S. Weir Mitchell," *Transactions of the American Neurological Association* 34 (1908): 217.

79. Robert N. Young, "Natural Theology, Victorian Periodicals, and the Fragmentation of a Common Context," in *Darwin to Einstein: Historical Studies of Science and Belief,* ed. Colin Chant and John Fauvel, 69–107 (New York: Longman's, Inc, 1980).

80. Young, "Natural Theology, Victorian Periodicals," 96.

81. Marvin, *Philosophy of Spiritualism,* 35.

82. Bonnie Blustein, *Preserve Your Love of Science: The Life of William A. Hammond, American Neurologist* (New York: Cambridge University Press, 1991), 95–96.

83. *Annual Report of the Board of Trustees of the New York State Hospital for Diseases of the Nervous System,* 1872, and minute book of the New York Neurological Society, 1872. New York Academy of Medicine, Rare Books and Manuscripts Division.

84. Hammond's works include "The Physics and Physiology of Spiritualism," *North American Review* (April 1870); *The Physics and Physiology of Spiritualism* (New York: Appleton, 1871); *Spiritualism and Allied Causes and Conditions of Nervous Derangement* (New York: G. P. Putnam's Sons, 1876); and *On Certain Conditions of Nervous Derangement: Somnambulism—Hypnotism—Hysteria—Hysteroid Affections, etc.* (New York: G. P. Putnam's Sons, 1883). As suggested by the titles, these works overlap a great deal.

85. Hammond, *Physics and Physiology of Spiritualism,* 48–49.

86. Ibid., 56.

87. Emily Apter makes a similar point about the genealogy of the fetishist, in which nineteenth-century French medicine comes to associate fetishism with libertinage, thus pathologizing the sexual excesses of the eighteenth century and, not incidentally, the politics associated with it. Emily Apter, *Feminizing the Fetish: Psychoanalysis and Narrative Obsession in Turn-of-the-Century France* (Ithaca, NY: Cornell University Press, 1991), 18.

88. It was not only doctors who linked Spiritualist mediums to their mystical foremothers. In 1859, Charles Dickens wrote in a London newspaper of Spiritualists: "Prophets and oracles, ghost-seers and visionaries, wonder-workers and miracle-mongers, troop in crowds through the pages of history, and the modern world is beset by the same, with nothing changed but dress and name." *All the Year Round,* November 5, 1859, 31.

89. Charcot also drew comparisons between nineteenth-century French hysterics and medieval Catholic mystics. See Charcot, "Hysteria and Spiritism."

90. W. B. Carpenter, "Epidemic Delusions," *Popular Science Monthly* 2 (1872–73): 16, 19.

91. Ibid., 36. See also Amos Craft, *Epidemic Delusions: Containing an Exposé of the Superstitions and Frauds which Underlie Some Ancient and Modern Delusions, Including Especial Reference to Modern Spiritualism* (New York: Phillips & Hunt, 1881). As well as bearing the same title as Carpenter's work, Craft's pamphlet reiterates many of the same ideas. For instance, Craft writes: "It is well known that fits

of hysteria and freaks of excited fancy, under the influence of popular delusion, may become epidemic" (186).

92. Bonnie Ellen Blustein, "'A Hollow Square of Psychological Science': American Neurologists and Psychiatrists in Conflict," in Scull, *Madhouses, Mad-Doctors*, 243.

93. George Miller Beard, *American Nervousness: Its Causes and Consequences* (New York: G. P. Putnam's Sons, 1881). On Beard, see Charles E. Rosenberg, "The Place of George M. Beard in Nineteenth-Century Psychiatry," *Bulletin of the History of Medicine* 36 (1962): 245–59, and Anson Rabinbach, "Neurasthenia and Modernity," in *Incorporations*, ed. Jonathan Crary and Sanford Kwinter (New York: Zone Books, 1992).

94. George M. Beard, *Psychology of Salem Witchcraft* (New York: G. P. Putnam's Sons, 1882), 42.

95. G. M. Beard, "The Delusions of Clairvoyance," *Scribner's Monthly* 18, no. 3 (1879): 438. See also Beard, "Trance," *Mind* 2 (1877): 568.

96. George Croom Robertson, ed., "Review of G. M. Beard, 'Trance,'" in *Mind: A Quarterly Review of Psychology and Philosophy* 2 (1877): 568. *Braidism* refers to therapy using hypnotic suggestion, named after the British doctor James Braid (1795–1860).

97. Rosenberg, "The Place of George M. Beard," 253, 254, and Beard, *American Nervousness*.

98. Anson Rabinbach also makes this argument about Beard's theories in "Neurasthenia and Modernity."

99. Gail Bederman, *Manliness and Civilization: A Cultural History of Gender and Race in the United States, 1880–1917* (Chicago: University of Chicago Press, 1995), 77–120.

100. Beard, *American Nervousness*, 92.

101. This finding seems contradictory, as the "lower orders"—women, children, nonwhites, and non-Europeans—were typically seen as more susceptible to suggestion. Yet Beard conducted a series of investigations into trance with a group of African Americans in the South, in which he described his trance experiments with these people as "somewhere between the highest order of animals and the lowest order of men," finding them somewhat difficult to entrance. G. M. Beard, "Trance State Artificially Produced in Negroes," Box 3, Folder 13, George Miller Beard Papers, Manuscripts and Archives, Yale University (hereafter Beard Papers).

102. G. M. Beard, "The Case of Guiteau—A Psychological Study," *Journal of Nervous and Mental Disorders*, 1882, quoted in Rosenberg, "The Place of George M. Beard," 255.

103. Robertson, "Review of G. M. Beard," 568–69.

104. Professional rivalries between neurologists and asylum keepers heated up during the 1880s, a key period in the development of the American psychiatric profession. In 1882, President James Garfield was shot by Charles J. Guiteau. At

Guiteau's trial, neurologists took the stand on his behalf, marking the first usage of the insanity defense. Asylum superintendents denounced the "insanity dodge," while neurologists (including Hammond and Beard) took the opposite view. See Charles Rosenberg, *The Trial of the Assassin Guiteau: Psychiatry and the Law in the Gilded Age* (Chicago: University of Chicago Press, 1968).

105. W. A. Hammond, *Journal of Psychological Medicine* 5 (1871): 576.

106. Henry Abelove, "Freud, Male Homosexuality, and the Americans," in *The Lesbian and Gay Studies Reader*, ed. Henry Abelove, Michele Aina Barale, and David M. Halperin (New York: Routledge, 1993), 381–93.

107. Ernest Earnest, *S. Weir Mitchell: Novelist and Physician* (Philadelphia: University of Pennsylvania Press, 1950), 227, 180.

108. J. M. S. Pearce, "Silas Weir Mitchell and the 'Rest Cure,'" *Journal of Neurology, Neurosurgery, and Psychiatry* 75, no. 381 (2004): 42; and Barbara Ehrenreich and Deirdre English, *For Her Own Good: 150 Years of the Experts' Advice to Women* (Garden City, NY: Doubleday, 1978), 133.

109. Jane F. Thrailkill, "Doctoring 'The Yellow Wallpaper,'" *ELH* 69, no. 2 (2002): 525–66.

110. S. Weir Mitchell, *The Autobiography of a Quack: And, the Case of George Dedlow* (New York: Century Company, 1900).

111. Earnest, *S. Weir Mitchell*, 62.

112. See Joan Jacobs Brumberg, *Fasting Girls: The Emergence of Anorexia Nervosa as a Modern Disease* (Cambridge, MA: Harvard University Press, 1988), 80, for "dyspeptic schoolgirl." "Dead and Yet Alive: The Extraordinary Case of Miss Fancher of Brooklyn," *Sun*, November 24, 1878, 1. As well as the copious press coverage in the New York *Sun, Herald, Evening Post,* and *Brooklyn Daily Eagle,* from September 1878 to January 1879, Mollie Fancher's story was detailed in a biography by Abram Dailey, a Spiritualist and friend of the family: *Mollie Fancher, the Brooklyn Enigma: An Authentic Statement of Facts in the Life of Mary J. Fancher* (Brooklyn, NY: Eagle Book Printing Dept., 1894); Brumberg, *Fasting Girls* (1988), 73–91, and, most recently, Michelle Stacey's popular *The Fasting Girl: A True Victorian Medical Mystery* (New York: Penguin, 2002).

113. "A Puzzle for the Psychologists," *Sun*, November 24, 1878, 4.

114. "Dead and Yet Alive," 1.

115. Quote from Abram Dailey, "Life of Mollie Fancher" (1894), unpublished manuscript, Beard Papers, n.p.

116. "Dead and Yet Alive," 1.

117. Dailey, *Mollie Fancher*, chapter 4.

118. "Dead and Yet Alive," 1.

119. "Life without Food: What the Physicians Say of the Remarkable Case, A Sad and Moving History," *Herald*, October 20, 1878, 12.

120. "Miss Fancher of Brooklyn: People of Two Cities Talking of Her Wonderful Powers," *Sun*, November 25, 1878, 3.

121. "Life without Food," 12.

122. On anorexia mirablis in the medieval tradition, see Carolyn Walker Bynum, *Holy Feast and Holy Fast: The Religious Significance of Food to Medieval Women* (Berkeley: University of California Press, 1987) and Bynum, *Fragmentation and Redemption: Essays on Gender and the Human Body in Medieval Religion* (New York: Zone Books, 1990).

123. William A. Hammond, *Fasting Girls: Their Physiology and Pathology* (New York: G. P. Putnam's Sons, 1876), 6.

124. "Miss Fancher of Brooklyn," 3.

125. George M. Beard, *Eating and Drinking: A Popular Manual of Food and Diet in Health and Disease* (New York: G. P. Putnam, 1871), 8.

126. For Beard's eating regimen and culinary confessions, see "Private Journal," March–May 1858, Box 1, Folder 3, Beard Papers.

127. Hammond, *Fasting Girls*, vi.

128. Brumberg, *Fasting Girls*, 83.

129. "Miss Fancher of Brooklyn" and "The Case of Miss Fancher: "If She Can Do All This, Then All Science Goes for Naught," *The Sun*, November 26, 1878, 1.

130. Sarah Jacob died in Wales in December 1869 after a group of London doctors set out to prove that she could not live without food by "miraculous means" and that her hysterical "religious enthusiasm" would not sustain her. Neither Hammond nor Beard was directly connected with Jacob's death, but the tragedy tainted the project of "testing" fasting girls.

131. M. Denslow to George M. Beard, September 25, 1879, Correspondence File, Box 1, Folder 10, Beard Papers.

132. "Correspondence and Clippings" File, Beard Papers. The Beard Papers contain many such letters from Spiritualists.

133. "The Case of Miss Fancher," *New York Herald*, November 26, 1878, with attached note, "Correspondence and Clippings" File, Beard Papers.

134. "The Case of Miss Fancher," *The Sun*, 1.

135. Ibid.

136. George M. Beard, *The Study of Trance, Muscle-Reading and Allied Nervous Phenomena in Europe and America, with a Letter on the Moral Character of Trance Subjects and a Defence of Dr. Charcot* (New York: n.p., 1882), Box 2, Folder 11, Beard Papers; "George M. Beard requests the honor . . . ," invitation to a public "experiment on a number of trained human subjects on whom Dr. Beard has been experimenting during the past year," Box 2, Folder 11, Beard Papers; and Beard, "Trance State Artificially Produced in Negroes," Box 3, Folder 13, Beard Papers.

5. SECULAR SPIRITS

1. The literature on secularization in Western culture is immense and, like much historical and sociological work that describes a long and gradual process of change

over time, secularization seems to "happen" for centuries. In the European literature, the timeline is typically written with the latter half of the seventeenth century standing in as the beginning of Enlightenment secularization and culminating, as it also does in historical literature on secularization in the U.S., at the end of the nineteenth-century with the supposed "elimination of magic as a technique of salvation." See Max Weber, *The Sociology of Religion,* trans. Talcott Parsons (1902; reprint, Boston: Beacon Press, 1963); Weber, *The Protestant Ethic and the Spirit of Capitalism,* trans. Talcott Parsons (New York: Charles Scribner's Sons, 1958); Émile Durkheim, *The Elementary Forms of Religious Life,* trans. Joseph W. Swain (1915; reprint, Glencoe, Ill: Free Press, 1926); Marcel Gauchet, *The Disenchantment of the World: A Political History of Religion,* trans. Oscar Burge (Princeton, NJ: Princeton University Press, 1997); Robert Darnton, *Mesmerism and the End of the Enlightenment in France* (Cambridge, MA: Harvard University Press, 1968); and Keith Thomas, *Religion and the Decline of Magic* (New York: Viking, 1971). On secularization in the U.S., see Charles Rosenberg, *No Other Gods: On Science and American Social Thought* (Baltimore, MD: The Johns Hopkins University Press, 1961); Bryan Wilson, "Secularization: The Inherited Model," in *Religion in American History,* eds. Jon Butler and Harry S. Stout (New York: Oxford University Press, 1998), 336–44; and Steve Bruce, ed. *Religion and Modernization: Sociologists and Historians Debate the Secularization Thesis* (New York: Oxford University Press, 1992). I have been especially aided by Janet R. Jakobsen with Ann Pellegrini, "World Secularisms at the Millennium: Introduction," *Social Text* 64 (Fall 2000): 1–27.

2. See Weber, *Protestant Ethic,* especially "The Religious Foundations of Worldly Asceticism."

3. Despite the foundational place of Foucault, in the United States his work was preceded by that of historians of sexuality working primarily outside the academy. In 1971, Jonathan Ned Katz began research that culminated his book *Gay American History: Lesbian and Gay Men in the U.S.A.* (New York: Avon Books, 1976). See also Jonathan Ned Katz, *Gay/Lesbian Almanac: A New Documentary* (New York: Harper and Row, 1983).

4. Michel Foucault, *The History of Sexuality, Volume 1: An Introduction,* trans. Robert Hurley (New York: Pantheon, 1978), 21, 37.

5. Ibid., 43.

6. Books on the history of sexuality that include the words *modern* or *modernity* in the title are too numerous to list here. I mean not to criticize the usage as much as point to the specificities that are erased in the recapitulation of this term.

7. The literature that emphasizes continuities in sexual identities over time is too varied to gather easily under one rubric. It ranges from the earliest attempts to find "gay" ancestors in the distant past to more recent excavations of premodern sexual or gender identities, including Judith M. Bennett, "Confronting Continuity," *Journal of Women's History* 9, no. 3 (1997): 73–94, and Randolph Trumbach, *Sex and the Gender Revolution: Heterosexuality and the Third Gender in Enlighten-*

ment London (Chicago: University of Chicago Press, 1998). The term "Great Paradigm Shift" is Eve Sedgwick's: "Axiom 5: The historical search for a Great Paradigm Shift may obscure the present conditions of sexual identity," *Epistemology of the Closet* (Berkeley: University of California Press, 1990), 44. For a recent reassessment of the divide between alterity and continuity, see Valerie Traub, "The Present Future of Lesbian Historiography," in *A Companion to LGBT/Q Studies,* ed. George E. Haggerty and Molly McGarry (London: Blackwell Publishing, 2007), 124–45.

8. Foucault, of course, never uses the term *identity* or any of its French cognates, instead wryly referring to homosexuals as a "species" distinguished from the "temporary aberration," the sodomite. Scholars have deployed this shift in discursive effects to both reify and trouble the notion of identity in the history of sexuality. See David M. Halperin, "Forgetting Foucault: Acts, Identities, and the History of Sexuality," *Representations* 63 (1998): 93–120. For a trenchant and concise take on the debate, see Carolyn Dinshaw, *Getting Medieval: Sexual Communities, Pre- and Postmodern* (Durham, NC: Duke University Press, 1999), 191–206, and Louise O. Fradenburg and Carla Freccero, eds., *Premodern Sexualities* (New York: Routledge, 1996).

9. See especially Jennifer Terry, "Theorizing Deviant Historiography," in *Feminists Revision History,* ed. Ann-Louise Shapiro, 276–303 (New Brunswick, NJ: Rutgers University Press, 1994); Frederik Silverstolpe, "Benkert Was Not a Doctor: On the Non-medical Origins of the Homosexual Category in the Nineteenth Century," in *Homosexuality, Which Homosexuality?* (Amsterdam: Free University/ Schorer Foundation, 1987), 206–20; and Lisa Duggan, *Sapphic Slashers: Sex, Violence, and American Modernity* (Durham, NC: Duke University Press, 2000).

10. Elizabeth Lapovsky Kennedy and Madeline D. Davis, *Boots of Leather, Slippers of Gold: The History of a Lesbian Community* (New York: Routledge, 1993); George Chauncey, *Gay New York: Gender, Urban Culture, and the Making of the Gay World, 1890–1940* (New York: Basic Books, 1994); and essays in *Creating a Place for Ourselves: Lesbian, Gay, and Bisexual Community Histories,* ed. Brett Beemyn (New York: Routledge, 1997).

11. Andrew Parker, Mary Russo, Doris Sommer, and Patricia Yaeger, eds., *Nationalisms and Sexualities* (New York: Routledge, 1991); Cindy Patton and Benigno Sánchez-Eppler, eds., *Queer Diasporas* (Durham, NC: Duke University Press, 2000); Jasbir Kuar Puar, ed., "Queer Tourism: Geographies of Globalization," *GLQ: A Journal of Lesbian and Gay Studies* 8, nos. 1–2, special issue (2000); Arnaldo Cruz-Malave and Martin F. Manalansan IV, eds., *Queer Globalizations: Citizenship and the Afterlife of Colonialism* (New York: New York University Press, 2002); and Gayatri Gopinath, *Impossible Desires: Queer Diasporas and South Asian Public Cultures* (Durham, NC: Duke University Press, 2005).

12. Halperin is essentially limning Foucault's later volumes on the history of sexuality, in which Foucault distanced himself somewhat from the distinction between acts and identities. Halperin, "Forgetting Foucault," 114 n. 8.

13. David M. Halperin, "Is There a History of Sexuality?" *History and Theory* 28 (1989): 257–74.

14. John D'Emilio, "Capitalism and Gay Identity," in *Powers of Desire: The Politics of Sexuality,* ed. Ann Snitow, Christine Stansell, and Sharon Thompson, 100–113 (New York: Monthly Review Press, 1983).

15. I take this formulation from Dilip Parameshwar Gaonkar, "On Alternative Modernities," in *Alternative Modernities,* ed. Dilip Parameshwar Gaonkar (Durham, NC: Duke University Press, 2001), 21.

16. Foucault distinguishes the argument he has sketched as "peculiar to the Catholic Church" but suggests that a "somewhat similar evolution takes place in Protestant countries, but through very different institutions and with a fundamental fragmentations of both religious theory and forms." For example, in English Puritan circles, Foucault traces "the practice of permanent autobiography in which each individual recounts his own life to himself and others" (Michel Foucault, *Abnormal: Lectures at the Collège de France, 1974–1974,* trans. Graham Burchell [New York: Picador, 2003], 184). For an account of confessional sexuality in the contemporary United States, see Joshua Gamson, *Freaks Talk Back: Tabloid Talk Shows and Sexual Nonconformity* (Chicago: University of Chicago Press, 1998).

17. On experiential religion in nineteenth-century Britain and America, see Henry Abelove, *The Evangelist of Desire: John Wesley and the Methodists* (Stanford, CA: Stanford University Press, 1990); Ann Taves, *Fits, Trances, and Visions: Experiencing Religion and Explaining Experience from Wesley to James* (Princeton, NJ: Princeton University Press, 1999); and Leigh Eric Schmidt, *Hearing Things: Religion, Illusion, and the American Enlightenment* (Cambridge, MA: Harvard University Press, 2000).

18. Georges Bataille, *Inner Experience* (1954; reprint, Albany: State University of New York Press, 1988) and I. M. Lewis, *Ecstatic Religion: A Study of Shamanism and Spirit Possession* (1971; reprint, New York: Routledge, 1989).

19. Michael Warner, "Tongues Untied: Memoirs of a Pentecostal Boyhood," in *Qu(e)erying Religion: A Critical Anthology,* ed. Gary David Comstock and Susan E. Henking (New York: Continuum, 1997), 229.

20. Elizabeth A. Castelli makes this point in "Women, Gender, Religion: Troubling Categories and Transforming Knowledge," *Women, Gender, Religion: A Reader,* ed. Elizabeth A. Castelli (London: Palgrave, 2001), 23 n. 9.

21. Uriah Clark, *Plain Guide to Spiritualism: A Hand-Book for Skeptics, Inquirers, Clergymen, Believers, Lecturers, Mediums, Editors . . .* (Boston: W. White & Co., 1863), 172.

22. Emma Hardinge Britten echoes this advice in her instructions for a spirit circle, writing that there "should be, as far as possible, of opposite temperaments, as positive and negative." Britten, "How to Investigate Spiritualism; or Rules for the Spirit Circle," *Two Worlds,* November 18, 1887, 1.

23. Andrew Jackson Davis, *The Magic Staff; An Autobiography* (New York: J. S. Brown, 1857), 383.

24. "Andrew Jackson Davis," *Shekinah* 3 (1853): 18.

25. This account is drawn from Emma Hardinge [Britten], *Modern American Spiritualism; A Twenty Years' Record of the Communion between Earth and the World of the Spirits* (1869; reprint, New York: University Books, 1970); Davis, *Magic Staff* (1857); and Catherine L. Albanese, "On the Matter of Spirit: Andrew Jackson Davis and the Marriage of God and Nature," *Journal of the American Academy of Religion* 60, no. 1 (Spring 1992): 1–17.

26. Britten, *Modern American Spiritualism*, 23.

27. Ibid., 23, 24, and Grimes, *The Mysteries of Human Nature Explained*, 401. Davis traveled with Dr. Silas Smith Lyon of Bridgeport as his new magnetizer and the Rev. William Fishbough, a Universalist clergyman, as his scribe. Three eminent men (the Rev. Y. N. Parker, R. Lapham, Esq., and Dr. L. Smith of New York) were called as "special witnesses." These lectures, compiled and edited by Fishbough, who described them as a "vast compendium of literary, scientific, philosophic, and historic knowledge," were published as Andrew Jackson Davis, *Nature's Divine Revelations: The Principles of Nature, Her Divine Revelations, and a Voice to Mankind* (New York: S. S. Lyon and Wm. Fishbough, 1851).

28. Britten, *Modern American Spiritualism*, 24.

29. Davis, *Magic Staff*, 415.

30. Samuel Byron Brittan, *Telegraph Papers* 4 (1856): 241.

31. Albanese, "On the Matter of Spirit," 10.

32. See especially "Spiritualism vs. Free Love," *Banner of Light*, November 1, 1862, 2; "The Beauty and Freedom of Love," *Banner of Light*, May 25, 1867, 2; and A.W., "An Answer to Mr. Peebles," *Banner of Light*, April 1, 1865, 6.

33. R. W. Shufeldt, "Dr. Havelock Ellis on Sexual Inversion," *Pacific Medical Journal* 45 (1902): 201, quoted in Katz, *Gay American History*, 243; and J. Murray Case, "Follies of Spiritualists," *Religio-philosophical Journal*, April 12, 1878, 1.

34. Case, "Follies of Spiritualists," 1.

35. She wore the medal every day until her death in 1919 and was buried in her frock coat. Walker's medal was restored, along with those of 910 other recipients, on June 10, 1977. Katz, *Gay American History*, 248.

36. "Mary Walker's Trousers: Patrolman Flannery Rebuked for an Illegal Arrest," New York *Sun*, December 6, 1878, 3.

37. "Dr. Mary Walker's Protest," New York *Sun*, December 7, 1878, 2.

38. There were many dress-reform appeals to female Spiritualists printed in the press, suggesting "rules and customs in regard to labor, dress, diet & most conducive to the development of both the physical and the spiritual." Eliza J. Robinson, "An Appeal to Women," *Banner of Light*, January 28, 1865, 2, and Juliet H. Stillman, "Hints on Dress," *Banner of Light*, January 23, 1865, 3.

39. Case, "Follies of Spiritualists," 1.

40. Katz notes that Walker is also mentioned in Edward Van Every, *The Sins of New York as "Exposed" by the Police Gazette* (New York: Stokes, 1931) in Katz, *Gay American History*, 574 n. 40. This suggests that Walker was a visible gender deviant in an urban context in which fairies were a part of the streetscape but cross-dressing women were rare. On the history of female dandyism in London, see Laura Doan, *Fashioning Sapphism: The Origins of a Modern English Lesbian Culture* (New York: Columbia University Press, 2001).

41. Henry Steel Olcott, *Old Diary Leaves: The True Story of the Theosophical Society* (New York and London: G. P. Putnam's Sons, 1895), 68; clipping, Folder 31, Box 1, Francis Grierson (Jesse Shepard) Papers, San Diego Historical Society.

42. Joy Dixon, *Divine Feminine: Theosophy and Feminism in England* (Baltimore, MD: Johns Hopkins University Press, 2001), 21.

43. Wm Emmette Coleman, "The Dangers Now Threatening Spiritualism: Sensuous Ultraism and Hindu Theosophy," *Carrier Dove*, February 4, 1888, 83.

44. Ibid.

45. Olcott, *Old Diary Leaves*, 68.

46. Ibid.

47. Ibid.

48. Jesse Shepard, 1872 entry, "Episodes and Interviews," unpublished MS, San Diego Historical Society, Francis Grierson (Jesse Shepard) Papers, MSS 55, Box 1, folder 1, n.p.

49. "Mr. Shepard, The Musical Medium," *Banner of Light*, August 29, 1868, 2.

50. Alma Whitaker, "Famed Author Dies in Want," *Los Angeles Times*, May 1927, from San Diego Historical Society, Francis Grierson (Jesse Shepard) Papers, MSS 55, Box 1, folder 6 (Reviews 1875–1928), and Erik Davis, *The Visionary State: A Journey through California's Spiritual Landscape* (San Francisco: Chronicle Books, 2006), 36.

51. Whitaker, "Famed Author Dies in Want."

52. "Portrait of the Medium," *Carrier Dove* 3, no. 7 (July 7, 1886): 153–54. Colville (1862–1917) was variously referred to in print as Wilberforce J., William Wilberforce Juvenal, and, most often, W. J. Colville.

53. H. D. Barrett and A. W. McCoy, eds., "W. J. Colville," in *Cassadaga: Its History and Teachings, with histories of Spiritualist Camp Meetings and Biographies of Cassadaga Pioneers and Others* (Meadville, PA: Gazette Printing Company, 1891), "taken by permission from an unpublished autobiography of this well-known speaker, carefully compiled by Cornelius Throgmorton" (179).

54. "Portrait of the Medium," 153, and Barrett and McCoy, "W. J. Colville."

55. "Portrait of the Medium," 153.

56. "Ibid.

57. Barrett and McCoy, "W. J. Colville," 178.

58. "Portrait of the Medium," 154.

59. W. J. Colville, *Ancient Mysteries and Modern Revelations* (New York: R. F. Fenno, 1910), 342.

60. "Portrait of the Medium," 153.

61. Raymond Williams, "Dominant, Residual, and Emergent," in *Marxism and Literature* (New York: Oxford University Press, 1977), 122.

62. "Portrait of the Medium," 154.

63. O. S. Fowler and L. N. Fowler, "Symbolical Head," in *The Illustrated Self-Instructor in Phrenology and Physiology* (New York: Fowler & Wells, 1855).

64. Michael Lynch, "'Here is Adhesiveness': From Friendship to Homosexuality," *Victorian Studies 29* (Autumn 1985): 68–96. Other accounts of Whitman's relation to phrenology include Edward Hungerford, "Walt Whitman and His Chart of Bumps," *American Literature 2* (1931): 366–81, and Betsy Erkkila, "Whitman and the Homosexual Republic," in *Walt Whitman: The Centennial Essays,* ed. Ed Folsom (Iowa City: University of Iowa Press, 1994), 153–171.

65. Lynch, "'Here is Adhesiveness,'" 84, 89. Lorenzo Fowler also worked with the publishers Orson Fowler and Samuel Wells. See Peter Coviello, "Intimate Nationality: Anonymity and Attachment in Whitman," *American Literature 73,* no. 1 (2001): 118 n. 36.

66. Edward Hungerford, quoted in Lynch, "'Here is Adhesiveness,'" 89.

67. Lynch, "'Here is Adhesiveness,'" 89.

68. Lorenzo Fowler, *Marriage: Its Histories and Ceremonies; With a Phrenological and Physiological Exposition of the Functions and Qualifications for Happy Marriages* (New York: Fowler and Wells, 1847), 76.

69. Michael Warner, "Whitman Drunk," in *Breaking Bounds: Whitman and American Cultural Studies,* ed. Betsy Erkkila and Jay Grossman (New York: Oxford University Press, 1996), 40.

70. Peter Coviello, *Intimacy in America: Dreams of Affiliation in Antebellum Literature* (Minneapolis: University of Minnesota Press, 2005), 127.

71. Michael Moon, *Disseminating Whitman: Revision and Corporeality in "Leaves of Grass"* (Cambridge, MA: Harvard University Press, 1991), 3.

72. Tenny Nathanson's description of Whitman's "'presence' and its capacity to compound the physical and the vaporous" speaks to this enmeshment. Nathanson, *Whitman's Presence: Body, Voice, and Writing in "Leaves of Grass"* (New York: New York University Press, 1996), 3.

73. "Poet of attachment" is Peter Coviello's term in *Intimacy in America,* 130.

74. "New York Conference. Session of July 21," *Spiritual Age,* August 1, 1857, 1.

75. The significant exception is Joy Dixon, "Sexology and the Occult: Sexuality and Subjectivity in Theosophy's New Age," in Castelli, *Women, Gender, Religion,* 288–309.

76. In his brief section "Dominant, Residual, and Emergent," Williams seems to suggest that the residual should reside in relationship to the dominant rather than to the emergent. *Marxism and Literature,* 122.

77. For instance, Krafft-Ebing refers to "the masculine soul, heaving in the female bosom," in Richard von Krafft-Ebing, "Congenital Sexual Inversion in Women," *Psychopathia Sexualis,* trans. Charles Gilbert Chaddock (Philadelphia: F. A. Davis Co., Publishers, [1886] 1893).

78. Edward Carpenter, "The Intermediate Sex" (1896) in *Sexology Uncensored: The Documents of Sexual Science,* ed. Lucy Bland and Laura Doan (Chicago: University of Chicago Press, 1998), 51. See also Edward Carpenter, *Intermediate Types among Primitive Folk: A Study in Social Evolution* (London: G. Allen, 1914).

79. Havelock Ellis and John Addington Symonds, *Sexual Inversion* (London: Wilson & MacMillan, 1897). Laura Doan and Chris Waters, "Introduction," in Bland and Doan, *Sexology Uncensored,* 42.

80. Quoted in Doan and Waters, "Introduction," 42.

81. Dixon, "Sexology and the Occult," 289–90.

82. The definitive history of Theosophy is Dixon, *Divine Feminine.*

83. Joscelyn Goodwin, glossing Madame Blavatsky's *Isis Unveiled* (1877) in *The Theosophical Enlightenment* (Albany: State University of New York Press, 1994), 341.

84. Terry Castle, *Noel Coward and Radclyffe Hall: Kindred Spirits* (New York: Columbia University Press, 1996), 14.

85. I use the terms *lesbian* and *invert* interchangeably here, but the two have distinct histories. Indeed, both Radclyffe Hall herself and *The Well* have been vexed sites in the history of critical and political reception of female masculinities. See Esther Newton, "The Mythic Mannish Lesbian: Radclyffe Hall and the New Woman," in *Hidden from History: Reclaiming the Gay and Lesbian Past,* ed. Martin Bauml Duberman, Martha Vicinus, and George Chauncey Jr. (New York: New American Library, 1989); Judith Halberstam, *Female Masculinity* (Durham, NC: Duke University Press, 1998); Jay Prosser, *Second Skins: The Body Narratives of Transsexuality* (New York: Columbia University Press, 1998); and Heather K. Love, "'Spoiled Identity': Stephen Gordon's Loneliness and the Difficulties of Queer History" *GLQ* 7, no. 4 (2001): 487–519.

86. "Psychical Research. The Spirits of the Dead Slander Action: King's Bench Division, Radclyffe Hall v. Fox Pitt," *The Times,* 19 November, 1920, 4, and Doan, *Fashioning Sapphism,* 31–32.

87. "Psychical Research," 4.

88. Ibid., and "The Psychical Research Case," *The Times,* 24 November, 1920, 4.

89. "Psychical Research Case," 4.

90. Quoted in Doan, *Fashioning Sapphism,* 33.

91. See Terry Castle, *The Apparitional Lesbian: Female Homosexuality and Modern Culture* (New York: Columbia University Press, 1993); Patricia White, "Female Spectator, Lesbian Specter: *The Haunting,*" in *Sexuality and Space,* ed. Beatriz Colomina (Princeton, NJ: Princeton Papers on Architecture, 1992), 131–

161; Patricia White, *Uninvited: Classical Hollywood Cinema and Lesbian Representability* (Bloomington: Indiana University Press, 1999); and Carla Freccero, "Queer Spectrality," *Queer/Early/Modern* (Durham, NC: Duke University Press, 2006), 69–104.

92. Castle, *Apparitional Lesbian,* 2.

93. Radclyffe Hall, *The Well of Loneliness* (1928; reprint, New York: Doubleday 1990), 437.

94. Ibid., 437, 436.

95. This is Carolyn Dinshaw's term from *Getting Medieval.*

SELECT BIBLIOGRAPHY

PRIMARY SOURCES

Manuscript Collections

THE LIBRARY OF CONGRESS, WASHINGTON, D.C.

Adelaide Johnson Collection
Harry Houdini Collection
McManus-Young Papers
National American Women's Suffrage Association Collection

NATIONAL ASSOCIATION OF SPIRITUALIST CHURCHES,
LILY DALE, NY

Marion Skidmore Library Special Collections
National Association of Spiritualist Churches Papers

NATIONAL MUSEUM OF AMERICAN HISTORY/
SMITHSONIAN INSTITUTION, WASHINGTON, DC

U.S. Political History Photograph Collection

NEW YORK ACADEMY OF MEDICINE, NEW YORK, NY

New York Neurological Society Records
Special Collections

THE NEW YORK PUBLIC LIBRARY,
RARE BOOKS AND MANUSCRIPTS, NEW YORK, NY

Beecher-Tilton Trial Scrapbook
New York Society for the Suppression of Vice Records
Theodore Tilton Papers

SAN DIEGO HISTORICAL SOCIETY

Francis Grierson (Jesse Shepard) Collection

YALE UNIVERSITY, MANUSCRIPTS AND ARCHIVES,
NEW HAVEN, CT

George Miller Beard Papers

Newspapers and Periodicals

Age of Progress (Buffalo), weekly, 1854–58. Edited by Stephen Albro, under the patronage of the Buffalo Harmonial Association.
American Spiritualist Magazine (Memphis), monthly, January 1875–December 1877. Edited by Samuel Watson; published by Southern Baptist Publication Society.
Banner of Light (Boston), weekly 1857–98. Edited by Luther Colby, John W. Day, and Epes Sargent; published by Isaac Rich.
Banner of Progress (San Francisco), weekly, 1867–68.
Brittan's Journal of Spiritual Science, Literature, Art, & Inspiration (New York), quarterly, January 1873–October 1874. Edited by Samuel Byron Brittan.
The Carrier Dove (Oakland), monthly, 1884–87; weekly, 1887–93. Edited by Elizabeth Lowe Watson and Julia Schlesinger; published by Julia Schlesinger and Dr. Louis Schlesinger.
The Friends of Progress (New York), monthly, 1864–65.
Gallery of Spirit Art. An Illustrated Magazine devoted to an Illustrative of Spirit Photography, Spirit Painting, the Photographing of Materialized Forms and Every Form of Spirit Art (Brooklyn, NY), August 1882–November 1883.
Golden Gate: A journal of practical reform . . . devoted to the elevation of humanity

in this life and a search for evidences of life beyond (San Francisco), weekly, 1885–90. Edited by J. J. Owen and Mattie P. Owen.

Herald of Progress (New York), weekly, 1860–64. Edited and published by Andrew Jackson Davis.

New England Spiritualist (Boston), 1855–57. Edited and published by Alonzo E. Newton.

The New York Daily Graphic (New York), daily, 1872–74.

The Popular Science Monthly (New York), monthly, 1874–89.

Religio-Philosophical Journal (Chicago), 1884–87.

Sacred Circle (New York), 1854–56.

Shekinah (Bridegport, CT), 1851–53. Edited by Samuel Byron Brittan.

Soul (Boston), 1888.

Spirit Messenger (Springfield, MA), 1850–52. Edited by R. P. Ambler and Apollos Munn.

Spiritual Telegraph (New York), 1853–57. Edited by Charles Partridge and Samuel Byron Brittan.

Univercoelum [or, Spiritual Philosopher] and Spiritual Philosopher (New York), 1847–49. Edited by Samuel Byron Brittan.

Woodhull & Claflin's Weekly (New York), weekly, 1872–74. Edited by Victoria Woodhull and Tennie C. Claflin.

Convention and Organizational Proceedings

American Spiritualist Association. *Address to the Public.* Chicago: Printed by the *Religio-Philosophical Journal,* 1865.

————. *Constitution and Some of the Resolutions Adopted at the Fifth Annual Convention held at Rochester, New York.* August 25–28, 1868.

National Spiritualists' Association. Cincinnati, Washington, 1894–95.

New England Spiritualist Association. *Constitution and By-Laws, List of Officers and Address to the Public.* Boston, 1854.

Rules and Regulations of a Spiritualist Association, at Their Rooms. Boston: Geo C. Rand & Avery, 1856.

Rutland Free Convention. *Proceedings of the Free Convention held at Rutland, VT, June 25th, 26th, 27th, 1858.* Boston: J. B. Yerrington & Son, 1858.

Books and Articles

Adams, Nehemiah. *Agnes and the Little Key: Or, Bereaved Parents Instructed and Comforted.* Boston: S. K. Whipple and Co., 1857.

Ballou, Adin. *An Exposition of Views Respecting the Principal Facts, Causes, and Peculiarities Involved in Spirit Manifestations.* Boston: B. Marsh, 1835.

Barrett, Harrison D. *Life Work of Mrs. Cora L. V. Richmond.* Chicago: Hack & Anderson, Printers, 1895.

Barrett, Harrison D., and A. W. McCoy, eds. *Cassadaga: Its History and Teachings, with Histories of Spiritualist Camp Meetings and Biographies of Cassadaga Pioneers and Others.* Meadville, PA: Gazette Printing Company, 1891.

Bartol, C. A. *Radical Problems.* Boston: Roberts Brothers, 1872.

Beard, George Miller. *American Nervousness: Its Causes and Consequences.* New York: G. P. Putnam's Sons, 1881.

———. "The Delusions of Clairvoyance." *Scribner's Monthly* 18, no. 3 (July 1879): 433–40.

———. *Eating and Drinking: A Popular Manual of Food and Diet in Health and Disease.* New York: G. P. Putnam, 1871.

———. "Physiology of Mind Reading." *Popular Science Monthly* (1876–77): 459–73.

———. *Psychology of Salem Witchcraft.* New York: G. P. Putnam's Sons, 1882.

———. "The Psychology of Spiritism." *North American Review* 129 (1879): 65–80.

———. "Scientific Lessons of the Mollie Fancher Case." *Medical Record* 14 (November 30, 1878).

———. "Trance." *Mind* 2 (1877): 568.

Beecher, Catherine. *Letter to the People on Health and Happiness.* New York: Harper & Bros., 1855.

Bennett, DeRobigne M. *Anthony Comstock: His Career of Cruelty and Crime.* New York: Liberal and Scientific Publishing House, 1878.

Blake, C. C. "Lunacy and Phrenology." *Anthropological Review* 1 (1863): 476–80.

Bowker, R. R. "Science and the Spirits." *Appleton's Journal* 7 (January 20, 1872): 67–69.

Brigham, Amariah. *An Inquiry Concerning the Diseases and Functions of the Brain, the Spinal Cord, and the Nerves.* 1840. Reprint, New York: Arno Press, 1973.

———. "Insanity and Insane Hospitals." *North American Review* 44 (January 1837): 91–121.

———. *Observations on the Influence of Religion upon the Health and Physical Welfare of Mankind.* 1835. Reprint, New York: Arno Press, 1973.

———. *Remarks on the Influence of Mental Cultivation and Mental Excitement upon Health.* Edinburgh: Fraser, 1836.

Britten, Emma Hardinge. *Autobiography of Emma Hardinge Britten.* Manchester, U.K.: John Heywood, Inc., 1900.

———. *Modern American Spiritualism: A Twenty Years' Record of the Communion between Earth and the World of the Spirits.* 1869. Reprint, New Hyde Park, NY: University Books, 1970.

———. *Nineteenth Century Miracles.* Manchester, U.K.: John Heywood, Inc., 1900.

———. *The Place and Mission of Women*. Boston: Hubbard W. Sweet, 1859.

Broun, Heywood, and Margaret Leech. *Anthony Comstock, Roundsman of the Lord*. New York: Albert & Charles Boni, 1927.

Brown, J. A. "Neurology and the Human Soul." *Lutheran Quarterly* (April 1878): 177–98.

Browne, J. Crichton. "Dr. Beard's Experiments in Hypnotism." *British Medical Journal* 27 (August 1881): 378–79.

Buntline, Ned. *Love at First Sight; Or, the Daguerreotype*. Boston: Jones's Publishing House, 1848.

Capron, Eliab Wilkinson. *Modern Spiritualism: Its Facts and Fanaticisms, Its Consistencies and Contradictions*. Boston: Bela Marsh, 1855.

———. *Singular Revelations: Explanation and History of the Mysterious Communion with Spirits*. Auburn, NY: Finn & Rockwell, 1850.

Carpenter, W. B. "Epidemic Delusions." *Popular Science Monthly* 2 (1872–73): 15–36.

———. "Mesmerism, Odylism, Table-Turning, and Spiritualism." *Popular Science Monthly* 11 (1877): 161–73.

"Case of Mania with the Delusions and Phenomena of Spiritualism." *American Journal of Insanity* 16 (1860): 321–41.

"A Cause of Insanity." *Alienist and Neurologist* 9 (1888): 343–44.

Charcot, J. M. "Hysteria and Spiritism." Translated by E. P. Hurd. *Medical Surgical Reporter* 59 (1888): 65–68.

———. *Lectures on the Diseases of the Nervous System*. Translated by George Sigerson, M.D. Philadelphia: Henry C. Lea, 1879.

Clark, Uriah. *Plain Guide to Spiritualism: A Hand-Book for Skeptics, Inquirers, Clergymen, Believers, Lecturers, Mediums, Editors, . . .* Boston: W. White & Company, 1863.

Coates, James. *Photographing the Invisible: Practical Studies in Spirit Photography, Spirit Portraiture, and Other Rare but Allied Phenomena*. Chicago: Advanced Thought Publishing Company, 1911.

Colville, W. J. *Ancient Mysteries and Modern Revelations*. New York: R. F. Fenno, 1910.

Comfort, S. "Religious Catalepsy." *Medical Review* 10 (April 1859): 218–27.

Comstock, Anthony. *Morals versus Art*. New York: J. S. Ogilvie and Co., 1887.

———. *Traps for the Young*. 1887. Reprint, edited by Robert Bremner, Cambridge, MA: Belknap Press of Harvard University Press, 1967.

———. "Vampire Literature." *North American Review* (August 1891): 160–71.

Cooke, Josiah P., Jr. *Religion and Chemistry: A Re-statement of an Old Argument*. 1864. Reprint, New York: Charles Scribner's Sons, 1880.

Craft, Amos. *Epidemic Delusions: Containing an Expose of the Superstitions and Frauds which Underlie Some Ancient and Modern Delusions, Including Especial Reference to Modern Spiritualism*. New York: Phillips & Hunt, 1881.

Crowe, Catherine. *Spiritualism and the Age We Live In.* London: Colburn, 1859.

Cuyler, Reverend Theodore. *The Empty Crib: A Book of Consolation.* New York: R. Carter and Brothers, 1868.

Dailey, Abram. *Mollie Fancher, the Brooklyn Enigma: An Authentic Statement of Facts in the Life of Mary J. Fancher.* Brooklyn, NY: Eagle Book Printing Dept., 1894.

Davenport, Reuben Briggs. *The Death-Blow to Spiritualism: Being the True Story of the Fox Sisters, as Revealed by Authority of Margaret Fox Kane and Catherine Fox Johnson.* New York: G. W. Dillingham, 1888.

Davis, Andrew Jackson. *The Great Harmonia.* 4 vols. New York: Fowler & Wells, 1851.

———. *Harbinger of Health: Containing Medical Prescriptions for the Human Body and Mind.* New York: A. J. Davis, 1861.

———. *The Magic Staff: An Autobiography.* New York: J. S. Brown, 1857.

———. *Nature's Divine Revelations: The Principles of Nature, Her Divine Revelations, and a Voice to Mankind.* New York: S. S. Lyon and Wm. Fishbough, 1851.

Davis, Nathan Smith. "Is There Such a Disease as Moral Insanity, Distinct From Intellectual Derangement?" *New Orleans Medical and Surgical Journal* 5 (1877–78): 834–35.

Davis, Paulina Wright. *A History of the National Woman's Rights Movement for Twenty Years, . . . from 1850 to 1870.* 1871. Reprint, New York: Kraus Reprint, 1971.

Dickens, Charles. "Hysteria and Devotion." *All the Year Round* (November 5, 1859): 31–34.

Doyle, Arthur Conan. *The Case for Spirit Photography.* New York: George H. Doran, 1923.

———. *The History of Spiritualism.* Vol. 1. 1926; reprint, New York: Arno Press, 1975.

Draper, John William. *The History of the Conflict between Science and Religion.* New York: D. Appleton and Company, 1875.

Duganne, Augustine J. H. *The DaguerreotypeMiniature; Or, Life in the Empire City.* Philadelphia: G. B. Zeiber, 1846.

Edmonds, John Worth. *Letters and Tracts on Spiritualism; also two inspirational orations by Cora L. V. Tappan; and particulars respecting the personal career and passing away of Judge Edmonds.* London: J. Burns Progressive Library and Spiritual Institution, 1875.

Edmonds, John Worth, and George T. Dexter. *Spiritualism.* Vol. 1. New York: Partridge and Brittan, 1853.

Ellis, John B. [James Towner]. *Free Love and its Votaries: Or, American Socialism Unmasked, Being an Historical and Descriptive Account of the Rise and Progress of the Various Free Love Associations in the United States, and of the Effects of*

Their Vicious Teachings on American Society. New York: United States Publishing Co., 1870.

Ellwood, George. *Some Earlier Public Amusements of Rochester, Read before the Rochester Historical Society, 1894.* Rochester, NY: Democrat and Chronicle, 1894.

Field, Matthew D. "Is Belief in Spiritualism Ever Evidence of Insanity per se?" *Medical Legal Journal* 61 (1888–89): 194–202.

Flint, Austin, M.D. "On the Discovery of the Source of the Rochester Knockings, and on the Sounds Produced by the Movements of Joints and Tendons." *Quarterly Journal of Medical Science* 3 (1869): 417–46.

Folio, Fred [pseud.]. *Lucy Boston: or, Women's Rights and Spiritualism, Illustrating the Follies and Delusions of the Nineteenth Century.* Auburn, NY: Alden & Beardsley, 1855.

Fowler, O. S., and L. N. Fowler. "Symbolical Head." In *The Illustrated Self-Instructor in Phrenology and Physiology.* New York: Fowler & Wells, 1855.

Gilman, Charlotte Perkins. *His Religion and Hers: A Study of the Faith of Our Fathers and the World of Our Mothers.* 1923. Reprint. Westport, CT: Hyperion Press, 1976.

Girdner, John. "Theology and Insanity." *North American Review* 168 (January 1899): 77–83.

———. "Insanity and Civilization." *Nation* 41 (October 29, 1885): 356–57.

Grimes, J. Stanley. *The Mysteries of Human Nature Explained by a New System of Nervous Physiology: To which is added, a review of the errors of spiritualism, and instructions for developing or resisting the influence by which subjects and mediums are made.* Buffalo, NY: R. M. Wanzer, 1857.

Hammond, William A. *Fasting Girls: Their Physiology and Pathology.* New York: G. P. Putnam's Sons, 1876.

———. *On Certain Conditions of Nervous Derangement: Somnambulism—Hypnotism—Hysteria—Hysteroid Affections, etc.* New York: G. P. Putnam's Sons, 1883.

———. "Phenomena of Spiritualism Explained." *North American Review* 110 (April 1870): 233–72.

———. *The Physics and Physiology of Spiritualism.* New York: D. Appleton & Company, 1871.

———. "Punishability of the Insane." *International Review* 11 (1881): 440–50.

———. *Spiritualism and Allied Causes of Nervous Derangements.* New York: G. P. Putnam's Sons, 1876.

Hartmann, Franz. *Buried Alive: An Examination into the Occult Causes of Apparent Death, Trance, and Catalepsy.* Boston: Occult Publishing, Co., 1895.

Hatch, Benjamin F. *Spiritual Iniquities Unmasked, and, the Hatch Divorce Case.* New York: B. F. Hatch, 1859.

Howells, William Dean. *Impressions and Experiences.* 1896. Reprint, Freeport, NY: Books for Libraries Press, 1972.

———. *Years of My Youth.* 1916. Reprint, Freeport, NY: Books for Libraries Press, 1972.

"The Inconstant Daguerreotype." *Harper's New Monthly Magazine.* 10, no. 60 (May 1855).

"Insanity and Spiritualism." *American Journal of Insanity* 33 (1876–77): 593–94.

James, Henry [Sr.]. "Faith and Science." *North American Review* 101 (October 1865): 335–78.

James, William. *The Varieties of Religious Experience.* 1902. Reprint, New York: Modern Library, 1929.

Jarvis, E. "Causes of Insanity." *Boston Medical and Surgical Journal* 45 (1851): 289–305.

Jastrow, Joseph. "The Psychology of Spiritualism." *Popular Science Monthly* 34 (1889): 721–32.

Jewell, J. S. "Hammond on Somnambulism, etc." *Dial* (March 1881): 231–33.

Jones, T. H. "Patent Medicines: What They Are, and How They Are Sold." *Good Words* 2 (1854): 371–75.

Lippitt, F. J. "Was it Katie King?" *Galaxy* 18, no. 6 (December 1874): 756–66.

Lombroso, Cesare. *After Death—What?* Translated by William Sloan Kennedy. Boston: Small, Maynard, & Co., 1909.

Lyman, C. S. "Literature of Spiritualism." *New Englander* 16 (August 1858): 666–90.

Marvin, Frederic R., M.D. *The Physiology of Spiritualism and the Pathology and Treatment of Mediomania: Two Lectures Read before the New York Liberal Club.* New York: Asa K. Butts & Co., Publishers, 1874.

Mattison, Hiram. *Spirit Rapping Unveiled! An Expose of the Origins, History, Theology and Philosophy of Certain Alleged Communications from the Spirit World, by Means of "Spirit Rapping," Physical Demonstrations, etc.* New York: J. C. Derby, 1855.

Maudsley, Henry, M.D. *Natural Causes and Supernatural Seemings.* London: Kegan Paul, Trench & Co., 1886.

———. *The Pathology of Mind.* London: Macmillan, 1879.

McCabe, Joseph. *Spiritualism: A Popular History From 1847.* London: T. Fisher Unwin, 1920.

McCauley, Clay. "Is Spiritual Science Possible?" *Religious Magazine and Monthly Review* 47 (March 1872): 201–18.

Melville, Herman. *The Confidence-Man: His Masquerade.* New York: Dix, Edwards, & Co., 1857.

Mitchell, S. Weir. *The Autobiography of a Quack: And, the Case of George Dedlow.* New York: Century Company, 1900.

———. *Lectures on Diseases of the Nervous System, Especially in Women.* Philadelphia: Lea Brothers & Co., 1885.

Mumler, William. *The Personal Experiences of William H. Mumler in Spirit Photography.* Boston: Colby & Rich, 1875.

Nichols, Thomas. "Free Love as a Doctrine of Spiritualism: A Discourse Delivered in Foster Hall, Cincinnati, December 22, 1855." Cincinnati, 1856.

Olcott, Henry S. *People from the Other World.* Hartford, CT: American Publishing Co., 1875.

Owen, Robert Dale. *The Debatable Land between This World and the Next.* New York: G. W. Carleton & Co., 1872.

———. *Footfalls on the Boundary of Another World.* Philadelphia: J. B. Lippincott & Co., 1860.

Packard, Elizabeth. *Great Disclosures of Spiritual Wickedness . . . With an Appeal to the Government to Protect the Inalienable Rights of Married Women.* Boston: For the Author, 1864.

———. *Modern Persecution, or Insane Asylums Unveiled,* 2 vols. Hartford, CT: Case, Lockwood, and Brainard, 1873.

Podmore, Frank. *Modern Spiritualism: A History and a Criticism, in Two Volumes.* London: Methuen and Company, 1902.

Powers, Grant. *Essay upon the Influence of the Imagination on the Nervous System, Contributing to False Hope in Religion.* Andover, MA: Flagg & Gould, 1828.

Report of the Mysterious Noises, Heard in the House of Mr. John D. Fox in Hydesville, Acadia, Wayne Co. Authenticated by the Certificates and Confirmed by the Statements of Citizens in that Place and Vicinity. Rochester, NY: D. M. Dewey, 1850.

Richards, J. H. "Studies on Hypnotism." *Nation* (April 29, 1880): 328–24.

Richmond, Cora L. V. *Is Materialization True?* Boston: Colby & Rich, Publishers, 1885.

———. *My Experiences While out of My Body and My Return After Many Days.* Boston: Christopher Press, 1915.

Robertson, George Croom, ed. "Review of G. M. Beard, 'Trance.'" *Mind: A Quarterly Review of Psychology and Philosophy* 2 (1877): 568–69.

Rogers, Edward C. *Philosophy of Mysterious Agents, Human and Mundane: Or, the Dynamic Laws and Relations of Man.* Boston: John P. Jewett, 1853.

Sargent, Epes. *The Proof Palpable of Immortality; Being An Account of the Materialization Phenomena of Modern Spiritualism.* 1876. Reprint, Boston: Colby and Rich, 1892.

Schlesinger, Julia. *Workers in the Vineyard: A Review of the Progress of Spiritualism.* San Francisco: By the Author, 1896.

Shindler, Mary Dana. *A Southerner among the Spirits.* Boston: Colby & Rich Publishers, 1877.

Simpson, Frederick T. "Hysteria: Its Nature and Treatment." *Psychotherapy* 3 (1909): 28–47.

Smith, Gerrit. *Lectures on the Religion of Reason.* Petersboro, NY: C. A. Hammond, 1864.

Smith, John. *The True Travels, Adventures and Observations of Captain John Smith*. 1630. Reprinted in Philip Barbour, ed., *The Complete Works of Captain John Smith*. 3 vols. Williamsburg, VA: Institute for Early American Culture, 1986.

Snow, Herman. *Visions of the Beyond, by a Seer of To-Day; Or, Symbolic Teachings from the Higher Life*. Boston: Colby & Rich; San Francisco: Herman Snow, 1877.

"Spiritualism and Its Recent Converts." *Quarterly Review* 131 (1871): 301.

"Spiritualism as Related to Religion and Science." *Fraser's Magazine* 71 (January 1865): 22–42.

"Spiritualism in America." *Chamber's Edinburgh Journal* 25 (1853): 81.

"Spiritual Rappers: Physiological Explanation." *American Journal of Insanity* 11 (1855): 294–95.

Stanton, Elizabeth Cady, Susan B. Anthony, and Matilda Joslyn Gage, eds. *History of Woman Suffrage*. Vol. 3. Rochester, NY: Charles Mann, 1887.

Stone, Elizabeth. *Exposing the Modern Secret Way of Persecuting Christians: Insane Hospitals Are Inquisition Houses*. Boston: For the Author, 1859.

Stone, William L. *Letter to Doctor A. Brigham on Animal Magnetism*. New York: George Dearborn & Co., 1837.

Stratchey, William. *The Historie of Travell into Virginia Britania*. 1612. Reprint, edited by Louis B. Wright and Virginia Freund, London: Hakluyt Society, 1953.

Theobald, Morell. *Spiritualism at Home*. London: E. W. Allen, 1884.

———. *Spirit Workers in the Home Circle*. London: T. Fisher Unwin, 1887.

Trumbell, Charles Gallaudet. *Anthony Comstock, Fighter*. New York: Fleming H. Revell, 1913.

"Vapors, Fears, and Tremors." *Blackwood's Magazine* 105 (January–June 1869): 228–27.

Viollet, Marcel. *Spiritism and Insanity*. London: Swan Sonnenschein, 1910.

Volckman, William. *Researches in the Phenomenon of Spiritualism*. London: James Burns, 1874.

Waisbrooker, Lois. *Alice Vale: A Story for the Times*. Boston: W. White and Company, 1869.

———. *Mayweed Blossoms*. Boston: W. White and Company, 1871.

———. *My Century Plant*. Topeka, KS: Independent Publishing Company, 1896.

———. *Nothing Like It: Or, Steps to the Kingdom*. Boston: Colby & Rich, Publishers, 1875.

———. *Perfect Motherhood: Or, Mabel Raymond's Resolve*. New York: Murray Hill Publishing, 1890.

Wallace, Alfred Russell. "A Defense of Modern Spiritualism." *Fortnightly Review* (1874): 630–807.

———. "Dr. Carpenter on Spiritualism." *Popular Science Monthly* 1 (1877): 435–40.

———. *Miracles and Modern Spiritualism.* London: G. Redway, 1896.

Weiss, John, ed. *Life and Correspondence of Theodore Parker.* London: Longmans, Green and Co., 1863.

White, Andrew Dickson. *A History of the Warfare of Science and Religion within Christendom.* New York: D. Appleton and Company, 1896.

Winslow, Forbes. "The Marvellous." *American Journal of Insanity* 18 (1861–62): 14–42.

Wright, George Frederick. *Studies in Science and Religion.* Andover, MA: Warren F. Draper, 1882.

Wundt, Wilhelm. "Spiritualism as a Scientific Question." *Popular Science Monthly* 15 (September 1879): 577–93.

SECONDARY SOURCES

Abelove, Henry. *The Evangelist of Desire: John Wesley and the Methodists.* Stanford, CA: Stanford University Press, 1990.

Abzub, Robert. *Cosmos Crumbling: American Reform and the Religious Imagination.* New York: Oxford University Press, 1994.

Ahlstrom, Sydney E. *A Religious History of the American People.* New Haven, CT: Yale University Press, 1972.

Albanese, Catherine L. *Nature Religion in America: From the Algonkian Indians to the New Age.* Chicago: University of Chicago Press, 1990.

———. *A Republic of Mind and Spirit: A Cultural History of American Metaphysical Religion.* New Haven, CT: Yale University Press, 2007.

Allen, Paula Gunn. *Pocahontas: Medicine Woman, Spy, Entrepreneur, Diplomat.* New York: HarperSanFrancisco, 2003.

Apter, Emily. *Feminizing the Fetish: Psychoanalysis and Narrative Obsession in Turn-of-the-Century France.* Ithaca, NY: Cornell University Press, 1991.

Ariès, Philippe. *L'homme devant la mort.* Paris: Éditions du Seuil, 1977.

———. *The Hour of Our Death.* Translated by Helen Weaver. Oxford: Oxford University Press, 1991.

———. *Images of Man in Death.* Cambridge, MA: Harvard University Press, 1985.

Ariès, Philippe, et al. *Death in America.* Edited by David E. Stannard. Philadelphia: University of Pennsylvania Press, 1974.

Asad, Talal. *Genealogies of Religion: Discipline and Reasons of Power in Christianity and Islam.* Baltimore, MD: Johns Hopkins University Press, 1993.

Auerbach, Nina. *Woman and the Demon: The Life of a Victorian Myth.* Cambridge, MA: Harvard University Press, 1982.

Baldwin, James. *The Evidence of Things Not Seen.* New York: Holt, Rinehart & Winston, 1985.

Barker-Benfield, Ben. *The Horrors of the Half-Known Life: Male Attitudes toward Women and Sexuality in Nineteenth-Century America.* New York: Harper and Row, 1976.

Barrow, Logie. *Independent Spirits: Spiritualism and English Plebeians, 1850–1910.* London: Routledge and Kegan Paul, 1986.

Basch, Norma. *Framing American Divorce: From the Revolutionary Generation to the Victorians.* Berkeley: University of California Press, 1998.

———. *In the Eyes of the Law: Women, Marriage, and Property in Nineteenth-Century New York.* Ithaca, NY: Cornell University Press, 1982.

Bataille, Georges. *Inner Experience.* 1954. Reprint, Albany: State University of New York Press, 1988.

Bates, Anna Louise. *Weeder in the Garden of the Lord: Anthony Comstock's Life and Career.* New York: University Press of America, Inc., 1995.

Bederman, Gail. *Manliness and Civilization: A Cultural History of Gender and Race in the United States, 1880–1917.* Chicago: University of Chicago Press, 1995.

Bednarowski, Mary Farrell. "Nineteenth-Century American Spiritualism: An Attempt at a Scientific Religion." Ph.D. diss., University of Minnesota, 1973.

———. "Outside the Mainstream: Women's Religion and Women Religious Leaders in Nineteenth-Century America." *Journal of the American Academy of Religion* 48, no. 2 (June 1980): 217–31.

———. "Women in Occult America." In *The Occult in America: New Historical Perspectives,* ed. Howard Kerr and Charles L. Crow. Urbana: University of Illinois Press, 1985.

Beemyn, Brett, ed. *Creating a Place for Ourselves: Lesbian, Gay, and Bisexual Community Histories.* New York: Routledge, 1997.

Beisel, Nicola. *Imperiled Innocents: Anthony Comstock and Family Reproduction in Victorian America.* Princeton, NJ: Princeton University Press, 1997.

Bender, Thomas. *New York Intellect: A History of Intellectual Life in New York.* New York: Knopf, 1987.

———. "The Rural Cemetery Movement: Urban Travail and the Appeal of Nature." *New England Quarterly* 47 (1974): 196–211.

Benjamin, Walter. "The Work of Art in the Age of Mechanical Reproduction." In *Illuminations.* New York: Schocken Books, 1968.

Berg, Barbara. *The Remembered Gate: Origins of American Feminism.* New York: Oxford University Press, 1978.

Bergland, Renée L. *The National Uncanny: Indian Ghosts and American Subjects.* Hanover, NH: University Press of New England, 2000.

Berkhofer, Robert F., Jr. *The White Man's Indian: Images of the American Indian from Columbus to the Present.* New York: Vintage Books, 1979.

Berlant, Lauren. "America, Post-Utopia: Body, Landscape, and National Fantasy in Hawthorne's Native Land." *Arizona Quarterly* 64, no. 1 (Winter 1989): 14–54.

——. "Fantasies of Utopia in the Blithedale Romance." *American Literary History* 1, no. 1 (Spring 1989): 30–62.

Bernheimer, Charles, and Claire Kahane, eds. *In Dora's Case: Freud—Hysteria—Feminism.* New York: Columbia University Press, 1985.

Bird, S. Elizabeth. *Dressing in Feathers: The Construction of the Indian in American Popular Culture.* Boulder, CO: Westview Press, 1996.

Blanchard, Mary Warner. *Oscar Wilde's America: Counterculture in the Gilded Age.* New Haven, CT: Yale University Press, 1998.

Bland, Lucy. *Banishing the Beast: Sexuality and the Early Feminists, 1880–1915.* New York: New Press, 1995.

Blustein, Bonnie. "A New York Medical Man: William Alexander Hammond, MD, 1828–1900." Ph.D. diss., University of Pennsylvannia, 1979.

——. *Preserve Your Love for Science: Life of William A. Hammond, American Neurologist.* New York: Cambridge University Press, 1991.

Boller, Paul F., Jr. *American Thought in Transition: The Impact of Evolutionary Naturalism, 1865–1900.* Chicago: Rand McNally & Company, 1969.

Bolt, Christine. *American Indian Policy and American Reform: Case Studies of the Campaign to Assimilate the American Indians.* London: Allen and Unwin, 1987.

Bowler, Peter. *The Invention of Progress: The Victorians and the Past.* Oxford: Blackwell, 1989.

Boyer, Paul. *Purity in Print: The Vice Society Movement and Book Censorship in America.* New York: Scribner, 1968.

Brandon, Ruth. *The Spiritualists: The Passion for the Occult in the Nineteenth Century.* Chicago: University of Chicago Press, 1983.

Braude, Ann. "News From the Spirit World: A Checklist of American Spiritualist Periodicals, 1847–1900." *Proceedings of the American Antiquarian Society* (October 1989): 399–462.

——. *Radical Spirits: Spiritualism and Women's Rights in Nineteenth-Century America.* Boston: Beacon Press, 1989.

——. "Spirits Defend the Rights of Women: Spiritualism and Changing Sex Roles in Nineteenth-Century America." In *Women, Religion and Social Change,* edited by Yvonne Yazbeck and Ellison Banks Findley. Albany: State University of New York Press, 1985.

Brodie, Janet Farrell. *Contraception and Abortion in Nineteenth-Century America.* Ithaca, NY: Cornell University Press, 1994.

Brooks, Daphne A. *Bodies in Dissent: Spectacular Performances of Race and Freedom.* Durham, NC: Duke University Press, 2006.

Brooks, Peter. *Body Work: Objects of Desire in Modern Narrative.* Cambridge, MA: Harvard University Press, 1993.

Brown, Burton Gates, Jr. "Spiritualism in Nineteenth-Century America." Ph.D. diss., Boston University, 1973.

Brown, E. M. "Neurology and Spiritualism in the 1870s." *Bulletin of the History of Medicine* 57 (1983): 563–57.

Bruce, Steve, ed. *Religion and Modernization: Sociologists and Historians Debate the Secularization Thesis.* London: Oxford University Press, 1992.

Brumberg, Joan Jacobs. *Fasting Girls: The Emergence of Anorexia Nervosa as a Modern Disease.* Cambridge, MA: Harvard University Press, 1988.

Bynum, Carolyn Walker. *Fragmentation and Redemption: Essays on Gender and the Human Body in Medieval Religion.* New York: Zone Books, 1990.

———. *Holy Feast and Holy Fast: The Religious Significance of Food to Medieval Women.* Berkeley: University of California Press, 1987.

Buse, Peter, and Andrew Stott, eds. *Ghosts: Deconstruction, Psychoanalysis, History.* New York: St. Martin's Press, 1999.

Butler, Jon. *Awash in A Sea of Faith: Christianizing the American People.* Cambridge, MA: Harvard University Press, 1990.

Butler, Jon, and Harry S. Stout, eds. *Religion in American History.* New York: Oxford University Press, 1998.

Butler, Judith. *Precarious Life: The Powers of Mourning and Violence.* London: Verso, 2006.

Campbell, Bruce F. *Ancient Wisdom Revived: A History of the Theosophical Movement.* Berkeley: University of California Press, 1980.

Carroll, Bret E. "The Religious Construction of Masculinity in Victorian America: The Male Mediumship of John Shoebridge Williams." *Religion and American Culture* 7, no. 1 (Winter 1997): 27–60.

———. *Spiritualism in Antebellum America.* Bloomington: Indiana University Press, 1997.

Cashman, Sean Dennis. *America in the Gilded Age.* New York: New York University Press, 1993.

Castelli, Elizabeth A. "Women, Gender, Religion: Troubling Categories and Transforming Knowledge." In *Women, Gender, Religion: A Reader,* edited by Elizabeth A. Castelli. London: Palgrave, 2001.

Castle, Terry. *The Apparitional Lesbian: Female Homosexuality and Modern Culture.* New York: Columbia University Press, 1993.

———. *Noel Coward and Radclyffe Hall: Kindred Spirits.* New York: Columbia University Press, 1996.

Castronovo, Russ. *Necro Citizenship: Death, Eroticism, and the Public Sphere in the Nineteenth-Century United States.* Durham, NC: Duke University Press, 2001.

Chakrabarty, Dipesh. "Radical Histories and Questions of Enlightenment Rationalism: Some Recent Critiques of *Subaltern Studies.*" *Economic and Political Weekly,* 8 April 1995, 752.

Chant, Colin, and John Fauvel, eds. *Darwin to Einstein: Historical Studies on Science and Belief*. London: Open University Press, 1980.

Chauncey, George. *Gay New York: Gender, Urban Culture, and the Making of the Gay World, 1890–1940*. New York: Basic Books, 1994.

Chesler, Phyllis. *Women and Madness*. New York: Doubleday, 1972.

Christ, Carol P., and Judith Plaskow, eds. *Womanspirit Rising: A Feminist Reader in Religion*. San Francisco: Harper & Row, 1979.

Clark, Clifford E., Jr. *Henry Ward Beecher*. Urbana: University of Illinois Press, 1978.

Clarke, Edwin, and L. S. Jacyna. *Nineteenth-Century Origins of Neuroscientific Concepts*. Berkeley: University of California Press, 1987.

Clifford, James, and George Marcus, eds. *Writing Culture: The Poetics and Politics of Ethnography*. Berkeley: University of California Press, 1986.

Cobb, Michael. *God Hates Fags: The Rhetorics of Religious Violence*. New York: New York University Press, 2006.

Cohen, Patricia Cline. "Unregulated Youth: Masculinity and Murder in the 1830s City." *Radical History Review* 52 (Winter 1992): 33–52.

Connor, Steven. *Dumbstruck: A Cultural History of Ventriloquism*. New York: Oxford University Press, 2000.

Cook, Noble David. *Born to Die: Disease and New World Conquest, 1492–1650*. Cambridge: Cambridge University Press, 1998.

Coon, Lynda L., Katherine J. Haldane, and Elisabeth W. Sommer, eds. *That Gentle Strength: Historical Perspectives on Women in Christianity*. Charlottesville: University Press of Virginia, 1990.

Coviello, Peter. *Intimacy in America: Dreams of Affiliation in Antebellum Literature*. Minneapolis: University of Minnesota Press, 2005.

Cox, Robert S. *Body and Soul: A Sympathetic History of American Spiritualism*. Charlottesville: University of Virginia Press, 2003.

Crary, Jonathan. *The Techniques of the Observer: On Vision and Modernity in the Nineteenth Century*. Cambridge, MA: MIT Press, 1990.

Crimp, Douglas. *Melancholia and Moralism: Essays on AIDS and Queer Politics*. Cambridge, MA: MIT Press, 2002.

Cross, Whitney. *The Burned Over District: The Social and Intellectual History of Enthusiastic Religion in Western New York, 1800–1850*. Ithaca, NY: Cornell University Press, 1950.

Cruz-Malavé, Arnaldo, and Martin F. Manalansan IV, eds. *Queer Globalizations: Citizenship and the Afterlife of Colonialism*. New York: New York University Press, 2002.

Czitrom, Daniel. *Media and the American Mind from Morse to McLuhan*. Chapel Hill: University of North Carolina Press, 1982.

Darnton, Robert. *Mesmerism and the End of the Enlightenment in France*. Cambridge, MA: Harvard University Press, 1968.

Davidoff, Lenore and Catherine Hall. *Family Fortunes: Men and Women of the English Middle Class, 1780–1850.* Chicago: University of Chicago Press, 1987.

Davidson, Cathy. *Revolution and the Word: The Rise of the Novel in America.* New York: Oxford University Press, 1986.

Davis, Erik. *The Visionary State: A Journey through California's Spiritual Landscape.* San Francisco, CA: Chronicle Books, 2006.

DeCarvalho, Roy Jose. "Methods and Manifestations: The Wallace-Carpenter Debate over Spiritualism." *Journal of Religion and Psychical Research* 12 (January 1989): 20–25.

———. "A Source on 19th-Century Spiritualism, Science, and Religion: Mason's Letter to Draper." *Journal of Religion and Psychical Research* 13 (July 1990): 124–28.

de Grazia, Edward. *Censorship Landmarks.* New York: R. R. Bowker, 1969.

———. *Girls Lean Back Everywhere: The Law of Obscenity and the Assault on Genius.* New York: Random House, 1992.

Deloria, Philip J. *Playing Indian.* New Haven, CT: Yale University Press, 1998.

Delp, Robert W. "The Southern Press and the Rise of American Spiritualism, 1847–1860." *Journal of American Culture* 7, no. 3 (Fall 1984): 88–95.

D'Emilio, John. "Capitalism and Gay Identity." In *Powers of Desire: The Politics of Sexuality,* edited by Ann Snitow, Christine Stansell, and Sharon Thompson. New York: Monthly Review Press, 1983.

D'Emilio, John, and Estelle Freedman. *Intimate Matters: A History of Sexuality in America.* New York: Harper & Row, 1988.

Denning, Michael. *Mechanic Accents: Dime Novels and Working-Class Culture in America.* New York: Verso, 1987.

Derrida, Jacques. *Specters of Marx: The State of the Debt, the Work of Mourning and the New International.* Translated by Peggy Kamuf. New York: Routledge, 1994.

Diamond, Irene, and Lee Quinby, eds. *Feminism and Foucault: Reflections on Resistance.* Boston: Northeastern University Press, 1988.

Dickerson, Vanessa D. "A Spirit of Her Own: Nineteenth-Century Explorations of Spirituality." In *That Gentle Strength: Historical Perspectives on Women in Christianity,* edited by Lynda L. Coon, Katherine J. Haldane, and Elisabeth W. Sommer. Charlottesville: University Press of Virginia, 1990.

Dinshaw, Carolyn. *Getting Medieval: Sexual Communities, Pre- and Postmodern.* Durham, NC: Duke University Press, 1999.

Dippie, Brian. *The Vanishing American: White Attitudes and U.S. Indian Policy.* Middletown, CT: Wesleyan University Press, 1982.

Dixon, Joy. *Divine Feminine: Theosophy and Feminism in England.* Baltimore, MD: Johns Hopkins University Press, 2001.

Doan, Laura. *Fashioning Sapphism: The Origins of a Modern English Lesbian Culture.* New York: Columbia University Press, 2001.

Douglas, Ann. *The Feminization of American Culture.* New York: Alfred A. Knopf, 1977.

Drinnon, Richard. *Facing West: The Metaphysics of Indian-Hating and Empire Building.* Minneapolis: University of Minnesota Press, 1980.

DuBois, Ellen Carol. *Feminism and Suffrage: The Emergence of an Independent Women's Movement in America, 1848–1869.* Ithaca, NY: Cornell University Press, 1978.

DuBois, Ellen Carol, and Linda Gordon. "Seeking Ecstasy on the Battlefield: Danger and Pleasure in Nineteenth-Century Feminist Sexual Thought." In *Pleasure and Danger,* edited by Carole S. Vance. New York: Routledge, 1984.

Duggan, Lisa. *Sapphic Slashers: Sex, Violence, and American Modernity.* Durham, NC: Duke University Press, 2000.

Durkheim, Émile. *The Elementary Forms of Religious Life.* Translated by Joseph W. Swain. 1915. Reprint, Glencoe, IL: Free Press, 1926.

Ehrenreich, Barbara, and Deirdre English. *For Her Own Good: 150 Years of Experts' Advice to Women.* Garden City, NY: Anchor Press, 1978.

Ellwood, Robert S., Jr. *Alternative Altars: Unconventional and Eastern Spirituality in America.* Chicago: University of Chicago Press, 1979.

Epstein, Barbara. *The Politics of Domesticity: Women, Evangelism, and Temperance in Nineteenth-Century America.* Middletown, CT: Wesleyan University Press, 1981.

Epstein, Julia. *Altered Conditions: Disease, Medicine, and Storytelling.* New York: Routledge, 1994.

Epstein, Julia, and Kristina Straub, eds. *Body Guards: The Cultural Politics of Gender Ambiguity.* New York: Routledge, 1991.

Ernst, Morris L., and Alan V. Schwartz. "The Post Office as Censor." In *Censorship: The Search for the Obscene.* New York: MacMillan, 1964.

Fabian, Ann Vincent. *Card Sharps, Dream Books, and Bucket Shops: Gambling in Nineteenth-Century America.* Ithaca, NY: Cornell University Press, 1990.

Fabian, Johannes. *Time and the Other: How Anthropology Makes Its Object.* New York: Columbia University Press, 1982.

Fellman, Anita Clair, and Michael Fellman. *Making Sense of Self: Medical Advice Literature in Late Nineteenth-Century America.* Philadelphia: University of Pennsylvania Press, 1981.

Fellman, Michael. *The Unbounded Frame: Freedom and Community in Nineteenth-Century American Utopianism.* Westport, CT: Greenwood Press, 1973.

Fogarty, Robert S. *All Things New: American Communes and Utopian Movements, 1860–1914.* Chicago: University of Chicago Press, 1990.

Foner, Eric. *Reconstruction: America's Unfinished Revolution, 1863–1877.* New York: Harper & Row, 1988.

Fornell, Earl Wesley. *The Unhappy Medium: Spiritualism and the Life of Margaret Fox.* Austin: University of Texas Press, 1964.

Foster, Lawrence. *Religion and Sexuality.* New York: Oxford University Press, 1981.

———. *Women, Family, and Utopia: Communal Experiments of the Shakers, the Oneida Community, and the Mormons.* Syracuse, NY: Syracuse University Press, 1991.

Foucault, Michel. *Abnormal: Lectures at the Collège de France, 1974–1975.* Translated by Graham Burchell and edited by Arnold I. Davidson. New York: Picador, 2003.

———. *The History of Sexuality, Volume 1: An Introduction.* Translated by Robert Hurley. New York: Vintage Books, 1980.

———. *Madness and Civilization: A History of Insanity in the Age of Reason.* Translated by Richard Howard. New York: Pantheon Books, 1965.

———. "What Is an Author?" In *Language, Counter-Memory, Practice,* translated by Donald F. Bouchard and Sherry Simon, edited by Donald F. Bouchard. Ithaca, NY: Cornell University Press, 1977.

Fox, Richard Wightman. *The Trials of Intimacy: Love and Loss in the Beecher-Tilton Scandal.* Chicago: University of Chicago Press, 1999.

Fradenburg, Louise O., and Carla Freccero, eds. *Premodern Sexualities.* New York: Routledge, 1996.

Frankiel, Sarah Sitzer. *California's Spiritual Frontiers: Religious Alternatives in Anglo-Protestantism, 1850–1910.* Berkeley: University of California Press, 1988.

Fraser, Nancy. "Rethinking the Public Sphere: A Contribution to the Critique of Actually Existing Democracy." In *Habermas and the Public Sphere,* edited by Craig Calhoun. Cambridge, MA: MIT Press, 1992.

Freccero, Carla. "Queer Spectrality." In *Queer/Early/Modern.* Durham, NC: Duke University Press, 2006.

———. "Queer Spectrality: Haunting the Past." In *A Companion to LGBT/Q Studies,* edited by George E. Haggerty and Molly McGarry. London: Blackwell Publishing, Inc., 2007.

Fredrickson, George. *The Inner Civil War.* New York: Harper and Row, 1965.

French, Stanley. "The Cemetery as Cultural Institution: The Establishment of Mt. Auburn and the 'Rural Cemetery' Movement." In Philippe Ariès et al., *Death in America,* edited by David E. Stannard. Philadelphia: Temple University Press, 1975.

Frisken, Amanda. *Victoria Woodhull's Sexual Revolution: Political Theater and the Popular Press in Nineteenth-Century America.* Philadelphia: University of Pennsylvania Press, 2004.

Gaonkar, Dilip Parameshwar. "On Alternative Modernities." In *Alternative Modernities,* edited by Dilip Parameshwar Gaonkar. Durham, NC: Duke University Press, 2001.

Garrett, Clarke. *Spirit Possession and Popular Religion: From the Camisards to the Shakers.* Baltimore, MD: Johns Hopkins University Press, 1987.

Gauchet, Marcel. *The Disenchantment of the World: A Political History of Religion*. Translated by Oscar Burge. Princeton, NJ: Princeton University Press, 1997.

Gay, Peter. *The Bourgeois Experience: Victoria to Freud*. 2 vols. New York: Oxford University Press, 1984.

Geertz, Hildred. "An Anthropology of Religion and Magic, I." *Journal of Interdisciplinary History* 6, no. 1 (Summer 1975): 71–89.

Gettings, Fred. *Ghosts in Photographs: The Extraordinary Story of Spirit Photography*. New York: Harmony Books, 1978.

Gilman, Sander L. *Difference and Pathology: Stereotypes of Sexuality, Race, and Madness*. Ithaca, NY: Cornell University Press, 1985.

———. *The Face of Madness: Hugh W. Diamond and the Origin of Psychiatric Photography*. New York: Brunner/Mazel, 1976.

Ginzburg, Carlo. *Nightbattles: Witchcraft and Agrarian Cults in the Sixteenth and Seventeenth Centuries*. Translated by John and Anne Tedeschi. New York: Penguin Books, 1985.

Gleach, Frederic W. *Powhatan's World and Colonial Virginia: A Conflict of Cultures*. Lincoln: University of Nebraska Press, 1997.

Godeau, Abigail Solomon. "The Legs of the Countess." *October* 39 (Winter 1986): 66–108.

Goldfarb, Russell M., and Clare R. Goldfarb. *Spiritualism and Nineteenth Century Letters*. London: Associated University Presses, 1978.

Goldsmith, Barbara. *Other Powers: The Age of Suffrage, Spiritualism, and the Scandalous Victoria Woodhull*. New York: Alfred A. Knopf, 1998.

Goldstein, Jan. *Console and Classify: The French Psychiatric Profession in the Nineteenth Century*. Chicago: University of Chicago Press, 1987.

Gopinath, Gayatri *Impossible Desires: Queer Diasporas and South Asian Public Cultures*. Durham, NC: Duke University Press, 2005.

Gordon, Avery. *Ghostly Matters: Haunting and the Sociological Imagination*. Minneapolis: University of Minnesota Press, 1997.

Gottschalk, Stephen. *The Emergence of Christian Science in American Religious Life*. Berkeley: University of California Press, 1973.

Greenwalt, Emmett A. *California Utopia: Point Loma, 1897–1941*. San Diego, CA: Point Loma Publications, 1978.

Hacking, Ian. *Rewriting the Soul: Multiple Personality and the Sciences of Memory*. Princeton, NJ: Princeton University Press, 1995.

Hale, Nathan G. *Freud and the Americans: The Beginning of Psychoanalysis in the United States, 1876–1917*. New York: Oxford University Press, 1971.

Hall, Trevor H. *The Medium and the Scientist: The Story of Florence Cook and William Crookes*. 1964. Reprint. Buffalo: Prometheus Books, 1984.

Halperin, David M. "Forgetting Foucault: Acts, Identities, and the History of Sexuality." *Representations* 63 (1998): 93–120.

———. "Is There a History of Sexuality?" *History and Theory* 28 (1989): 257–74.

Halttunen, Karen. *Confidence Men and Painted Women: A Study of Middle-Class Culture in America, 1830–1870.* New Haven, CT: Yale University Press, 1982.

Haney, Robert W. *Comstockery in America: Patterns of Censorship and Control.* Boston: Beacon Press, 1960.

Harring, Sidney. *Policing a Class Society: The Experience of American Cities, 1865–1915.* New Brunswick, NJ: Rutgers University Press, 1983.

Harris, Neil. *Humbug! The Art of P. T. Barnum.* Boston: Little Brown & Company, 1973.

Hendler, Glenn. *Public Sentiments: Structures of Feeling in Nineteenth-Century American Literature.* Chapel Hill: University of North Carolina Press, 2001.

Herndl, Diane Price. *Invalid Women: Figuring Feminine Illness in American Fiction and Culture, 1840–1940.* Chapel Hill: University of North Carolina Press, 1993.

Hertz, Robert. *Death and the Right Hand.* Translated by Rodney and Claudia Needham. Aberdeen: University Press, 1960.

Hess, David J. *Science in the New Age: The Paranormal, Its Defenders and Debunkers, and American Culture.* Madison: University of Wisconsin Press, 1993.

Higginbotham, Evelyn Brooks. *Righteous Discontent: The Women's Movement in the Black Baptist Church, 1880–1921.* Cambridge, MA: Harvard University Press, 1992.

Higham, John. *From Boundlessness to Consolidation.* Ann Arbor: University of Michigan Press, 1969.

Hine, Robert. *California's Utopian Colonies.* New Haven, CT: Yale University Press, 1966.

Holden, Pat, ed. *Women's Religious Experience.* London: Croom Helm, 1987.

Holland, Sharon Patricia. *Raising the Dead: Readings of Death and (Black) Subjectivity.* Durham, NC: Duke University Press, 2000.

Hollinger, David. "Justification by Verification: The Scientific Challenge to the Moral Authority of Christianity in Modern America." In *Religion and Twentieth-Century American Intellectual Life,* edited by Michael J. Lacey. New York: Cambridge University Press, 1989.

Homans, Peter. "Introduction: The Decline of Mourning Practices in Modern Western Societies; A Short Sketch." In *Symbolic Loss: The Ambiguity of Mourning and Memory at Century's End,* edited by Peter Homans. Charlottesville: University Press of Virginia, 2000.

Horowitz, Helen Lefkowitz. *Rereading Sex: Battles over Sexual Knowledge and Suppression in Nineteenth-Century America.* New York: Alfred A. Knopf, 2002.

———. "A Victoria Woodhull for the 1990s." *Reviews in American History* 87, no. 2 (September 2000): 403–34.

Houlbrooke, Ralph, ed. *Death, Ritual, and Bereavement.* New York: Routledge, 1989.

Howe, Daniel Walker. "Victorian Culture in America." In *Victorian America*. Philadelphia: University of Pennsylvania Press, 1976.

Hunter, Tera W. *To 'Joy My Freedom: Southern Black Women's Lives and Labors after the Civil War*. Cambridge, MA: Harvard University Press, 1997.

Isaacs, Ernest Joseph. "A History of Nineteenth-Century American Spiritualism as a Religious and Social Movement." Ph.D. diss., University of Wisconsin, 1975.

Isenberg, Nancy, and Andrew Burstein, eds. Introduction to *Mortal Remains: Death in Early America*, edited by Nancy Isenberg and Andrew Burstein. Philadelphia: University of Pennsylvania Press, 2003.

Jakobsen, Janet R. *Working Alliances and the Politics of Difference: Diversity and Feminist Ethics*. Bloomington: University of Indiana Press, 1998.

Jakobsen, Janet R., and Ann Pellegrini. *Love the Sin: Sexual Regulation and the Limits of Religious Tolerance*. New York: New York University Press, 2003.

James, Janet Wilson, ed. *Women in American Religion*. Philadelphia: University of Pennsylvania Press, 1980.

Jenkins, Philip. *Moral Panic: Changing Concepts of the Child Molester in Modern America*. New Haven, CT: Yale University Press, 1998.

John, Richard. *Spreading the News: The American Postal System From Franklin to Morse*. Cambridge, MA: Harvard University Press, 1995.

Kahane, Claire. "Hysteria, Feminism, and the Case of *The Bostonians*." In *Feminism and Psychoanalysis*, edited by Richard Feldstein and Judith Roof. Ithaca, NY: Cornell University Press, 1989.

——. *Passions of the Voice: Hysteria, Narrative, and the Figure of the Speaking Woman, 1850–1915*. Baltimore, MD: Johns Hopkins University Press, 1995.

Kaplan, E. Ann. "Is the Gaze Male?" In *Powers of Desire: The Politics of Sexuality*, edited by Ann Snitow, Christine Stansell, and Sharon Thompson. New York: Monthly Review Press, 1983.

Karp, Ivan, and Steven D. Lavine, eds. *Exhibiting Cultures: The Poetics and Politics of Museum Display*. Washington, DC: Smithsonian Institution Press, 1991.

Keller, Morton. *Affairs of State: Public Life in Late Nineteenth-Century America*. Cambridge, MA: Belknap Press of Harvard University Press, 1977.

Kennedy, Elizabeth Lapovsky, and Madeline D. Davis. *Boots of Leather, Slippers of Gold: The History of a Lesbian Community*. New York: Routledge, 1993.

Kerber, Linda K. "The Abolitionist Perception of the Indian." *Journal of American History* 62, no. 2 (September 1975): 271–95.

Kern, Louis J. *An Ordered Love: Sex Roles and Sexuality in Victorian Utopias, the Shakers, the Mormons, and the Oneida Community*. Chapel Hill: University of North Carolina Press, 1981.

Kerr, Howard. *Mediums, Spirit Rappers and Roaring Radicals: Spiritualism in American Literature*. Urbana: University of Illinois Press, 1972.

Kerr, Howard, and Charles L. Crow, eds. *The Occult in America: New Historical Perspectives*. Chicago: University of Illinois Press, 1983.

Kerr, Howard, John W. Crowley, and Charles L. Crow, eds. *The Haunted Dusk: American Supernatural Fiction, 1820–1920.* Athens: University of Georgia Press, 1983.

Kete, Mary Louise. *Sentimental Collaborations: Mourning and Middle-Class Identity in Nineteenth-Century America.* Durham, NC: Duke University Press, 2000.

Kibbey, Ann. *The Interpretation of Material Shapes in Puritanism: A Study of Rhetoric, Prejudice, and Violence.* London: Cambridge University Press, 1986.

Kucich, John J. *Ghostly Communion: Cross-Cultural Spiritualism in Nineteenth-Century American Literature.* Hanover, NH: Dartmouth College Press, 2004.

Kucich, John, and Dianne Sadoff, eds. *Victorian Afterlife: Postmodern Culture Rewrites the Nineteenth Century.* Minneapolis: University of Minnesota Press, 2000.

Kuper, Adam. *The Invention of Primitive Society: Transformations of an Illusion.* New York: Routledge, 1988.

Kupperman, Karen Ordahl. *Indians and English: Facing Off in Early America.* Ithaca, NY: Cornell University Press, 2000.

Laqueur, Thomas. *Making Sex: Body and Gender from the Greeks to Freud.* Cambridge, MA: Harvard University Press, 1990.

Latour, Bruno. *We Have Never Been Modern.* Translated by Catherine Porter. Cambridge, MA: Harvard University Press, 1993.

Leach, William. *True Love and Perfect Union: The Feminist Reform of Sex and Society.* New York: Basic Books, 1980.

Lears, T. J. Jackson. *No Place of Grace: Antimodernism and the Transformation of American Culture, 1880–1920.* New York: Pantheon, 1981.

Leja, Michael. *Looking Askance: Skepticism and American Art from Eakins to Duchamp.* Berkeley: University of California Press, 2004.

Lewis, I. M. *Ecstatic Religion: A Study of Shamanism and Spirit Possession.* 1971. Reprint, New York: Routledge, 1989.

Lunbeck, Elizabeth. *The Psychiatric Persuasion: Knowledge, Gender, and Power in Modern America.* Princeton, NJ: Princeton University Press, 1994.

Lutz, Tom. *American Nervousness, 1903: An Anecdotal History.* Ithaca, NY: Cornell University Press, 1991.

Macherey, Pierre. "Marx Dematerialized, or the Spirit of Derrida." In *Ghostly Demarcations,* edited by Michael Sprinker. London: Verso, 1999.

Mann, Arthur. *Yankee Reformers in the Urban Age.* New York: Harper & Row, 1966.

Mardock, Robert Winston. *The Reformers and the American Indian.* Columbia: University of Missouri Press, 1971.

Mavor, Carol. *Pleasures Taken: Performance of Sexuality and Loss in Victorian Photographs.* Durham, NC: Duke University Press, 1995.

McCandless, Peter. "Dangerous to Themselves and Others: The Victorian Debate over the Prevention of Wrongful Confinement." *Journal of British Studies* 23 (Fall 1983): 84–104.

———. "Liberty and Lunacy: The Victorians and Wrongful Confinement." *Journal of Social History* 11 (1978): 366–86.

McDannell, Colleen. *Material Christianity: Religion and Popular Culture in America.* New Haven, CT: Yale University Press, 1995.

McDonald, Michael. *Mystical Bedlam: Madness, Anxiety and Healing in Seventeenth-Century England.* New York: Cambridge University Press, 1981.

Melish, Joanne Pope. *Disowning Slavery: Gradual Emancipation and "Race" in New England, 1780–1860.* Ithaca, NY: Cornell University Press, 1998.

Melton, J. Gordon. *Cults and New Religions: Sources for Study of Nonconventional Religious Groups in Nineteenth- and Twentieth-Century America.* New York: Garland Publishing, 1990.

Meyer, Donald. *The Positive Thinkers: A Study of the American Search for Health, Wealth and Personal Power from Mary Baker Eddy to Norman Vincent Peale.* Middletown, CT: Wesleyan University Press, 1988.

Micale, Mark. *Approaching Hysteria: Disease and its Interpretations.* Princeton, NJ: Princeton University Press, 1995.

Mitchell, Timothy. *Questions of Modernity.* Minneapolis: University of Minnesota Press, 2000.

Moore, R. Laurence. *In Search of White Crows: Spiritualism, Parapsychology and American Culture.* New York: Cambridge University Press, 1977.

———. "Insiders and Outsiders in American Historical Narrative and American History." In *Religion in American History,* edited by Jon Butler and Harry S. Stout. New York: Oxford University Press, 1998.

Morrison, Toni. "Unspeakable Things Unspoken: The Afro-American Presence in American Literature." *Michigan Quarterly Review* 28 (Winter 1989): 1–34.

Murphy, Teresa Anne. *Ten Hours' Labor: Religion, Reform and Gender in Early New England.* Ithaca, NY: Cornell University Press, 1992.

Nelson, Geoffrey K. *Spiritualism and Society.* London: Routledge and Kegan Paul, 1969.

Nissenbaum, Stephen. *Sex, Diet, and Debility in Jacksonian America: Sylvester Graham and Health Reform.* Westport, CT: Greenwood Press, 1980.

Norton, Mary Beth. *In the Devil's Snare: The Salem Witchcraft Crisis of 1692.* New York: Alfred A. Knopf, 2002.

Numbers, Ronald L. *Prophetess of Health: Ellen G. White and the Origins of Seventh-Day Adventist Health Reform.* Knoxville: University of Tennessee Press, 1992.

Oppenheim, Janet. *The Other World: Spiritualism and Psychical Research in England, 1850–1914.* New York: Cambridge University Press, 1985.

Owen, Alex. " 'Borderland Forms': Arthur Conan Doyle, Albion's Daughters, and the Politics of the Cottingley Fairies." *History Workshop Journal* 38 (1994): 48–85.

———. *A Darkened Room: Women, Power and Spiritualism in Late Victorian England*. London: Virago, 1989.

———. *The Place of Enchantment: British Occultism and the Culture of the Modern*. Chicago: University of Chicago Press, 2004.

Parker, Andrew, Mary Russo, Doris Sommer, and Patricia Yaeger, eds. *Nationalisms and Sexualities*. New York: Routledge, 1991.

Patton, Cindy, and Benigno Sánchez-Eppler, eds. *Queer Diasporas*. Durham, NC: Duke University Press, 2000.

Paul, James C. N., and Murray L. Schwartz. *Federal Censorship: Obscenity in the Mail*. New York: Free Press of Glencoe, Inc., 1961.

Perry, Lewis. *Radical Abolitionism: Anarchy and the Government of God in Antislavery Thought*. Ithaca, NY: Cornell University Press, 1973.

Pfister, Joel, and Nancy Schnog, eds. *Inventing the Psychological: Toward a Cultural History of Emotional Life in America*. New Haven, CT: Yale University Press, 1997.

Pike, Martha, and Janice Gray Armstrong, eds. *A Time to Mourn: Expressions of Grief in Nineteenth-Century America*. Stony Brook, NY: Museums at Stony Brook, 1980.

Pivar, David. *Purity Crusade: Sexual Morality and Social Control, 1868–1900*. Westport, CT: Greenwood Press, 1973.

Poovey, Mary. *Uneven Developments: The Ideological Work of Gender in Mid-Victorian England*. Chicago: University of Chicago Press, 1988.

Porterfield, Amanda. *Feminine Spirituality in America: From Sarah Edwards to Martha Graham*. Philadelphia: Temple University Press, 1980.

Potter, Stephen R. "Early Effects on Virginia Algonquian Exchange and Tribute in the Tidewater Potomac." In *Powhatan's Mantle: Indians in the Colonial Southwest*, edited by Peter H. Wood, Gregory A. Waselkov, and M. Thomas Hatley. Lincoln: University of Nebraska Press, 1989.

Prothero, Stephen. "From Spiritualism to Theosophy: 'Uplifting' a Democratic Tradition." *Religion and American Culture* 3, no. 2 (Summer 1993): 197–216.

Puar, Jasbir Kuar, ed. "Queer Tourism: Geographies of Globalization." *GLQ: A Journal of Lesbian and Gay Studies* 8, nos. 1–2, special issue. 2000.

Rabinbach, Anson. "Neurasthenia and Modernity." In *Incorporations*, edited by Jonathan Crary and Sanford Kwinter. New York: Zone Books, 1992.

Reuther, Rosemary Radford, ed. *Religion and Sexism*. New York: Simon and Schuster, 1974.

Reuther, Rosemary Radford, and Rosemary Skinner Keller, eds. *Women and Religion in America*. New York: Harper & Row, 1981.

Reynolds, David. *Beneath the American Renaissance: The Subversive Imagination in the Age of Emerson and Melville*. New York: Alfred A. Knopf, 1988.

Rhodes, D. L. *Justice and Gender.* Cambridge, MA: Harvard University Press, 1989.

Ricciardi, Alessia. *The Ends of Mourning: Psychoanalysis, Literature, Film.* Stanford, CA: Stanford University Press, 2003.

Roach, Joseph. *Cities of the Dead: Circum-Atlantic Performance.* New York: Columbia University Press, 1996.

Rogers, Daniel T. "Socializing Middle-Class Children: Institutions, Fables, and Work Values in Nineteenth-Century America." In *Growing Up in America: Children in Historical Perspective,* edited by N. Ray Hiner and Joseph M. Hawes. Chicago: University of Illinois Press, 1985.

Rogin, Michael Paul. *Fathers and Children: Andrew Jackson and the Subjugation of the American Indian.* New York: Knopf, 1975.

Ronell, Avital. *The Telephone Book: Technology—Schizophrenia—Electric Speech.* Lincoln: University of Nebraska Press, 1989.

Rosen, George. *Madness in Society.* Chicago: University of Chicago Press, 1968.

Rosenberg, Charles. *The Cholera Years: The United States in 1832, 1849, and 1866.* Chicago: University of Chicago Press, 1962.

———. *No Other Gods: On Science and American Social Thought.* Baltimore, MD: Johns Hopkins University Press, 1961.

———. "The Place of George M. Beard in Nineteenth-Century Psychiatry." *Bulletin of the History of Medicine* 36 (1962): 245–59.

———. *The Trial of the Assassin Guiteau: Psychiatry and the Law in the Gilded Age.* Chicago: University of Chicago Press, 1968.

Rosenberg, Charles, and Morris Vogel, eds. *The Therapeutic Revolution: Essays in the Social History of American Medicine.* Philadelphia: University of Pennsylvania Press, 1979.

Rothman, David J. *The Discovery of the Asylum: Social Order and Disorder in the New Republic.* Boston: Little, Brown and Company, 1971.

Rousseau, G. S. *Enlightenment Crossings: Pre-and Post-modern Discourses.* Manchester, U.K.: Manchester University Press, 1991.

———, ed. *The Languages of Psyche: Mind and Body in Enlightenment Thought.* Berkeley: University of California Press, 1990.

Rubin, Gayle. "Thinking Sex: Notes for a Radical Theory of the Politics of Sexuality." In *Pleasure and Danger,* edited by Carole S. Vance. New York: Routledge, 1984.

Russett, Cynthia Eagle. *Sexual Science: The Victorian Construction of Womanhood.* Cambridge, MA: Harvard University Press, 1989.

Ryan, Mary P. *Cradle of the Middle-Class: The Family in Oneida County, New York, 1790–1865.* New York: Cambridge University Press, 1981.

Samuels, Shirley ed. *The Culture of Sentiment: Race, Gender, and Sentimentality in Nineteenth-Century America.* New York: Oxford University Press, 1992.

Sánchez-Eppler, Karen. "Bodily Bonds: The Intersecting Rhetorics of Feminism and Abolition." *Representations* 24 (Fall 1988): 28–59.

Sapinsley, Barbara. *The Private War of Mrs. Packard*. New York: Paragon House, 1991.

Satter, Beryl. *Each Mind a Kingdom: American Women, Sexual Purity, and the New Thought Movement, 1875–1920*. Berkeley: University of California Press, 1999.

Sawicki, Jana. *Disciplining Foucault: Feminism, Power, and the Body*. New York: Routledge, 1991.

Schlesinger, Arthur. *The American as Reformer*. Cambridge, MA: Harvard University Press, 1950.

Schmidt, Leigh Eric. *Hearing Things: Religion, Illusion, and the American Enlightenment*. Cambridge, MA: Harvard University Press, 2000.

Schorsch, Anita. *Mourning Becomes America: Mourning Art in the New Nation*. Clinton, NJ: Main Street Press, 1976.

Schrager, Cynthia D. "Both Sides of the Veil: Race, Science, and Mysticism in W. E. B. DuBois." *American Quarterly* 48, no. 4 (December 1996): 551–86.

Scull, Andrew T., ed. *Madhouses, Mad-Doctors and Madmen: The Social History of Psychiatry in the Victorian Era*. Philadelphia: University of Pennsylvania Press, 1981.

———. *Museums of Madness: The Social Organization of Insanity in Nineteenth-Century England*. New York: St. Martin's Press, 1979.

Sears, Hal D. *The Sex Radicals: Free Love in High Victorian America*. Lawrence: Regents Press of Kansas, 1977.

Sedgwick, Eve Kosofsky. *Epistemology of the Closet*. Berkeley: University of California Press, 1990.

Sered, Susan Starr. *Priestess, Mother, Sacred Sister: Religions Dominated by Women*. New York: Oxford University Press, 1994.

Shortt, S. E. D. "Physicians and Psychics: The Anglo-American Medical Response to Spiritualism, 1870–1890." *Journal of the History of Medicine and Allied Sciences* 39, no. 3 (July 1984): 339–55.

Showalter, Elaine. *The Female Malady: Women, Madness and English Culture, 1830–1980*. New York: Penguin Books, 1985.

———. *Sexual Anarchy: Gender and Culture at the Fin de Siècle*. New York: Viking, 1990.

Skultans, Vieda. *Intimacy and Ritual: A Study of Spiritualism, Mediums, and Groups*. London: Routledge and Kegan Paul, 1974.

———. "Mediums, Controls, and Eminent Men." In *Women's Religious Experience,* edited by Pat Holden. New York: Pantheon, 1987.

Smith-Rosenberg, Carroll. *Disorderly Conduct: Visions of Gender in Victorian America*. New York: Oxford University Press, 1985.

Sloan, David Charles. *The Last Great Necessity: Cemeteries in American History*. Baltimore, MD: Johns Hopkins University Press, 1991.

Sobel, Mechal. *Trabelin' On: The Slave Journey to An Afro-Baptist Faith*. Westport, CT: Greenwood Press, 1979.

Spurlock, John C. *Free Love: Marriage and Middle-Class Radicalism in America, 1825–1860*. New York: New York University Press, 1988.

———. "The Free Love Network in America, 1850–1860." *Journal of Social History* 21, no. 4 (Summer 1988): 765–79.

Stannard, David E. "Where All Our Steps Are Tending: Death in the American Context." In *A Time to Mourn: Expressions of Grief in Nineteenth-Century America*, edited by Martha Pike and Janice Gray Armstrong. Stony Brook, NY: Museums at Stony Brook, 1980.

Stansell, Christine. *City of Women: Sex and Class in New York, 1789–1860*. New York: Knopf, 1986.

Steele, Jeffrey. "The Gender and Racial Politics of Mourning in Antebellum America." In *An Emotional History of the United States*, edited by Peter N. Stearns and Jan Lewis. New York: New York University Press, 1998.

Stein, Stephen J. *The Shaker Experience in America: A History of the United Society of Believers*. New Haven, CT: Yale University Press, 1992.

Stern, Madeline B. *The Pantarchy: A Biography of Stephen Pearl Andrews*. Austin: University of Texas Press, 1968.

———. *The Victoria Woodhull Reader*. New York: M & S Press, 1974.

Stevens, Laura M. "The Christian Origins of the Vanishing Indian." In *Mortal Remains: Death in Early America*, edited by Nancy Isenberg and Andrew Burstein. Philadelphia: University of Pennsylvania Press, 2003.

Stewart, Garret. *Death Sentences: Styles of Dying in British Fiction*. New York: Cambridge University Press, 1984.

Stoehr, Taylor. *Free Love in America*. New York: AMS Press, 1979.

Sword, Helen. *Ghostwriting Modernism*. Ithaca, NY: Cornell University Press, 2002.

Tagg, John. *The Burden of Representation: Essays on Photographies and Histories*. Amherst: University of Massachusetts Press, 1988.

Tambiah, Stanley Jeyaraja. *Magic, Science, Religion, and the Scope of Rationality*. New York: Cambridge University Press, 1990.

Taves, Ann. *Fits, Trances, and Visions: Experiencing Religion and Explaining Experience from Wesley to James*. Princeton, NJ: Princeton University Press, 1999.

Taylor, Barbara. *Eve and the New Jerusalem: Socialism and Feminism in the Nineteenth Century*. New York: Pantheon Books, 1983.

Terry, Jennifer. *An American Obsession: Science, Medicine, and Homosexuality in Modern Society*. Chicago: University of Chicago Press, 1999.

Thomas, John L. "Romantic Reform in America, 1815–1865." In *Intellectual History in America*, edited by Cushing Strout. New York: Harper & Row, 1968.

Thomas, Keith. *Religion and the Decline of Magic*. New York: Viking, 1971.

Thompson, E. P. "Anthropology and the Discipline of Historical Context." *Midland History* 1 (1972): 53–54.

Thurschwell, Pamela. *Literature, Technology, and Magical Thinking, 1880–1920.* New York: Cambridge University Press, 2001.

Tiryakian, Edward A. *On the Margin of the Visible: Sociology, the Esoteric, and the Occult.* New York: Wiley, 1974.

Tompkins, Jane. *Sensational Designs: The Cultural Work of American Fiction.* New York: Oxford University Press, 1985.

Torgovnick, Marianna. *Primitive Passions: Men, Women, and the Quest for Ecstasy.* Chicago: University of Chicago Press, 1996.

Townsend, Camilla. *Pocahontas and the Powhatan Dilemma.* New York: Hill and Wang, 2004.

Trachtenberg, Alan. *The Incorporation of America: Culture and Society in the Gilded Age.* New York: Hill and Wang, 1982.

Tucker, Jennifer. *Nature Exposed: Photography as Eyewitness in Victorian Science.* London: Johns Hopkins University Press, 2006.

Turner, Frank M. *Between Science and Religion: The Reaction to Scientific Naturalism in Late Victorian England.* New Haven, CT: Yale University Press, 1974.

Turner, Victor. *The Forest of Symbols: Aspects of Ndembu Ritual.* Ithaca, NY: Cornell University Press, 1967.

Tyler, Alice Felt. *Freedom's Ferment: Phases of American Social History to 1860.* Minneapolis: University of Minnesota Press, 1944.

Underhill, Lois Beachy. *The Woman Who Ran For President: The Many Lives of Victoria Woodhull.* Bridgehampton, NY: Bridge Works Publishing Co., 1995.

Utley, Robert M. *The Indian Frontier of the American West, 1846–1890.* Albuquerque: University of Mexico Press, 1984.

Veith, Ilza. *Hysteria: The History of a Disease.* Chicago: University of Chicago Press, 1965.

Viswanathan, Guari. *Outside the Fold: Conversion, Modernity, and Belief.* Princeton, NJ: Princeton University Press, 1998.

Walker, Mary. "Between Fiction and Madness: The Relationship of Women to the Supernatural in Late Victorian Britain." In *That Gentle Strength: Historical Perspectives on Women in Christianity,* edited by Lynda J. Coon, Katherine J. Haldane, and Elizabeth W. Somer. Charlottesville: University of Virginia Press, 1990.

Walkowitz, Judith R. *City of Dreadful Delight: Narratives of Sexual Danger in Late Victorian London.* Chicago: University of Chicago Press, 1992.

———. *Prostitution and Victorian Society: Women, Class and the State.* New York: Cambridge University Press, 1980.

Waller, Altina L. *Reverend Beecher and Mrs. Tilton: Sex and Class in Victorian America.* Amherst: University of Massachusetts Press, 1982.

Wallis, Roy ed. *On the Margins of Science: The Social Construction of Rejected Knowledge.* Sociological Review Monograph 27. Keele, Staffordshire: University of Keele Press, 1979.

Walters, Ronald G. *American Reformers, 1815–1860.* New York: Hill and Wang, 1978.

Ward, Gary L., ed. *Cults and New Religions: Spiritualism I and Spiritualism II; The Movement.* New York: Garland Publishing, 1990.

Warner, Michael. "Tongues Untied: Memoirs of a Pentecostal Boyhood." In *Qu(e) erying Religion: A Critical Anthology,* edited by Gary David Comstock and Susan E. Henking. New York: Continuum, 1997.

Watkin, William. *On Mourning: Theories of Loss in Modern Literature.* Edinburgh: Edinburgh University Press, 2004.

Weber, Max. *The Protestant Ethic and the Spirit of Capitalism.* Translated by Talcott Parsons. New York: Charles Scribner's Sons, 1958.

———. *The Sociology of Religion.* Translated by Talcott Parsons. 1902. Reprint, Boston: Beacon Press, 1963.

Weeks, Jeffrey. *"Invented Moralities: Sexual Values in An Age of Uncertainty.* New York: Columbia University Press, 1995.

———. *Sex, Politics, and Society: The Regulation of Sexuality Since 1800.* London and New York: Longman Group, Ltd., 1981.

Weisberg, Barbara, *Talking to the Dead: Kate and Maggie Fox and the Rise of Spiritualism.* New York: HarperCollins Publishers, 2004.

Wells, Robert V. *Facing the "King of Terrors": Death and Society in an American Community, 1750–1990.* Cambridge, MA: Harvard University Press, 2000.

Wessinger, Catherine, ed. *Women's Leadership in Marginal Religions: Explorations outside the Mainstream.* Chicago: University of Illinois Press, 1993.

Welter, Barbara. "The Cult of True Womanhood, 1820–1860." *American Quarterly* 18 (Summer 1966): 151–74.

———. "The Feminization of American Religion, 1800–1860." In *Religion in American History,* edited by Jon Butler and Harry S. Stout. New York: Oxford University Press, 1998.

White, Patricia. "Female Spectator, Lesbian Specter: *The Haunting."* In *Sexuality and Space,* edited by Beatriz Colomina. Princeton, NJ: Princeton Papers on Architecture, 1992.

———. *Uninvited: Classical Hollywood Cinema and Lesbian Representability.* Bloomington: Indiana University Press, 1999.

Wicker, Christine. *Not in Kansas Anymore: A Curious Tale of How Magic Is Transforming America.* San Francisco, CA: HarperSanFrancisco, 2005.

Wiebe, Robert H. *Search for Order, 1877–1920.* New York: Hill and Wang, 1967.

———. *The Segmented Society,* New York: Oxford University Press, 1975.

Williams, Raymond. "Dominant, Residual, and Emergent." In *Marxism and Literature.* New York: Oxford University Press, 1977.

Wilson, Bryan. "Secularization: The Inherited Model." In *Religion in American History,* edited by Jon Butler and Harry S. Stout. New York: Oxford University Press, 1998.

Wilson, David B. "The Thought of Late Victorian Physicists: Oliver Lodge's Ethereal Body." *Victorian Studies* 15 (1971–72): 29–48.

Winter, Alison. *Mesmerized: Powers of Mind in Victorian Britain*. Chicago: University of Chicago Press, 1998.

Wood, Mary Elene. *The Writing on the Wall: Women's Autobiography and the Asylum*. Urbana: University of Illinois Press, 1994.

Yellin, Jean Fagan. *Harriet Jacobs: A Life*. New York: Basic Civitas Books, 2004.

Young, Robert N. "Natural Theology, Victorian Periodicals, and the Fragmentation of a Common Context." In *Darwin to Einstein: Historical Studies of Science and Belief,* edited by Colin Chant and John Fauvel. New York: Longman's, Inc., 1980.

Zelizer, Viviana A. "From Useful to Useless: Moral Conflict over Child Labor." In *The Children's Culture Reader,* edited by Henry Jenkins. New York: New York University Press, 1998.

INDEX

abolitionism, 4, 19, 31, 54–55, 79, 81, 89, 92, 99, 118

Adams, Nehemiah, 24

adhesiveness, as phrenological category, 168–69

affinities, spiritual, 2, 98–99, 161

African Americans, 53–54, 84, 118–19, 146, 219n101; and African religious practices, 10

Agassiz, Louis, 128

Ahlstrom, Sydney, 44

AIDS epidemic, 7, 203n3

Albanese, Catherine L., 3, 9, 178nn7,9

alienists, 135, 136, 140, 141, 147

Allen, Paula Gunn, 13, 198n9

amativeness, as phrenological category, 168–69

American Association for the Advancement of Science, 128

American Association of Spiritualists, 98

American Journal of Insanity, 129, 135

American Society for Psychical Research, 17

Andrews, Stephen Pearl, 206n27

animal magnetism, 2, 145

anorexia, 150–52, 221n130

Anthony, Susan B., 47

antiauthoritarianism, 19, 98, 99

anti-imperialism, 2, 49

antiobscenity legislation, 15, 94–96, 115–18, 119, 204nn9–10

antislavery movement. *See* abolitionism

antivice movement, 114–20, 203n3, 211n85

Apter, Emily, 218n87

Ariès, Philippe, 7, 25–26

Asad, Talal, 13

asylums, 106, 126, 135–36, 140, 144, 147, 219–20n104

automatic writing, 20

Ballou, Adin, 34–35

Banner of Light (newspaper): and abolitionism, 54–55; and California spirit circles, 61, 62; and free love, 98; and mediums, 32, 37, 40, 178n12; and mourning practices, 21, 24; and Native American rights, 81, 88, 89–90, 93; and Native American spirits, 73, 86, 89–90; and pacifism, 49, 50–51; and premature burial, 137; and reform, 42, 56, 57; and religious insanity, 139–40; and spirit bodies, 60; and women's rights, 47, 56, 195n174

Banner of Progress (newspaper), 62, 196n189

Barnum, P. T., 110, 123, 150

Freud, Sigmund, 133, 138–39, 147, 148
Frost, Mary E., 48
Fuller, Margaret, 45

Garfield, James, 219n104
Garrison, William Lloyd, 54, 65, 79
Geertz, Hildred, 13
gender: and balance of positive and negative forces, 46, 51, 158–59; and equality, 42, 45–46, 51, 58; and mediumship, 125, 131–32, 170; and mourning practices, 22; and theology, 42, 45, 46
Gilded Age, 52, 53
Gilman, Charlotte Perkins, 148
Golden Gate (periodical), 63, 196n189
Gordon, Avery, 8
Gordon, Laura De Force, 62, 63
Graham, Sylvester, 47, 48
Gray, John P., 147
Great Britain, 2, 16, 99, 104, 105, 115, 144, 171–75, 178n6, 189n79, 218n88, 221n130
Greeley, Horace, 35, 36, 214n11
Grimes, Stanley, 130–31
Grimké sisters (Angelina and Sarah), 79
Guiteau, Charles J., 219–20n104

Habermas, Jürgen, 53
Hall, Radclyffe, 16, 172, 173–76, 228n85
Hall's Journal of Health, 55
Halperin, David M., 156, 223n12
Halttunen, Karen, 23–24, 123
Hammond, William Alexander, 140, 141, 142–43, 145, 147, 149–53, 220n104
Hardinge, Emma, 3, 4, 29, 30, 32, 33, 34, 42, 50, 57, 61, 78–79, 161, 213n6, 224n22
Hare, Robert, 129
Hatch, Benjamin F., 35–36, 39
Hatch, Cora L. V. *See* Scott, Cora L. V.
Hayes, Rutherford B., 180n20
Hazard, Thomas, 51
Helmholtz, Hermann, 145
Helms, Jesse, 203n3
Henderson, Anna M., 39–40
Herald of Progress (newspaper), 49–50, 54, 55, 60, 76, 82, 84
homosexuality, 131, 155–57, 168–69, 171, 223n8. *See also* inversion, sexual

Hopedale, 35
Howells, William Dean, 52, 106
hysteria: as bodily performance, 133–34, 137–38; case studies of, 127, 135–36, 152–53; female, 64, 65, 125–28, 132, 133, 139, 143–44, 146, 152, 159; Foucault on, 133–34; and mediumship, 15, 125–28, 132, 143, 152–53; and narrativity, 134, 216n53; and neurology, 143–45; and possession, 135–36; and psychoanalysis, 133, 138–39; religious, 143–44, 218n89, 221n130; and suffragists, 64, 65

immigrants, 25, 41
Indians, American. *See* Native Americans
individualism: and free love, 98–99; and mourning practices, 25–26; and reform, 44
insanity, 15, 77, 125, 129, 136–37, 139, 141, 142, 145, 147, 220n104
internationalism, 51
International Workingmen's Association, 97
Internet, 15, 120
inversion, sexual, 157, 162, 163, 170–71, 173, 174, 175, 228n85
Isenberg, Nancy, 22–23

Jackson, Andrew, 70, 72
Jackson, Jane M., 73
Jacob, Sarah, 221n130
Jacobs, Harriet, 37
James, Henry, 10, 37, 65
James, William, 17, 140–41, 147, 172
Jesup, Morris K., 114
Joan of Arc, 143
Johnson, Andrew, 54

Katz, Jonathan Ned, 222n3, 226n40
Kerr, Michael C., 204n9
King, Katie, 104–6, 108*fig,* 109*fig,* 114
Kirby, Georgiana B., 61
Krafft-Ebing, Richard von, 171
Kucich, John J., 184n6
Kuhn, Thomas, 12

Leaves of Grass (Whitman), 168, 169
Lee, Ann, 45

Shakers, 2, 10, 45, 139
Shekinah (newspaper), 21, 22, 24
Shepard, Jesse, 103, 104, 164–66, 170
Shields, James, 2
Shindler, Mary Dana, 104
Showalter, Elaine, 138
Simpson, Frederick, 127
Sitting Bull, 72
skepticism, 6, 12, 55, 106, 122–23, 124, 213n6
Slocum, Amanda M., 62, 196n189
Slocum, W. N., 62, 196n189
Smith, Gerrit, 4
Smith, John, 69
Smith-Rosenberg, Carroll, 139
Snow, Herman, 75, 200n13
socialism, 97, 106
Society for Psychical Research, 129, 173, 189n79
South Carolina, 118
Southcott, Joanna, 143
Spence, Amanda, 46
Spence, Payton, 51–52, 53
Spencer, Herbert, 147
spirit circles, 2, 3, 21, 31, 32, 48, 61, 114; Native American spirits at, 66, 86, 91; structure of, 51, 158, 224n22. See also séances
Spiritualism: and abolitionism, 4, 54–55; in California 2–3, 61–64, 86, 87, 165–66; and childhood, 28–29; as consolation, 24–25; conversion to, 22, 44; cosmology of, 46, 51–52, 67, 73, 75, 81, 124, 158–59, 169; and debunkers, 3, 6, 31, 105–6, 124, 125, 129, 133, 143; and health, 47–48, 58, 63–64; in home circles, 3–4; and ideologies of progress, 6, 52, 71, 137; and magic, 10–13; and Native American rights, 67, 78–93; and new media, 14, 20–21; origins of, 2, 30–32; and pacifism, 49–51; performances of freedom in, 118–19; and politics, 4, 19, 31, 54–55, 79, 81, 89, 92, 99, 118; and queer subjects, 16, 159, 169, 175, 176; and racial science, 84; recasting of feminine passivity in, 32, 37, 39, 44, 126, 127, 131–32, 159; and revolutions of 1848, 1; and scandal, 94–95, 99–101, 173–74; and science, 17; scope of 2–3; and temperance, 4, 41, 42, 43fig, 115, 211n77; and utopia-

nism, 1, 4, 21, 34–35, 52, 64; and women's rights, 1, 41, 42, 46–49, 58, 64–65, 98–99; and witchcraft, 10
Spiritual Magazine, 178n6
spiritual telegraph, 2, 8, 14, 20, 68, 177n1
Spiritual Telegraph (newspaper), 66, 77, 162
Squire, Orson, 47
Stanton, Elizabeth Cady, 47
Steele, Jeffrey, 24
stereopticon cards, 11, 160fig
Stevens, Laura M., 71, 199n20
Stillman, Juliet, 47
Stone, John Augustus, 71
Story, Joseph, 72
Stowe, Harriet Beecher, 99
Stowe, Mrs. C. M., 62
suffrage: African-American, 54; women's, 4, 42, 46–47, 48, 56, 64–65, 97, 100, 167, 195n174
Summerland, 2, 19, 63, 67, 93, 184n3
Swedenborgians, 10, 45

Talbot, William Henry Fox, 111
talking cure, 133
Taves, Ann, 127
technology, 8, 14, 17, 20, 107, 120
telegraph, 14, 20, 68, 101, 146, 184n9. See also spiritual telegraph
temperance movement, 4, 41, 42, 43fig, 115, 211n77
Theosophical Society, 104, 129, 164
Theosophy, 2, 16, 45, 64, 104, 163–64, 171–74
Theresa, Saint, 143
Thomas, Keith, 12, 13
Thompson, E. P., 12
Thomson, Samuel, 64
Tilton, Elizabeth, 99
Tilton, Theodore, 100
Todd, Benjamin, 196n189
Trachtenberg, Alan, 52
trance: disembodiment, 48–49; and hysteria, 126–27, 137–38; and neurasthenia, 145; and passivity, 161, 166–67; and racial difference, 219n101; and Cora L. V. Scott's mediumship, 35, 36, 38, 39, 166, 169, 170, 188n68; Whitman's interest in, 169–70, 173

Text:	11.25/13.5 Adobe Garamond
Display:	Adobe Garamond, Perpetua
Index:	Andrew Joron
Compositor:	BookMatters, Berkeley
Printer and binder:	Maple-Vail Manufacturing Group